Logic and Contemporary Rhetoric

The Use of Reason in Everyday Life

Fourth Edition

Howard Kahane

University of Maryland
Baltimore County

Wadsworth Publishing Company
A Division of Wadsworth, Inc.
Belmont, California

Philosophy Editor: *Kenneth King*
Production Editor: *Leland Moss*
Managing Designer: *Paula Shuhert*
Copy Editor: *Bill Reynolds*
Signing Representative: *Robert Gormley*

Printed in the United States of America
1 2 3 4 5 6 7 8 9 10—88 87 86 85 84

ISBN 0-534-03188-9

Library of Congress Cataloging in Publication Data
Kahane, Howard, 1928–
    Logic and contemporary rhetoric.

    Bibliography: p.
    Includes index.
    1. Fallacies (Logic) 2. Reasoning. 3. Judgment
(Logic) I. Title.
BC175.K25 1984   160   83-16797
ISBN 0-534-03188-9

For Bonny sweet Robin . . .

Ignorance is preferable to error; and he is less remote from the truth who believes nothing, than he who believes what is wrong.
—Thomas Jefferson

It ain't so much the things we don't know that get us in trouble. It's the things we know that ain't so.
—Artemus Ward

Nothing is so firmly believed as what we least know.
—Montaigne

Contents

I do not pretend to know what many
ignorant men are sure of.
　　　　　　　—Clarence Darrow

To know that we know what we know,
and that we do not know what we do not
know, that is true knowledge.
　　　　　　　—Henry David Thoreau

We have met the enemy and he is us.
　　　　　　　—Walt Kelly's "Pogo"

Many people would sooner die than
think. In fact, they do.
　　　　　　　—Bertrand Russell

Preface

The purpose of this fourth edition of *Logic and Contemporary Rhetoric* remains the same as its predecessors: to help students improve their ability to reason about everyday political and social issues (and thus to help raise the level of political discussion in our society). This text differs from others by concentrating on everyday issues and problems and by drawing examples and exercises from a broad range of actual political rhetoric, advertisements, and other current sources, rather than traditional or made-up examples.

This edition is superior to the previous versions in many respects:

1. Hundreds of exercise items, examples, cartoons, and other boxed materials have been updated, and new items added, to broaden the text's scope.

2. The discussion of self deception and wishful thinking in the first chapter has been greatly improved, especially by inclusion of new material on several varieties of self deception.

3. The discussion of some of the key fallacies, such as *appeal to authority,* has been improved, and several fallacies previously not discussed are now considered, including *appeal to ignorance* and the master fallacy *lack of proportion.* Yet despite these additions, the subject of fallacies is covered more concisely in three rather than four chapters.

4. A new section on common rhetorical devices has been added to the chapter on language, including discussions of slanting, the use of weasel words, and fine print qualifications.

5. The chapter on analyzing extended arguments has been largely rewritten, and now includes sections on quick appraisals of arguments and constructing good arguments.

In addition, almost every page of the text has been rewritten to improve organization, style, and flow. The mark of *Logic and Contemporary Rhetoric* is more than ever ease of comprehension, and more interesting material for students.

The book divides into five parts:

1. Chapter 1 concerns good reasoning and the impediments to its mastery (such as wishful thinking and self deception), and provides an overview of the rest of the book.

2. Chapters 2 through 4 deal with fallacious reasoning, concentrating on how to avoid fallacies by becoming familiar with the types most frequently encountered (illustrated by live specimens).

3. Chapter 5 concerns language itself, demonstrating that good reasoning develops from an awareness of how language can manipulate.

4. Chapter 6 provides hints for, as well as practice in, analyzing extended passages. It also contains a section on constructing good arguments.

5. And Chapters 7, 8, and 9 discuss students' three main sources of information: advertising (singling out political advertising for special scrutiny); the media (television, newspapers, radio, magazines, and books); and public school textbooks.

This book is unique in bringing together all of these apparently diverse elements, and unique among books on logic or fallacy in dealing with information sources. The ability to evaluate available information, sources—which, in the case of social and political information, means primarily learning how best to use the media, advertising, and books—is an essential step in acquiring a good world view, or philosophy.

Although it contains much discussion of theory, this is *not* a textbook on the theory of cogent and fallacious reasoning. Rather, it is designed to help students learn how to reason cogently and avoid fallacy, in particular when dealing with social and political issues. That's why so many examples and exercise items have been included. And that's why perhaps the most important exercises in the text require students to do things on their own—for instance, to find examples from the mass media of the fallacies and linguistic ploys discussed in the text, or to analyze news stories and other textbooks for points of view, slanting, or bias. Discussing in class examples that students themselves have found is an excellent way to bring the material to life. Another teaching device that dovetails nicely with the use of this text is to organize classroom debates on current social/political issues. By constructing their own arguments, which are then discussed in class by peers, students will improve not only their ability to evaluate arguments encountered in everyday life, but also their effectiveness in expressing their own views and convincing others.

The word *fallacy* comes from the Latin *fallere,* to deceive. Latin commentators referred to the 13 kinds enumerated by Aristotle as *fallaciae,* no doubt because they were regarded as devices used to deceive. Through the years, however, the term *fallacy* has taken on many different but related meanings. The use of the term in this book is much broader than in most, both in removing the idea of deliberate deception as a condition of fallacy and in extending the term to cover all *errors of reasoning.*

Fallacy classifications have also undergone many changes since Aristotle's time. The organization used here is fairly standard except in its use of an overarching division into three master fallacies—*questionable premise, suppressed evidence, and invalid inference*—and in its inclusion of a few fallacies not generally considered (for instance, *lack of proportion*). The classic text that comes closest to utilizing this classification system is Richard Whately's *Elements of Logic,* written in 1826.

Acknowledgments

I'd like to thank the publisher's reviewers for this fourth edition: Professors Larry Friedman, University of Illinois; Paul J. Haanstad, University of Utah; W. J. Holly, University of Oregon; Glenn Kessler, University of Virginia; Ilona Lappo, Boston University; David L. Morgan, University of Northern Iowa; and Paul Roth, University of Missouri.

Many thanks also to all those mentioned in earlier editions, and to Douglas Stalker, University of Delaware; John George, Central State University (Oklahoma); Ben Starr, Modesto Junior College; Perry Weddle, California State University, Sacramento; James Gould, University of South Florida; Donald Lazere, California Polytechnic State University; Richard Paul, Sonoma State University; Dr. Margaret Penn, San Francisco Unified School District; Robert Cogan, Edinboro State College (Pennsylvania); Nelson Pole, Cleveland State University; Lee Creer, Central Connecticut State College; Alan Hausman, Ohio State University; and in particular Nancy Cavender, College of Marin. And finally many thanks to students of the University of Kansas, Bernard Baruch College of CUNY, and the University of Maryland Baltimore County.

HOWARD KAHANE
Sausalito, California

Logic and Contemporary Rhetoric

Drawing by H. Martin; © 1974 The New Yorker Magazine, Inc.

"If the coach and horses and the footmen and the beautiful clothes all turned back into the pumpkin and the mice and the rags, then how come the glass slipper didn't turn back, too?"

Two important factors in critical or creative thinking are: (1) the ability to bring relevant background information to bear on a problem, and (2) the ability to carry through the relevant implications of an argument or position to determine whether they hang together. The above cartoon illustrates the second of these factors: The child carries through the reasoning in the Cinderella story and finds it wanting. The first factor might be illustrated by a child who brings relevant background information to bear on the Santa Claus story (for instance, a child who realizes there are millions of chimneys for Santa to get down in one night and wonders how he could manage to do so in time).

It's much easier to do and die than it is to reason why.
—G. A. Studdert Kennedy

You can lead a man up to the university, but you can't make him think.
—Finley Peter Dunne

Habit is stronger than reason.
—George Santayana

Clopton's Law: *For every credibility gap, there is a gullibility fill.*
—Richard Clopton

The curse of man, and cause of nearly all his woe, is his stupendous capacity for believing the incredible.
—H. L. Mencken

Read not to contradict and confute, nor to believe and take for granted, . . . but to weigh and consider.
—Francis Bacon

Cohodas's Observation: *If it looks too good to be true, it is too good to be true.*
—Howard Cohodas

1

Good Reasoning

There is much truth to the old saying that life is just one damned problem after another. That's why problem solving is life's chief preoccupation. **Reasoning**— giving reasons in favor of doing this or that—is the essential ingredient in problem solving. When confronted with a problem, we reason from what we already know or believe to new beliefs useful for solving that problem. The trick, of course, is to reason *well*.

1. Arguments, Premises, Conclusions

Consider the following simple example of reasoning:

> Identical twins often have different IQ test scores. Yet such twins inherit the same genes. So environment must play some part in determining IQ.

Logicians call this kind of reasoning an **argument.** In this case, the argument consists of three statements:

1. Identical twins often have different IQ test scores.
2. Identical twins inherit the same genes.
3. So environment must play some part in determining IQ.

The first two statements in this argument give *reasons* for accepting the third. In logic talk, they are said to be **premises** of the argument, and the third statement is called the argument's **conclusion**.

In everyday life, few of us bother to label premises or conclusions. We usually don't even bother to distinguish one argument from another. But we do sometimes give clues. Such words as *because, since,* and *for* usually indicate that what follows is a premise. And words like *therefore, hence, consequently, so,* and *it follows that* usually signal a conclusion. Similarly, expressions like "It has been observed that . . . ," "In support of this . . . ." and "The relevant data . . ." generally introduce premises, while expressions like "The result is . . . ," "The point of all this is . . . ," and "The implication is . . ." usually signal conclusions. Here is a simple example:

> *Since* it's wrong to kill a human being, *it follows that* abortion is wrong, *because* abortion takes the life of (kills) a human being.

In this example, the words *since* and *because* signal premises offered in support of the conclusion signalled by the phrase *it follows that.* Put into textbook form, the argument reads:

1. It's wrong to kill a human being.
2. Abortion takes the life of (kills) a human being.
∴ 3. Abortion is wrong.[1]

(Of course, an argument may have any number of premises and may be surrounded by or embedded in other arguments.)

In addition to using transitional words like *since, because,* and *therefore,* we sometimes use other devices, such as sentence order, and may even mask a conclusion in the form of a question. For example, during the 1980 election a speaker gave all sorts of reasons for believing that Ronald Reagan would balance the budget if elected and then stated his conclusion in the form of a rhetorical question: "Can anyone doubt that Ronald Reagan will balance the federal budget?"

While we don't usually bother to label the premises and conclusions of our own arguments in daily life, it's sometimes useful to do so when evaluating the arguments of others. One quick way is to underline (or bracket) premises and conclusions, using a single underline to indicate a premise and a double underline to indicate a conclusion, like this:

> Since it's wrong to kill a human being, it follows that capital punishment is wrong, because capital punishment takes the life of a human being.

Notice that one of the premises is given *after* the conclusion. Psycho-logic doesn't always mirror formal logic: Premises needn't come before conclusions. What makes a statement a premise of an argument is that it is offered in support of some other statement.

Exposition and Argument

Arguments are not formed by all groups of sentences, but only by those that provide *reasons* for believing something. Thus anecdotes are generally not arguments, nor

---

[1]The symbol "∴" is used to indicate that a conclusion follows.

are most other forms of *exposition* or *explanation*. But even in these cases, arguments are often implied. Here is a television sales clerk explaining the difference between a 19-inch Sony and a 21-inch house brand: "Well, Sony has a one-gun picture tube, while our own Supremacy set doesn't; so the Sony picture will be a bit better in areas where reception is good to start with. Of course, if reception isn't that good in your area, the picture won't be that clear anyway—unless you have cable. On the other hand, our own brand, Supremacy, is $175 cheaper for a 21-inch set than Sony is for a 19-inch set."

While the clerk's remarks contain no explicit argument because no conclusion is drawn (no reasons are given in support of another statement), still a conclusion is *implied*—namely, you should choose the Sony if you're willing to pay $175 more for a slightly better picture (especially if you're on cable); otherwise you should choose the house brand.

The point is that explanations and expositions are not generally aimless: A good deal of everyday talk, even gossip, is intended to influence the beliefs and actions of others. In the television set example, the clerk gave information intended to convince the customer to draw either the conclusion, "I'll buy the 19-inch Sony because a small picture improvement is worth $175 to me," or the conclusion, "I'll buy the 21-inch Supremacy set because the difference in picture quality isn't worth $175 to me." In other words, the point of the chatter about Sony and the house brand was to *sell a TV set*.

Similarly, advertisements often restrict themselves to information about a product, rather than advancing any specific arguments. Yet clearly every ad has an implied conclusion—that you should buy the advertised product. Information given in an ad is thus offered as premises or reasons for drawing the conclusion that you should buy the product.

Still, it's important to understand the difference between rhetoric that is primarily expository or explanatory and rhetoric that is basically argumentative. A passage that contains only exposition gives us no reason to accept the "facts" in it other than the authority of the writer or speaker, whereas passages that contain arguments allege to give reasons for some of their claims (the conclusions) and call for a different sort of evaluation than merely an evaluation of the authority of the writer.

Exercise 1-1

Here are some passages from student papers and exams (modestly edited). Determine which contain arguments and which do not. Label the premises and conclusions of those that do, and *explain* your answers. (Starred (*) items are answered in a section at the back of the book.)

*1. At the present rate of consumption, the oil will be used up in 20–25 years. And we're sure not going to reduce consumption in the near future. So we'd better start developing solar power, windmills, and other "alternative energy sources" pretty soon.

2. My thesis is that the doomsayers are wrong to believe we're going to run out of oil in the near future, because necessity is the mother of discovery (ha, ha), and my geology text says we have only discovered a small fraction of the oil in the ground.

*3. I don't like big-time college football. I don't like pro football on TV either. In fact, I don't like sports, period.

4. Well, I have a special reason for believing in big-time college football. After all, I wouldn't have come here if Ohio State hadn't gone to the Rose Bowl, because that's how I heard about this place in the first place.

5. Big-time football doesn't belong at a university. Look at Ohio State— everything here revolves around football, at least in the fall. You can't even park within a mile of campus on a football Saturday, and that's why this assignment is late.

6. My summer vacation was spent working in Las Vegas. I worked as a waitress at the Desert Inn and made tons of money. But I guess I got addicted to the slots and didn't save too much. Next summer my friend Hal and I are going to work in Reno, if we can find jobs there.

7. We've had open admission here at KU [the University of Kansas] ever since living memory can remember, and things work swell here, don't they? I suppose that's because those that don't belong here flunk out, or don't come here in the first place. So who needs restricted enrollment?

8. The abortion issue is blown all out of proportion. How come we don't hear nearly as much about the evils of the pill? After all, a lot more potential people are "killed" by the pill than by abortion.

9. People say too much is made of abortion. Hogwash. Didn't they say over a million babies don't get born every year because of it? Yes, they did. Boy, if they killed a million congressmen every year, they'd sure think it was important.

10. You ask me what claims made by my textbooks are wrong. Well, I'll tell you. My science book says whales are mammals. But everyone knows whales live in the sea. And that's what a fish is, an animal that lives in the sea. So there.

11. I don't know of any claims in my textbooks that are wrong. But there must be some, because authors are human beings, just like everybody else. So I have to say there must be some wrong statements in my textbooks, even if I'm not smart enough to spot them.

12. I've often wondered how they make lead pencils. Of course, they don't use lead, they use graphite. But I mean how do they get the graphite into the wood? That's my problem. The only thing I can think of is maybe they cut the lead into long round strips and then cut holes in the wood and slip the lead in.

---

2. Cogent Reasoning

Reasoning—and any argument into which reasoning is cast—is either **cogent** (good) or **fallacious** (bad). To reason cogently, three criteria must be satisfied:

> Life is the art of drawing sufficient conclusions from insufficient premises.
> —Samuel Butler

(1) We must start with **justified** or **warranted** premises; (2) We must include all available relevant information;[2] and (3) our reasoning must be **correct** or **valid,** which means roughly that being justified in accepting the premises justifies acceptance of the conclusion.[3] (The second criterion is important only with respect to what is called *inductive* reasoning, to be discussed below.)

3. Two Basic Kinds of Valid Argument

There are two basic kinds of correct or valid argument: **deductive** and **inductive.** The essential property of a **deductively valid argument** is this: *If its premises are true, then its conclusion must be true also.* To put it another way, if the premises of a deductively valid argument are true, then its conclusion *cannot be false.*

On the other hand, the premises of an **inductively valid argument** provide good but not conclusive grounds for accepting its conclusion. The truth of its premises does not guarantee the truth of its conclusion, although it does make the conclusion *probable.* (That's why the expression "probability argument" is often used instead of "inductive argument.")

Here is an example of an inductively valid argument:

   1. So far, very few presidents of U.S. colleges and universities have been brilliant intellectuals.
∴ 2. Probably very few future presidents of U.S. colleges and universities will be brilliant intellectuals.

There may be a few readers who will want to deny the truth of the premise of this argument. But even they will have to admit that *if* they were to accept it as true (on good grounds), then it would be reasonable to accept the argument's conclusion also. And yet, the conclusion may turn out to be false, even if the premise is true, since boards of overseers, regents, and state legislators could conceivably start selecting more intellectual college presidents.

Contrast the above inductive argument with the following deductively valid argument:

   1. Every U.S. president has lied to us.
   2. Jimmy Carter was a U.S. president.
∴ 3. Jimmy Carter lied to us.

---

[2]This is an extremely stringent requirement that in real life is beyond the ability of most of us most of the time. The point is to come as close as possible to satisfying it, bearing in mind the seriousness of the problems to be solved and the cost (in time and effort) of obtaining or recalling relevant information. (One of the marks of genius is the ability to recognize that information is relevant to a topic when the rest of us aren't likely to notice.)

[3]For a more detailed account of valid reasoning, see the author's *Logic and Philosophy,* 4th ed. (Belmont, Calif.: Wadsworth, 1982).

Assuming for the moment that the first premise is true (we all know that the second premise is true), it is inconceivable that the conclusion could be false. It would be inconsistent (contradictory) to believe both premises yet deny the conclusion. For in saying the two premises we have implicitly said the conclusion.

We have here a fundamental difference between deductive and inductive reasoning: The conclusion of a deductively valid argument is just as certain as its premises, while the conclusion of an inductively valid argument is less certain than its premises. Inductive conclusions have that extra element of doubt (however slight) because they make claims not already made by their premises. In contrast, the conclusion of a deductively valid argument is no more doubtful than its premises because its conclusion is already contained in its premises (although often only implicitly).

Induction Is a Kind of Patterning

Perhaps the basic idea behind valid induction is that of *pattern* or *resemblance*. We want our conception of the future, our idea about what this or that will be like, to fit a pattern we glean from what this or that was like in the past. We feel justified in expecting the pattern of the future to match the pattern of the past. (The problem, of course, is to find patterns that fit all of what we have experienced of the past.)

4. Deductive Validity

Different arguments may have the same **form,** or **structure.** Here are two arguments that share the same form:

(1) 1. If the president doesn't act forcefully, he'll lose points in the polls.
     2. He won't act forcefully.
∴   3. He'll lose points in the polls.

(2) 1. If Russian hawks get their backfire bomber, our hawks will have to be given something.
     2. The Russian hawks will get their backfire bomber.
∴   3. Our hawks will have to be thrown a bone. (That is, our hawks will have to be given something.)

And here is the form or structure they share:

1. If [some sentence] then [a second sentence].
2. [The first sentence].
∴ 3. [The second sentence].

Or, using *A* and *B* to stand for the two sentences:

1. If *A* then *B*.
2. *A*.
∴ 3. *B*.

(This form is traditionally called **Modus Ponens.**)

Now, here is another commonly used and intuitively valid deductive form, called **Modus Tollens:**

Form:
1. If *A* then *B*.
2. Not *B*.
∴ 3. Not *A*.

Example:
1. If blacks are genetically less intelligent than whites, then mixed racial blacks should have higher average test scores than pure blacks.
2. They don't have average scores higher than pure blacks.[4]
∴ 3. Blacks aren't genetically less intelligent than whites.

Here is the argument form called **Disjunctive Syllogism:**

Form:
1. *A* or *B*.
2. Not *A*.
∴ 3. *B*.

Example:
1. Either it is our African policy to support majority rule or else our policy is antiwhite.
2. It can't be that our policy is to support majority rule.
∴ 3. Our African policy must be antiwhite. (See Chapter 6, where this argument is used in the analysis of a political column.)

And here is the valid argument form called **Hypothetical Syllogism:**

Form:
1. If *A* then *B*.
2. If *B* then *C*.
∴ 3. If *A* then *C*.

Example:
1. If the industrial countries get tough with OPEC, oil will become cheap and plentiful.
2. If oil becomes cheap and plentiful, then the energy problem will be solved.
∴ 3. If the industrial countries get tough with OPEC, then we can forget about the energy crisis (the problem will be solved).

Finally, here are three argument forms of a slightly different nature:[5]

Form:
1. All *F*s are *G*s.
2. This is an *F*.
∴ 3. This is a *G*.

Example:
1. All politicians are liars.
2. Ted Kennedy is a politician.
∴ 3. Ted Kennedy is a liar.

Form:
1. No *F*s are *G*s.
∴ 2. It's false that some *F*s are *G*s.

Example:
1. No policemen accept bribes.
∴ 2. It's false that some policemen accept bribes.

---

[4]See the box on page 28.
[5]See the author's *Logic and Philosophy,* 4th edition (Belmont, Calif.: Wadsworth, 1982), for more on the difference between these three and the others just mentioned.

Form: 1. All *F*s are *G*s.
                 2. All *G*s are *H*s.
        ∴ 3. All *F*s are *H*s.

Example: 1. All hetero males without women resort to masturbation.
                 2. Those who masturbate eventually go crazy.
        ∴ 3. Hetero males who don't have women eventually go crazy.

In everyday life, arguments tend to come bunched together in extended passages that are usually designed to justify one grand conclusion or theme. Here is a very simple example containing just three related arguments (with structure exhibited to the left):

1. If *A* then *B*.

     1. If the politicians have their way, we'll increase our nuclear arsenal faster than the Russians.

2. If *B* then *C*.

     2. But if we do (increase our stockpile faster), there will be no nuclear disarmament.

∴ 3. If *A* then *C*.

     3. So if the politicians have their way, there won't be any nuclear disarmament.

4. If *C* then *D*.

     4. But then (if there is no nuclear disarmament), an all-out nuclear war will be inevitable.

∴ 5. If *A* then *D*.

     5. All of which proves that if the politicians have their way, we'll all end up fighting a nuclear war.

6. Not *D*.

     6. But it's ridiculous to think we'll actually have an all-out nuclear holocaust (that is, it's false that we'll have an all-out nuclear war).

∴ 7. Not *A*.

     7. So the politicians aren't going to have their own way this time.

Beetle Bailey cartoon reprinted by permission of King Features Syndicate.

Humorous use of disjunctive syllogism. Gen. Halftrack's reasoning is this: Either the box is too small or we're not running this camp right. It's false that we're not running this camp right—that is, we are running it right. So the box is too small—build a bigger one. Halftrack omits as understood the premise that the camp is not being run wrong, just as we often do in daily life.

Deductive Invalidity

Any argument that doesn't have a deductively valid form is said to be *deductively invalid.*[6] The number of deductively invalid argument forms is legion, but a few are so common they've been given names. Here are two (to give the flavor):

Fallacy of Denying the Antecedent:

Form:
1. If *A* then *B*.
2. Not *A*.
∴ 3. Not *B*.

Example:
1. If abortion is murder, then it's wrong.
2. But abortion isn't murder.
∴ 3. Abortion isn't wrong.

(The conclusion doesn't follow because abortion may still be wrong for other reasons.)

Fallacy of Asserting the Consequent:

Form:
1. If *A* then *B*.
2. *B*.
∴ 3. *A*.

Example:
1. If Carter is still president, then a liar is now president.
2. A liar is now president.
∴ 3. Carter is still president.

(The conclusion doesn't follow because some other liar may now be president.)

Exercise 1-2

Invent deductively valid arguments having the forms of *Modus Ponens, Modus Tollens, Disjunctive Syllogism,* and *Hypothetical Syllogism.* Then invent arguments having the forms of the fallacies *Denying the Antecedent* and *Asserting the Consequent,* and show that they are deductively invalid.

---

5. Inductive Validity

We can think of induction, or patterning, as a principle of reasoning that moves from evidence about some members of a class to a conclusion about all members of that class.[7] What is called **induction by enumeration** is the simplest form of induction (and according to some, the foundation for all the other forms). In induction by enumeration, we infer from the fact that all *A*s observed so far are *B*s to the conclu-

---

[6]A deductively invalid argument isn't necessarily bad. It may still be inductively valid. The examples about to be given are bad because they're both deductively and inductively invalid.
[7]Or, in the case of analogical reasoning, to a conclusion about *some* other members. See below for more on analogies.

sion that all *A*s whatsoever are *B*s. For instance, a study of 100 members of Congress which revealed that all 100 support the FBI in its effort to reduce crime would count as good evidence for the inductive conclusion that *all* members of Congress support the FBI in this effort. Similarly, a check of, say, 15 secondary school civics texts from major publishing houses indicating that each one falsifies the extent of the difference between American ideals and actual practice would be good evidence that all such texts stray from the truth in this way.

Obviously, some inductions of this kind are better than others, and make their conclusions more *reliable,* or *probable.* While there are several different theories about how to determine the probability of the conclusion of a particular induction by enumeration, almost all agree on a few points.

Greater sample size yields greater probability.   The more instances in a sample, the greater the probability of a conclusion based on that sample. If our sample of civics texts had included 20 books instead of 15, and if we had checked 200 members of Congress instead of 100, then the conclusions drawn from these larger samples would be more probable. The point is that more of the same sort of evidence doesn't change the conclusion of an inductively valid argument; it changes the degree of probability of that conclusion, and thus changes the strength of belief a rational person should have in that conclusion.

More representative samples yield higher probabilities.   In addition to sheer size, the quality of a sample is important. We want a sample to be *representative* of the population it was drawn from. It won't do, for instance, to ignore the civics texts of a particular publisher if we have any reason to suspect that that company's texts might be substantially different from the rest. Similarly, we don't want our sample of members of Congress to contain only Democrats or only Republicans because of the possibility that one party supports the FBI more than the other. In other words, we want to make sure that our sample is not *biased,* that it is as representative of the population as possible. The more representative a sample, the greater the probability of a conclusion drawn from it.

One definite counterexample refutes a theory.   One definite counterexample to an enumerative induction shoots it down. If we run across even one member of Congress who does not support the FBI in its war on crime, then our theory that all members of Congress do so is obviously false.

However, it's often hard to be sure that what looks like a counterexample really is. Suppose a woman taking a certain birth control pill becomes pregnant. Does this disprove the manufacturer's claim that the pill in question is 100 percent effective? Should it count as a genuine counterexample? Yes, if there is good evidence that the woman in question really did take her pills in the prescribed way and didn't, say, accidentally skip a day. Otherwise, no. The trouble is that in everyday life the needed evidence may be hard to come by. The moral is that it's risky to reject a theory or idea because of one or two counterexamples unless we're very sure that at least one is the genuine article.

Reasoning by Analogy

In addition to induction by enumeration, there are also several closely related forms of reasoning by **analogy**. In one version, we reason from the similarity of two things in several respects to their similarity in another. Thus, if we know that Smith and Jones have similar tastes in books, art, food, music, and TV programs and find out that Smith likes Buñuel movies, we're justified in concluding that Jones does so also.

In another version of reasoning by analogy, we reason from the fact that all items of a certain kind, *A,* that have been checked so far have some property, *B,* to the conclusion that some as yet unexamined *A* has the property *B*. We use this form of analogy, for instance, when we reason from evidence that 100 members of Congress improperly use franked mail to the conclusion that a certain other member is going to campaign via franked mail in the next election (and thus have an advantage over his challenger).

Reasoning by analogy is safer than induction by enumeration, since analogies have much weaker conclusions. We inferred above that one particular member of Congress would abuse his right to free official mail, which clearly is a weaker (and thus safer) prediction than that all members of Congress will abuse that privilege.

The strength of an analogy is judged in pretty much the same way as that of an induction by enumeration. For instance, the more tastes Smith and Jones share, the better our analogical conclusion that they share a liking for Buñuel flicks. And the more members of Congress we discover abusing their franking privileges, the better our analogical conclusion that a certain other member will do so in the next election.

Statistical Induction

Suppose we wish to investigate the acceptance of illegal campaign contributions from large corporations, instead of the misuse of franked mail. We would almost certainly find that some members of Congress never engage in such thievery. Checking on 100 randomly selected incumbents in Congress, we might find that only 15 have accepted illegal campaign contributions (so far as we can tell). We can't then conclude that all members of Congress accept illegal contributions, but we can conclude that about 15 percent of them do, based on the evidence that 15 percent of our sample did so. Such an inference is called a **statistical induction.**

It should be obvious that statistical induction is very much like induction by enumeration. In fact, some claim that induction by enumeration is just a special case of statistical induction in which the percentage of *A*s that are *B*s happens to be 100 percent. (In other words, they interpret the *all* in the conclusion of an enumerative induction to mean "100 percent.") So it should be obvious that, just as in the case of induction by enumeration, the conclusion of a valid statistical induction becomes more probable as we increase sample size and instance variety—since it is then more likely that our sample will be representative of the population as a whole.

Higher Level Induction

Induction of a broader, more general, or higher level can be used to evaluate (correct or support) lower level inductions. For centuries, Europeans noted that every swan they'd ever seen was white. Using induction by enumeration, many concluded that all swans are white. But some ornithologists, observing that bird species often vary in color in different locations, reasoned by means of a broader, **higher level induction** to the conclusion that swans might vary in color also. They reasoned (roughly) like this: Most bird species observed so far vary in color. Therefore, probably, swans vary in color also (a conclusion that turned out to be correct, since some Australian swans are black).

Higher level inductions of this kind are used all the time in daily life. For example, we use higher level induction when we conclude than an automobile will break down eventually and need repairs even though it has run perfectly so far. Our higher level induction goes roughly like this: All mechanical devices with moving

Joseph Farris cartoon. Copyright © 1982 by *Playboy*

"How can we know that no one can win a nuclear war unless we try it and see?"

Most readers of Playboy *magazine no doubt smiled when they read the caption under the above cartoon. But few would have been able to explain the nature of the folly in the respondent's reasoning. He seems to assume that the only way to establish or justify factual beliefs is by low-level induction by enumeration (or perhaps by statistical induction)—trying out several nuclear wars to see whether any nation can win them. He overlooks the use of higher level induction (plus deductive reasoning) by means of which many of us conclude that the destruction caused by an all-out nuclear war would leave neither side a winner.*

parts eventually wear out and need repairs. So, *very* probably (because our evidence is so overwhelming), this particular mechanical device with moving parts (it happens to be an automobile) will wear out eventually and have to be repaired.[8]

Causal Connections

When we reason inductively, we are often looking for explanations or **causes**. For example, early investigators of the connection between cigarette smoking and lung cancer, emphysema, and heart disease wanted to determine by means of statistical inductions whether smoking *causes* these death-dealing diseases. They found that smokers get these diseases much more often than nonsmokers, and heavy smokers more than light. That is, they discovered a statistical connection between smoking cigarettes and contracting these diseases. Finding no higher level evidence to the contrary, they concluded that cigarette smoking does indeed *cause* these life-threatening illnesses.

But finding a statistical connection does not always mean that we can claim a causal connection. This is true even if the statistical connection is 100 percent, and even if we're convinced that the 100 percent connection will continue indefinitely. It all depends on what other beliefs we have that are relevant.

To take a famous example, before Newton some scientists believed that the earth would circle the sun forever, revolving on its axis every 24 hours. They thus believed in a constant connection, a one-to-one correlation, between occurrences of night and of day. That is, they believed that every time one occurred it would be followed by the other. But they did not believe night *causes* day, nor day night. For they knew that *if* the earth stopped rotating on its axis (of course, they believed this would never be the case), then night would not follow day, nor day night. Thus, for them, night could not be the cause of day, nor day the cause of night.

By way of contrast, we assume that the constant connection between, say, putting sugar into coffee and the coffee tasting sweet *is* a causal connection, because (unlike the day/night case) we have no higher level theories that show how this constant connection might be broken. In other words, we feel justified in assuming that the 100 percent statistical connection between sugar and sweet-tasting coffee is a causal connection because doing so does not conflict with higher level (and thus better confirmed) inductive conclusions.

---

[8]This use of higher level evidence to support or refute a lower level conclusion is a familiar one in science. Physicists, for instance, used evidence about the tides and about objects falling toward the earth as evidence for Isaac Newton's very general law of universal gravitation. (Each observed case in which the tides or objects falling toward the earth conform to Newton's law constitutes an instance of the enumerative induction whose conclusion is Newton's law.) This law in turn implies Kepler's laws, which describe the orbits of planets around the sun as ellipses of a certain kind. So evidence about the motion of the tides and the velocity of objects falling toward the earth confirms Kepler's laws by confirming Newton's higher level law, of which Kepler's laws are a special case. (More precisely, Newton showed that Kepler's laws are very close approximations to the truth.) The relevance of watches wearing out to automobile durability is thus no more mysterious than the relevance of the tides to Kepler's laws about planetary motion.

A Misconception about Deduction and Induction

There is a widespread but erroneous idea about the difference between deductive and inductive validity. This is the idea that in deductively valid reasoning we go from the general to the particular, while in inductively valid reasoning we move from the particular to the general. But there is little to be said for this idea. For instance, the deductively valid argument

    1. All Republican politicians are to the right of Tip O'Neill.
∴ 2. All who are not to the right of Tip O'Neill are not Republican politicians.

moves from the general to the equally general, while the inductively valid argument

    1. Richard Nixon made promises in 1960 and 1968 he didn't intend to keep.
∴ 2. Richard Nixon made promises in 1972 he didn't intend to keep.

moves from the particular to the equally particular. And the inductively valid argument

    1. So far, all Democratic party presidential candidates have been white.
∴ 2. The next Democratic party presidential candidate will be white.

moves from the general to the particular, not the other way around.

So there isn't much truth to the old idea that deductive reasoning moves from the general to the particular while inductive reasoning moves from the particular to the general. More accurately, when we reason deductively, we reason to conclusions already contained (implicitly or explicitly) in our premises; when we reason inductively, we move to conclusions by extending patterns or resemblances observed in our experiences to predict our future experiences.

6. World Views and Background Beliefs

When evidence linked high White House officials to the Watergate burglary during the 1972 presidential campaign, a great many Americans dismissed it as just campaign rhetoric—it couldn't be true because President Nixon himself said it wasn't, and presidents of the United States don't lie to the American people about such matters. But other Americans responded differently, dismissing Nixon's denials as what one would expect from a politician running for office, even a president of the United States. Nixon's earlier denials that American forces had invaded Cambodia met with a similar mixed response.

Could it be true that officials of the American government, from the president on down, would lie about invading a foreign country? Yes, it could be true, and it was. Why then did so many Americans accept their government's denials, even in the face of clear-cut evidence to the contrary? Because of some of their basic beliefs about human nature, and in particular about how the American system works. Given these beliefs, which formed part of what might be called their **world views**, it *was* unlikely that Nixon, Henry Kissinger, and other top officials would lie about such a serious matter; it *was* sensible to believe what their government—in particular their president—told them and to reject what otherwise would have been overwhelming evidence.

World views are crucial. Accurate world views help us to assess information accurately; inaccurate world views lead us into error. A world view is like a veil through which we perceive the world—a filter through which all new ideas or information must pass. Reasoning based on a grossly inaccurate world view yields grossly inaccurate conclusions (except when we're just plain lucky), no matter how good our reasoning may be otherwise.

This means that if we want to draw sensible conclusions, we must pay a good deal of attention to our world views (or, as they are also called, our *philosophies*), constantly checking them against newly acquired information and revising them when necessary, so that our evidence and beliefs form as coherent a package as possible.

What we have called a *world view* or *philosophy* is just the most general and theoretical part of what can be called our package of **background beliefs**, a package that includes particular facts as well as general theories. In judging arguments, we need to bring to bear *all* relevant background beliefs, particular as well as general. Thus, in trying to decide whether President Nixon was telling the truth about Watergate or Cambodia, intelligent citizens tried to bring to bear not only their overall world views but also particular facts they knew about Nixon (and about those who contradicted what Nixon said). For example, this writer tended not to believe the president, first because his overall world view told him that national leaders often do lie about such matters, and second because of what he knew about Nixon's record as a shady liar[9] (as well as his knowledge of what European and non-mass media correspondents in the Far East were claiming). But many Americans were fooled by Nixon, not just because of their defective world views but also because they didn't know the details of Nixon's past record of dishonesty, or hadn't heard (or believed) what European correspondents and the American non-mass media were saying.

Exercise 1-3

Find at least one item in the mass media (a newspaper or magazine article, or something from TV) that reflects a typically American world view and explain what makes it typically American.

---

7. Self-Deception and Wishful Thinking

If life consists of one damned problem after another, and if world views are crucial to the solution of these problems, it might be supposed that intelligent people would constantly strive to have the most accurate world views possible. And, according to some world views, they do. But in fact (or, more modestly, according to the world view of the author), this cannot be true. Allegedly reasonable human beings have always differed seriously in their world views (as well as in their particular beliefs), even when exposed to roughly the same evidence. Think, for instance, of the differing views intelligent people hold on issues such as national defense, the "energy crisis," and how to reduce unemployment. The same relevant evidence

---

[9]See, for instance, page 78 for earlier Nixon chicanery.

Andy Capp by Reggie Smythe, © 1976 Daily Mirror Newspapers Ltd. Dist. Field Newspaper Syndicate.

Self-deception at work.

concerning these subjects is available to all the "experts," yet their use of this information (including, sometimes, just ignoring it) varies greatly, largely because it fits differently into their different world views. When people differ on factual questions, some people—in fact lots of quite intelligent people—must either be reasoning incorrectly or, more likely, be wedded to grossly inaccurate world views.

But how can this be? The answer (according to the author's view of human nature—an important part of his world view) is **self-deception** or **wishful thinking**. It is a very human trait indeed to believe that which we want to believe, and in particular to deny that which we find too unpleasant. To take an extreme case, Jews in Nazi-controlled Europe during World War II overlooked all sorts of evidence about what was in store for them (extermination) and grasped at every straw in the wind that favored a less horrible fate (thereby making it more certain that they would in fact be exterminated). The point of facing reality is precisely to increase one's chances of enjoying a satisfying life.

But human beings deceive themselves about ordinary problems also. Take cigarette smoking. The evidence linking cigarette smoking to all sorts of fatal illnesses (lung cancer, heart diseases, emphysema) is overwhelming. Yet several tobacco

---

Silver Linings

Our rationalization of the month award goes to W. Clement Stone, the wealthy Chicago insurance executive who donated $201,000 to Richard Nixon's campaign in 1968 and $2 million more in 1972. Asked at his seat in the Illinois delegation at Kansas City if he had second thoughts about those contributions, he replied, "No, I'm not sorry. I'm glad I gave to Nixon. Watergate was good for the country. It allowed us to define standards of public morality."

—*New Times* (September 17, 1976)

Rationalization—*convincing oneself of (usually) plausible but untrue reasons for conduct*—is an important component of self-deception. *(The best way to fool others is to first fool ourselves.) This item shows that even the rich and powerful need to forestall public embarrassment by rationalizing away foolish mistakes.*

company presidents have publicly denied the conclusiveness of this evidence. They may be lying, but then again they may simply be deceiving themselves—it's hard to accept the idea that one's life is being spent selling a product that kills people. And legions of habitual cigarette smokers tell themselves they have to quit, or that they can quit any time they want to, while lighting up still another Marlboro or Winston. It takes a great deal of effort to reduce such self-deception, but that effort is very much worthwhile, given that the truths we conceal from ourselves so often return to haunt us (in the case of cigarettes, perhaps to kill us). Straight thinking, unlike wishful thinking, pays off by giving us better estimates of what life has to offer, of what we should seek or avoid, and of our strengths and weaknesses, thus giving us a better chance to succeed at whatever we want to do with our lives.

Yet many people consciously prefer wishful thinking or childlike fantasy to facing reality. They seem to reason this way: "How can I arrange my beliefs so I'll feel most comfortable?"—rather than arranging them so as to agree with reality.[10]

Self-deception and wishful thinking lead to all sorts of prejudices. Millions of Americans today believe in astrology, "pyramid power," and many other pseudo-scientific "theories" for which there is no supporting evidence and overwhelming negative evidence. Millions more believe that there have been many "close encounters of the third kind" and that astronauts from outer space landed on Earth in ancient times. The lack of supporting evidence and the higher level inductions that make such beliefs totally improbable don't seem to have any serious effect on these beliefs. Here is an excerpt illustrating this kind of irrational, self-deceptive prejudice.

O Tempora, O Cult

"Bending . . . bending," the students chanted, as they "helped" a magician "bend" a solid brass rod by gently stroking it—a standard trick. Then, the students watched as the performer did two other tricks that are found in many children's magic books: he "read" three-digit numbers "by ESP" while blindfolded, and "teleported" ashes from the back of a volunteer's fist to the inside of her palm.

The 189 students, enrolled in introductory psychology classes at California State University at Long Beach, were part of an experiment that revealed the considerable depth of their belief in paranormal or psychic processes. Surveys consistently show that a majority of Americans believe in occult or paranormal events, such as ESP, UFOs, and exorcism, or in supposedly psychic feats like Uri Geller's spoon bending. In this experiment, psychologists Victor Benassi

---

[10]It's true that self-deception does have some advantages. For example, terminally ill patients who refuse to believe that they are dying may increase their chance of survival just by believing they're going to live.

and Barry Singer found that among students, brief skeptical comments from teachers leave such beliefs virtually unshaken.

Benassi and Singer asked the magician to enhance his psychic aura by wearing a choir robe and medallion instead of the usual top hat and tails. However, they asked instructors to introduce him to three different, randomly selected groups, using speeches designed to encourage increasing degrees of skepticism about paranormal events. For the first group, the instructor described the performer as someone "interested in the psychology of paranormal or psychic abilities," but the instructor firmly stated his own doubts about such powers. In the second group, the instructor described the performer as a magician. With the third group, the instructor again said the performer was a magician, and added that he would only "pretend to read minds and demonstrate psychic abilities . . . what you'll be seeing are only tricks."

When the students wrote down their reactions after the performances, 75 percent of those in the first group said they believed in the performer's psychic powers, despite the instructor's expressed skepticism. In the second group, which had explicitly been told the performer was a magician, more than 60 percent felt he was using psychic powers to perform his tricks. In the third group, despite the instructor's clear warning that they would be seeing "only tricks," more than half the students still believed the performer was psychic. In each group, many students said their belief in the paranormal had increased because they had finally seen it "with their own eyes."

Benassi and Singer hypothesize that prior belief in psychic power among the students (which they did not measure) was so strong that the students simply disavowed contrary information and interpreted the evidence to suit their prejudices.

Berkeley Rice in *Psychology Today* (March 1979). Reprinted by permission.

S. Gross cartoon. *Psychology Today* (February 1983)

The ancient Romans had a saying: "Populus vult decipi"—The people want to be deceived. Yes, on the whole they often do. But not every person every time (one reason for Abraham Lincoln's famous remark about not being able to fool all the people all the time). We can, by conscious effort and attentiveness, catch ourselves in the act and, over time, reduce self-deception to more manageable proportions.

The trouble is that most people are unwilling to face the fact that *they* engage in self-deception and wishful thinking, even though they may believe that other people are self-deceivers. One way to get yourself to notice your own self-deceptions is to become familiar with some of the more common varieties so that if you pull some of these tricks on yourself, you may notice that reason has flown out the window. Here are just a very few of the more common self-deceptive devices:

Rationalization or false motive.   We often tell ourselves "good" motives for doing something when our strongest motive is one we'd rather not face. The author of this text has a rather embarrassing fear of telephoning in certain situations, which he papers over with believable excuses—so believable that he tends to believe them himself (except, of course, later on, when as in this case there is mileage to be gained by owning up).

Guilt avoidance.   This is a kind of rationalization that is so common it deserves separate mention. When we want very much to do something we're not supposed to do, even by our own standards, we often avoid guilt by finding other ways to describe and justify the action. Or, in extreme cases, we simply "forget" the rule and *do it* (whatever we want to do). Perhaps the classic example of this is sexual seduction, which works precisely because the parties in question want it to work, even though one of the parties is not supposed to want it to work. Similarly, dieters may "forget" they're on a diet, often until the forbidden food is in their mouth, when, of course, it's "too late" to stop.

Here is an excerpt from an analysis by N. W. Ayer of a Daniel Yankelovich opinion survey.

Women are in unanimous agreement that they want to be surprised with gifts. . . . They want, of course, to be surprised for the thrill of it. However, a deeper, more important reason lies behind this desire, . . . "freedom from guilt." Some of the women pointed out that if their husbands enlisted their help in purchasing a gift (like diamond jewelry), their practical nature would come to the fore and they would be compelled to object to the purchase.

Quoted by Edward J. Epstein in *The Atlantic* (February, 1982)

Typical example of self-deception—allowing selfish motives to overcome more high-minded ones of familial cooperation.

Blindness to evil.   One way to deal with the bad news life presents us with is to ignore it, or better yet to avoid finding out about it. This is so common it's captured in a cliché: "Don't tell me that; I don't want to know about it." Many members of minority groups, for instance, seem to go out of their way not to find out how the deck is stacked against them. This sometimes is advantageous—not knowing the extent of prejudice occasionally increases one's chances of beating it. But usually, such blindness to evil yields an immediate advantage only to backfire in the long run.

Rehearsing and posing.   In our attempt to look the best we can for other people, all of us often rehearse to ourselves what we plan to tell others later, and then sometimes come to believe the rehearsed version of reality, even though deep down we may know the truth. (The same is true of pretending.)

Similarly, we all know that most social life involves posing, although we tend not to pay attention to our own poses. When we go to a party, say one where we don't know many people, we may be bored or afraid, but most of us paste smiles on our faces and pretend we're having a great time. Later, we may remember the party as more fun than it really was. Liars pose as truth tellers (what else would they do?) and eventually come to believe some of their own lies. Self-serving politicians eventually come to believe part of their own campaign rhetoric.[11] The list of such deceptions is endless.

Of course, this idea that human beings are self-deceivers contradicts the entrenched belief that human beings are essentially rational animals, a belief many of us have incorporated into our world view. Now there can be no doubt that human beings are the smartest animals, and no doubt that some of us on occasion perform marvelous feats of reasoning. But those who watch themselves and others carefully and *without bias* will find that rationality is only part of the story and that self-deception is the other part. In particular, when we are of divided minds or hearts on a topic, we tend somehow or other to deceive ourselves so as to favor one internal force against the others, and when faced with extremely harsh reality, we often deny what the evidence clearly implies. Those of us willing to face this nonrational element in human nature have a much better chance of overcoming it and living better, happier lives than those (a large majority) who are more or less blind to that part of their nature.

One of the functions of great humorists—in particular great satirists, like Jonathan Swift and Henry Fielding—is that they effectively puncture our self-deceptive defenses and reveal true human nature with all its warts. Here is Mark Twain skewering the naïve idea that human beings are essentially honest and truthful.

As I understand it, what you desire is information about "my first lie, and how I got out of it." I am well along, and my memory is not as good as it was. If you had asked about my first truth it would have been easier for me and kinder of you, for I remember that fairly well. I remember it as if it were last week. The family think it was the week before, but that is flattery and probably has a selfish project back of it. . . .

---

[11]We don't want to go overboard. All posing does not result in believing one's own pose. Politicians don't always believe their own lies, any more than do the rest of us. But they, like us, tend to be caught up in their own lies.

I do not remember my first lie, it is too far back; but I remember my second one very well. I was nine days old at the time, and had noticed that if a pin was sticking in me and I advertised it in the usual fashion, I was lovingly petted and coddled and pitied in a most agreeable way and got a ration between meals besides.

It was human nature to want to get these riches, and I fell. I lied about the pin—advertising one when there wasn't any. You would have done it; George Washington did it, anybody would have done it. During the first half of my life I never knew a child that was able to raise above that temptation and keep from telling that lie. Up to 1867 all the civilized children that were ever born into the world were liars—including George. Then the safety pin came in and blocked the game. But is that reform worth anything? No; for it is reform by force and has no virtue in it; it merely stops that form of lying, it doesn't impair the disposition to lie, by a shade. . . .

To return to that early lie. They found no pin and they realized that another liar had been added to the world's supply. For by grace of a rare inspiration a quite commonplace but seldom noticed fact was borne in upon their under-standings—that almost all lies are acts, and speech has no part in them. Then, if they examined a little further they recognized that all people are liars from the cradle onward, without exception, and that they begin to lie as soon as they wake in the morning, and keep it up without rest or refreshment until they go to sleep at night. If they arrived at that truth it probably grieved them—*did*, if they had been heedlessly and ignorantly educated by their books and teachers, for why should a person grieve over a thing which by the eternal law of his make he cannot help? He didn't invent the law; it is merely his business to obey it and keep still; join the universal conspiracy and keep so still that he shall deceive his fellow-conspirators into imagining that he doesn't know that the law exists. It is what we all do—we that know. I am speaking of *the lie of silent assertion;* we can tell it without saying a word, and we all do it—we that know. In the magnitude of its territorial spread it is one of the most majestic lies that the civilizations make it their sacred and anxious care to guard and watch and propagate.

For instance. It would not be possible for a humane and intelligent person to invent a rational excuse for slavery; yet you will remember that in the early days of the emancipation agitation in the North the agitators got but small help or countenance from anyone. Argue and plead and pray as they might, they could not break the universal stillness that reigned, from pulpit and press all the way down to the bottom of society—the clammy stillness created and maintained by the lie of silent assertion—the silent assertion that there wasn't anything going on in which humane and intelligent people were interested.

From the beginning of the Dreyfus case to the end of it, all France, except a couple of dozen moral paladins, lay under the smother of the silent-assertion lie that no wrong was being done to a persecuted and unoffending man. . . .

Now there we have instances of . . . prominent ostensible civilizations working the silent-assertion lie. Could one find other instances . . . ? I think so.

Not so very many perhaps, but say a billion—just so as to keep within bounds. Are those countries working that kind of lie, day in and day out, in thousands and thousands of varieties, without ever resting? Yes, we know that to be true. The universal conspiracy of the silent-assertion lie is hard at work always and everywhere, and always in the interest of a stupidity or a sham, never in the interest of a thing fine or respectable. Is it the most timid and shabby of all lies? It seems to have the look of it. For ages and ages it has mutely labored in the interest of despotisms and aristocracies and chattel slaveries, and military slaveries, and religious slaveries, and has kept them alive; keeps them alive yet, here and there and yonder, all about the globe; and will go on keeping them alive until the silent-assertion lie retires from business—the silent assertion that nothing is going on which fair and intelligent men are aware of and are engaged by their duty to try to stop.

What I am arriving at is this: When whole races and peoples conspire to propagate gigantic mute lies in the interest of tyrannies and shams, why should we care anything about the trifling lies told by individuals? Why should we try to make it appear that abstention from lying is a virtue? Why should we want to beguile ourselves in that way? Why should we without shame help the nation lie, and then be ashamed to do a little lying on our own account? Why shouldn't we be honest and honorable, and lie every time we get a chance? That is to say, why shouldn't we be consistent, and either lie all the time or not at all? Why should we help the nation lie the whole day long and then object to telling one little individual private lie in our own interest to go to bed on? Just for the refreshment of it, I mean, and to take the rancid taste out of our mouth. . . .

Mr. [William Cullen] Bryant said, "Truth crushed to earth will rise again." I have taken medals at thirteen world's fairs, and may claim to be not without capacity, but I never told as big a one as that. Mr. Bryant was playing to the gallery; we all do it. Carlyle said, in substance, this—I do not remember the exact words: "This gospel is eternal—that a lie shall not live." I have a reverent affection for Carlyle's books, and have read his *Revolution* eight times; and so I prefer to think he was not entirely at himself when he told that one. . . .

To sum up, on the whole I am satisfied with things the way they are. There is a prejudice against the spoken lie, but none against any other, and by examination and mathematical computation I find that the proportion of the spoken lie to the other varieties is as 1 to 22,894. Therefore the spoken lie is of no consequence, and it is not worth while to go around fussing about it and trying to make believe that it is an important matter. The silent colossal national lie that is the support and confederate of all the tyrannies and shams and inequalities and unfairnesses that afflict the peoples—that is the one to throw bricks and sermons at. But let us be judicious and let somebody else begin.

And then— But I have wandered from my text. How did I get out of my second lie? I think I got out with honor, but I cannot be sure, for it was a long time ago and some of the details have faded out of my memory. I recollect that

> I reversed and stretched across someone's knee, and that something happened, but I cannot now remember what it was. I think there was music; but it is all dim now and blurred by the lapse of time, and this may be only a senile fancy.
>
> From "My First Lie and How I Got Out of It," in *Mark Twain on the Damned Human Race*, edited by Janet Smith (New York: Hill and Wang, 1962).

8. Hints for Constructing Cogent World Views

World-view construction should be a lifelong activity, a habitual response to the flood of information we all are exposed to. One way to become good at this activity is to develop rough-and-ready rules, or hints, to guide us. Here are a few that may prove useful.

Check World Views for Consistency

To the extent that a world view is *internally inconsistent* (that is, one part contradicts another) or *inconsistent with our experiences* of the world, it must be incorrect. Truths do not contradict each other.

A world view that frequently leads us to beliefs contradicted by experience should be changed so as to accord more closely with reality—that, after all, is the point of world-view building. Failure to bring a world view into conformity with experience renders cogent reasoning less and less likely and makes a person's fate just that much more a matter of luck. So the first and most important hint for good world-view construction is to *habitually check one's world view for consistency with experience,* amending it when necessary to make it as consistent as possible.

This hint needs to be emphasized, because people find it hard to give up cherished or long-held beliefs. Beliefs about drugs are a good example. Medical evidence and everyday experience strongly indicate that the drugs in cigarettes (nicotine), hard liquor (alcohol), and coffee, tea, and cola drinks (caffeine), as well as several widely used prescription drugs (Valium, Quaaludes), are much more harmful than, say, marijuana or cocaine. Yet most Americans simply will not accept this, because it violates long-held and somehow psychologically more comfortable beliefs to the contrary.

A world view tends to be a hodgepodge of beliefs on different levels of generality—one reason it's so hard to root out inconsistencies. World views, at least for mere mortals, are thus unlike scientific theories (although a good world view will have lots of scientific theories in it). Science also contains theories on different levels of generality—physics, for example, certainly is more general than geography or geology. But a geological theory concerning, say, how valleys of a certain kind are formed over the ages is expected to be consistent with the rest of scientific theory. World views, on the other hand, rarely, if ever, are examined so carefully, although a few brave souls—true philosophers—do try. (For this and other reasons, smart people *always* revise their world views when they contradict well established scientific theories.)

Evaluate Information Sources for Accuracy

The crucial factor in formulating a reasonably accurate world view is the quality of information we are exposed to. As computer experts say, "Garbage in, garbage out." If we allow the usual (poor) information to just wash over us, using it uncritically in forming our basic beliefs as most people do, it is unlikely that our world views will be much better than those of most people—which means not very good at all.

So it's vital that we form an accurate theory concerning the quality of various sources of information, in particular the information obtained from professional "experts" (doctors, lawyers, teachers, elected officials), the media (television, radio, newspapers, magazines), friends and relatives, and textbooks (including this one). Under what conditions are these sources likely to give us the truth (in particular, give us information not colored by wishful thinking)? And, equally important, when are they likely to lie, or conceal the truth, and when tell it to us straight? The average person tends to believe what is said by those in positions of authority and to digest whole what appears on television or in the newspaper. But some authorities and some media sources are better than others, because they are positioned better to know the truth, or because they are more highly motivated to tell the truth (or less highly motivated to conceal it). So hint number two for constructing a cogent world view is to *evaluate sources of information for their likely accuracy.* And the key to such evaluation is *past performance:* we should conclude by low-level induction that on the whole, sources which have proved more (or less) accurate in the past will prove to be so in the future. (It's important to see that this rule applies to friends, also, since friends are an important source of information, and lots of otherwise fine friends are congenital bull slingers.)

Construct Theories of Human Motivation

Low-level induction by enumeration is a relatively slow process and often leads us astray. So we sometimes need to use higher level theories to correct lower level conclusions. For example, higher level theories about how human beings will respond to economic and other factors should have convinced us that the trend toward true investigative reporting started by the Woodward and Bernstein *Washington Post* Watergate exposés would prove too costly in time and political good will, and that reporters would tend to return, more or less (there has been some improvement), to the same old ways of gathering the news (described in Chapter 8).

The key to higher level conclusions about news sources is a general theory of human motivation. Experts, friends, and those who run the media are just people, more or less like the rest of us. How much will what they tell us be motivated by personal goals or desires? Almost all journalists are economically dependent on their jobs; to what extent is this likely to color their reporting of the news? Most television stations and newspapers are privately owned businesses that are expected to turn a profit for their owners; how is this likely to be reflected in the information they provide us? Most members of Congress almost without thinking fall into the exciting, seductive lifestyle of those at the center of power; will this usually lead to a strong desire for continual reelection, which in turn will influence their performance and rhetoric? Information sources need to be evaluated in terms of human motivation for acquiring and telling the truth. We cannot assume, for instance, that members of Congress are "supposed" to tell the truth and therefore can be relied upon to do so, or that television stations "wouldn't be allowed" to mangle the news for private purposes.

So hint number three for cogent world-view construction is to *develop and continually update general theories of human motivation.* Of course, induction is the main tool to use in doing this—the past is our only key to what reason can tell us about the future. But we don't have to start from scratch. A good deal of the experience of the species is captured in everyday sayings, such as "Blood is thicker than water" and "Power tends to corrupt," that are good candidates for inclusion in a theory of human motivation (not that we should accept them uncritically).

Beware of Self-Deception and Wishful Thinking

We've already seen how self-deception and wishful thinking are the chief villains that reduce our ability to reason. This is especially true in constructing world views.

One good way to reduce self-deception and wishful thinking is to ask yourself of each prospective belief, "Would I accept it if I didn't *want* it to be true?"

Avoid Thinking in Terms of Unverified Stereotypes

A **stereotype** is a conventional, usually oversimplified or overblown conception, view, or belief. Most stereotypes are accepted because of prejudice, resulting from

---

The third edition of this text had a box at this point containing fourteen examples of sayings of a particular kind (a bit cynical or irreverent, with a twist, yet usually containing serious truth) that have been extremely popular in recent years. The three best known of those quoted were the Peter Principle ("In every hierarchy, each employee tends to rise to his or her level of incompetence"), Parkinson's Law of the Bureaucracy ("Work expands to fill the time available for its completion"), and the most famous of the lot, Murphy's Law ("If anything can go wrong, it will").

Now it turns out (illustrating this *version of Murphy's Law) that Edward A. Murphy, Jr., himself had something different in mind. What he actually said was: "If there is a wrong way to do something, then someone will do it."*[12] *And what he meant was this: Anyone working with or designing equipment or machinery should try to figure out every possible way in which someone could misuse it, and then try to make such misuses as difficult as possible. In other words, he meant that "If there are two or more ways to do something, and one of those ways can result in a catastrophe, then someone will choose that way, so we should design things to have only one method of operation—the right way." Murphy was seriously trying to reduce human error and definitely* not *proclaiming a fatalistic slogan. Well, let's hope we've got Murhphy right this time.*

---

[12]See *Science 83*, Jan/Feb 83.

the desire to conform to group beliefs or the desire to draw quick and convenient conclusions even though lacking sufficient evidence.

Stereotypes concerning particular classes of people are especially dangerous. It is a stereotype that the French are great lovers, women more fickle than men, blacks very rhythmic, men emotionally tough, Indians good only when dead, Jews and Scots unusually frugal, and so on.

Since stereotypes are on the whole cultural in origin, a world view based on stereotypes is unlikely to be much better than the average in a given culture, which means not very good at all. A person who wants to think more subtly than the herd needs to pay attention to the hint to *avoid thinking in terms of stereotypes except where there is good evidence that a stereotype is accurate.*

Scientific theories can get extremely complicated and technical, to the point that few nonscientists understand them. But the structure of good scientific reasoning usually is rather simple. Here is an example of simple and good scientific reasoning in psychology, on the touchy question of IQ differences between whites and blacks. The excerpt quoted here forms just a small part of a very well-thought-out theory. While the test referred to is not by itself conclusive, it does provide some confirmation (and others mentioned in the article much more) for its conclusion.

Attitudes, Interests, and IQs

Some people who believe in genetic differences [in IQ] between blacks and whites think that there is an easy way to prove their point: Blacks who have more European and less African ancestry should have higher IQs than blacks with less European and more African ancestry. . . . We tested this notion by giving several tests of intellectual skill to a sample of 350 blacks in the Philadelphia area. Instead of asking the participants directly what their heritage was, we could estimate each person's degree of African and European ancestry from blood samples, because Africans and Europeans differ in the average frequencies of certain types of blood groups and serum protein. If a person had a particular blood group or serum protein gene, the researchers could assign a probability that he got it from a European or African ancestor. The estimates were based on 12 genes. Though some error undoubtedly crept into the estimates, they were accurate enough, because they matched up with skin color and were similar for siblings.

The results were unequivocal. Blacks who had a large number of European ancestors did no better or worse on the tests than blacks of almost total African ancestry. These studies dispute the hypothesis that IQ differences between blacks and whites are in large part the result of genetic differences.

Sandra Scarr and Richard A. Weinberg, in *Human Nature* (April 1978). Copyright © 1978 by Human Nature, Inc. Reprinted by permission of Harcourt Brace Jovanovich, Inc.

Become Familiar with the Scientific View of the Universe

While no information is absolutely reliable, some kinds are more reliable than others. The safest kind, without question (if successful application is any guide), is information gained from the physical sciences—and biology, now that the genetic code is being cracked. (The basic principles of the social sciences are still a matter of great controversy and all sorts of foolish ideas flourish alongside penetrating insights. But here also rapid progress is being made and these sciences have a good deal to tell discriminating readers.)

One reason why the sciences are so accurate is that science is an organized, world-wide, ongoing activity, which builds and corrects from generation to generation. Another is that the method of science is just the rigorous, systematic application of cogent inductive reasoning from what has been observed of the world to expectations about future experiences that can be and are checked up on.[13] No one starting from scratch could hope to obtain in one lifetime anything remotely like the sophisticated and accurate conclusions of the physical or biological sciences.

Grasping the general outline of the scientific picture of the universe and of the way we fit in it is doubly valuable. First, that picture can serve as the core onto which we can sketch increasingly sophisticated ideas as to how this or that works, so that new information can be systematically integrated with old. And second, it can help us to understand the vital issues of the day (for example, whether we're likely to run out of oil soon if present rates of consumption continue, the consequences of making abortion illegal, whether any "close encounters of the third kind" have actually occurred, the effectiveness of SALT treaties and negotiations, or the risks connected with nuclear power plants), and help us deal with life's day-to-day mundane problems (for instance, whether to take large doses of various vitamins, whether a particular "hair restorer" may actually work, how to choose the best painkiller for the money, how to safely siphon gasoline from one gas tank to another, or which breakfast foods are healthiest).

So a fourth hint for good world-view building is to *learn the basics of the scientific view of the world.* This means that world-view building is not something that can be done in a day, or even a few months. It is an ongoing lifetime activity with increasing benefits in terms of more accurate judgments—*provided* it is done carefully.

Don't Fall for Pseudoscience

Since so many people tend to believe what they want to believe, pseudoscience prospers. We therefore have to be able to tell the difference between it and the genuine article. Obviously, the best way to learn how to do this is to become scientists ourselves, or learn as much as we can about basic scientific theory. It is physicists, chemists, and astronomers, after all, who are in the best position to evaluate a theory such as, say, Immanuel Velikovsky's brainstorm that Venus broke away from Jupiter in biblical times.

But most of us are not scientists. So we sometimes have difficulty distinguishing science from pseudoscience, in particular since there is no sharp line between the

---

[13]For another reason, see the box on pages 32–33.

two. Roughly speaking, a theory is not acceptable to scientists if it contradicts well-confirmed theories or if there is no good evidence in its favor. But spotting examples where this is the case can be difficult, in particular because pseudoscientists do often present what looks like good evidence to the lay person. For example, Erich von Daniken presented all sorts of "evidence" in favor of his "Chariot-of-the-Gods" theory that ancient astronauts from outer space landed on Earth in ancient times, including "evidence" of their landing site in South America. Real scientists easily showed his evidence to consist primarily of misinterpreted relics of ancient human civilizations (the landing strip is just a level area with lots of ancient Indian ceremonial markings). But nonexperts could not be expected to see through von Daniken's "proof" so easily.

Still, there are a few marks of pseudoscience to help us avoid it.

1. *Pseudoscience often conflicts with everyday experiences.* The trick is to get the knack of bringing your everyday experiences to bear when relevant. Take astrology—in particular, the unsophisticated versions peddled by the

---

In the fight between you and world, back the world.
>—Franz Kafka

Natural laws have no pity.
>—Robert A. Heinlein

Nature, to be commanded, must be obeyed.
>—Francis Bacon

Those who fail to remember the laws of science are condemned to rediscover some of the worst ones.
>—Harold Gordon (in a takeoff on George Santayana)

Most men of education are more superstitious than they admit—nay, than they think.
>—G. C. Lichtenberg

We are never deceived. We deceive ourselves.
>—Johann von Goethe

Habit is stronger than reason.
>—George Santayana

There are two reasons for doing things—a very good reason and the real reason.
>—Anonymous

Every man is encompassed by a cloud of comforting convictions, which move with him like flies on a summer day.
>—Bertrand Russell

Every dogma has its day.
>—Abraham Rotstein

mass media—the most popular of all pseudosciences. The basic idea behind the various popular versions of astrology is that the positions of the planets (or "stars") at the time of birth influence the whole course of a person's life. Millions of people accept this theory even though it runs counter to their own everyday experiences. Pliny, the Elder, put this experience into words a very long time ago when he said: "If a man's destiny is caused by the star under which he is born, then all men born under that star should have the same fortune. However, masters and slaves and kings and beggars all are born under the same star." If astrology were true, all people born at the same time would have the same sorts of personalities, experiences, or opportunities, yet everyday experience shows that this conclusion is completely false.

2. *Pseudoscience suppresses negative evidence.* Astrology buffs often claim that their everyday experiences do in fact confirm astrological theory. For instance, they say they often can tell which sign a person is born under just by seeing how that person behaves. They often say things like, "You must be a Taurus." And then they remember the times when they guess right and forget those when they guess wrong. Or, when told that the person in question isn't a Taurus, they rationalize: "Oh, Leo! Yes, yes, how could I have missed it. You are *so* Leo." And so on. For them, one good guess outweighs ten bad ones.

3. *Pseudoscience doesn't fit in with the rest of science.* The first thing a true scientist does when he hears some new cockamamie pseudo claim is to see if it conflicts with accepted scientific theories. Take Immanuel Velikovsky's theory that Venus broke away from Jupiter in biblical times (thus accounting for the sun standing still for Joshua, and other biblical miracles). On hearing this theory, a good scientist would immediately make some quick calculations and find that the path Venus is supposed to have taken from Jupiter past the Earth and into its present orbit around the sun could not possibly have conformed to Newton's law of motion. Nor could the Earth possibly have its present orbit, or be in its current condition. Having much more evidence in favor of Newton than Velikovsky, scientists dismissed Velikovsky's theory as nonsense.

4. *Pseudoscience usually lacks detail.* True scientists always consider the details that make all the difference. Pseudoscientists generally pass over these details, perhaps because they would show their theories to be false. For instance, it's not just that Velikovsky miscalculated the path Venus would have had to take, but rather that he never even bothered to go into the "little detail" of whether the path he proposed did or didn't conform to Newton's laws. Like most pseudoscientists, he didn't bother to do the required mathematical calculations.

5. *Pseudoscience smacks of wishful thinking.* Most people believe what they want to believe and not necessarily what they have evidence for. They *want* to believe that there have been "close encounters of the third kind," or that astrology is true, or that people like Jeanne Dixon can actually predict the future—so they *do* believe, and then find "reasons" to support their beliefs.

When tempted to believe a theory that mainstream scientists scoff at, the crucial question to ask yourself is this: Would you believe the theory if you had exactly the same evidence but didn't want to believe it? For instance, would you believe in astrology if it predicted your doom? When the answer is *no,* your belief is just wishful thinking, not the intelligent use of reason.

Learn from the Experiences of Past Generations

There is, finally, an important rule for young people, namely to *learn from the experiences of past generations.*

In general, the young are perfectly willing to learn from their own experiences (or those of friends) and from current science. But anything that happened before they were born tends to get treated as very ancient history. There is a certain legitimate optimism in this, the feeling that the accomplishments and knowledge of past generations can and will be improved on, that old champions will be replaced by new (and better) ones. But Santayana was right when he said that "those who fail to remember the past are condemned to relive it." Past inflations may tell us a great deal about the latest one, past wars how to avoid the next one. And even ancient history has its timely lessons: knowing why the Roman empire fell may give us clues as to how to

---

Here is Isaac Asimov, one of the best known popularizers of science (also famous for his science fiction), explaining why cheating in science is so rare, why getting caught is almost inevitable sooner or later, and thus why scientists on the whole are so much more trustworthy (when they're doing science!) than, say, politicians and other "public servants."

Self-correction

Every once in a while—not often—scientists discover that one of their number has published false data or has plagiarized someone else's work.

This is always deeply embarrassing, especially since these days such news usually receives wide publicity in the nonscientific world.

In some ways, however, these scandals actually reflect credit upon the world of science. Consider:

1) Scientists are, after all, human. There is enormous pressure and competition in the world of science. Promotion and status depend on how much you publish and how *soon* you publish, for the lion's share of credit comes if you are *first* with an important theory or observation. Under these circumstances, there is great temptation to rush things; to make up some data you are sure you will eventually find anyway that will support your theory; or to help yourself to someone else's work. The surprise, really, is not that it sometimes happens, but that it doesn't happen much more often. Scientists resist the pressure marvelously well.

keep our own western civilization from crumbling. Every generation does *not* have to repeat the mistakes of previous ones, either as a group or in their individual private lives. After all, there are plenty of new ones available.

Realistically Appraise One's Own Abilities and Chances

While not directly relevant to this text's concentration on the social-political arena, an accurate *assessment of one's own abilities and chances* for success in life is a valuable part of anyone's world view. While there is often a certain advantage to be gained by (very) modestly overestimating one's own abilities and opportunities (for one thing because it may help overcome apprehension), still many more people fail from overinflated self-opinions or expectations than from underestimations.

For instance, being blind to one's own abilities and weaknesses often leads to a terrible waste of time and effort pursuing a will-o'-the-wisp. A friend of this writer spent over twenty years of his life trying to make it as a political cartoonist in spite of having no drawing talent whatsoever. Another, a modestly talented athlete, sweated blood between the ages of 15 and 25 trying to succeed as a football player but was never offered a pro contract (in spite of trying three times). (He did finally face reality and happily discovered that he was a natural born salesman.)

---

2) When it does happen, the mere fact that it is so publicized is a tribute to scientists. If it were a common event, or if people expected scientists to be corrupt, it would make smaller headlines and drop out of sight sooner. Single cases of scientific corruption, however, will be talked about for years and inspire articles and books by the score. It's really a compliment.

3) Cases of scientific misbehavior point out how difficult it actually is to carry them out successfully, or even for very long. . . . [A] vital principle in scientific research is that nothing counts until observations can be repeated independently and there, almost inevitably, anything peculiar is uncovered. Science is *self-correcting* in a way that no other field of intellectual endeavor can match.

4) It is scientists themselves who catch the frauds; no one else is equipped to do so. The point is that scientists *do* catch them. There is never any cover-up on the grounds that science itself must not be disgraced. However embarrassing the facts may be, the culprit is exposed pitilessly and publicly. Science is *self-policing* in a way that no other field is.

5) Finally, the punishment is absolute. Anyone who proves to have violated the ethics of scientific endeavor is ruined for life. There is no second chance, no vestige of status. He or she must drop out, forever disgraced.

Add to all this the fact that scientific ethics requires all scientists to labor to find flaws in their *own* observations and theories—and to publicize these flaws when they find them—and you will understand how stern the requirements are and how astonishing it is that scandal is so infrequent.

From *SciQuest* (February 1982). Reprinted by permission of the author.

9. Hints for Evaluating Particular Arguments

The point of constructing world views (aside from simple curiosity about how the world works) is to be better able to solve particular problems and deal with particular arguments. Waiting in line to buy gasoline is annoying; running out of gas, extremely disruptive. When service stations run out of gas, is that due to a genuine gasoline shortage? If so, what is the cause of the shortage? The government asks Americans to buy series E bonds; is the rate of inflation likely to be greater than the rate of interest on such bonds during the time they take to mature, so that investors in E bonds end up with less than when they started?

Of course, world views don't answer questions like these all by themselves. We have to *reason* from our world views, coupled with particular facts, to sensible conclusions. While the general theory for evaluating the validity of particular reasons or arguments of this kind has been modestly well worked out, effective theories have not been discovered for *finding* sensible conclusions to consider or for bringing all relevant information to bear on a proposed solution. (One reason may be that, as remarked before, some people do better using one method, some another). But again, a few rules or hints may prove useful.

Look For and Evaluate Presuppositions

In the first place, we should try to *figure out and evaluate the unspoken presuppositions of an argument.* Life is short—no one spells out everything. Does a particular argument rest on a presupposition you don't share? If so, no matter how valid that argument may be, it would be a mistake to accept its conclusion.

This sounds obvious, but it takes practice to become good at it. Consider the argument that the quality of life in the United States must have improved considerably between 1960 and 1970, because productivity increased by about 40 percent during that period. The unspoken presupposition of this argument is that increased productivity results in increased quality of life, or (put another way) that increases in goods and services result in increases in human satisfaction. Lots of people, including some economics experts, seem not to have noticed that this presupposition needs to be added to the argument as a premise if the argument is to be valid (or perhaps they haven't bothered testing to see whether it stands up to experience).

Well, does the premise that increased productivity results in increased quality of life square with your experience, with your world view? If yes, then (neglecting questions of wealth distribution) you should accept the conclusion that the quality of life in the U.S. improved a great deal from 1960 to 1970. But if no, then this conclusion has to be rejected.[14] (In fact, there are all sorts of reasons for supposing that increased productivity does not necessarily lead to increased quality of life. For example, the private automobile has taken a great deal of the increase in U.S. productivity since World War II, in part because we have neglected short-distance public transportation while the average distance from home to work has increased. Enduring rush-hour traffic jams alone in one's private auto takes a great deal more material wealth than does walking to work or taking a commuter train or bus, but is it more satisfying?)

---

[14]This doesn't mean its negation, that the quality of life has not improved, should be accepted. It means that this argument should not convince us either way.

Test Premises Against Background Beliefs

Obviously, it isn't only implicit premises (presuppositions) of an argument that need to be looked into. Explicit (stated) premises also need to be evaluated. In particular, we need to *test the premises of arguments for consistency with our other beliefs*—especially the basic ones that make up our world view.

Read Between the Lines

A person who has a reasonably accurate world view and lots of background facts often can get more information from a statement or argument than is expressly contained in it. Doing this is called "reading between the lines" and often is the essential ingredient in assessing political rhetoric as well as (interestingly) advertisements.

Take the Bufferin ad, "No regular aspirin product reduces fever better." Reading between the lines of this ad, we should conclude that Bufferin does *not* reduce fever better than some competing products, because if they did their ad would make that stronger claim ("Bufferin reduces fever better than any other aspirin product"), rather than the weaker one that none reduces fever better. The point is that we should expect an advertiser to make the strongest claim possible, and thus conclude that a less strong claim is made because stronger ones are false.[15]

Reading between the lines often requires great sophistication or subtlety, but

At certain moments, as we have seen, athletes have feelings of floating and weightlessness. Sometimes, in fact, they even have out-of-body experiences. Now we would like to consider the possibility that the athlete is literally able to suspend himself in midair. In the earlier chapters we discussed the athletes' subjective feelings that they were floating or outside themselves. But is there an objective reality involved, something that can be verified by others? We think that there is. We have collected many statements by sportswriters, coaches, and other observers that attest to the fact that some athletes actually can, for brief moments, remain suspended in the air. Basketball players and dancers, especially, seem to demonstrate this amazing ability.

Human Behavior (March 1979)

This *writer's world view tells him that if better evidence could have been obtained to prove this kind of levitation it would have been—first, because really proving it exists would have created a sensation, and second, because it would have been so easy to get (motion pictures would show it). Since they didn't get this proof, it's reasonable to suppose they couldn't, because, as the basic laws of physics suggest, no one can suspend himself in midair, even for a brief moment.*

---

[15]Reading between the lines is the linguistic equivalent of "sizing up" a person. A good poker player, for instance, looks for telltale signs of bluffing in personal mannerisms, since some players systematically signal a bluff by increased chatter or nervousness, while others do so by feigning unconcern. Similarly, an intelligent voter sizing up a political candidate looks for nonverbal as well as verbal signs of that candidate's true intent once in office.

sometimes it just requires adding or subtracting a few figures. Here is a quote from *Inquiry* magazine (October 15, 1979) illustrating this:

> Consider the state of agriculture between the Civil War and World War I, a period of immense growth in the American economy. Agriculture shared in that growth: The number of farms tripled, the number of acres of farmland doubled, the net farm income increased more than fourfold. Despite this growth, two stark figures stand out. Farm population decreased from 60 percent to 35 percent of the national total population, and agriculture's share of the national income dropped from 31 percent to 22 percent. In other words, agriculture did not keep pace with the rest of the economy.

Interesting figures. But by doing a little calculating, we can come up with two more interesting statistics. First, while lots of farmers must have gone broke, those that remained seem to have improved their financial position compared to nonfarm workers. And second, surprisingly, the average farm, contrary to what one might think, seems to have decreased in size during the period in question (figure out why).

An alleged case of reading between the lines during World War II may have changed the course of human history. Here is the story, according to some sources:[16] "In May of 1942, . . . a young Soviet physicist noted the abrupt absence of articles on nuclear fission in the American journal *Physical Review.* He drew the obvious conclusion—security measures often point an unmistakable finger—and wrote Stalin a letter reporting that the Americans were trying to build an atomic bomb. Early in 1943, Stalin appointed the physicist Igor Kurchatov to run a small Soviet bomb project." Even supposing the story isn't true, the point about reading between the lines remains the same. The information was there for an astute physicist in the Soviet Union (or Germany! or Japan!) to discover by reading between the lines.

There is a technical reason why the intelligentsia in the Soviet Union consume more books than their Western colleagues. Where a Western scholar or writer can refer to just one source book, a Russian must often gather the same information bit by bit from various sources. Information about the history of religion is gleaned from quotes in antireligious brochures, the opinions of modern philosophers from Marxist articles condemning bourgeois or revisionist philosophy, and so on. For many years, for example, the only reference book on modern music was Shneerson's *Music Serving the Reactionaries,* which branded Stravinsky, Messiaen, Menotti, and others as agents of imperialism. But at least there one could pick up the names, dates, names of compositions, and a few ideas about these composers.

—Lev Lifshitz-Losev,
in *New York Review of Books (May 31, 1979)*

Reading-between-the-lines pickings are slim in the Soviet Union, but vital.

---

[16]See *The Atlantic* magazine (March 1983) book review of *The Soviet Union and the Arms Race* (New Haven: Yale University Press, 1982), or read the book.

Bring Unstated but Relevant Information to Bear

One of the crucial differences between geniuses and the rest of us is that a genius is able to bring information to bear on an issue which the rest of us tend not to recall or not to realize is relevant. Of course, only a few of us can be geniuses, but we can all try to get into the habit of searching our minds for relevant information.

Take the question of why American industry has lost the competitive edge it enjoyed over other industrial nations since World War II. One answer sometimes heard is that ever increasing energy costs, in particular high oil prices, have raised production costs of goods to levels which make American goods uncompetitive with foreign manufactured products. But if we think about it for a minute we should see that we know a fact which is not consistent with this explanation, so that it can't be correct. The fact is simply that other industrial nations also have a problem with high energy costs (chiefly high oil prices), so that lower energy costs cannot be their advantage. We cannot expect others to give us information which would destroy their positions; we have to try to think of that information by ourselves. The hint this suggests is that we should try to *bring all the relevant information we know to bear on an issue or argument.*

One kind of information authors rarely provide is any bias or pressure that might have influenced their judgment. It's asking too much to expect to get such information (although on rare occasions we do get it). Take the question of animal over-population, starvation, and hunting. In a letter (*Harper's,* September 1978), Lewis Regenstein, executive vice-president of The Fund for Animals, suggests an interesting motive that wildlife officials themselves were unlikely to mention for the oft-proposed defense of the "sport" of deer hunting:[17]

> Hunters consistently claim that deer herds must be "culled" to prevent over-population and starvation. . . . The main reason some areas temporarily end up with more deer than the habitat can support is that wildlife management officials deliberately try to create a "surplus" of deer—through stocking programs and manipulation of habitat—*in order to stimulate a demand for, and sell, a maximum number of hunting licenses, their main source of revenue.* [Italics added.]

Of course, finding out who gets what is always useful, because most of us are under pressure to make ends meet and therefore just might hold back information harmful to our financial interests.

Apply Principles Consistently

In the example above concerning oil and the loss of our competitive edge, the trick was to apply an alleged answer to similar cases: If it works for them, then it's more

---

A wise man hears one word and understands two.

—Jewish proverb

---

[17]Notice how important it is what name we give a thing.

likely that it will work in the case in question. When we apply the high-energy-costs answer to the similar cases of other industrial nations, it doesn't work, which should tell us that perhaps it doesn't work in the case of the United States either. This is a variation on the overarching principle that we should *reason consistently*.

A related kind of mistake is to reason inconsistently by appealing to one principle in a given circumstance and a contradictory principle in another (or by appealing to a principle in one circumstance while denying it in another), without showing a *relevant* difference between the two. A humorous example occurred at a poker game recently when someone argued that he wouldn't smoke marijuana because it's illegal. When confronted with the fact that the poker game was also illegal, he replied, "So who's going to tell on us?" Inconsistent reasoning of this kind is really more an attempt to prop up or paper over wishful thinking or prejudice than to arrive at justified beliefs or decisions.

Draw Undrawn Relevant Conclusions

In late spring of 1979, a radio news program reported that while oil imports were down from a year earlier, demand was down slightly more. The announcer then quoted a Department of Energy explanation that oil companies (following a suggestion of President Carter's) were trying to build up reserves to avoid a fuel shortage the following winter. But there was a much better explanation available, so the DOE explanation should have been questioned. For it is precisely the oil companies, owners of increased stocks of oil, who benefit the most from the increased prices likely to result from a temporary shortage at the gas pump. The big oil corporations could have eliminated all shortages by pumping and refining more domestic oil. But our world view should tell us that corporations tend to act in the interests of their stockholders and (to a lesser extent) their high-level employees; in this case, the oil corporations had a strong motive for reducing the supply of gasoline (rather than, say, building up reserves by temporarily pumping more domestic oil)—namely, to drive up the price of gasoline so as to maximize profits.

The trick is to learn habitually to bring our world views and other relevant information to bear and then *draw relevant conclusions not drawn for us by others*. (Sometimes, all that is required is just to "add up" the information in an argument to reach a conclusion not reached by the arguer.)

Consider the Strongest Version of an Argument

In connection with the idea of bringing unstated but relevant information to bear on an argument, there is an additional rule to use when we're tempted to reject an argument, namely, to *be sure we have considered the strongest version of the argument* (the point of avoiding the "straw man" fallacy to be discussed in Chapter 3).

This is an important rule, because all of us are tempted to reject conclusions we don't like much more quickly than those we do. (The corollary to this rule is that we should be doubly suspicious of the things we are eager to believe.)

Become Aware of an Information Source's Bias

One of the problems in evaluating information is that much of the news is often presented from a point of view we don't share. Most political magazines, for example, give us information within the context of articles which presuppose (in the case of many left-wing publications) that big business is the main villain in American society or (in the case of some right-wing publications) that labor unions and welfare government are the chief villains. Given the natural human tendency to want to hear what we already believe to be true rather than to investigate different points of view, readers tend to choose magazines and newspapers that reflect their own point of view, particularly with respect to political/social issues. A publication thus tends to reflect a particular world view shared by its readers but not often critically evaluated within its pages. So we should *bear in mind the bias of the publications and writers we read,* for one thing so as not to be persuaded by rhetoric meant for the already converted.[18]

Indeed, knowing where an information source is coming from is important even in understanding *what* is being said, much less in determining its bias or accuracy. For instance, is the following quote, in particular its last line, intended to be ironic, or are we supposed to take it straight?

> The best parts . . . [of Henry Kissinger's book *Years of Upheaval*] are those that deal with the Middle East. Kissinger's part in the beginning of the peace process between Israel and Egypt is his most notable single personal accomplishment, one which goes far to justify his place on the list of Nobel Peace Prize winners. *One shares his view that this work outranks his labors on Vietnam.* [Italics added.]

Once we know that the writer is McGeorge Bundy, the air is cleared (assuming we know something of Bundy's role in American foreign policy). We then know he intended the passage to be taken literally.

Beware of Oversimplification

Sometimes we can tell the real from the fake, in part, by the relative lack of detail, depth, or subtlety of the fake. (Recall from our previous discussion that the high degree of detail and subtlety found in real science helps to distinguish the genuine article from pseudoscience.) A good current example of this is "Creation Science," which has practically no detail or depth. Its competitor, the truly scientific theory of evolution, is a marvelously detailed and complicated theory. For instance, a chemical archaeologist whose specialty is the prehistoric trade routes of Europe chemically investigates amber beads dug up at archaeological sites in order to help trace the movements of prehistoric peoples. The lack of comparable detail or depth in "Creation Science" is one of several reasons why that theory has next to no predictive power.

Break the Complicated into Simpler Parts

One difficulty in trying to reason well is that problems often get very complicated and thus are hard to digest whole. So to make them easier to digest, try to *break complicated problems, ideas, or arguments into more easily grasped component parts.*

---

[18]The charlatan's corollary: Don't fall for your own rhetoric.

The Fixation of Belief

Charles Peirce (1839–1914) is the father of Pragmatism, the only important philosophical position to originate in the United States. The following is from his 1877 article "The Fixation of Belief."

Few persons care to study logic, because everybody conceives himself to be proficient enough in the art of reasoning already. But I observe that this satisfaction is limited to one's own ratiocination, and does not extend to that of other men. . . .

Doubt is an uneasy and dissatisfied state from which we struggle to free ourselves and pass into the state of belief; while the latter is a calm and satisfactory state which we do not wish to avoid, or to change to a belief in anything else. On the contrary, we cling tenaciously, not merely to believing, but to believing just what we do believe. . . .

If the settlement of opinion is the sole object of inquiry, and if belief is of the nature of a habit, why should we not attain the desired end, by taking any answer to a question, which we may fancy, and constantly reiterating it to ourselves, dwelling on all which may conduce to that belief, and learning to turn with contempt and hatred from anything which might disturb it? This simple and direct method is really pursued by many men. I remember once being entreated not to read a certain newspaper lest it might change my opinion upon free-trade. . . . A similar consideration seems to have weight with many persons in religious topics, for we frequently hear it said, "Oh, I could not believe so-and-so, because I should be wretched if I did."

But this method of fixing belief, which may be called the method of tenacity, will be unable to hold its ground in practice. The social impulse is against it. The man who adopts it will find that other men think differently from him, and it will be apt to occur to him in some saner moment that their opinions are quite as good as his own, and this will shake his confidence in his belief. This conception, that another man's thought or sentiment may be equivalent to one's own, is a distinctly new step, and a highly important one. It arises from an impulse too strong in man to be suppressed, without danger of destroying the human species; so that the problem becomes how to fix belief, not in the individual merely, but in the community.

Let the will of the state act, then, instead of that of the individual. Let an institution be created which shall have for its object to keep correct doctrines before the attention of the people, to reiterate them perpetually, and to teach them to the young; having at the same time power to prevent contrary doctrines from being taught, advocated, or expressed. . . .

This method has, from the earliest times, been one of the chief means of upholding correct theological and political doctrines, and of preserving their universal or catholic character. . . .

For the mass of mankind, then, there is perhaps no better method than this. If it is their highest impulse to be intellectual slaves, then slaves they ought to remain.

But in the most priest-ridden states some individuals will be found who are raised above that condition. These men possess a wider sort of social feeling; they see that men in other countries and in other ages have held to very different doctrines from those which they themselves have been brought up to believe; and they cannot help seeing that it is the mere accident of their having been taught as they have . . . that has caused them to believe as they do and not far differently. Nor can their candor resist the reflection that there is no reason to rate their own views at a higher value than those of other nations and other centuries; thus giving rise to doubts in their minds.

A different method of settling opinions must be adopted, that shall not only produce an impulse to believe, but shall also decide what proposition it is which is to be believed. Let the action of natural preferences be unimpeded, then, and under their influence let men, conversing together and regarding matters in different lights, gradually develop beliefs in harmony with natural causes. This method resembles that by which conceptions of art have been brought to maturity. The most perfect example of it is to be found in the history of metaphysical philosophy. Systems of this sort have not usually rested upon any observed facts, at least not in any great degree. They have been chiefly adopted because their fundamental propositions seemed "agreeable to reason." This is an apt expression; it does not mean that which agrees with experience, but that which we find ourselves inclined to believe. Plato, for example, finds it agreeable to reason that the distances of the celestial spheres from one another should be proportional to the different lengths of strings which produce harmonious chords. Many philosophers have been led to their main conclusions by considerations like this.

This method is far more intellectual and respectable from the point of view of reason than either of the others which we have noticed. But its failure has been the most manifest. It makes of inquiry something similar to the development of taste; but taste, unfortunately, is always more or less a matter of fashion, and accordingly metaphysicians have never come to any fixed agreement, but the pendulum has swung backward and forward between a more material and a more spiritual philosophy, from the earliest times to the latest. And so from this, which has been called the *a priori* method, we are driven, in Lord Bacon's phrase, to a true induction. . . . [For] some people, among whom I must suppose that my reader is to be found, who, when they see that any belief of theirs is determined by any circumstance extraneous to the facts, will from that moment not merely admit in words that that belief is doubtful, but will experience a real doubt of it, so that it ceases in some degree to be a belief. . . . To satisfy our doubts, therefore, it is necessary that a method should be found by which our beliefs may be caused by nothing human, but by some external permanency—by something upon which our thinking has no effect. Some mystics imagine that they have such a method in a private inspiration from on high. But that is only a form of the method of tenacity, in which the conception of truth as something public is not yet developed. Our external permanency would not be external, in our sense, if it was restricted in its influence to one individual. It must be something which affects, or might affect, every man. And, though these affections are necessarily as various as are individual conditions, yet the method must be such that the ultimate conclusion of every man shall be the same. Such is the method of science. Its fundamental hypothesis, restated in more familiar language, is this: There are Real things, whose characters are entirely independent of our opinions about them; those realities affect our senses according to regular laws, and, though our sensations are as different as are our relations to the objects, yet, by taking advantage of the laws of perception, we can ascertain by reasoning how things really are; and any man, if he have sufficient experience and he reason enough about it, will be led to the one True conclusion. . . .

This is the only one of the four methods which presents any distinction of a right and a wrong way. If I adopt the method of tenacity, and shut myself out from all influences, whatever I think necessary to doing this, is necessary according to that method. So with the method of authority: the state may try to put down heresy by means which, from a scientific point of view, seem very ill-calculated to accomplish its purposes; but the only test *on that method* is what the state thinks; so that it cannot pursue the method wrongly. So with the *a priori* method. The very essence of it is to think as one is inclined to think. All metaphysicians will be sure to do that, however they may be inclined to judge each other to be perversely wrong. . . . above all, let it be considered that what is more wholesome than any particular belief is integrity of belief, and that to avoid looking into the support of any belief from a fear that it may turn out rotten is quite as immoral as it is disadvantageous. The person who confesses that there is such a thing as truth, which is distinguished from falsehood simply by this, that if acted on it will carry us to the point we aim at and not astray, and then, though convinced of this, dares not know the truth and seeks to avoid it, is in a sorry state of mind indeed.

Again, take the vexing question whether we have to worry about running out of oil, a very large question indeed. Here is one way to divide this large question into smaller ones (a way that flows from the author's background beliefs about the issue plus his general world view—different beliefs and views are likely to yield a different list):

1. What are the so-called "proven reserves" of oil, for the whole world and for the United States?

2. How much more recoverable oil—in addition to proven reserves—is there likely to be?

3. What is the current consumption of oil, in the whole world and in the United States?

4. Assuming sufficient supply, what is the most likely rate of increase in oil consumption in the world and in the United States?

5. What economically feasible alternative energy sources are there now?

6. What economically feasible alternative energy sources are there likely to be in the future?

7. Who benefits the most from a failure to solve the problem?

Even if these are not the best possible questions to ask, answering them is certain to help us formulate better ones, and to understand better the energy issue as a whole.

Of course, to answer questions such as those just posed, considering that most of us are nonexperts, we must inevitably appeal to experts or to the media, at least to obtain facts and figures (for instance, on crude oil imports and domestic production). In doing so, we naturally want to be sure that our appeals to expert opinion are cogent, not fallacious. And that's why the fallacy called *appeal to authority* is discussed first in the next chapter.

Summary of Chapter One

Reasoning is the essential ingredient in solving life's problems. Chapter 1 concerns good (and bad) reasoning about such problems.

1. Reasoning can be cast into *arguments,* which consist of one or more *premises* supporting a *conclusion.* In real life (as opposed to in textbooks), rhetoric does not divide easily into arguments or have premises and conclusions neatly labeled. Still, clues are given: for example, the words *because, since,* and *for* usually signal premises, and *hence, therefore,* and *so* conclusions. But remember that not all groups of sentences form arguments. They may, for example, form anecdotes or other types of exposition or explanation.

2. Reasoning is either *cogent* (good) or *fallacious* (bad). Cogent reasoning has to satisfy three criteria; it must: (1) start with *justified* or *warranted* premises; (2) use all relevant available information; and (3) be *valid,* or correct.

3. There are two basic kinds of valid reasoning: *deductive* and *inductive.* An argument is *deductively valid* provided that if its premises are true, its conclusion must be true. And, roughly, an argument is *inductively valid* when it projects a pattern gleaned from past experiences onto future ones. An inductively valid argument at best only makes its conclusion very probable— never certain.

4. Different arguments may have the same *form,* or *structure. Modus Ponens, Modus Tollens, Hypothetical Syllogism,* and so on, are deductively valid argument forms. *Asserting the Consequent* and *Denying the Antecedent* are deductively *in*valid argument forms.

5. The basic kind of induction is *low-level induction by enumeration,* in which we infer from the fact that all observed *A*s are *B*s to the conclusion that all *A*s whatsoever are *B*s (for example, assuming that since all our friends cheat on their income tax, everybody does).
    Here are a few hints for constructing and evaluating inductive inferences:
    a. Greater sample size yields greater probability.
    b. The more representative a sample (set of observations) is, the higher the probability of an induction based on it.
    c. One definite counterexample shoots down an induction. (But we have to make sure that it really is a counterexample.)

d. We can check up on lower level inductions by means of higher level (more general) ones.

Analogical reasoning is just like induction by enumeration, except that it yields a singular conclusion rather than a general one (and thus has a greater chance of being correct). *Statistical inductions* are also similar, except that they infer from the fact that *N* percent of a sample has a certain property to the conclusion that *N* percent of the population has that property (rather than that all do).

One very important reason for using induction is to discover *causal connections*. In the absence of contrary evidence, we usually can conclude that an observed constant connection is a causal connection. It isn't true that the difference between a deductively valid and inductively valid argument is that the former goes from the general to the particular while the latter goes from the particular to the general.

6. A person's basic beliefs about how the world and things in it work are called a *world view* or *philosophy*. How we construct our world view is vital, because we use it every day in reasoning about practically all problems of any import. A world view is the most theoretical part of our general stock of *background beliefs*. (And, of course, some of these other background beliefs may be relevant to a particular argument.)

7. *Self-deception* and *wishful thinking* are serious impediments to good world-view construction, as well as to all other reasoning. One important species is *rationalization,* another is *guilt avoidance,* a third is being blind to evil, and a fourth is believing one's own poses.

8. There are several good hints for world-view constructing. We should:
   a. Check our world view for internal consistency and for consistency with our experiences.
   b. Evaluate information sources for accuracy (some "experts" can't distinguish accurate information from a hole in the ground).
   c. Construct theories of human motivation, in particular so as to better evaluate information sources.
   d. Guard against self-deception and wishful thinking.
   e. Avoid thinking in terms of unverified stereotypes.
   f. Become aware of the basics of the scientific conception of the world, because science itself is just a systematic accumulation of inductively derived theories that are well supported by vast amounts of evidence. (We should also learn the difference between science and pseudo-science.)
   g. Try to learn from the experiences of past generations, so that we don't commit their mistakes over again.

9. There also are several hints for evaluating particular arguments. We should:
   a. Look for and evaluate the presuppositions of an argument, to make sure they fit with what we already know or believe.
   b. Do the same with respect to stated premises.
   c. Try to pick up useful information or ideas by reading between the lines of a passage.

d. Bring unstated but relevant information to bear on an issue. (We can't expect others to tell us everything.)
e. Apply principles consistently.
f. Draw undrawn relevant conclusions (again because we can't expect others to do this for us every time).
g. Consider the strongest versions of arguments, so that we don't knock over "straw positions."
h. Become aware of the biases of information sources.
i. Beware of oversimplification.
j. Get the knack of breaking complicated arguments or topics into their simpler parts, so that we can handle them more easily.

Exercise 1-4

Find a magazine or newspaper article that *disagrees* with your world view on some point. Show either why you still think your world view is correct and the article wrong or how the article led you to change your mind.

Exercise 1-5

Find a magazine or newspaper article that involves some omission or misstatement of fact or theory that could plausibly be attributed to self-deception, wishful thinking, or other forms of bias on the part of the writer. Explain.

Exercise 1-6

Describe a situation where you changed your mind on some more or less fundamental belief, and explain what convinced you. (Do *not* use the example you mentioned in answering Exercise 1–4.)

Exercise 1-7

This text characterizes human beings as liars as well as truth tellers (it silently asserts agreement with Mark Twain on this simply by selecting his point of view rather than others). Does this fit *your* world view? Defend your answer, especially by appeal to actual cases (in particular those where you have had firsthand experience).

Exercise 1-8 (for the energetic)

Construct a cogent argument (or group of related arguments) supporting one viewpoint on the issue of abortion, capital punishment, drug laws, or some other controversial social-political topic. Explain why you think the argument is both valid and persuasive.

Truth Is Booty, Booty Is Truth

"There is already an inclination to trust the Veep-designate precisely because he is rich. 'When somebody is one of the wealthiest men in the world,' said Rep. John Rhodes of Arizona, the Republican leader in the house, 'he's got so much money there would be no point in cheating.'"

—*Newsweek* (September 2, 1974)

Does this Edward Sorel political cartoon from The Village Voice *(September 17, 1974) illustrate a fallacious appeal to the authority of former Vice President Nelson Rockefeller's money?*

Half of being smart is knowing what you're dumb at.
                              —David Gerrold

Two wrongs don't make a right, but three do.
          —Unofficial slogan of the
          American military in Vietnam

It would be a very good thing if every trick could receive some short and obviously appropriate name, so that when a man used this or that particular trick, he could at once be reproved for it.
                    —Arthur Schopenhauer

2

Fallacious Reasoning—I

We said in Chapter 1 that to reason cogently, or correctly, we must: (1) reason from justified premises, (2) include all relevant information at our disposal, and (3) reason validly. *Fallacious reasoning* is just reasoning that fails to satisfy one or more of these three criteria. In other words, we reason **fallaciously** whenever we (1) reason from unjustified premises, (2) fail to use relevant information, or (3) reason invalidly.

Of course, we must remember that the fallacious arguments encountered in daily life tend to be vague and ambiguous, and can thus be taken in different ways, depending on how we construe them. Consider the following line from a beer commercial:

> More people in America drink Budweiser than any other beer.

Taken literally, this isn't even an argument, much less a fallacious one. But it clearly implies that the listener should also drink Bud. So we can restate it to say:

  1. More people in America drink Budweiser than any other beer. (Premise)
∴ 2. So you, too, should drink Budweiser. (Conclusion)

Stated this way, the argument is defective because it contains an *invalid inference*. Yet we could just as well restate it this way:

  1. More people in America drink Budweiser than any other beer. (Premise)
  2. The most popular beer is the best beer. (Premise)
  3. You should drink the best beer. (Premise)
∴ 4. So you should drink Budweiser. (Conclusion)

Now the argument is valid but contains a *questionable premise* —that the most popular beer is the best beer. Interpreted this way, the commercial can't be faulted for

47

invalid reasoning, but if we're persuaded by it, we become guilty of accepting a *questionable premise.*

Like the Budweiser example, most fallacious arguments can be restated in various ways. So there is no point in worrying too much about exactly which fallacy label we apply to a particular fallacious argument. Fallacy categories aren't built in heaven; they're just useful tools for spotting bad reasoning.

Logically, of course, all fallacies fall naturally into one of the three broad categories—*questionable premise, suppressed evidence,* and *invalid inference*— corresponding to the three ways that reasoning can be fallacious. But over the years a number of other fallacy categories have been invented that cross-cut the three logical categories. These other categories have come into common use because experience has shown them to be helpful in spotting fallacious reasoning.[1]

Let's now look at some of these other fallacy categories, remembering that in the last analysis, what makes reasoning fallacious is that it either uses *questionable premises,* or *suppresses relevant evidence,* or is *invalid.*

1. Appeal to Authority

None of us knows everything. So we all often have to appeal to other people or sources for information or advice. Improper appeals—in particular improper appeals to alleged experts—constitute the fallacy called **appeal to authority**.

But which appeals are proper and which improper? Roughly speaking, an appeal to another person or source is proper (not fallacious) when we're reasonably sure that this "authority" has the knowledge or judgment we need, we can expect the authority to tell the truth, *and* we don't have the time, inclination, or ability to form an expert opinion on our own. The more sure we are of these three things, the more legitimate or proper is our appeal to an authority; the less sure we are, the more likely it is that our appeal is fallacious. (There are other complications, of course, in particular when dealing with "sensitive" questions that involve values or taste.)

This means that there are three basic questions that need to be asked when we seriously want to know whether a particular appeal to an authority would be legitimate:

1. Does this source have the information or judgment we need?

2. If so, can we trust this authority to tell it to us truthfully?

3. Do we have the time, the desire, and the ability to reason this out for ourselves (or to understand the expert's reasoning, so we don't have to merely accept his conclusion)?

In everyday life, we usually know right away whether we've got the needed time and inclination. But the other questions can usually be answered only by bringing

---

[1]Over 100 different fallacies are discussed in one or another logic text, but no single book discusses them all. Only those that occur frequently are discussed in this text, which means our list is not exhaustive by any means. But the division into the master fallacies *questionable premise, suppressed evidence,* and *invalid inference* is exhaustive. (So far as this writer is aware, it's the only exhaustive fallacy classification in the literature.)

background information to bear. This process is usually not easy, but the rules of thumb about to be discussed should prove useful.

Authorities in One Field Aren't Necessarily Experts in Another

Famous athletes and movie stars who endorse all sorts of products in television commercials are good examples of experts speaking out of their fields of expertise. They may know how to act, or how to hit home runs, but there's no reason to suppose they know any more about beer or shaving cream than anyone else. The fact that Cheryl Tiegs recommends the Canon AE1 camera, for instance, proves next to nothing about its quality.

Beware of Paid Endorsements

Of course, many people are persuaded by celebrity commercials simply because they want to imitate famous people. Their main concern is fashion, not quality. Looking good to other people is crucial in life, and one way to do this is to follow the lead of the rich, the powerful, or the famous. So if a movie star wears Jordache designer jeans, others will want to also. The error these people make in being persuaded by celebrity endorsements lies in assuming that celebrities actually prefer the

Al Ross—Rothco Cartoons

"When Paul Newman says the arms race should stop, then the arms race *should* stop!"

products they endorse. Recommending a product and actually using it are two quite different things. It's very unlikely, for instance, that members of the "famed British wine tasting team" who endorsed Taylor Empire Cream Sherry actually serve that relatively cheap product when friends come over for dinner. Remember, celebrities are paid handsomely to tout these products. So if you really want to use the products famous people use, you'll have to find out what they are in some other way.

We Need to Become Experts on Controversial Topics

When experts disagree, the rest of us must become our own experts, turning to acknowledged authorities for evidence, reasons, and arguments, but not for conclusions or opinions. This is especially true with respect to political matters, because of the tremendous controversies they arouse. But it applies elsewhere, too. A judge, for example, rather than merely accepting a psychologist's opinion concerning the sanity of an accused person, ought instead to ask for the reasons that led the psychologist to this opinion. After all, a different opinion could be obtained just by asking another psychologist.[2] Similarly, American presidents need to go into the complex details that lie behind the opinions of their economic advisors, rather than confining themselves (as President Eisenhower is said to have done) to whatever can be typed onto one side of one page.

Some Experts Are More Trustworthy than Others

Experts with an axe to grind are less trustworthy than just about anybody. It is to be expected, for instance, that corporation executives will testify to "facts" that place their corporations or products in a good light. Thus, we should expect that the executives of corporations dealing in products with harmful side effects (such as cigarettes, birth control pills, coffee, refined sugar, and nuclear power) will tend to deny or play down the unhealthy nature of their products. (Can there be any doubt that the president of, say, R. J. Reynolds would be fired if he publicly stated that cigarettes do indeed cause lung cancer, emphysema, and heart disease?)

Check the Past Records of Alleged Experts

Finally, anyone who has to appeal to an expert in a way which violates any of the above rules should at least consult the past record of that authority. Experts who have been right in the past are more likely to be right in the future than those who have been wrong. It is surprising how often even this rule of last resort is violated. (Think of the many Americans who as late as 1983 still believed President Reagan would balance the budget and significantly reduce the size of the federal bureaucracy.)

---

[2]This conforms to B. Duggan's *Law of Expert Testimony:* "To every Ph.D. there is an equal and opposite Ph.D." See Paul Dixon's *The Official Rules* (New York: Delacorte, 1978) for more on irreverent, pithy sayings like Duggan's Law.

Most of us have much too high an opinion of the knowledge of government officials. We forget, if we ever knew, that elected government officials—in particular members of Congress and the President of the United States—have to spend enormous amounts of time campaigning, leaving too little time to think about or study the great issues on which they have to decide. Here are two little snippets illustrating this sad fact, and another illustrating a related problem with appointed government officials:

Since taking office, the thing that really shocks me is how little time a Congressman has to devote to any one issue. There's simply no way you can cram your way to knowledgeability on any one subject in three or four hours. We have so many issues to contend with that, with all our research facilities, the best we can do is pick up information in bits and snatches.

> —Representative James M. Shannon of
> Massachusetts, quoted in *Parade Magazine*
> (May 13, 1979)

[Maine Republican William S. Cohen's] first act after his Senate victory is a trip to Arizona to address the Traveling Salesmen of America. Then off on a whirlwind tour of the Far East. Then back to pose for *Life* magazine on the Capitol steps, dressed in a jogging suit.

During this time he is playing intricate political games to position himself on the Armed Services Committee. Yet Cohen has not had the time to learn anything about military affairs before the committee actually meets—a fact he notes in passing as if it were a mere procedural detail. He boasts of confronting the secretary of defense with an impressive-sounding question about the AV-8B Harrier, an assault plane well-known to anyone with a modest interest in defense matters, even though "I had no idea what the AV-8B aircraft was." (Not to worry; little more than a month later, he is writing an Op-Ed piece about the intricacies of the SALT II treaty for the *Washington Post* .)

> —*Inquiry* (March 30, 1981)*

*From a review of Cohen's book, *Roll Call* (New York: Simon & Schuster, 1980).

Former Public School Honor Student Named Ambassador

[U.S.] Ambassador [to Singapore] Richard Kneip didn't know there were two Koreas or that India and Pakistan had fought a war in 1971, says [Edward Ingraham,] a career diplomat dismissed by Kneip after eight months as his chief deputy.

One day, during a discussion of the resurgence of Islam, Ingraham said Kneip had asked him, "What's Islam?"

He said Kneip, shortly after his arrival, had asked senior staff members:

"Did you say there are two separate Korean governments? How come?"

"You mean there has been a war between India and Pakistan? What was that all about?"

> —*San Francisco Chronicle* (January 31, 1980)

The Media as Experts

Since we get so much of our information from the mass media, it's particularly important that we check up on their accuracy (as mentioned in Chapter 1). For example, Jack Anderson is one of the more popular newspaper muckrakers—but is he accurate? He makes lots of predictions—do they come true? Here's a prediction he made in November 1982, when Yuri Andropov replaced Leonid Brezhnev as leader of the Soviet Union:

> What this means for Soviet–American relations is that detente is dead. As long as Andropov is in charge at the Kremlin, the United States can expect a tough Soviet policy on all fronts. The man who supervised the crushing of the Hungarian uprising as Soviet ambassador in 1956 can hardly be expected to take a lenient postion on Poland or other restive satellites.

Was Anderson right on this extremely important question of detente with Russia? If he was, this should increase our confidence in his other predictions; if he wasn't, it should lower our confidence. Most readers never bother to find out; they just keep on reading his column.

Usually, the media lead us astray in fairly ordinary, predictable ways. But occasionally, their failures are surprising and deceptive. For instance, the *New York Times*, thought by many to be the best newspaper in the world, whose slogan is "All

---

Experts on economic matters have notoriously poor track records, yet they are still listened to as though they have a direct wire to the truth. Here are a few predictions made by some of the nation's top money market experts in July 1982. The experts were asked to predict what interest rates would be at the end of 1982 (more precisely, what the prime rate charged by banks to top customers and the discount rate on three-month Treasury bills would be on December 31, 1982): [3]

	Prediction for:	
	Prime Rate	**Treasury Bills**
Irwin Kellner (Manufacturers Hanover Bank)	16%	12%
Donald Maude (Merrill Lynch)	15.5%	11.75%
Robert Parry (Security Pacific National Bank)	16%	12%
Thomas Thomson (Crocker Bank)	15%	11.75%
John Wilson (Bank of America)	14%	12%

The prime rate on July 2, 1982, was 16.5 percent, and three-month Treasury bills were paying 12.43 percent. At the end of the year, the prime was at 11.0–11.5 percent and T-bills were going at a discount rate of 7.9 percent. In other words, every one of these experts underestimated the decline in interest rates by a wide margin. (Note the implication of precision in a prediction like "11.75 percent"!) It's fiendishly hard to predict such things as how the economy is going to move. You should know that when you hear experts prognosticate.

---

[3] See Donald K. White's business column that appears in the *San Francisco Chronicle* (among others) on April 13, 1983.

the news that's fit to print," systematically omits religious books from its highly regarded and supposedly authoritative best-seller book list, even though books on religion frequently outsell all others. Few people are aware of this, and the lists themselves don't say so—all of which puts a bit of tarnish on the *Times's* reputation as *the* newspaper of record. (They also omit "Harlequin" type romance novels, perhaps because they don't poll supermarket, drugstore, or news vendors.)

Appeal to Authority and Questionable Premise

As we mentioned before, the everyday fallacy categories like *appeal to authority* crosscut the three basic logical categories. But most fallacious appeals to authority happen to fall into the broad logical category *questionable premise.* In other words, they are fallacious precisely because they involve acceptance of a questionable premise: Appeals to authority generally involve the implicit premise that the source or person appealed to has the information we want and will answer our appeal truthfully. In the case of fallacious appeals to authorities this is often a very *questionable premise.*

Consider, for instance, a woman who is convinced to buy Chanel No. 5 perfume by a Catherine Deneuve commercial. Her implicit reasoning may be something like this:

1. Catherine Deneuve knows good perfume from bad.

2. In the commercial, she honestly tells us her opinion (or tells us which perfume she wears).

3. In the commercial, she says Chanel No. 5 is best (or she says she uses Chanel No. 5).

4. I should believe Chanel No. 5 is best (or believe that Catherine Deneuve uses Chanel No. 5).

But as we mentioned before, it is a mistake to suppose that celebrities who are paid to tout a product actually believe that product is best or use that product themselves. Catherine Deneuve may or may not use Chanel No. 5, but her saying that she does is not a good reason to believe she does, given that she makes a tidy part of her living by endorsing fancy cosmetics. So the woman who is convinced by such a commercial is guilty of the fallacy *appeal to authority* because she accepts a *questionable premise* (that the star in the commercial will tell the truth). This is the most common reason for an appeal to an authority to be fallacious.

2. Two Wrongs Make a Right

The fallacy **two wrongs make a right** is committed when we try to justify an apparently wrong action by charging our accusers with a similar wrong. The idea is that if "they" do it, it's all right if we do.

An example is Interior Department official Richard Hite's defense of Interior Secretary James Watt's spending $8,000 of government money on Republican

"Watt's parties."[4] Hite said he believed the spending was legitimate because Cecil Andrus, the Democrat Watt replaced, used such funds to buy $2500 worth of paperweights. But Cecil Andrus's error in no way justifies errors by James Watt. Two wrongs do *not* automatically make a right.

Fighting Fire with Fire

Like many other fallacies, *two wrongs* seems plausible because of its resemblance to a more sensible way of reasoning—in this case to the plausible idea that we are

---

A true expert is someone who knows a good deal more than most of us on a subject or who has acquired a skill most of us have not. Experts are not miracle workers. It is important to know the "state of the art" so that we can judge whether experts really know or can do what they (or others) claim. Here are some excerpts from an article showing the true limits to the expert ability of most wine tasters.

Challenged to identify a wine about to be served, the smart taster can learn much from details that have nothing to do with the wine itself. He will watch the cork being drawn, for instance, noticing its length, shape, firmness and branding. The shape of the neck and color of the glass of the bottle are also useful. So is the shape of the bottle.

A good example of this process occurred at one of the weekly tasting sessions I attend. One member presented a bottle from which cork and capsule— usually good hints to a wine's identity—had already been removed, and the label had been soaked off. It looked bad. But then I noticed that the label had left faint traces of glue on the bottle and that this glue had been applied in broad horizontal bands. I knew of only one winery doing that at the time. The outline of the glue showed that the label had been both tall and wide. Same winery. Finally, the bottle was of a dark tint not then widely used. Those three clues made it almost certainly a wine from Ridge Vineyards. . . .

After a bit of purely ceremonial peering, sniffing and tasting, I named the wine. Cheers all around! I had identified the wine "blind." But tasting had had little to do with it. I would have made the same guess without it. . . .

An exceedingly interesting experiment was conducted with nine of these judges not long ago to determine just how well they really could identify not specific wines, but simply the grape varieties from which certain wines had been made. Here was an experiment conducted under the best conditions, with some of the best judges in existence. These were no "wizard palates" on TV talk shows or "guest experts" performing at riotous public tastings. They were university professionals with an average of nineteen years of daily tasting experience each. Their task was simplified by the fact that all the wines in each

---

[4]See, for example, the UPI story which appeared in the *Baltimore News American* and other newspapers (February 27, 1982).

sometimes justified in fighting fire with fire, or in getting our hands as dirty as our opponents'. A good example is the killing of someone in self-defense: we're justified in fighting one evil (the taking of our own life) with what would otherwise be another evil (the taking of our attacker's life).

So the fallacy *two wrongs make a right* is not automatically committed every time one apparent wrong is justified by appeal to an opponent's wrong; the crucial question is whether the second wrong indeed is necessary to fight or counteract the first wrong.[5] In the case of justified self-defense against physical attack, the evil of killing the attacker is necessary; in the case of James Watt and his "Watt's parties," the evil

---

group they tasted were of the same year. All the wines had been made at the university. Grape variety was the only variable.

The judges failed. The only variety identified correctly more than half the time was the muscat—one of the most distinctive and easily recognizable grapes there is. Cabernet sauvignon was identified a bit more than a third of the time and chardonnay less than a quarter of the time. Zinfandel was correctly identified about a third of the time, but it was called cabernet almost as often. Cabernet wasn't called zinfandel as often, but it *was* called pinot noir, petite sirah and several other things.

These sobering results show how limited is the success to be attained when wine judges are rigorously denied all information about the wines they are considering. It is undoubtedly true that there are a few people with an extraordinary ability to identify wines, but this ability . . . is a matter of the elusive gift of taste memory and of specialization and luck—and . . . of the opportunity to sample vast numbers of wines.

A person who tastes, say, dozens of white burgundies of the Côte de Beaune every day will become adept at identifying these wines—but he still will not recognize them as one would recognize Lloyd George. He will have learned the personalities of each vintage, the characteristics of each district, the quirks of each producer, even details as specialized as the influence on the wine of various kinds of barrels. Faced with a sample, he begins to decide what it may be and what it may not be. Successively eliminating, he narrows down the possibilities to a few, or, with luck, to one. But take him to Bordeaux and he is as helpless as thee and me. . . .

The distinguished English wine taster Harry Waugh—himself a director of Château Latour—notes that he has been to many blind tastings in Bordeaux and elsewhere at which vineyard proprietors failed to pick out their own wines—and they had a great advantage over a true blind taster because they knew that their own wines were present. And once asked if he had ever confused bordeaux and burgundy, Waugh ruefully replied, "Not since lunch." That's the way an honest wine taster sounds.

Excerpts from Roy Brady, "Secrets of a Wine Taster Exposed," *New West,* Oct. 1978.
Reprinted with permission of Roy Brady.

---

[5]This overlooks the issue of retributive justice. If retributivists are right, then we're sometimes justified in inflicting harm (punishment) on those guilty of harming others, even though in doing so we fail to fight the original harm.

was not necessary, or even helpful, in fighting any other evil—certainly not the evil of Cecil Andrus spending government money on trivial items. On the contrary, Watt's spending just added another evil to the already existing large supply.[6]

Two Wrongs and Hypocrisy

The fallacy *two wrongs make a right* also often seems plausible for another reason. Most of the time, someone arguing this way implies that his or her opponent is being hypocritical—and often this is correct, so that there is some justification in the attack. The town drunk isn't the one to tell us we've had too many and are making a fool of ourselves, even if it's true. Similarly, the philanderer who finds out about his wife's infidelity is hardly the one to complain that she is deceiving him. But when we become outraged at the "chutzpah" of our accuser, we sometimes lose sight of the fact that our accuser's hypocrisy doesn't justify our own failures.

Common Practice and Traditional Wisdom

In addition to the fallacies of *appeal to authority* and *two wrongs make a right,* there are several similar, overlapping fallacies. One is *common practice,* where a wrong is justified by claiming lots of people do that sort of thing. An example is the German soldier in World War II who justified machine-gunning unarmed civilian Russians by pointing out that lots of other German soldiers did the same thing.

A related fallacy is *traditional wisdom* or *past practice,* where the wrong is justified because it's the traditional or accepted way of doing things. Of course, we want to learn from the experiences of others. But we don't want to assume that *just because* something has been done in the past, it must be right.

However, we don't want to go overboard on this. Many organizations try to write their rules so as to conform to past practice because experience shows past practice has worked, or because there is no good reason to think some new way will be better. And an appeal to the fact that many (perhaps most) people fail to live up to a certain standard or to resist a certain sort of temptation may function at least as a mitigating excuse, even if not an exonerating one (examples: a loyal spouse who commits adultery for the first time after 30 years of marriage; a cigarette smoker who's "quit" smoking a dozen times).

Popularity

A related but somewhat different fallacy is that of *popularity,* where the fact that something is popular is taken to prove that it's right. This fallacy is committed, for instance, when someone argues that smoking marijuana must be harmful since most people think it is. (That the appeal to popularity is fallacious is easily seen by recalling that at one time almost everybody believed the earth was flat.)

---

[6]Fighting fire with fire raises a moral issue outside the scope of this book. A few people hold the extreme view that evil is always wrong, even to fight a worse evil. Most people believe fighting one evil with another is sometimes justified, but they are hazy about exactly when. For instance, in football, is illegal roughness against an illegally rough opponent justified? What about cheating on exams when everyone else is cheating?

Of course, the usual precautions are in order. For instance, those who rushed out to see *E. T.* because it was so popular didn't necessarily commit a fallacy—they may have learned from experience that they tend to like popular movies, or they may just want to have seen the movie everyone is talking about so they can talk about it too.

3. Irrelevant Reason

Traditional textbooks often discuss a fallacy called *non sequitur* ("it does not follow"), usually described as a fallacy in which the conclusion does not follow logically from the given premises. In this sense, any fallacy in the broad category *invalid inference* can be said to be a *non sequitur.* But other writers describe this fallacy more narrowly.

Let's replace the ambiguous term *non sequitur* with the expression **irrelevant reason**, to refer to reasons or premises that are or come close to being totally irrelevant to a conclusion (provided another fallacy name, for instance, *appeal to authority,* does not apply).

As an example of *irrelevant reason,* consider those who replied to charges that the United States had no business in Vietnam, either morally or to satisfy our national interests, by arguing that such talk only prolonged the war by making the enemy believe America's will to fight was declining. This reply in all likelihood was true, but was irrelevant to the question of our justification for being in Vietnam.

(It should be noticed that a reason is not automatically irrelevant just because it is false. For instance, the old idea that masturbation causes insanity is false, but it isn't irrelevant to the question whether a person should or shouldn't engage in that practice, because if true it would be a good reason not to masturbate.)

The fallacy of *irrelevant reason* fools us as often as it does because in typical cases the reasons presented support a conclusion that somehow resembles, or appears to resemble, the one supposedly argued for. Indeed, a special form of this fallacy, in which the issue is evaded deliberately while it appears not to be, is the stock in trade of many politicians. Their trick is to speak in favor of solving some general problem that all agree must be solved while ignoring the specific proposed solution that is in fact the issue in question. Everyone is in favor of freedom, equality, the elimination of poverty, and so on (politicians refer to this as being in favor of mom and apple pie). It's proposed ways for achieving these obvious goals that are controversial. So when we provide arguments in favor of mom and apple pie, our reasoning is generally irrelevant to what is at issue.

For example, in a discussion of a public housing bill, a particular congressman went on and on about the need for more housing for the citizens of this great country, while saying nothing about the merits of the bill in question, confident that some of his listeners would fail to notice the irrelevance of his remarks to the specific bill before the House.

4. Equivocation

A term or expression is used ambiguously or equivocally in an argument when used in one sense in one place and another sense in another place. Clearly, an argument containing such an ambiguous use of language is invalid. Those who are convinced by such an argument are guilty of the fallacy called **equivocation** or **ambiguity** (which usually falls into the broad logical category *invalid inference*).

When an evangelist on TV said we all should stop sinning and "be like Jesus," a member of the audience expressed doubt that he was up to that. He pointed out that, after all, "Jesus was the son of God." In reply, the evangelist told the doubter that he could indeed stop sinning because, "You're the son of God, too." But the evangelist was guilty of *equivocation,* since the doubter meant that Jesus is the son of God in the special way that (according to Christian doctrine) only Jesus is held to be, while the evangelist had to mean that the doubter was the son of God in the metaphorical sense in which (according to Christian theology) we all are children of God.

Equivocation is a common fallacy because it is often quite hard to notice that a shift in meaning has taken place. But sometimes people are set up to commit this fallacy. For example, an ad touting sugar consumption (of all things) supported its pitch by stating, "Sugar is an essential component of the body . . . a key material in all sorts of metabolic processes." The ambiguity in this case centers on the word "sugar." If taken to mean glucose (blood sugar), the statement is true. But if taken to mean ordinary table sugar (and the average reader could be expected to take it that way), then it is false. The advertiser can claim the ad tells the truth by construing the word "sugar" to mean glucose, knowing that most readers, taking it to mean ordinary table sugar, would conclude erroneously that table sugar is an essential food.

Ambiguity Serves Useful Functions

Students sometimes get the idea that every ambiguity, certainly every equivocation, is fallacious. But nothing could be further from the truth. Ambiguous uses of language, in particular metaphoric ones, have all sorts of good purposes. So do equivocations. Here is an example from the writings of oldster Carl Rogers in which

---

It is he that sitteth upon the circle of the earth.

—Isaiah 40:22

Ambiguity

Almost any statement can be interpreted in various ways if we have a mind to do so. The Bible is a happy hunting ground for those intent on taking advantage of the ambiguity of natural languages because many people take what it says to be the word of the Ultimate Authority on most important issues. The above passage from Isaiah, once used to prove that the earth is flat, was cited after Copernicus, Kepler, and Newton as proof that it is a sphere.

the deliberate equivocation is successfully used to emphasize that he is still young at heart:

> As a boy I was rather sickly, and my parents have told me that it was predicted I would die young. This prediction has been proven completely wrong in one sense, but has come profoundly true in another sense. I think it is correct that I will never live to be old. So now I agree with the prediction. I believe that I will die *young*. [7]

Ambiguous uses of language also serve many other functions, such as the politeness needed to grease the skids of social intercourse. Benjamin Disraeli, nineteenth-century British prime minister, used ambiguity to soften his reply when someone sent him an unsolicited amateur manuscript: "Many thanks; I shall lose no time in reading it," a response similar to that of H. L. Mencken's "Thanks for your letter. You may be right."

So-called token reflexive terms, such as *you* and *me,* are ambiguous in the sense that they refer to different people depending on who uses them and who's listening. However this ambiguity of reference fools very few people other than professional philosophers. But some terms that can be used either relatively or absolutely, like *rich* and *poor,* occasionally cause trouble for everybody. Poverty, for example, is exceedingly unpleasant anywhere, at any time. But the poor in America today are richer in absolute terms than most people were in nineteenth-century Europe (or are today in India or Africa). This important truth is masked by the fact that the term *poor,* in its relative sense, does apply to those Americans who are poor (in the relative sense) compared to most Americans although rich (in the absolute sense) compared to most non-Americans. (Clear?)

So long as the economic system meets these demands [of the middle class for more jobs, higher income, more consumer goods, and more recreation], and so long as the demands take these forms, the perennial questions about *power* and *control* need never be asked. Or, better, those whose demands are being met can be congratulated on having "power," *for what is power but the ability to have one's demands met?*

—Ben Wattenberg*

Ambiguity (Very Subtle)

Do we have power if we have the ability to get all *of our demands met,* some *met, or even* one? *Just about everyone has some power. The political question Wattenberg evaded is whether average Americans have power equal to their numbers— Wattenberg's opponents don't deny that members of the middle class have power; they just deny they have their fair share.*

The Real America (Doubleday, N.Y., 1974).

---

[7]Carl Rogers, in the *Journal of Humanistic Psychology* (Fall 1980).

5. Appeal to Ignorance

When good reasons or evidence are lacking, the rational conclusion to draw is that we just don't know. But it's often tempting to take the absence of evidence for a claim as proof that the claim is false. Doing this sometimes leads to the fallacy called **appeal to ignorance** (traditionally known as *argumentum ad ignorantiam*). Thus, some have argued fallaciously that there can't be such a thing as ESP or psycho-kinesis since no one has been able to prove their existence. On the other hand, others have argued that flying saucers do in fact exist since no one has ever proved they don't.

The fallacy in such reasoning is easily seen by turning these arguments around. If appeals to ignorance could prove, say, that ESP claims are false (since we haven't proved they're true), then they would also prove ESP claims are true (since we haven't proved they're false). Obviously, in the absence of good evidence for a claim, the right thing to do is become *agnostic* on the issue and neither believe nor disbelieve it. Ignorance proves nothing, except, of course, that we are ignorant.

However, there are cases in which failure of a search does count as evidence against a claim. These are the cases in which the thing searched for would very likely be found if it were really there. Thus, if someone were to claim that a planet exists between Earth and Mars, the absence of favorable evidence would count against the existence of such a planet, given all the sky watching that has gone on in the last 10,000 years. Similarly, when a careful test fails to find blood in a urine specimen, a doctor is justified in concluding that no blood is there. These are not cases of reasoning from ignorance, but rather of reasoning from the *knowledge* that we've appropriately looked and yet failed to find the thing in question. (Note the importance of *appropriate* looking. The fact that telescopes have searched the sky for several hundred years, and naked eyes for thousands of years, without spotting God up there proves absolutely nothing about the existence of a God in the sky, since no one supposes you can see God just by looking through a telescope.)

6. Ad Hominem Argument

The fallacy of arguing **ad hominem**, sometimes called the **genetic fallacy,** consists of an irrelevant attack on an opponent, rather than his or her argument. (An *ad hominem* argument, literally, is an argument "to the person.")

In 1950, Senator Joseph R. McCarthy responded to a doubting question about the fortieth name on a list of eighty-one case histories he claimed were of communists working for the United States State Department by saying, "I do not have much information on this except the general statement of the agency that there is nothing in the files to disprove his Communist connections."

Many of McCarthy's followers took this absence of evidence proving that the person in question was not a communist as evidence that he was, a good example of the fallacy of appeal to ignorance.

Senator Jennings Randolph was guilty of *ad hominem* argument in a U.S. Senate debate on the Equal Rights Amendment to the Constitution (ERA) when he dismissed women's liberationists, and thus their arguments, with the remark that they constituted a "small band of bra-less bubbleheads." This may have been good for a laugh in the almost all-male Senate, but it was irrelevant to arguments the women's rights representatives had presented. Randolph attacked *them* (through ridicule) rather than their arguments. So he argued fallaciously.

In ridiculing women's liberationists as "bra-less bubbleheads," Senator Randolph resorted to namecalling on a rather low level. But ad hominem namecalling need not be so crude. Here is an example with a good deal of literary merit, representing Vice President Spiro Agnew at his very best:

> A spirit of national masochism prevails, encouraged by an effete corps of impudent snobs who characterize themselves as intellectuals.[8]

Agnew attacked his intellectual opponents without bothering to consider their arguments.

Now here is an excerpt from an article on George Michanowsky, a lone maverick without formal credentials who had attacked a theory of Hans Goedicke, Chairman of the Near Eastern Studies Department of Johns Hopkins University:[9]

> "I notice that he [Michanowsky] sports a rather interesting title," says Goedicke, . . . "Scientific Advisor to the Explorers Club for the field of archoastronomy." He smiles at the absurdity of it all and pulls a yellow paperback from his bookcase. "This is the *International Directory of Egyptology*. It has the name of every Egyptologist in the world—about 70 of them. Michanowsky's name is not here." Goedicke holds it up triumphantly. The matter is settled. "You know, I've never met the man," Goedicke says casually. "If you see Mr. Michanowsky, give him my regards. And tell him he is an idiot."

All of which says next to nothing about the truth or falsity of Michanowsky's claims.

Attacks on Character or Credentials May Be Cogent

Lawyers who attack the testimony of courtroom witnesses by questioning their character or expertise are not necessarily guilty of *ad hominem* argument. For courtroom witnesses, doctors, auto mechanics, lawyers, and other experts often present opinions against which we, as nonexperts, are unable to argue directly. Sometimes, the best we can do is try to evaluate their honesty and judgment. Thus, testimony that a psychological expert has been convicted of perjury, or spends more time testifying in court than on any other job, would be good reason to prefer the conflicting opinion of an expert for the other side.

In these cases we certainly do not prove that expert opinion is incorrect. At best, character attacks provide grounds only for canceling or disregarding the opinion of

---

[8]From a speech delivered in New Orleans (October 19, 1969).
[9]Goedicke's theory is that the parting of the Red Sea waters in front of the ancient Hebrews escaping from Egypt was caused by a tidal wave produced by a volcanic eruption. Michanowsky had several at least plausible objections to Goedicke's theory. See *Science 83* (March 1983).

an expert, not for deciding that that opinion is false. If a doctor who advises operating on a patient turns out to be a quack, it's rash to conclude that no operation is necessary. In disregarding the doctor's opinion, we don't thereby judge it false, but rather in need of other support before we can accept it.

Further, in avoiding *ad hominem* reasoning, we don't want to also avoid assessing information partly in terms of its source. That someone is a genuine expert in a field or has a good record as a predictor is relevant to accepting or rejecting her or his claim, even though it's usually not conclusive.

Guilt by Association

One of the important variations on *ad hominem* arguments is **guilt by association**. Many believe that people are to be judged by the company they keep. But many others hold that you should not judge people by their associates, any more than you judge books by their covers. Which view is correct?

The answer is that it *is* rational under certain circumstances to judge people by their associates. However, only rarely will such judgments have a *high degree of probability* attached to them. In the absence of other evidence, a man frequently seen in the company of different women known to be prostitutes is rightly suspected of being connected with their occupation in a way that casts doubt on his moral character. Similarly, a person who associates frequently and closely with men known to be agents of a foreign government is rightly suspected of being an agent of that government.

But caution is needed in dealing with indirect evidence of this kind. Suspecting that Smith uses the services of prostitutes is different from knowing that he does. (It is, of course, good reason for looking further—assuming we care enough to expend the effort.) The man who frequently associates with prostitutes may turn out to be a sociologist conducting an investigation. The close associate of foreign spies may be a friendly counterspy.

Even so, when decisions must be made and our only evidence is indirect, it is prudent to judge people on the basis of their associates.[10] There is no fallacy in this.

Does Carter Know It from a Hole in the Ground?

— Front page headline in *The Village Voice*

Ad hominem *headline, more common in left- and right-wing publications than in the mass media, which tend to stay pretty much in the center politically. (You'll never see this nasty a headline in* Time, Newsweek, *or the* New York Times. *On the other hand,* The Village Voice *comes through with many more juicy "how society really works" articles than any establishment publication.)*

---

[10]But doing so sometimes generates serious moral or political problems. For instance, auto insurance companies judge blacks who live in certain big city ghettos to be poor risks on the basis of indirect statistical evidence rather than on more direct evidence concerning particular applicants (because the statistical evidence is much cheaper). But is this fair to a ghetto resident who is a hard-working, bill-paying, careful driver, who in fact is a better than average risk?

The fallacy of *guilt by association* occurs when suspicion is taken to be knowledge, when more direct evidence is available but not used, or when association with "that kind of person" is not truly derogatory.

Summary of Chapter Two

We reason fallaciously when we: (1) reason from unjustified premises, (2) fail to use relevant information, or (3) reason invalidly. Standard everyday fallacy classifications, however, often crosscut these categories.

1. *Appeal to authority:* Accepting the word of alleged authorities when you shouldn't, either because it's not likely that they have the needed knowledge or because they might not tell us truthfully, or because experts disagree on the issue (in which case we should become our own expert and form our own opinion). *Example:* Taking the word of power industry executives on the safety of nuclear power plants.

2. *Two wrongs make a right:* Defending a wrong by pointing out that our opponent has done the same (or an equally wrong) thing. *Example:* Arguing it isn't so wrong of James Watt to use public funds to host parties, since his predecessor (Cecil Andrus) also used funds wastefully.

    However, sometimes two wrongs do make a right, in particular when "fighting fire with fire."

    a. *Common practice* and *traditional wisdom* (or *past practice*): Claiming something isn't wrong, or at least is excusable, since it's commonly or traditionally done. *Example:* A soldier who defends his commission of atrocities on the grounds that soldiers commonly do such things.

    b. *Popularity:* Appealing to the crowd to determine truth. *Example:* Arguing that marijuana must be harmful since most people think it is.

3. *Irrelevant reason:* Trying to prove something using evidence that may appear to be relevant but really isn't. *Example:* Arguing against the claim that we shouldn't have been fighting in Vietnam on grounds that such talk only showed the enemy that America's will to fight was declining.

4. *Equivocation:* Using ambiguous locutions to mislead (or which in fact mislead). *Example:* The TV evangelist's use of the expression "son of God."

    It's important to note, however, that intentional ambiguity, and even equivocation, can be very useful and perfectly proper.

5. *Appeal to ignorance:* Arguing that since we can't prove something is false (true), we're entitled to believe it's true (false). *Example:* Arguing that ESP must be false, since no one has ever proved it's true.

    Note, however, that when an *appropriate* search has failed to turn up an item, we're generally justified in believing that it doesn't exist (example: a doctor's failure to find blood in a urine sample).

6. *Ad hominem argument:* An irrelevant attack on one's opponent rather than his or her argument. *Example:* Senator Jennings Randolph's attacking

women's libbers as "bra-less bubbleheads" instead of dealing with their arguments head-on.

But note that in some circumstances, the best we can do is to attack (or evaluate) a person's character (example: a courtroom expert or a doctor.)

a. *Guilt by association:* Judging a person by associates when more sensible evidence is available. *Example:* The CIA and FBI, during the 1950s, when they judged people who associated with "security risks" to themselves be security risks.

Exercise 2-1

Which of the fallacies discussed in Chapter 2 occur in the following passages? (Some may contain no fallacies.) Explain the reasons for your answers. (For instance, if the fallacy is *equivocation,* show the different senses that are involved and how they lead to confusion; if the fallacy is *appeal to authority,* show what is unwise about this particular appeal — why we should not listen to this authority this time.) Remember that fallacy categories sometimes overlap, and that a given item may contain more than one fallacy. Remember also that the material is quite controversial and thus open to differing interpretations. So your *explanations* are more important than the fallacy labels you put on an argument. Getting the label right but the explanation wrong means that you have answered incorrectly.

*1. *Article in college newspaper:* A committee on teaching evaluation in colleges is the coming thing.

2. *Senator Sam Ervin of North Carolina (*New York Times, *September 30, 1970) telling how he replied to women who were in favor of the Equal Rights Amendment to the Constitution:* I tell them, "Why, ladies, any bill that lies around here for 47 years without getting any more support than this one has got in the past *obviously* shouldn't be passed at all. Why, I think *that affords most conclusive proof that it's unworthy of consideration.* "

3. Baltimore Sun *(August 24, 1976):* "Jimmy Carter says he'll never lie," [Senator Howard] Baker noted, but he is "the nominee of the party which created more than 1,000 new federal programs and planned them so poorly that they made Washington sound like a dirty word."

4. *Overheard in line at the movies:* "Raiders of the Lost Ark *should have gotten the best picture Oscar, since so many people liked it better than* Chariots of Fire [which won the Oscar]."

5. *Comment in the* Skeptical Inquirer *(Winter 1978) on astronaut Gordon Cooper's belief that some UFOs are ships from outer space:* What does Cooper do, now that he is no longer with NASA? He is currently employed, appropriately enough, by Walt Disney Enterprises.

6. *Adelle Davis, in* Let's Eat Right to Keep Fit: Namecalling, derogatory articles, and adverse propaganda are other methods used to belittle persons refusing to recommend refined goods. We have long been called crackpots and faddists regardless of training or of accuracy in reporting research.

The words "quacks" and "quackery" are now such current favorites that you can be fairly sure that anyone using them is receiving benefits from the food processors.

*7. Hartford Courant *(December 20, 1972), in an article on the possibility of women priests in the Catholic Church:* Citing the historic exclusion of women from the priesthood, however, the study [of a committee of Roman Catholic bishops] said ". . . the constant tradition and practice, interpreted as of divine law, is of such a nature as to constitute a clear teaching of the Ordinary Magisterium [teaching authority] of the Church."

8. *Beginning of a book review:* Erich Segal's *Love Story—Romeo and Juliet* it isn't. But who cares. It's guaranteed to give you a good cry now and then. And it couldn't have gotten off to such a flying start for nothing. Everybody is going to be reading this novel, so you better go down to your nearest bookstore and pick up a copy.

9. It's all right for President Reagan to impound funds voted by the Congress. Every recent president—Carter, Ford, Nixon, Johnson—did so. In fact, Nixon did so on a grand scale.

10. Hartford Courant *(December 20, 1970), from an AP story on Soviet efforts to crush political dissent in Russia:* Minister of Culture Yekaterina Furtseva publicly berated an American correspondent for "poking his nose into our internal affairs" when he asked a question related to the case of disgraced novelist Alexander Solzhenitsyn. "If you cannot punish the killers of your government leaders, you have no right to be interested in such questions," the [Soviet] culture minister retorted.

11. *In reply to a Clarence Darrow remark that "in spite of all the yearnings of men, no one can produce a single fact or reason to support the belief in God and in personal immortality," a religious fundamentalist replied:* "It is easy to answer such an extravagant and boastful defense of atheism. We point to the fact that belief in God is universally held by all peoples of all times. There has never been a race of atheists."

12. *Here is a reply on TV to political science professor Robert Lekachman's attack on "Reaganomics":* "What do these professors know? Have they ever met a payroll?"

13. *Mike Royko, in the* Chicago Sun-Times *(June 30, 1978), commenting on the very bad publicity Senator Edward Brooke of Massachusetts was getting because of the way he was handling his divorce:* What Brooke did was try to cheat his wife out of some money when they made a divorce settlement. In other words, he did what tens of thousands of desperate American men do every year. And for this perfectly normal effort at survival, his career is threatened with ruin. . . . I'm not siding with Brooke against his wife. I have no idea who was in the right or wrong. But lying during a divorce case is not unusual. If anything, it is the rule. Most people who come to divorce courts lie their heads off.

Momma by Mell Lazarus. Courtesy of Mell Lazarus and Field Newspaper Syndicate.

14. (In this case, the question is what fallacy Momma failed to perpetrate on her son.)

*15. *John P. Roche, in his political column (October 1970):* Every society is, of course, repressive to some extent—as Sigmund Freud pointed out, repression is the price we pay for civilization.

16. *Popular magazine article in 1874:* Louis Agassiz, the greatest scientist of his day, examined Darwin's claims for his theory of evolution very carefully and finally decided that it could not be true that man was descended from the ape and its earlier animal ancestry. Within six months the greatest German biologists, and the most learned anthropologists now living, have declared that the Darwin theory of the origin of man could not be true. In spite of the opinions of these, the . . . leading investigators of the century, the theory of Darwinism is being taught in the universities of America. There is such a thing as a little knowledge leading to a great error, and this is an example.[11]

17. *American Medical Association ad against smoking:* 100,000 doctors have quit smoking cigarettes. (Maybe they know something you don't.)

18. *Lewis Carroll, in* Through the Looking Glass: "You couldn't have it if you *did* want it," the Queen said. "The rule is jam tomorrow and jam yesterday—but never jam *today.* "

    "It *must* come sometimes to jam today," Alice objected.

    "No it can't," said the Queen. "It's jam every *other* day: today isn't any *other* day, you know."

19. Washington Monthly, *June 1983:* According to Lou Cannon of *The Washington Post,* Fred F. Fielding recently objected to inviting Teamsters President Jackie Presser to a White House state dinner on the grounds that Presser's former Ohio local is under federal investigation for racketeering. An unnamed Reagan adviser rejected Fielding's advice by pointing out, "Teamsters are always under investigation."

20. *Vivekananda:* There is no past or future even in thought, because to think it you have to make it present.[12]

---

[11]Quoted in Richard L. Purtill's *Logic: Argument, Refutation, and Proof* (New York: Harper & Row, 1979).

[12]Quoted in Henry C. Byerly's *A Primer of Logic* (New York: McGraw-Hill, 1978).

21. *Benedetto Croce, in* Philosophy of the Practical: The Inquisition must have been justified and beneficial, if whole peoples invoked and defended it, if men of the loftiest souls founded and created it severally and impartially, and its very adversaries applied it on their own account, [funeral] pyre answering to pyre.

*22. *Dr. Norman Geisler, witness for the state of Arkansas in the 1981 Creation-Evolution trial, testified in favor of belief in God, citing the line in the Bible to the effect that the Devil acknowledges but refuses to worship God, and then cinched his point by stating:* "The *Devil* believes there is a God!"

23. *St. Augustine, in* De Libero Arbitrio: See how absurd and foolish it is to say: I should prefer nonexistence to miserable existence. He who says, I prefer this to that, chooses something. Nonexistence is not something; it is nothing. There can be no real choice when what you choose is nothing.

24. [Secretary of Defense Caspar] Weinberger said [Israeli Premier Menachem] Begin's behavior [the bombing of Beirut, which killed 300 civilians] "cannot really be described as moderation," and [Deputy Secretary of State William] Clark added that the bombing had "embarrassed and disappointed" the Administration. Mr. Begin, however, was in no mood for moralizing from Washington. "I don't want to hear anything from the Americans about hitting civilian targets," he was reported to have said. "I know exactly what Americans did in Vietnam."[13]

25. *Column by John Cunniff (July 1970):* Do Americans eat well in comparison with other nations? Millions of Americans still have poor diets, but generally speaking most Americans can afford to eat well. In the U.S. and Canada less than 20 percent of all "personal consumption expenditures" are for food. In less developed countries, the figures are much higher.

*26. ". . . Our own death is . . . unimaginable, and whenever we make the attempt to imagine it we can perceive that we really survive as spectators. . ."—Freud

27. *President Carter, justifying the government's bailout of the then virtually bankrupt Chrysler Corporation:* "This legislation does not violate the principle of letting free enterprise function on its own, because Chrysler is unique in its present circumstances."

*28. *Nicholas von Hoffman, in the* New York Post *(October 1, 1974):* The trouble with such propositions [that there was a second murderer of John F. Kennedy] is that . . . they are seldom able to give us much of a clue as to who the "real" killer may be. It is for that reason that nobody has been able to discredit the Warren Commission report. If Lee Harvey Oswald didn't murder President Kennedy, then who did?

---

[13]*New York Times,* July 26, 1981. Reprinted in *Inquiry* magazine.

29. *Dialogue from the movie* Fun with Dick and Jane *about whether to keep the money Jane stole:*

> *Jane Fonda:* We've always done things the straight way.
> *George Segal:* Yeah. Well I'm tired of belonging to a minority group.

30. *From an interview with Ronald Reagan (taken from the* New York Review of Books):

> *Mr. Otis:* We would like to know . . . what the Bible really means to you.
> *President Reagan:* I have never had any doubt about it being of divine origin. And to those who . . . doubt it, I would like to have them point out to me any similar collection of writings that have lasted for as many thousands of years and is still the best seller worldwide. It had to be of divine origin.

31. *President Reagan (*New York Times, *July 29, 1982) on how he could certify progress in human rights in El Salvador given that their government wasn't cooperating in the investigation of the murder of three American nuns:* I'm quite sure that there are unfortunate things that are going on and that are happening.

32. *E. F. Schumacher, famous economist, in an article in* The Atlantic *(April 1979):* Fifteen months [after I had advised that rural India should have a technology intermediate between the hoe and the tractor,] an all-India conference on intermediate technology was arranged. (They still didn't like the term [*intermediate*], so they called it appropriate technology. That's all right: when I come to India and somebody says, "Oh, Mr. Schumacher, I don't believe in appropriate technology," I just look him straight in the face and say, "Oh, that's splendid. Do you believe in inappropriate technology?")

33. *Asked how he could support a constitutional amendment requiring balanced budgets while his administration had the biggest deficits in history, President Reagan replied (*New York Times, *July 29, 1982):* The budget deficits I don't think can be laid at any individual's door.

34. Mother Jones *article (August 1983) on Ronald Reagan appointee Marjory Mecklenburg, whose legislative mandate was to promote chastity and self-discipline and "to explore family-centered approaches to the problem of adolescent sexual relations and adolescent pregnancy":* . . . she herself would just as soon keep quiet about those aspects of her personal history that do not conform to her "Little House on the Prairie" moral creed. Back home, where Mecklenburg was an outspoken opponent of abortion rights, sources have revealed to us that the chastity crusader was pregnant before she was married. . . . How does Mecklenburg justify her efforts to impose an official morality on the nation's young when she herself conceived a child out of wedlock? "No comment. . . . It's a family matter."

35. *After the Soviet Union refused to accept a U.S. note demanding compensation for relatives of those in the Korean jet shot down by the Russians, the U.S. appealed to the Soviets to accept the note on grounds that it had been diplomatic common practice to do so for several centuries.*

Exercise 2-2

Find examples in the mass media (television, magazines, newspapers, radio) of fallacies discussed in Chapter 2, and explain why they are fallacious.

The Village Voice. Reprinted by permission of Edward Sorel.

O! Little Clown of Bethlehem

Complaining about the "commercialization of Christmas," Mike Douglas told his television audience: "Christmas has virtually lost its true religious significance. It's tragic to see the tradition of gift-giving perverted into nothing more than an excuse for stores to run sales." Oddly enough, one of the items on sale in stores this Christmas is Mr. Douglas's recording of "Happy Birthday, Jesus," written by Lee Pockriss and Estelle Levitt. Mr. Pockriss is perhaps best remembered for his "Itsy-Bitsy, Teeny-Weeny Yellow Polka-Dot Bikini." In keeping with the Christmas spirit, Mr. Douglas has decided to keep all his royalties from the record.

—*New York Daily News* (December 6, 1977)

Mike Douglas's fans don't want to think of him as just another money grubber. So he keeps them happy (fools them?) with a little inconsistency between words and actions.

Arguments, like men, often are
pretenders.

—Plato

It don't even make good nonsense.
—Davy Crockett, remarking on a statement
by President Andrew Jackson

3

Fallacious Reasoning—II

Let's now discuss some other common fallacies.

1. Provincialism

The fallacy of **provincialism** stems from the natural tendency to identify with our own group and to perceive experience largely in terms of "in-group" and "out-group." (It also stems from our identification with our own time and place.) This tendency has some good things to be said for it, since our own well-being so often depends on that of the group. But when it begins to determine the content of our beliefs, the result is fallacy.

Provincialism influences our beliefs in basically two ways: (1) It tends to make us concentrate on our own society and what it knows and believes, to the exclusion of other cultures and what they know or believe; and (2) it tends, via *loyalty,* to influence our acceptance or rejection of alleged facts or theories, whatever the nature of the evidence.[1] Here is an example of the first, from an American newspaper series on Japan:

> The [Japanese] empire supposedly was founded about 600 B.C., but for the next 24 centuries the Japanese people lived in almost complete isolation from *the rest of the world.*[2] [Italics added]

"The rest of the world," of course, meant the western world. The writer ignored the great influence of China on Japan during much of that 24-century period.

Provincialism is a problem for all of us, including experts. Countless psychological experiments conducted on American subjects have reached conclusions that could be shown wrong by observing even a few people of other cultures. The same is

---

[1]The fallacy of *provincialism* is similar to but different from that of *traditional wisdom.* The error in *traditional wisdom* results from assuming that traditional ways of doing things are right because they are traditional. The error in *provincialism* results from relative blindness to cultures and groups other than our own, or from loyalty to our own group. Being blind to other groups, for instance, does not imply accepting the traditions of one's own group.

[2]*Lawrence* (Kansas) *Daily Journal World* (August 8, 1970).

true of many commonly held ideas. An example is the widely held belief that lefties write with a hooked motion because the left-to-right direction of English (and most written languages) is unnatural for them, while quite natural for right-handers. Even experts have made this claim. Yet lefties in Israel often write Hebrew (written from right to left) with that same hooked motion, while righties do not, a fact experts could discover by just removing their provincial blinders.

Doonesbury Copyright, 1973, G. B. Trudeau.
Used by permission of Universal Press Syndicate. All rights reserved.

Provincialism leads us to inflate the importance and size of our own nation at the expense of the rest of the world. China is larger in size than the United States, and has about one-third of the human race within its borders (close to 1 billion *people, compared to about 230 million in the United States). In this comic strip, Garry Trudeau pokes fun at our provincial ignorance of the rest of the world. In addition, of course, it doesn't make much sense to refer to Samoans as a minority group in their own island.*

> Man is a social animal; only in the herd is he happy. It is all one to him whether it is the profoundest nonsense or the greatest villainy—he feels completely at ease with it—so long as it is the view of the herd, and he is able to join the herd.
>
> —Sören Kierkegaard

Loyalty

The second way our provincial natures push us into committing the fallacy of *provincialism* is by making us believe, or disbelieve, because of our *loyalty* to the group. We want to believe we're the greatest and the other guys are second rate, so we tend to make our beliefs conform to this desire, whatever the facts of the matter indicate.

The reactions of many Americans to the My Lai massacre in Vietnam are a good example.[3] On reading about My Lai, a teletype inspector in Philadelphia is reported to have said he didn't think it happened: "I can't believe our boys' hearts are that rotten." This response was typical, as was that of the person who informed the *Cleveland Plain Dealer,* which had printed photos of the massacre: "Your paper is rotten and anti-American." Surveys taken after wide circulation of news about the massacre revealed that large numbers of Americans refused to believe "American boys" had done such a thing. The myth of American moral superiority seems to have been a better source of truth for them than evidence at hand. They were like the clerics who refused to look through Galileo's telescope to see the moons of Jupiter because they *knew* Jupiter could not possibly have moons.

2. Lack of Proportion

Perhaps the most overlooked error of reasoning in the literature is the failure to see things in proper perspective or proportion. Let's name this the fallacy of **lack of proportion**.

Here is an excerpt from a newspaper column by George F. Will making that very point:

> When polio was killing 300 people annually, parents feared for their children. Drunk drivers will kill 86 times that many people this year, yet few Americans are alarmed. They are rightly alarmed about violent crime, and about handguns, yet drunk drivers account for the most common form of violent death.
>
> When toxic shock killed some women, the publicity killed a product. A few instances of botulism destroyed a soup company. But the public that reacts

> These times are the ancient times, when the world is ancient, and not those which we account ancient . . . by a computation backward from ourselves.
>
> —Francis Bacon

Provincialism *crops up in all sorts of unexpected places.*

---

[3]See Seymour M. Hersh's *My Lai 4: A Report on the Massacre and Its Aftermath* (New York: Random House, 1970), pp. 151–52.

swiftly to such dangers is not comparably aroused by the fact that a life is lost every 21 minutes in an alcohol-related crash, and one out of every two Americans will eventually be involved in an alcohol-related crash. . . .

If Americans used seat belts, they would save 28,000 lives this year. But seat belt use is declining while anxieties about remote dangers are rising.[4]

Failure to see things in perspective is especially common among those who work for what they believe to be a worthy cause—they tend to get caught up in what they're doing and exaggerate its importance all out of proportion. Women caught up in the women's rights movement, blacks working for civil rights, and religious fundamentalists caught up in the fight against the theory of evolution, all are good examples. Such people often become overzealous and tend to see the less concerned as callous, unthinking, or prejudiced, forgetting that there are plenty of other evils in the world, even some worse ones. (They also sometimes drive the rest of us crazy by turning every conversation into a political harangue.) Here is a magazine excerpt showing how our rhetoric often reveals a lack of a sense of proportion, generated by missionary zeal:

"Genocide" was a word used to describe the Atlanta murders. "Fascist" was the word Norman Mailer used to characterize a society unwilling to take chances on literary murderers [the particular literary murderer Mailer had in mind proceeded to murder again when Mailer's efforts helped win him a chance]. Senator Larry Pressler was detained by the Polish police for half an hour during his visit to Warsaw a couple of weeks ago, and came back saying that now he understands how repressive martial law can be.[5]

Tokenism

One of the important variations on the fallacy *lack of proportion* is **tokenism**—mistaking a token gesture for the real thing. We do so, usually, because we fail to see the lack of proportion between the token gesture and the amount of effort actually required.

Tokenism is one of the politician's best friends. When action is demanded but is politically inexpedient, politicians frequently turn to it. They make a token gesture (set in motion only a small proportion of what is required) and shout about it as loudly as they can. For example, in 1970, an earthquake in Peru killed about 50,000 people and left an emergency of major proportions in its wake. (That many people have probably not been killed in the United States in all the earthquakes, hurricanes, and tornadoes in our history.) Relief aid was desperately needed by the Peruvians. The American response was a trip to Peru by Mrs. Nixon (widely publicized—a picture of Mrs. Nixon hugging a little earthquake victim appeared on page one in many newspapers around the country). But very little effective aid ever reached Peru from the United States.[6] Clearly, our hearts were not really in the relief venture: the American effort was only a token gesture designed to pacify the few in the United States who wanted to aid the Peruvians. Given the lack of complaints from Americans after Mrs. Nixon's trip to Peru, we can assume most of us here were satisfied by this token gesture.

---

[4]*Washington Post* (May 2, 1982).
[5]*New Republic* (February 10, 1982).
[6]See Roger Glass's article in *New Republic* (September 19, 1970).

Tokenism

Note that Clint equates his notion of halfway with fairness.

Names Change but Tokenism Never Does

Proctor & Gamble is making an all-out effort to eliminate sexist language from company reports and job titles. The firm is focusing its attention on a cake plant being built near Jackson, Tenn. There, "manpower curves" have become "effort curves," "man-hours" are now "effort hours" and "he"—"he/she."

Craftsmen became artisans but that term left the plant's building contractor speechless. Now they're crafters. Other terms have been harder to replace: Foreman are now called first-line supervisors, but they've yet to come up with a suitable replacement for journeyman.

As could be expected, the new terminology is not being taken too seriously by the people actually building the plant. And why should it be? Of the 340 wage earners at the cake factory, only five are women.

—*New Times* (October 2, 1978)
© 1978 by New Times Publishing Co. Reprinted by permission.

Corporate tokenism on the women's rights front.

The Double Standard

We are guilty of the fallacy of the **double standard** when we judge or evaluate two or more things, groups, or people, according to inconsistent standards (without some legitimate reason for doing so.) Usually, this means holding our opponents to higher standards than we do our friends (or ourselves) just because they are our opponents. (And usually, we don't notice that we've used a double standard, because of *self deception*.)

While the fallacy of the *double standard* is usually a variation of the fallacy *inconsistency* (to be discussed soon), a lack of proportion is often the psychological mechanism that puts it into motion. In other words, we often unwittingly adopt a double standard because we don't realize that a lack of proportion or perspective has led us into inconsistency.

The way the media portrayed Israel's role in the 1982 Beirut massacre is a good example. In the first place, "only" a few hundred people were killed in this massacre—many fewer than the number of Lebanese murdered by the PLO, the Syrians, and other Lebanese. Yet the coverage of the Beirut massacre was much greater (so was the public outrage). And second, while the Israelis surely were guilty of negligence (they expected the Lebanese Christian militia to kill PLO soldiers who were hiding in refugee camps, in violation of the peace agreement just reached, and didn't pay attention when civilians were killed), it was, after all, Lebanese Christian militia who committed the slaughter—in retaliation for previous atrocities that were in turn in retaliation for still prior atrocities. But it was the Israelis who received most of the condemnation.[7]

---

[7]For more in this vein, see the Norman Podhoretz article that appeared in the *International Herald Tribune* and many other papers on September 27, 1982. And see Chapter 8 on Managing the News for more on the principles of news reporting that led the media to play the story the way they did.

3. Questionable Premise

We're guilty of the fallacy of **questionable premise** when we violate the requirement of cogent reasoning that we use only justified or warranted premises. (Of course, what a given person finds justified depends on that person's background information and world view.[8])

To become a pro at spotting questionable premises, we have to overcome certain natural tendencies and beliefs. Recall the misplaced faith many Americans had—almost to the end—that President Nixon did not take part in the Watergate coverup and therefore should not be impeached.[9] Why did they believe this in the face of increasingly strong evidence that he was lying? The answer spotlights several of the natural tendencies we need to hold in check.

In the first place, we all are strongly moved to accept the official "myths" about our own society. And one of those myths is that our leaders, in particular our presidents, do not lie to us (the point of the George Washington cherry tree myth), except perhaps for very high-minded reasons (for instance, to keep vital secrets from the enemy). Good thinkers go beyond official myths to formulate more accurate theories as to how their societies actually function.

Second, when we're young, most of us accept our parents as genuine authorities, perhaps even the best authorities (when we're kids, *we* obviously don't know enough to survive without their knowledge). Other authority figures, such as religious ministers and especially leaders of nations, receive some of that parental aura by virtue of their positions of authority. Good thinkers learn from experience that authority figures come in all shapes, sizes, and qualities—our parents and leaders may be brilliant people of sterling integrity, but then again they may not. (Nixon, obviously, was not a leader of sterling integrity.)

Third, our feelings get bound up with issues and personalities, making it hard for us to be objective. (Gamblers know, for instance, that in a stadium sports crowd, better odds can be obtained by betting *against* the home team.) Thus, the feelings of those who voted for Nixon became bound up with his innocence. It's hard after all, to admit we voted for a liar. Good thinkers learn to give up discredited opinions.

Fourth, we tend to deceive ourselves in ways that favor our own narrow interests. Nixon, like any president, favored certain social and economic interests over others. Selfish desire led some people who had those interests to deceive themselves into believing in his innocence. Those who reason well don't let selfish desires influence their perception of reality.

Fifth, we tend to hang on to beliefs out of tenacity or loyalty, even in the face of contrary evidence (recall the earlier discussion of loyalty). Some diehard Nixon supporters didn't want to be "quitters" or "fair-weather friends," and thus they

---

[8]Some logicians, who conceive of the notion of fallacious reasoning more narrowly than we do in this text, refuse to call acceptance of a questionable premise a fallacy. They do, of course, admit that acceptance of questionable premises is a mistake.

[9]Their fallacy was *questionable premise* because the conclusion Nixon wanted us to draw was that he shouldn't be forced out of office. (Premise: I'm innocent. Conclusion: Don't fire me.) In everyday life, however, it's often difficult to tell premises from conclusions—an argument should be questioned if it contains a questionable *statement*, whether or not we can figure out that it was a premise rather than a conclusion.

believed the president long after overwhelming evidence of his guilt was available. Loyalty is a wonderful human trait, but not for finding out the truth about things.

And, finally, most of us simply aren't trained in the art of critical thinking—in particular, in the knack of dredging up from memory old information relevant to current issues. Nixon should have been doubted on Watergate because of his past record (see below about the lies he told in campaigning against, say, Helen Gahagan Douglas in 1950); but even among those Americans who once knew this, there was a tendency to let the past rest. This tendency is the reason why, for instance, a sitting president can campaign for reelection on a platform contradictory to the one on which he originally was elected.

Reading between the lines, or adding up the figures, is one way to avoid accepting questionable statements. For example, an article on Ann Landers (of advice column fame) states she personally reads every one of more than 1000 letters she receives every day, considering it a sacred trust. The article states that this conscientious practice has paid off for her not just with fame and a high salary but also with income from about 100 speeches she's asked to deliver every year. But even if she spent eight hours every day reading those letters, that would mean reading about two every minute (no time off for coffee breaks), a task even Ann Landers isn't likely to be up to—and when would she get time to write her column or prepare and deliver 100 speeches? So the claim that she actually reads every letter she receives is questionable indeed.

4. Straw Man

While the broad fallacy category of *questionable premise* is seldom mentioned in traditional logic texts, several specific varieties of that fallacy are quite common. One of these is the fallacy **straw man**.[10] We're guilty of this fallacy when we misrepresent an opponent's position to make it easier to attack, or attack a weaker opponent or position while ignoring a stronger one.

Politicians running for office frequently use this fallacy, Richard Nixon being one of the best examples. He used *straw man* (along with *ad hominem* argument and *false dilemma,* to be discussed soon) as the cornerstone of his rhetorical style in every campaign he waged. In 1950, when he ran for the Senate against Congresswoman Helen Gahagan Douglas, Nixon's speeches and political ads were full of *ad hominem* and *straw man* arguments. Here is an example from a political ad:

> The real import of the contest between Mr. Nixon and Helen Gahagan Douglas is whether America shall continue to tolerate COMMUNIST CONSPIRACIES within our own borders and Government, persist in condoning BUREAU-CRATIC PROFLIGACY and appeasing TOTALITARIAN AGGRESSION, or whether America shall victoriously resist these deadly dangers.[11]

---

[10]Should a time-honored name such as this one be replaced by, say, *straw person,* on grounds of reforming sexist features of language? Is the name *straw man* derogatory to women?

[11]For more on early Nixon campaign rhetoric, see the article on Helen Gahagan Douglas in *Ms* magazine, October 1973 and the book *The Strange Case of Richard Milhous Nixon* (New York: Popular Library, 1973) by former Congressman Jerry Voorhis, Nixon's opponent in 1946.

The later Nixon played down communism in distorting his opponents' positions, preferring instead to associate them in the public eye with the views of "radical liberals," hippies, the youth counterculture, and militant left-wing groups like the Weather Underground. Here is an example from his acceptance speech at the 1972 Republican Convention:

> Let me illustrate the difference in our philosophies. Because of our free economic system, what we have done is build a great building of economic wealth and might in America. It is by far the tallest building in the world, and we are still adding to it. Now, because some of the windows are broken, they say tear it down and start again. We say, replace the windows and keep building. That's the difference.

The "they" was the radical left; Nixon wanted voters to think the position of his opponent, George McGovern, was just like that of the radical left, because Nixon's version of the radical left position was so easy to caricature and then attack. Nixon rarely mentioned the specifics either of McGovern's program or of his actual record. The straw McGovern was, after all, such an inviting target.

Why are *ad hominem* argument and *straw man* so powerful in the hands of a skilled practitioner like Richard Nixon? One reason is that voters rarely do the small amount of work necessary to discover that the position attacked is a straw one—a distortion of the position actually held. Those who fail to follow through on the facts are condemned to be easy marks for the clever politicians who hawk *straw man* and other fallacies as their stock in trade.

A twenty-seventh amendment, which would provide full representation in the House and Senate for Washington, D.C., is defended on grounds that to oppose it is racist. And now the twenty-eighth, or Equal Rights Amendment, is recommended to recalcitrant states on the basis that to resist it will invite economic reprisals [against states that did not ratify the amendment].

—Walter Berns, in *The Atlantic* (May 1979)

The fallacy straw man *is committed either when conclusions are distorted or when* reasons *for espousing those conclusions are mangled. Failing to achieve passage of the Equal Rights Amendment on the basis of fairness or justice (their reasons for championing ERA), equal rights advocates tried economic force to push hesitant states into ratifying ERA (considerations of fairness rarely are sufficient alone to bring about social change). But there is a great deal of difference between the reasons a person gives in the sense of justifications for holding a view and reasons in the sense of motivators to action. Analogy: A mother might tell her daughter to clean up her room because it's fair for everyone to pitch in and do part of the work but, when that fails, tell the child that if she doesn't clean up her room she'll have to stay in it all evening and miss her favorite television programs. (Incidentally, these attempts at coercion by ERA advocates seem to have backfired.)*

Exaggeration

The fallacy of the *straw man* is perpetrated by distorting the argument of one's opponent and then attacking that distorted version. However, distortion itself is not necessarily bad or fallacious. In the form of *exaggeration,* for instance, it is a time-honored literary device used by most great writers for satirical or poetic effect. Great satirists, such as Jonathan Swift, use exaggeration in order to shock people into seeing what they take to be humanity's true nature, and in an attempt to reduce that strange gap in most of us between mere belief and belief that serves as an impetus to action.

So exaggeration in itself is not fallacious. The purpose of the exaggeration determines whether or not a fallacy is committed. A satirist who exaggerates the evil in human nature doesn't intend us to believe that human beings are as bad as he portrays them. He exaggerates to help us realize the actual extent of human evil. But when the intent is to make us believe that the exaggeration is literally true, then the fallacy *straw man* enters into the picture.

5. False Dilemma

The fallacy called **false dilemma** (or the *either-or* fallacy) occurs when we reason or argue on the assumption that there are just two plausible solutions to a problem or issue, when in fact there are at least three. (However, it's convenient to stretch the term *false dilemma* to cover false "trilemmas," and so on.) *False dilemma* is a species of *questionable premise,* because any statement that sets up a *false* dilemma ought to be questioned.

Here is the lead-in blurb for an article: "Society and Sex Roles":

Economics, not biology, may explain male domination.[12]

This statement suggests that there are just two possibilities: either biology explains male dominance, or economic success does so. And it suggests that the second possibility, economic success, "may" (weasel word) be the true explanation of male domination. Yet there are many other possibilities, such as social custom, religious conviction, and various *combinations* of economic and biological factors. By tempting us to think of the cause of male domination as either economics or biology, the

---

In the case of Richard Nixon, he got where he got by . . . dogged and intelligent perseverance: *ten million* town hall appearances for local candidates over a period of 20 years.
— William F. Buckley, Jr., in the *New York Post* (October 1974)

We don't want to be foolishly strict in labeling items fallacious. Obviously, Buckley didn't intend readers to take the 10 million figure literally. So he isn't guilty of a fallacy, although he surely did exaggerate. He used exaggeration to impress on us that, as Vice President and then President, Nixon made an unusually large number of appearances for local candidates, and in fact Nixon did just that.

---

[12]*Human Nature* (April 1978).

quote leads us to overlook other possibilities and thus to commit the fallacy of *false dilemma.*

Which brings to mind the familiar question whether it is differences in heredity or in environment (nature or nurture) that are responsible for individual differences in intelligence. Put as a question of heredity *or* environment, the problem becomes a *false dilemma,* because it should be clear by now that heredity and environment both shape intelligence. The sensible question to ask is not whether heredity or environment is responsible but rather how much effect each of these has on intelligence.

Arguments or statements posing *false dilemmas* often mask the fact that they contain a dilemma of any kind, so that noticing their fallaciousness takes watchfulness. Here is an example, a 1978 statement by Harvard University President Derek Bok:

> If you think education is expensive, try ignorance.

This has lots of truth to it, of course; some sort of education is certainly more valuable than no education at all. But Bok's statement, in particular because uttered by the president of Harvard, invites us to think that our choice is either *formal* education or ignorance. So it invites us to accept the *false dilemma* of either getting a formal education or remaining ignorant—omitting the alternatives of *informal* education or becoming *self-taught* (as many important thinkers have been).

Since World War II, a good deal of the discussion in the mass media (as on the floor in Congress—but not nearly as much in the *non-*mass media) concerning the extremely serious question of military budgets has been based on some sort of *false dilemma.* The issue has usually been characterized in the media as though there are two basic positions on the question: increased defense spending, leading to increased military strength and safety; and decreased defense spending leading to decreased military strength and safety. (The 1983 *Time* magazine article on military equipment discussed in Chapter 8 is interesting because it was an important recent exception.)

Yet this has never been the way the forces have lined up. There have always been *several* camps on this issue. Some people have indeed favored increased military spending as the way to get increased military protection from the Russians (in terms of political power, this has been the dominant view). And a few have favored reduced military spending and reduced military capability—often on the grounds that an all-out war with Russia is unthinkable, but sometimes for strictly pacifistic reasons. However, others have argued not for an increase or decrease in military spending as much as for an improvement in the *quality* of the weapons and training we buy for all those billions spent. And still others have argued for both reduced spending and a (selective) improvement in our military might. Their point has been that we spend too much on atomic overkill and on a few very complicated ineffective weapons—battleships, the F-16 fighter plane, etc.—rather than on simpler, cheaper weapons.

By reducing as much of the debate as possible into a simplistic *false dilemma* between more spending and better defense versus less spending and poorer defense, those favoring the first of these alternatives increase their chances of prevailing, since the other alternative in their dilemma is not acceptable to most Americans. (Note the connection between falling for this kind of *false dilemma* and simplistic, unsubtle, undetailed reasoning.)

6. Begging the Question

When arguing, it's impossible to provide reasons for every assertion. Some of what we say or do must go unjustified, at least for the moment. But if, in the course of a discussion or debate, we endorse without proof some form of the very question at issue, we are guilty of the fallacy generally called **begging the question.**[13] Here is an example excerpted from a recent magazine interview:

> *Question:* Why do you think Argentina will go socialist?
> *Answer:* Because of the force of "world historical circumstances."

In other words, we're told that the circumstances in the world today that will lead Argentina to socialism are the historical circumstances in the world today that will lead Argentina to socialism.

Drawing by Booth: © 1975 The New Yorker Magazine, Inc.

"Having concluded, Your Highness, an exhaustive study of this nation's political, social and economic history, and after examining, Sire, the unfortunate events leading to the present deplorable state of the realm, the consensus of the council is that Your Majesty's only course, for the public good, must be to take the next step."

Question-begging *advice, following oracular rule number one: make pronouncements as vague as possible to minimize the chance of being wrong.*

---

[13]*Begging the question* falls into the broad logical category *questionable premise* because a statement questionable as a conclusion is equally questionable as a premise.

Political arguments frequently beg questions at issue. For example, in 1972, an expert in Massachusetts testifying against legalizing abortion argued that abortion is wrong since a baby shouldn't have to suffer because of the selfish desires or the illness of the mother. By calling the fetus a *baby,* the arguer implicitly asserted that it is a human being, thus begging one of the more serious points at issue (whether a fetus is a human being).

Question begging occurs frequently in disputes between partisans of extremely different positions. Thus, the rejoinder "But that amounts to socialism!" often is heard in disputes over public medical care, even though the other side is perfectly aware of this fact, and may even be attracted to the proposal precisely because it *is* socialistic. To avoid begging the question, the antisocialist must present *reasons* for rejecting anything that smacks of socialism. (This example illustrates the point that the fallacy of *begging the question* is relative. For instance, when two died-in-the-wool advocates of capitalism argue, the claim "But that amounts to socialism" doesn't beg a question at issue between them, and so isn't necessarily fallacious.)

7. Inconsistency

One of the most important fallacies is that of **inconsistency.** We reason or argue *inconsistently* when we argue from contradictory premises, or argue for contradictory conclusions. Obviously, if two premises contradict each other, one of them must be false. So even though the argument in which they occur is *valid,*[14] we commit a fallacy in accepting its conclusion. (Similar remarks apply to cases in which we reason to inconsistent conclusions.)

It should be clear that the fallacy of *inconsistency* is a species of the larger fallacy category of *questionable premise.* This is because at least one of a set of inconsistent premises must be false, so that the set as a whole should be questioned.

Politics being what it is, government officials and other politicians are frequently (one might even say continually) inconsistent, although their inconsistency is not usually explicit or even exact (for one thing because political rhetoric is so vague and ambiguous). Their inconsistency is of several kinds, the simplest being to contradict themselves within a single speech, article, or news conference. Of course, such inconsistency is rarely explicit—that would be too obvious. Instead, it tends to be concealed in some way or other. Typical is the candidate who in the same speech favors large increases in government services (to attract voters who will benefit from them) and important tax reductions (to attract voters burdened by heavy taxes). Since government services cost money (and since most government expenditures are fixed), a package of increased services and decreased taxes can be regarded as inconsistent in the absence of a plausible explanation as to how it can be done. Requiring that figures "add up" is a way of requiring candidates to be consistent.

Inconsistency over Time

Another way in which politicians are often guilty of *inconsistency* is by saying one thing at one time and place and another thing at another, without justifying the

---

[14]*Valid* because contradictory premises validly imply any and every conclusion (for technical reasons).

change or retracting the earlier pronouncement. (The expression is "blowing with the wind.")

Ronald Reagan campaigned on a platform of lower taxes (who doesn't?) and tried to stick to his guns when elected. Of course, he had to backtrack when it became evident that monstrous deficits were piling up, but he tried his best to hold the rhetorical line. Thus, in October 1982, he was asked whether he could still assure the American people that he would "rule out any tax increases, revenue enhancers, or specifically an increase in the gasoline tax." His reply was, "Unless there's a palace coup and I'm overthrown, there will be no tax increases."[15] But soon after, we heard that Reagan would ask for an increase in the federal gasoline tax from four to eight cents a gallon.[16]

Politicians often are forced by circumstances to commit the fallacy of *inconsistency* when, by rising in office, they come to represent different constituencies with different viewpoints. Similarly, they often commit this fallacy in order to "keep up with the times"; what is popular at one time often is unpopular at another.

Lyndon Johnson's position on civil rights legislation illustrates both of these. As a congressman and (for a while) as a senator from Texas, he consistently voted and spoke *against* civil rights legislation. But when he became a power in the Senate his tune modified, and as president it changed completely. Here are two quotes that illustrate Johnson's fundamental *inconsistency over time* on the question of race and

HIS FANTASY, TATTOO?... HE WANTS TO CUT TAXES, INCREASE DEFENSES AND BALANCE THE BUDGET ALL AT THE SAME TIME...

Mike Peters, *Dayton Daily News*

---

[15] *New York Times* (October 29, 1982).
[16] *New York Times* (November 24, 1982).

civil rights legislation. The first statement was made in 1948 at Austin, Texas, when he was running for the Senate:

> This civil rights program [part of President Truman's "Fair Deal"], about which you have heard so much, is a farce and a sham—an effort to set up a police state in the guise of liberty. I am opposed to that program. I have fought it in Congress. *It is the province of the state to run its own elections.* I am opposed to the antilynching bill because the federal government has no more business enacting a law against one form of murder than another. I am against the FEPC [Fair Employment Practices Commission] because if a man can tell you whom you must hire, he can tell you whom you cannot employ.

But in 1964 Johnson was president of the United States. He had a larger constituency, and, equally important, the average American's views on race and civil rights were changing. In that year Congress passed an extremely important civil rights act *at his great urging*. And in 1965 he delivered a famous speech at the predominantly black Howard University, in which he said in part:

> Nothing in any country touches us more profoundly, and nothing is more freighted with meaning for our own destiny, than the revolution of the Negro American.
>
> In far too many ways American Negroes have been another nation, deprived of freedom, crippled by hatred, the doors of opportunity closed to hope.
>
> In our time change has come to this nation, too. The American Negro, acting with impressive restraint, has peacefully protested and marched, entered the courtrooms and the seats of government, demanding a justice that has long been denied. The voice of the Negro was the call to action. But it is a tribute to America that, once aroused, the courts and the Congress, the President and most of the people, have been the allies of progress. . . . [W]e have seen in 1957 and 1960, and again in 1964, the first civil rights legislation in this nation in almost an entire century.
>
> As majority leader of the United States Senate, I helped to guide two of these bills through the Senate. And as your president, I was proud to sign the third. And now, very soon *we will have the fourth—a new law guaranteeing every American the right to vote.*
>
> No act of my entire administration will give me greater satisfaction than the day when my signature makes this bill, too, the law of this land.

And on August 6, 1965, he did sign the Voting Rights Act into law. But he didn't explain why it was no longer ". . . the province of the state to run its own elections." He didn't explain his about-face on civil rights legislation.

Organizational Inconsistency

Large organizations, such as governments, generally have several different people who can "speak for" the organization. Perhaps we can think of an organization as being guilty of *inconsistency* when different authorized representatives who are speaking or acting for that organization contradict each other, or where there is a contradiction between the organization's announced policies and its actual practices.

For example, during the Reagan administration, the Commerce Department investigated several Japanese electronics firms for "dumping" 64K RAM computer chips on the U.S. market. (*Dumping* means selling below cost in foreign markets.) At the same time, the Justice Department was investigating the same companies to determine if they'd violated antitrust laws by conspiring to set (presumably too high) prices.

Similarly, President Reagan said in a speech to the Costa Rican National Assembly that "any nation destabilizing its neighbors by protecting guerrillas and exporting violence should forfeit close and fruitful relations with . . . any people who truly love peace and freedom." But soon after, we learned that the CIA was recruiting, arming, and directing "clandestine military operations against Nicaragua."[17]

Because of the vagueness and ambiguity of most everyday language, organizations often can get away with what appears to be *inconsistency* simply by reinterpreting. For instance, in a nationally televised speech on July 27, 1981, President Reagan said, "I will not stand by and see those of you who are dependent on Social Security deprived of the benefits you've worked so hard to earn. You will continue to receive your checks in the full amount due you." Listeners certainly got the impression the President was against Social Security payment cuts. But the next day, David Gergen, a White House spokesman, "interpreted" Reagan's statement to mean that President Reagan reserved the right to decide who was dependent on Social Security benefits, who had earned such benefits, and who, accordingly, was due them.[18] (Since Reagan tended to wander from prepared texts, reinterpreting his remarks back on course became a common feature of the Reagan administration.)

Inconsistency between Words and Actions

Another common variety of inconsistency is to *say* one thing but *do* something else. (Calling this a "fallacy" stretches that concept a bit to serve everyday purposes.) During the 1976 campaign, Jimmy Carter and his representatives kept assuring us that Carter would appoint "fresh talent" if elected. Here, for instance, is a statement by then campaign manager Hamilton Jordan:

> If we end up appointing people like Cyrus Vance and Zbigniew Brzezinski, we will have failed.

Washington Post (July 17, 1980)

---

[17] *Philadelphia Inquirer,* December 5, 1982 and January 11, 1983.

[18] *Philadelphia Inquirer* (July 31, 1981); also reported in the *Quarterly Review of Doublespeak* (November 1981).

So after winning election, Carter appointed Vance Secretary of State and Brzezinski head of the National Security Council. (His other appointments tended to be equally stale "fresh talent," like James Schlesinger as energy chief.)

When Gerald Ford, chosen by Richard Nixon as his successor, became the first unelected president, he assured the American people he would not run for president in 1976. But when the time came, he ran, an inconsistency between his words and actions that hardly caused a ripple.

During the hearings held before Ford's confirmation as vice president, he was asked: "If a president resigned his office before his term expired, would his successor have the power to prevent or to terminate any investigation or criminal prosecution charges against the former president?" His reply was: "I do not think the public would stand for it," a clear indication that he would not use such power. And then, eleven days before issuing the pardon, when asked if he intended to pardon Mr. Nixon, he replied that until legal procedures had been undertaken, ". . . I think it's unwise and untimely for me to make any commitment." In the absence of an explanation of his change of mind, it's clear that President Ford was guilty of the fallacy of *inconsistency* when he pardoned Richard Nixon.

Of course, high government officials are not the only ones whose words are inconsistent with their actions. Cigarette smokers who argue against legalizing marijuana on the grounds that marijuana is unhealthy are inconsistent in this way. And so are those women's liberationists who argue against different "roles" for each sex, yet play the feminine role when it's in their interest to do so (for instance, expecting men to drive on long trips, buy them expensive engagement rings, or spank errant children).

The breaking of campaign promises is so common that you'd think no one would pay any attention to them. The rule seems to be to promise them anything, even Arpege. In the 1982 election for governor of California, George Deukmejian campaigned on a promise to balance the state budget without raising taxes (not the usual promise of this kind because of Proposition 13—his opponent, Tom Bradley, refused to make such a promise). But after winning the election, Deukmejian faced reality and (no fooling) gave in to increased taxes.

Like all candidates, Ronald Reagan promised all sorts of things to attract voters in his 1980 election campaign. Perhaps the nastiest example concerns the air traffic controllers. In October 1980, he wrote to Robert Poli, their union president, saying:

> I have been thoroughly briefed by members of my staff as to the deplorable
> state of our nation's air traffic control system. They have told me that too few

© 1959 United Feature Syndicate, Inc.

This Peanuts comic strip illustrates another way in which we tend to be inconsistent. Linus is all for a generality (he loves humanity in general), but not the individual cases that fall under it (he doesn't love individual people).

people working unreasonable hours with obsolete equipment has placed the nation's air travelers in unwarranted danger. In an area the Carter Administration has failed to act reasonably.

You can rest assured that if I am elected President, I will take whatever steps are necessary to provide our air traffic controllers with the most modern equipment available, and to adjust staff levels and work days so they are commensurate with achieving the maximum degree of public safety. . . .

I pledge to you that my administration will work very closely with you to bring about a spirit of cooperation between the President and the air traffic controllers. Such harmony can and must exist if we are to restore the people's confidence in the government. . . .

On the strength of this letter and Reagan's public pronouncements, the air traffic controller's union (PATCO) naïvely endorsed Reagan over Jimmy Carter. But when elected, Reagan sold the union and its striking members down the river in an especially brutal case of union busting (he had military personnel take over their jobs and barred strikers from ever again serving as air traffic controllers).

Another way to look at *inconsistency between words and actions* is that the person who believes someone who is frequently inconsistent between what she says and what she does should not automatically be believed when she says she'll do this or that. In other words, we can think of the fallacy in these cases as that of *questionable premise*, since experience has shown the speaker is not to be believed on words alone.

The Double Standard (Again)

Since the fallacy of the *double standard* (mentioned when discussing the fallacy *lack of proportion*) is a variety of *inconsistency,* let's look at one example here. When abortion and birth control became big issues a few years ago, many liberal pundits (such as *New York Times* columnist Anthony Lewis) attacked Catholic priests and bishops who spoke out against both of these measures on the grounds that the church and the clergy should stay out of politics; yet in the 1960s and 1970s, these same writers were loud in their praise of Catholic and other clergy who worked hard and risked their necks championing civil rights.

Summary of Chapter Three

1. *Provincialism:* Assuming that the familiar, the close, or what is one's own is *therefore* the better or more important. Also, the failure to look beyond one's own group, in particular to the ideas of other cultures. *Example:* Assuming that left-handed people write with a hooked motion because English is written from left to right, an idea that can easily be proved false by checking on lefties in cultures where the language is written from right to left.
   a. *Loyalty:* Deciding the truth of an assertion on the basis of loyalty. *Example:* Refusing to believe the overwhelming evidence that U.S. soldiers had shot and killed defenseless women, children, and babies at My Lai 4 in South Vietnam.

2. *Lack of proportion:* This failure to see things in proper perspective or proportion.
   a. *Tokenism:* Mistaking a token gesture, usually ineffective, for an adequate effort. *Example:* Accepting General Motors's spending of 0.1 percent of its gross annual sales on air pollution research as a genuine effort at pollution control.
   b. *Double standard:* Judging according to inconsistent standards, a variety of the fallacy of *inconsistency,* but often committed because of a lack of proportion. *Example:* Holding Israel to a higher standard of conduct than its enemies.

3. *Questionable premise:* Accepting a premise when there is no good reason to accept it (and the argument in question doesn't provide any). *Example:* Having believed the premise that President Nixon had no part in the Watergate coverup, without having a good reason to believe it (leading to acceptance of his conclusion that he shouldn't be impeached).

4. *Straw man:* Attacking a position similar to but significantly different from an opponent's position (or attacking weaker opponents while ignoring stronger ones). *Example:* Richard Nixon branding his opponent, Helen Gahagan Douglas, as a pinko.

   Note that exaggeration of an opponent's position only counts as a fallacy if there is an implication that the exaggeration is literally true.

5. *False dilemma:* Erroneous reduction of alternatives of possibilities—usually a reduction to just two. *Example:* Implying that male domination is due to either economics or biology, while omitting all sorts of other possibilities.

6. *Begging the question:* Asserting without justification all or part of the very question at issue. *Example:* Answering the question why Argentina will go socialist by saying it's because of "world historical circumstances."

7. *Inconsistency:* Using or accepting contradictory statements to support a conclusion or conclusions. These statements may be presented: (1) by one person at one time; (2) by one person at different times (without explaining the contradiction as a change of mind and providing evidence to support the change); or (3) by different representatives of one institution. It also is committed by someone who *says* one thing but *does* another. *Example:* Lyndon Johnson's stand on racial questions as a candidate for the U.S. Senate and his stand on racial questions as President of the United States.

Exercise 3-1

Determine which fallacies (if any) occur in the following passages and state the reasons for your answers, following the instructions given for Exercise 2-1.

1. *Soviet sociologist Geunadi Gerasimov, quoted in the* Village Voice *(May 5, 1975):* Communism will replace capitalism because private ownership of the means of production is obsolete.

*2. *Private conversation:* I asked the doctor why my mouth was so dry, and he said it was because my salivary glands are not producing enough saliva.

3. *Henry J. Taylor, in the* Topeka Daily Capital *(July 1970):* The great Declaration of Independence begins: "When in the course of human events . . ." and for the first time in man's history announced that all rights came not from a sovereign, not from a government, but from God.

4. San Francisco Chronicle *(March 28, 1972);* "I'm all for women having equal rights," said Bullfight Association president Paco Camino. "But . . . women shouldn't fight bulls, because a bullfighter is and should be a man."

5. *Editorial in the* Hartford Times *(September 11, 1970) on the topic of an extra twenty minutes of school time for teachers (the extra time was objected to by the teachers' union):* Insisting that teachers be in school [twenty minutes] longer than children may seem to some teachers like a factory time-clock operation, but it probably troubles the conscientious teacher far less than those who leave school at the final bell.

*6. *Aristotle:* Oh my friends! There are no friends.

7. *Letter from Robert Rodale touting his* Complete Book of Minerals for Health: That's just one small part of the story of these magnificent elements called minerals—the cornerstones of good health. The fact is, minerals are every bit as important to you as are your vitamins. Good health cannot exist without *both!* But still, many doctors and nutritionists continue to relegate minerals to some minor status.

8. *Private conversation:*

> *Miana:* You'll be rich someday, How.
> *How:* What makes you think so?
> *Miana:* You were born for it.

9. *Lyndon B. Johnson:* I believe in the right to dissent, but I do not believe it should be exercised.

10. *Bumper sticker:* America—Love It or Leave It!

*11. *From Ohio State University* Lantern *story, "Study of Pot Uses Eyed":* Marijuana may be used to treat glaucoma and cancer patients if legislation introduced Wednesday before the Ohio Senate is passed. Under the bill, a research program would be set up to study the medicinal uses of marijuana as it affects . . . glaucoma patients. . . . OSU glaucoma specialist, Dr. Paul Weber, is . . . against the bill. "There is no question in my mind that marijuana eases eye pressure, but not enough studies have been done," Weber said.

12. *John F. Kennedy:* Why, some say, the moon? Why choose this as our goal? They may [as] well ask why climb the highest mountain? Why thirty-five years ago fly the Atlantic? Why does Rice play Texas?

13. High Times *magazine interview with once-Deputy Director of the Bureau of Narcotics and dangerous drugs John Finlator (Fall 1974):*

> *High Times:* One of the excuses for keeping grass illegal is that it causes fatal car accidents.
> *Finlator:* I'd rather be riding with a guy who's stoned than with a guy who's drunk, or on heroin.

14. *Patient:* Doctor, my wife left me four months ago, and I've been shot ever since. I'm beginning to wonder. Will I ever pull out of this?
    Shrink: It's normal to feel a lot of anxiety and depression after a severe loss. But let me assure you that everyone does recover from this sort of thing. So you will too. Unless, of course, the trauma has been so severe that the ego is shattered.

*15. *From "Intelligence Report" by Lloyd Shearer, in* Parade Magazine *(November 5, 1978);* This past September, [Bob Hope] refused to cross a picket line at the Chicago Marriot Hotel, where 1500 guests were waiting for him at a dinner of the National Committee for Prevention of Child Abuse. W. Clement Stone, the insurance tycoon who contributed $2 million to the Nixon campaign fund in 1972, tried to negotiate a temporary halt of picketing so that Hope could enter the hotel. When Stone failed, Hope returned to the Drake Hotel, where he videotaped a 15-minute spot to be shown at the dinner. Hope, who belongs to four show business unions, later explained that he had crossed a picket line many years ago and subsequently had to apologize to labor leader George Meany. He promised then never to cross another.

*16. *From the television show* The Advocates *(December 1972), a story on a proposed "shield law" granting reporters immunity from prosecution if they refuse to reveal their sources to the police or courts:* Contempt of court is a crime for an ordinary citizen. since it is a crime for every citizen, it ought to be a crime for a news reporter who refuses to disclose his sources to a court which has subpoenaed him.

17. *House Judiciary Committee hearing on vice presidential nominations, November 1973:*
    > *Chairman Rodino:* Would you think that the president could, by use of executive privilege, . . . terminate any criminal investigation involving even the president or vice president?
    > *Gerald Ford:* I do not think the president should have the authority to terminate a criminal investigation of anybody in any branch of the federal government.

    Same committee, October 1974:
    > *Representative Mann:* Was it your intention by the pardon [of President Nixon] to terminate the investigation by the special prosecutor's office in the ten areas [in which Nixon was under investigation]?
    > *President Ford:* I think the net result of the pardon was in effect just that, yes, sir.

18. *From a student exam in critical thinking:* The problem with this is that anyone can quit smoking if they have enough willpower and really want to do it.

19. *Newspaper article entitled "Reagan's Remedy for His 'Woman Problem'":* The Reagan administration has launched a campaign to close the political "gender gap" by attempting to improve its negative image to women. In recent days the administration has appointed two women to Cabinet positions, filed a brief supporting women's pension benefits and is hinting at taking further initiatives.

    At the same time, there is no indication that President Reagan plans to change his opposition to many fundamental rights that would strengthen women—from abortion to equal pay.

20. *Los Angeles Chief of Police Daryl F. Gates's response to criticism of the police department by a retiring Deputy Chief of Police (Los Angeles Times, June 29, 1981):* For police department officials to talk to reporters, . . . the board of police commissioners, people in the mayor's offices, council members—that is serious. There is a theme of disloyalty about that kind of thing.

21. *Howard Smith and Brian Van derHorst, in the* Village Voice *(October 18, 1976):* Sri Swami Swanandashram, Hindu holy man from India, after criticizing other Hindu swamis [for instance, Maharishi Mahesh Yogi of TM fame, Swami Muktananda, Sri Chinmoy, and Baba Ram Dass (Richard Alpert)] for making lots of money in the United States from their teaching: "They should have no house, no foundation, no bank accounts. . . . Our laws strictly forbid selling spirituality. But that's what they're doing." When asked what will happen when *he* starts making money, his chosen ally, the Divine Mother Swami Lakshmy Devyashram Mahamandaleshwari, responded: "Money itself is not bad. It's how it's used. Money should all be given away to schools, hospitals, and needy children, or something. It shouldn't be held on to." When asked if it wasn't against their own rules to criticize anyone else's spiritual path, that each must find his own way, Swami Swanandashram answered: "Oh, yes, it's true. Nobody is supposed to do it. But I'm in America. In India we wouldn't criticize. But we are not actually criticizing here. When they are deviating from the real path, we are just telling the truth."

22. An article in *New Times* (May 30, 1975, p. 13) on the Catholic Church reported its efforts to reduce the divorce rate among Catholics by instituting rules that prospective couples must satisfy to gain the Church's blessing for their marriage. A church spokesman stated that the right to marry is a natural right, but restrictions are justified when the proposed marriage "poses a threat to the common good of society."

23. *Senator Jacob Javits, on Senator Mike Gravel's amendment to cut off funds for bombing Indochina (October 5, 1971):* I have decided to vote against the amendment [which he then did], because on balance, I think it would be a

mistake to single out this one aspect of U.S. military activity in Indochina. . . . I want to make it clear that my decision to vote against the Gravel amendment in no way lessens my deep, anguished concern over the continuing ravage being rained on civilians throughout Indochina through the massive U.S. bombing program. I want this war to end now.

24. *Ad for a debate at North Texas State University:* The arena has been set. The contestants are preparing themselves. The event—the Warren–Barnhart debate. On the timely question of ethics and morality.

Dr. Barnhart's position is that if an act brings pleasure, then it is right. If an act is unpleasant, then it is wrong. But if two actions bring pleasure, then the one with the greatest amount of pleasure should be adopted.

Dr. Warren's position is that an act is right or wrong based upon God's word—the New Testament.

The stances have been made. The time is drawing nigh for the confrontation. The only thing lacking now are the spectators. And their judgment of which position is right.

25. *From a high school civics exam:* The white settlers brought civilization to the Indians in America. So now their descendants are suing everybody in sight—total injustice, I say—even ingratitude.

26. *Congressman Frank T. Bow:* How did this so-called leak get out with regard to Kent State?

FBI Director J. Edgar Hoover: That did not come from the FBI. But it did cause me great concern. The first time I knew of it was when the *Akron Beacon-Journal* had a great headline—it is part of the Knight chain of newspapers—saying "FBI: No Reason for Guard to Shoot at Kent State." I knew this was untrue. We never make any conclusions. . . . These were certainly extenuating circumstances which caused the guard to resort to the use of firearms. Perhaps they were not as completely trained as they should have been, but certainly some stated they feared for their lives and then fired; some of the students were throwing bricks and rocks and taunting the National Guardsmen.

Congressman Bow: Do you mind this being on the record?

Hoover: Not at all.[19]

27. *Thomas A. Porter, Dean, School of Arts and Sciences, Central Connecticut State College (in a November 1970 report titled "School of Arts and Sciences: 1970–1980"):* Each department of the school should begin at once to plan how to utilize various instructional patterns and/or new instructional techniques so as to make quality instruction available to all students who seek it. The problem of closing students out of classes which they want and need can only become more serious as our enrollments increase. Efforts in this direction by departments may include the creation of large lecture classes (not always at the lower division level) and utilization

---

[19]From House Appropriations hearings on the 1971 supplemental (released December 8, 1970). Reported in *I. F. Stone's Bi-Weekly* (December 28, 1970).

of TV, auto-instructional labs, and other technological aids. It can be argued, of course, that this approach sacrifices individual communication between faculty and student and dehumanizes education. On the other hand, nothing sacrifices communication so much as being closed out of a class entirely.

*28. *Pope Pius XII (in 1944):* If the exclusive aim of nature [for sexual intercourse] or at least its primary intent had been the mutual giving and possessing of husband and wife in pleasure and delight; if nature had arranged that act only to make their personal experience joyous in the highest degree, and not as an incentive in the service of life; then the Creator would have made use of another plan in the formation of the marital act.

29. *Naval Investigative Service Director (reported to AP, January 3, 1971):* A Naval Investigative Service office will not initiate any investigation . . . when the prediction [provocation?] for the investigation is mere expression of views in opposition to official U.S. policy. . . . Nothing herein is intended to inhibit or preclude normal reporting of information . . . on those individuals whose expressed controversial views may be adjudged to have a potential for embarrassment to the Department of the Navy.

30. *Interior Secretary James G. Watt replying to the claim that he wouldn't be able to perform his duties in the face of mounting criticism:* I have only one loyalty and that's to the President [Reagan] and to the oath of office and to the American people. The criticism I knew would come with a change of government. We represent a change in philosophy . . . and we recognize that there will be a segment that opposed the President's election, opposed my nomination and will faithfully oppose most of my actions.[20]

Exercise 3-2

Find several examples in the mass media television, magazines, newspapers, radio) of fallacies discussed in Chapter 3 and explain carefully and fully why they are fallacious.

---

[20](*Los Angeles Times,* July 16, 19812. Reprinted in Vincent Barry, *Good Reason For Writing* (Belmont, Calif.: Wadsworth, 1983).

It's dangerous to conclude that A is the cause of B just because B follows A.

Figures don't lie, but liars figure.
—Old saying

Peter's Calculation: *No executive devotes much effort to proving himself wrong.*
—Laurence J. Peter

There are lies, damn lies, and statistics.
—Benjamin Disraeli

How happy are the astrologers, who are believed if they tell one truth to a hundred lies, while other people lose all credit if they tell one lie to a hundred truths.
—Guicciardi

It is a well-known fact that in human memory the testimony of a positive case always overshadows the negative one. One gain easily outweighs several losses. *Thus the instances which affirm magic always loom far more conspicuously than those which deny it.*
—Bronislaw Malinowski

4

Fallacious Reasoning—III

Let's now continue our discussion of common fallacies.

1. Suppressed Evidence

We commit the fallacy of **suppressed evidence** when we violate the requirement of cogent reasoning that our starting points (premises) contain as much as possible[1] of the relevant evidence at our disposal (in particular, when we pass over or "forget" evidence contrary to what we want to believe). That is, we commit this fallacy when we fail to use relevant information that we should have thought of or known to look for, or deliberately neglect evidence we know contradicts our theory.

The United Way, which used to discourage donations earmarked for individual member charities, has given in to public pressure and how "honors designation" of a particular member charity. This sounds like progress, but it isn't; the suppressed evidence—what the United Way doesn't choose to tell us—is that it subtracts the amount so designated from the amount it would have given that charity anyway. So in

---

[1]Up to the point of proof, of course. Every time we flick a switch and thus turn on a light, we have evidence relevant to the "theory" that copper conducts electricity. But with much better evidence having proved the point a long time ago, it would be silly to bother with such evidence now.

fact there is no "designation" honored by the United Way. (Not very charitable of them, either.)

As the competitive position of American industrial goods declined during the 1970s, some economic "experts" attributed this decline primarily to rapidly rising gas and oil prices. But this could not possibly have been an important reason for the decline, since America produces more of its own oil than any of its major industrial competitors, who, therefore, were even more at the mercy of OPEC blackmail than we were. They also blamed our high rate of inflation on OPEC extortion, perhaps forgetting that Japan and Germany had much lower inflation rates (or didn't the experts in question know this? What does your world view tell you about this?)

Since most of us tend to suppress evidence when it suits our purposes, it's reasonable for us to suspect that others do so also and to be on our guard against such practices. And we do need to be on our guard when dealing with high-powered, persuasive rhetoric. Television commercials that praised the Shell gasoline ingredient Platformate illustrate this well. In these commercials, the automobile using Shell with Platformate always obtained better mileage than autos using gasoline without Platformate. What was the suppressed evidence? Simply that just about every standard brand of gasoline at the time contained the basic ingredient in Platformate (under a different name). Thus, Shell pitted its gasoline against a decidedly inferior product most auto owners did not use. The viewer's attention was directed away from this fact by the way the claim was worded and also by the general presentation of the commercial.

One good way to avoid being taken in by arguments that suppress evidence is to ask yourself whether additional information isn't needed to come to a sensible conclusion. Take the *Soviet Life* article, "About Millionaires, Family Budgets and Private Business, Soviet Style," which implied that Soviet citizens can indeed become rich, even millionaires:[2]

> Can Soviet citizens accumulate considerable savings? Of course they can. Here are some figures to prove it:

Savings Bank Deposits

Item	1970	1976
Total accounts (in millions [of accounts])	80.1	113.1
Accounts in urban banks (in millions)	58.9	84.0
Accounts in rural banks (in millions)	21.2	29.1
Total deposits (in billions of rubles)	46.6	103.0

But taken alone, these figures don't prove much of anything. For example, simple calculation yields the information that the average deposit was about 910 rubles. But,

[2]April 1978. *Soviet Life* is a Soviet magazine published especially for American readers and distributed in the United States by a reciprocal agreement between the U.S. and U.S.S.R.

first, how much is a ruble worth? (In Italy, 910 lira won't buy much more than a couple of cans of garbanzo beans at the local grocery.) It turns out that 910 rubles were worth about $1,400 in U.S. dollars in 1975. That'll buy a lot of borscht but hardly makes anyone rich. Second, how many people, if any, have savings of, say, 100,000 rubles? (That amount would at least make a person paper rich.) Third, what can be bought in the Soviet Union for 100,000 rubles? (Being paper rich without much to buy doesn't make a person actually rich.) Finally, does even one private person have a million rubles saved up? (The article wants very much for you to conclude that there are such persons in Russia, but it doesn't say that there are.) Until we get the answers to questions like these, suppressed by *Soviet Life,* we're in no position to evaluate their claims about all those rich people in Russia.

In early 1971, then Democrat John Connally, ex-governor of oil-rich Texas, testified before the U.S. Senate Finance Committee concerning his nomination as Secretary of the Treasury. He testified that the allegations of his "vast wealth" in oil and gas were false and that his total wealth in oil and gas was $7,240. But when the *New York Times* revealed that Connally had received money from the Richardson Foundation (set up by the late Texas oil millionaire Sid Richardson), Connally admitted he had been paid $750,000 by the Richardson Foundation for services rendered to Richardson's estate.[3]

This example illustrates how a person may attempt to conceal evidence while not actually lying. Connally's original testimony conveyed the impression that he had not profited from his proximity to vast oil wealth. And he managed to convey that impression without committing what is politely called an "error of commission" (that is, he did not actually lie). But his suppression of the very kind of information that he knew his questioners were looking for did amount to an "error of *omission*" (that is, he did mislead by omitting information he knew the Committee was seeking).

Statistics seem to baffle almost everyone. Here is a choice item illustrating that fact:

We once gave a test to 200 educators, asking what percent of children read at grade level or below. Only 22 percent answered correctly—50 percent of children.

—*Human Behavior* (April 1977)

Even teachers have a hard time keeping straight on the difference between comparative and absolute scales.

Another comparative rating that causes confusion is the IQ rating: Half of all who take the test must be rated below 100, given that 100 merely marks the halfway point in results.

---

[3]For more details, see the *New Republic* (February 13, 1971).

In cases where inconclusive evidence or reasons are given to us when it would be reasonable to expect something more conclusive—for instance, when some easily obtained fact necessary to prove a point is omitted from an argument—we should suspect that the arguer didn't provide us with the information because he didn't have it or perhaps because he knew it to be false. The question we should ask is why that relevant fact hasn't been given to us.

When the New York Times settled a sex discrimination suit for $350,000 (plus promises to hire more women), it tried to reduce its guilt by pointing out that the $350,000 was less than female employees at the Readers Digest and NBC received from their suits. But before we can accept their implied conclusion (that they discriminated less than the others), we need to know whether there are as many women employed by the Times as by these other corporations, so as to calculate average compensation. Since the Times didn't provide this needed information, we should suspect that negative evidence was suppressed and therefore not accept their conclusion that they discriminated less. (This turned out to be a suspicion confirmed: In fact, New York Times women received more per person than the women at the other organizations, which certainly does not support the Times in its claim to have discriminated less.)

2. Slippery Slope

The fallacy of **slippery slope** consists in objecting to a particular action on the grounds that once that action is taken, it will lead inevitably to a similar but less desirable action, which will lead in turn to an even less desirable action, and so on down the "slippery slope" until the horror lurking at the bottom is reached. (Members of the Texas State Legislature sometimes refer to this fallacy as "the camel's nose in the tent," since once the camel's nose enters, the rest of the camel, it is alleged, will follow close behind.)

According to a slightly different version of *slippery slope,* whatever would justify taking the first step over the edge also would justify all the other steps. But, it's argued, if the last step isn't justified, then the first step isn't either.

People frequently argued against Medicare in the late 1960s on the grounds that it was socialized medicine for the aged and would lead to socialized medicine for all, and then to socialized insurance of all kinds, socialized railroads, airlines, and steel mills. It was also argued that whatever justified socialized medicine for the aged justified it for everyone, and justified as well socialized railroads, and so on, all the way down the slope to a completely socialistic system.

The *slippery slope* fallacy is committed when we accept *without further argument* the idea that once the first step is taken, the slide all the way down is inevitable. In fact, the first step sometimes does and sometimes doesn't lead to more steps. Further argument is needed to determine the facts in particular cases like that of Medicare.

Slippery slope is a surprisingly common fallacy. We're exposed to it in watered-down form all the time. For instance, we often hear that smoking marijuana sooner or later leads to snorting cocaine, and then to injecting heroin and leading the life of a junkie, without proof that the progression is anywhere near inevitable (or even frequent). Similarly, it's often argued that premarital sex inevitably gives one a taste for philandering and leads to adultery and broken marriages later on, and that failure to severely punish rowdy children leads them to petty thievery as adolescents and a life of crime as adults. The mistake in all these cases is *not* that the slope isn't slippery. Without more information, we can't know whether it is or isn't. It may be, for instance, that failure to severely punish children who steal makes them think that crime does indeed pay. The error is to assume *without good evidence* that the slope is slippery—that failure to punish errant children turns them into criminals, and so on.

The Domino Theory

The variations on *slippery slope* are almost limitless. One, the **domino theory,** has been employed quite frequently in recent years, notably concerning the war in Vietnam (Indo-China). Everyone seems to have used it at one time or another, starting with the French:

> Once Tongking [Northern Indo-China] is lost, there is really no barrier before Suez.[4]

The Americans then joined in, one of the first being John Foster Dulles:[5]

> If Indo-China should be lost, there would be a chain reaction throughout the Far East and South Asia.

A Quick About-Face

Perhaps intimidated by flack from Capitol Hill, the Social Security Advisory Council has backed away from a proposal to increase the maximum pay subject to Soc-Sec taxation from $14,000 to $24,000 to keep the plan on a pay-as-you-go basis. Instead, it has recommended shifting the cost of Medicare to the general fund.

The proposal, if adopted, would begin the process of transforming Social Security into an out-and-out welfare program. Once we start in that direction, where do we stop?

—*New York Daily News* (January 21, 1975)

Slippery slope, *a favorite of the* New York Daily News. *(The answer to the* News's *question, by the way, is that we can stop whenever—collectively—we want to.)*

---

[4]Spoken by General Jean de Lattre de Tassiguy, general in charge of French forces in the Far East (September 20, 1951). This, and several of the examples which follow, are mentioned in the book *Quotations Vietnam: 1945–1970,* compiled by William G. Effros (New York: Random House, 1970), Chapter Three.
[5]Secretary of State under Eisenhower (April 5, 1954).

Then there was William P. Bundy:[6]

> If South Vietnam falls, the rest of Southeast Asia will be in grave danger of progressively disappearing behind the Bamboo Curtain, and other Asian countries like India and even in time Australia and your own [country—Japan] will in turn be threatened.

Even Bob Hope got into the act:

> Everybody I talked to there [Vietnam] wants to know why they can't go in and finish it, and don't let anybody kid you about why we're there. If we weren't, those Commies would have the whole thing, and it wouldn't be long until we'd be looking off the coast of Santa Monica [California].[7]

All of these versions of the *domino theory* reveal the simplistic attitude that is characteristic of *slippery slope* in any of its variations, the attitude that once the first step is taken, the rest are inevitable. But sometimes that first step will lead to others, sometimes it won't. We must examine each case individually for the details that make all the difference. If we fail to do so, we reason fallaciously.

(It should be noted that we're much more likely to fall for a fallacy like *slippery slope* when we read and think in a simplistic manner. For *slippery slope* arguments typically omit the subtle details that might support, or refute, the claim that the slope is in fact slippery—details without which no one can accurately evaluate such a claim.)

3. Hasty Conclusion

The fallacy of *hasty conclusion* is generally described as the use of an argument which presents evidence that, while relevant to its conclusion, is not sufficient by itself to warrant acceptance of that conclusion.

Voters often judge their representatives by how they vote on a few supposedly key roll calls. But frequently these roll calls are just for show—for the voters back home—the issue already having been decided by committee votes or back-room dealing. To adequately assess the performance of representatives, even on a single important issue, without being guilty of *hasty conclusion,* we have to look behind the facade every elected body erects to make it appear the members are doing roughly the job they're supposed to do, whether they are or not. (Remember, the best elected officials need PR techniques just as much as the worst.)

The *Saturday Review* (February 9, 1974) ran an article stating that college entrance scholastic aptitude test scores are declining in America, indicating, according to the article, that students in the United States are not as bright (or well-educated) as they used to be.

But their conclusion was hasty. For it failed to take account of the fact (mentioned in the article) that the percentage of the total high school population taking these tests has increased—in particular, many more academically poor students now take them.

---

[6]Assistant Secretary of State for Far Eastern Affairs under President Johnson (September 1964, in Tokyo, Japan).

[7]Quoted in Anthony J. Lukas's "This is Bob (Politician-Patriot-Publicist) Hope." In *New York Times Magazine* (October 4, 1970).

(The fallacy of *hasty conclusion* often goes hand in hand with that of *suppressed evidence*.)

4. Small Sample

Statistics frequently are used to project from a sample to the "population" from which the sample was drawn. This is the basic technique behind all polling (as well as a good deal of inductive reasoning), from the Gallup Poll to the Nielsen television ratings. But if the sample is too small to be a reliable measure of the population,[8] then to accept it is to commit the fallacy of the **small sample,** a variety of the fallacy of *hasty conclusion*.

Rowland Evans and Robert Novak (in their newspaper column) are perhaps the all-time *small sample* fallacy champions. At election time, they poll about 50 to 75 voters in "key" districts and then predict statewide elections on that basis. Their batting average, as you might suspect, is a good deal better than chance, but not as good as most successful politicians can achieve (after all, knowing which way voters will go is a key factor in political success). Typical was one of their columns that rated the chances of Democratic State Senator Sander Levin as poor in his effort to become Michigan's governor. This prediction was based on the fact that only 42 percent of those polled in an overwhelmingly Democratic stronghold where he had

---

Courts and legislatures continually try to resuscitate the average person. But as we learn to appreciate the pluralistic nature of our society and the complexity of the human personality, the idea that there is a central point that adequately describes members of our society seems more and more ludicrous. . . . At least one state is resisting [the] trend to do away with the concept of the average person. The Tennessee Obscenity Act of 1978, which was signed into law last April, maintains that: "The phrase 'average person' means a hypothetical human being whose attitude represents a synthesis and composite of all the various attitudes of all individuals, irrespective of age, in Tennessee society at large, which attitude is the result of human experience, understanding, development, cultivation, and socialization in Tennessee, taking into account relevant factors which affect and contribute to that attitude, limited to that which is personally acceptable, as opposed to that which might merely be tolerated."

—*Human Nature* (March 1979)

When we hear statistics about the average this or that, it's important to remember that some averages make sense while others do not. The "average" Tennesseean is a bit over 50 percent female, has about 1.9 children (if married), is mulatto (with a touch of oriental), and owns a home part of the year, renting the other part. In other words, the idea of an average Tennesseean is not just useless, it's ridiculous.

---

[8]An extremely well-conceived poll, which takes care to obtain a truly representative sample, may be quite small and still be reliable. (How small depends on the nature of the sample.) The trouble with most small samples is that they're not selected with sufficient care, because it's too expensive to do so.

to win big favored Levin (36 percent were for his opponent, and 22 percent were undecided). The trouble was that exactly 64 blue-collar workers in one suburb (Warren, Michigan) made up the entire sample. No one today knows enough to categorize voters so that such a small sample is sufficiently representative to predict accurately, except by accident.

An interesting related fallacy concerns statistical trends in small populations. An article in the University of Maryland Baltimore County *Retriever* (September 19, 1977) argued that the "crime wave" on campus was decreasing. Aggravated assaults decreased by 50 percent from 1975 to 1976 and car thefts by 20 percent. This sounded convincing until we read that the 50 percent decrease was from four to two aggravated assaults, and the 20 percent decrease was from five to four cars stolen.

Scientists, of all people, aren't supposed to commit statistical fallacies. But they're human too. An interesting article on vocal responses during mating among different primate species in *Human Nature* (March 1979) turned out to be based on a sample of three human couples (each observed engaging in sex exactly once), a pair of gibbons, and one troop of chacma baboons.

5. Unrepresentative Sample

In addition to being large enough, a good sample must be *representative* of the population from which it is drawn. (Indeed, the more representative it is, the smaller it can be and still be significant.) When we reason from a sample that isn't sufficiently representative, we commit the fallacy of the **unrepresentative sample.** (This fallacy is sometimes called the fallacy of **biased statistics,** although that name also applies to cases where known statistics that are unfavorable to a theory are deliberately suppressed.)

The example above about primate mating responses illustrates the fallacy of the *unrepresentative sample* as well as the *small sample*. For one thing, only three of dozens of primate species were checked—chimpanzees, gorillas, tarsiers, and so forth may be quite different. For another, there is reason to believe that no sample of three human couples could possibly be representative of human beings, given the tremendous variety our species exhibits in its sex habits.

6. Questionable Classification

The fallacy of **questionable classification** or **questionable correlation** is committed when we classify something incorrectly, given the evidence we have or could have. The program of NOW (National Organization for Women) once included in its list of recommendations for securing equality of the sexes the proposal that facilities be established to rehabilitate and train divorced *women.* They further recommended that the ex-husbands in question, if financially able, should pay for the education of divorced *women.*

But stated this way, their recommendation exhibited *questionable classification* (to say nothing of female chauvinism). The group in need of rehabilitation clearly was not divorced women but divorced *persons,* or better yet divorced *homemakers.* For if a man happened to be the partner who took care of the home while his wife earned the bread, surely he would be entitled to help in the event of a divorce, just as a woman would in the same situation. Of all groups, NOW, with its concern for equality between the sexes, should not have classified the needy group as divorced *women*.

Note that in this example of *questionable classification* the correct and incorrect classes (divorced homemakers and divorced women) are close to being identical in membership: There are relatively few divorced males in the United States who fit the classification *divorced homemaker*. Close overlap of this kind is frequent when the fallacy of *questionable classification* occurs and is a major reason why this fallacy is so common.

But it also is a major reason why avoiding questionable classifications is so important. In some areas of the United States, the overwhelming majority of "deprived children" (whatever that means) are nonwhite (whatever *that* means). Deprived children, as a group, do less well in school than nondeprived children. Hence, nonwhites do less well than whites. But to classify backward students as nonwhites leads naturally to the conclusion that their being nonwhite is the *cause* of their backwardness. And we are all familiar with the way in which this conclusion has been used to defend racial prejudice and segregation in the United States.

7. Questionable Cause

We commit the fallacy of **questionable cause** when we label a given thing as the cause of something else on the basis of insufficient or inappropriate evidence, or in the face of reasonable contrary evidence.

The fallacy of *questionable classification* frequently entails *questionable cause,* because we classify partly in order to determine causes. As just stated, once we classify slow learners as mostly nonwhite, it's easy to take the next step and conclude that their being nonwhite is the *cause* of their being slow learners. But even in cases where the classification is correct, it doesn't follow that we've discovered a causal connection; the connection we've discovered may be *accidental*.

Dubious Fact

Citing high housing costs, unemployment, and divorce among newlyweds, recent reports in *The New York Times* and *U.S. News and World Report* have proclaimed that more and more young adults are finding it necessary to live with their parents. Indeed, as *The Times* correctly reported, the number of people over 25 still living with their parents has jumped by 25 percent since 1970 to 4.3 million. But the statistic hardly marks a change in the proportion of young people living at home. According to Steve Rawlings, a housing analyst at the Census Bureau, most of the increase simply parallels a similar increase in the number of people over 25. Since 1970, the proportion of young adults who haven't left the nest has only increased by 1 percent.

Richard Camer, in *Psychology Today* (January 1983)

For example, a 1977 story by College Press Service (catering to student newspapers) was headlined in some papers: "Pot Improves Grades." The article started out, "Men who get high at an early age get higher grades later in college, a University of Vermont study has found," and then went on to explain that researchers didn't know why this should be so. Supposing their research is correct, all it would prove is that there is a correlation between smoking dope and getting higher grades. (It appeared from the rest of the article, however, that even this conclusion was somewhat hasty.) It certainly wouldn't prove that early pot smoking *causes* students to get better grades later. There are all sorts of more likely explanations.

But some pot-smoking students apparently were influenced more by the article's headline than by the fine print later in the story. They concluded that smoking marijuana at an early age does indeed cause a person to get better grades later on—a completely foolish idea, whose acceptance without tons of favorable evidence required a good deal of self-deception on the part of these dopeheads.

On a level not much higher, a *Newsweek* article on the My Lai massacre[9] raised the question whether the GIs involved "should be punished for, in effect, *trying too hard*—by gunning down civilians in a village long sympathetic to the Viet Cong?" But is it reasonable to say that the *cause* of the massacre of tiny babies in mothers' arms at point blank range was overconscientiousness on the part of the soldiers in question?

Statistical Versions

Perhaps the most common variety of *questionable cause* is the statistical one—taking a mere statistical correlation as proof of a causal connection. Of course, every statistical connection has some significance and increases the probability, however slightly, that there is also a causal connection between the things correlated. But when we have background information strongly opposed to such a causal con-

---

Ninety percent of our breakfast cereal comes from Kellogg, General Mills, Quaker Oats or General Foods; it is they who have decided that breakfast cereal and sugar are almost inseparable.

Jeffrey Schrank, *Snap, Crackle, and Popular Taste* (New York: Delacorte, 1977)

Yes and no. The big four does sell most of our breakfast cereal, but what they decide to sell depends to a great extent on another factor, namely, what sells best to consumers, who are the ultimate deciders on this matter—witness the many brands of nonsugary cereals on the market, none of which are big sellers. That the big cereal manufacturers are the cause of so much sugar in cereals is thus, to say the least, a case of questionable cause. *(As Americans become more and more health conscious, cereals with no added sugar are selling better and better. So manufacturers are marketing more low sugar brands.)*

---

[9]*Newsweek*, August 31, 1970. (Recall the discussion in Chapter 3 of American reactions to news of this massacre.)

nection, or the statistical sample in question is too small or unrepresentative, then we make a mistake in jumping to the conclusion that we've found a causal connection.

Sometimes, alleged causal connections of this kind are so silly hardly anyone who is thinking takes them seriously (*silly* here means obviously contrary to well-supported background beliefs). The dope-smoking-causes-better-grades bit, above, is an example. But sometimes the dubious connection is quite appealing and indeed leads to serious disputes within the scientific community.

An interesting and timely example (more complicated than most) is the dispute concerning the relationship between the intake of high-cholesterol fats and heart disease. According to recent studies, there was a decline of 27 percent in heart disease in the United States between 1968 and 1977, a time when Americans were seriously reducing their intake of fatty foods and serum cholesterol (believed to be linked to heart disease by other studies). This shows that there is certainly a statistical correlation between fat intake and heart disease in the sample in question (the American population between 1968 and 1977).

Confronted with statistical jungles like the one above concerning fat intake and heart disease, many people throw up their hands and just accept the latest "expert" opinion. And sometimes that's all the nonexpert can do. But we can learn a few simple ways to evaluate statistical classifications alleged to indicate causal connections. The following excerpt from an article on statistical reasoning illustrates one such method:

"What do the other three cells look like?" This slogan should always be invoked to assess covariation [statistical connection] of events. . . . To determine the effectiveness of chiropractic treatment, for example, one needs numbers from four "cells." How many people were cured after being treated by a chiropractor? How many were not cured after such treatment? How many people got better without treatment? How many people didn't get better and went untreated?

—*Psychology Today* (June 1980)

Most of us are impressed when we see statistics on the first cell and fail to realize that we usually need to know about one or more of the others to determine whether we've found a causal connection as well as a mere statistical one. For example, finding out, say, that two-thirds of those treated by chiropractors get better proves nothing about the effectiveness of chiropractors; it may be that two-thirds of those with similar complaints who weren't so treated also got well, or even that three-quarters of them did (in which case we would have evidence that chiropractors harm patients more than they help them). We might, of course, find that chiropractors cure nine-tenths of their patients, which would indicate that they do help some patients. (Similarly, before going to a chiropractor with a certain kind of ailment, it would be useful to know not just the success rate of chiropractors in these cases but also that of MDs and osteopathic physicians. Of course, figures like these are often hard to come by.)

On the other hand, lots of evidence points in the other direction. First of all, during the period in question, Americans also reduced their cigarette smoking significantly (and there is independent evidence linking smoking and heart disease), did more strenuous exercise, and took greater care to reduce high blood pressure (also associated with heart disease). Further, in both Switzerland and Japan, fat intake increased during that period while heart disease decreased. And finally, a report, in spring 1980, of the Food and Nutrition Board of the National Research Council of the National Academy of Science (a name like that would snow anybody) said they had found no persuasive reason for healthy people to eat less fatty foods containing cholesterol. One serious factor leading them to this conclusion was summed up as follows:

> The distinct differences that emerge when one population is compared with another tend to vanish among people *within* a population. The Japanese, for example, will show marked differences from Americans in fat intake, serum cholesterol, and heart disease rates. But when Japanese are compared to other Japanese (in Japan), or Americans to other Americans, differences in fat intake or dietary habits show no consistent relationship to either serum cholesterol levels or heart disease incidence. In part, this is because the range of dietary variation within a country tends to be relatively narrow. Countries, on the other hand, may vary greatly from one another in eating habits and lifestyles.[10]

8. Questionable Analogy

We reason by analogy (as described in Chapter 1) for much the same reason that we classify and assign causes, namely to understand and control ourselves and our environment. In fact, analogical reasoning is a common way in which we reason to causes. But analogical reasoning can go wrong, and when it does, the result is the fallacy of **questionable analogy,** or **false analogy.**

A high-fashion hairdresser, Marc DeCoster, complained that some of his customers tried to save money by shampooing their own hair before getting a DeCoster set:

> Some are trying to wash their hair at home and then ask why I charge them for a shampoo. So I ask them, *do you bring your own salad to the restaurant?*[11]

If we have to teach the Bible account of the creation along with evolution theory, we ought to have to teach the stork theory of creation along with biological theory.

　　　　—Response to a demand that the Bible account of creation get equal time with evolution theory in biology classes

---

This is a typical case in which our opinion about whether the fallacy of questionable analogy *has been committed depends almost entirely on our world view. Those whose religious convictions lead them to a literal acceptance of the Bible will tend to find this analogy questionable; others will tend to find it apt.*

---

[10]*Consumer Reports* (May 1981).
[11]*New York Times* (December 12, 1971).

Spelled out, DeCoster's analogy is this: Washing your hair at home before getting it set at the beauty parlor is like bringing your own salad to a restaurant before eating their roast beef. It would be wrong to bring your salad to the restaurant, so it's wrong to shampoo your hair first at home. Therefore, claims DeCoster, it's not unfair to charge for the shampoo he doesn't give you, when he does give you a set.

But DeCoster's analogy is not apt. Shampooing your hair at home before going to the hairdresser is more like eating your own salad *at home* before going to the restaurant than it is like bringing your own salad to the restaurant to eat there before eating their roast beef. The two cases he considers thus differ in a relevant way. So the analogy fails.

Faulty Comparison

Analogies are a kind of *comparison*. For example, in the *questionable analogy* mentioned above, Marc DeCoster compared shampooing your hair before getting a DeCoster set to bringing your own salad to a restaurant (before, say, ordering a steak). So looked at another way, a *questionable analogy* can be thought of as a **faulty comparison** (sometimes called *comparing apples with oranges*).

A 3-in-1 Oil television commercial pictured a saw oiled with 3-in-1 Oil outperforming an unoiled saw—the intended conclusion being that you should use 3-in-1 Oil on your saws. But the comparison was faulty. It should have shown a saw oiled with 3-in-1 outperforming a saw oiled with some other standard brand of oil. Otherwise, all it proves is that oiled saws work better than unoiled ones (something every user of saws knows perfectly well), not that saws oiled with 3-in-1 Oil work better than those oiled with a competing product. So their faulty comparison gave no "reasons why" you should use their brand rather than another.

Faulty Statistical Comparisons

Although they are just variations on the general theme of *faulty comparisons,* mistaken statistical comparisons are so widespread that they deserve special mention. For example, because statistics are often cited showing that the percentage of births

Reprinted by permission of the Washington Star Syndicate, Inc.

It's not easy to determine what is the cause of what.

to adolescent mothers compared to more mature women has increased significantly since 1960, it is widely believed that American teenage women have become more promiscuous. Various sets of statistics showing an increase in births to teenagers from about $1/7$ or $1/8$ to $1/6$ or $1/5$ of all births are often cited by those pining for the "good old days" when, they say, morality meant more than it does now.

But even though the statistics cited are no doubt reasonably accurate, this sort of comparison is faulty, to say the least. Here is an excerpt from an article in *The Atlantic* explaining why it is faulty and showing that the correct comparison indicates a significant *decline* in births to American teenage women:

> Amid all the anxious words that have been published, few people have considered . . . the fact that the rate of births to teenagers is actually lower now than it was in 1976, and lower still than it was in the 1950s. The birthrate among adolescents peaked in 1957, when there were 96.3 births per thousand young women, married and single, between the ages of fifteen and nineteen. Since then, the rate for this age group has fallen sharply and steadily; by 1980 it had dropped to 53 births per thousand. But over the same period there was a still sharper decline, of almost 50 percent, in births to women between the ages of twenty and twenty-nine. Thus, when the number of childbearing teenagers is expressed relative to the population of childbearing women as a whole ("one out of six"), it appears inordinately high. In fact, however, it accounts only for a significant fraction of a shrunken total.[12]

Quality of Statistics Differs Widely

Comparisons using statistics may also be faulty because the quality or accuracy of statistics differs so widely from time to time and place to place. Crime statistics are a good example. In many parts of the country, apparent increases in the crime rate can be achieved simply by changing the recording habits of police officers—for instance, by recording minor crimes by blacks against blacks, Chicanos against Chicanos, or Indians against Indians. In New York City, police can increase the crime total simply by walking down almost any main street and arresting hot dog, pretzel, or ice cream vendors; if a decrease is desired, they simply become blinder than usual to these everyday violations of the law. The same is true of prostitution, gambling, and homosexual activity, areas of crime in which the police generally have a special interest (a euphemistic way of indicating that police often get their "taste" of this kind of action). Police statistics simply do not accurately reflect the actual incidence of lawbreaking. Hence, if we compare figures on lawbreaking for one place or time with those for another, the result is apt to be ludicrous.

Equally silly are many of the statistical comparisons which fail to take account of inflation or (occasionally) deflation. Perhaps the classic inflation example is the one inadvertently furnished by Marvin Kitman in his book, *Washington's Expense Account* (New York: Simon & Schuster, 1970). Mr. Kitman was trying to prove that George Washington had lived relatively high on the hog during the Revolutionary War, which is true,[13] and also that he padded expense accounts, which is possible but not proved by Kitman's figures.

---

[12]Jo Ann S. Putnam-Scholes, in *The Atlantic* (July 1983).
[13]But you won't find this truth in public school history textbooks, because it runs counter to an official myth.

Washington's accounts were kept primarily in Pennsylvania pounds. Mr. Kitman translated them into dollars via the Continental (Congress) dollar, equating twenty-six Continental dollars with one Pennsylvania pound. The trouble is that the value of the Continental dollar fluctuated widely, mostly downward, eventually becoming just about worthless (the origin of the phrase "not worth a Continental").

Kitman listed Washington's total expenses as $449,261.51 (note the aura of authority in that last 51¢!). An "expert" (who preferred to remain anonymous—perhaps because of the amount of guesswork involved) suggested $68,000 was a better figure.

In these examples, the comparisons themselves are faulty. Often, however, while the comparison is on the up and up, the *conclusion* is misleading. It is frequently stated that the American Indian has less to complain about than is usually supposed—that we can't have treated the Indian all that badly, since there are more Indians in the United States now than when Columbus "discovered" America. (This is disputed by some experts, who think the standard estimates on the Indian population in 1492 are too low. But in any event, the population then was probably not greatly different from what it is now.)

But even supposing the cited figures are correct, what do they prove? A more significant figure would be this (but still not terribly significant, given the immense amount of direct evidence that white men mistreated Indians): Take the number of whites and blacks in the United States in, say, 1783 (the end of the Revolutionary War), and compare that to the number of their descendants alive today (that is, don't count later immigrants and their progeny—a good trick because of interbreeding, but not impossible to estimate). Now compare this increase with that of the American Indian. What we would no doubt find is that the white and black populations

The
General Surgeon
has determined that breathing
is dangerous to your health.
This conclusion
was drawn from a survey
of 100 Canadian rats
that have died
within the past 5 years.
All were
habitual breathers.

Greeting card humor illustrating some fallacy or other, no doubt.

doubled many times over, while the number of Indians remained fairly stable.[14] If we had no direct evidence, then this comparison would be significant; but it would support the idea that the white man did, after all, mistreat the Indian.

9. Unknowable Statistics

Statistics always seem precise and *authoritative*. But statistical facts can be just as unknowable as any others. Here is a letter received several years ago which contains examples of **unknowable statistics** that would be hard to top:

> Dear Friend: In the past 5,000 years men have fought in 14,523 wars. One out of four persons living during this time have been war casualties. A nuclear war would add 1,245,000,000 men, women, and children to this tragic list.

It's ludicrous to present such precise figures as facts. No one knows (or could know) the exact number of wars fought up to the present time, to say nothing of the number of war casualties. As for the number of casualties in some future nuclear war, it would depend on what kind of war, and in any event is a matter on which even so-called experts can only speculate.

10. Questionable Statistics

But it is not just unknowable statistics that should be challenged. Some kinds of statistics are knowable in theory but not in fact. Business statistics, a case in point, often are *questionable*. Or at least there are those who think so.

Take the statistics published by the federal government on business conditions in the United States. Oskar Morgenstern is one expert who argues that these statistics are very questionable indeed.[15]

One of the major problems with government statistics is that their *margin of error* (not usually reported) is often greater than the "significant" differences they report. We read in the newspapers that the economy grew in a given month at a rate amount-

---

The average American child by age eighteen has watched 22,000 hours of television. This same average viewer has watched thousands of hours of inane situation comedy, fantasy, and soap opera and an average of 4,286 separate acts of violence.

> D. Stanley Eitzen in *Social Structure and Social Problems in America* (Boston: Allyn & Bacon, 1975)

Statistics—knowable, or unknowable? And if knowable roughly, what about that precise figure of 4,286?

---

[14]Actually, the Indian population steadily declined until the Indians were completely conquered at the end of the nineteenth century. But in the past 75 years or so, their number has increased.

[15]Oskar Morgenstern, *"Qui Numerare Incipit Errare Incipit"* (roughly, "He who begins to count begins to err"). In *Fortune* (October 1963).

ing to 5 percent a year, perhaps an increase of 1 percent over the previous year. Everyone is pleased at this increase in the growth rate of the economy. But the margin of error on government growth rate statistics very likely is much greater than

---

It has recently been said that the Warsaw Pact nations (the Soviet Union and its Eastern European satellites) have surpassed their NATO rivals (the United States and its Western European allies) in military strength in Europe. (This claim is sometimes used to prove that the Warsaw Pact countries are planning an invasion of Western Europe.) President Reagan lent support to this hypothesis in his 1981 State of the Union address:

> I believe my duty as President requires that I recommend increases in defense spending over the coming years. Since 1970, the Soviet Union has invested $300 billion more in its military forces than we have.

His administration then attempted to counter this trend by increasing United States military spending.

But is there such a trend to counter? It all depends on how you throw figures around. As pointed out in an article in The Atlantic, *much of this speculation is based on CIA estimates that the U.S.S.R. is currently outspending the U.S. in military matters by about 50 percent—$300–400 billion more in the past decade.* [16] *However, reviewed more closely, these figures appear to be misleading. For one thing, our NATO allies (West Germany, France, Britain, etc.) are much richer than the Soviets' East European puppets (East Germany, Rumania, Poland, etc.) and spend much more on military forces. Comparing the total NATO military expenditures (instead of just the U.S. effort) with total Warsaw Pact expenditures (not just Soviet military spending), even the CIA estimates that NATO is the bigger military spender (by about $250 billion in the last ten years).*

Further, the CIA estimates that about 12–20 percent of the Soviet military effort is directed against China, and thus is not easily available for combat in Europe.

In addition, CIA estimates of Soviet versus American expenditures are calculated both in rubles and in dollars, but the figures generally quoted are those calculated in dollars. Yet for several reasons the dollar calculations are much higher than those in rubles; for one thing, Soviet spending for complicated military equipment is calculated on the basis of higher American costs. (See the Atlantic *article for more on this point.) Therefore, both figures should be used—one to give the highest estimate, one the lowest. As the CIA itself has said, "Dollar cost calculations tend to overstate Soviet defense activities relative to those of the United States."*

Adjusting the often quoted figures in the three ways just described, it appears that NATO outspent the Warsaw Pact in the ten years in question by about $550 billion. (Of course, this doesn't prove we've spent enough, or too much, since dollar figures say nothing about what is bought for all that money.)

---

[16] Franklyn D. Holzman, "Are We Falling Behind the Soviets?" *The Atlantic* (July 1983). Most of the facts and figures quoted here can be found in this article.

1 percent, as Morgenstern indicated, citing one of the government's own revisions:

> If the rate for the change [in growth] from 1947 to 1948 was determined in
> February, 1949, when the first figures became available, it was 10.8 percent. In
> July, 1950, using officially corrected figures, it became 12.5 percent; in July,
> 1956, it fell to 11.8 percent—a full percentage point. All this for the growth rate
> from 1947 to 1948!

Add to this the fact that even the officially corrected figures cannot take account of
the deliberately misleading or false figures businessmen sometimes provide the
government (to cover their tracks or to mislead rival companies), and it becomes
clear that the margin of error on figures for the gross national product has to be
fairly large.

In addition, there is the problem arising from the need to use a base year (because
of price fluctuations):

> If a year with a high (or low) gross national product is chosen as base year,
> this will depress (or raise) the growth rate of subsequent years. . . . An un-
> scrupulous or politically oriented [!] writer will choose that base year which
> produces the sequence of (alleged) growth rates best suited to his aims and
> programs. . . . These are, of course, standard tricks, used, undoubtedly, ever
> since index numbers were invented.

In other words, if you want to show that a given year had a high rate of growth,
choose a low base year, and vice versa for a low growth rate. Meanwhile, the true
rate of growth remains unknown, except for broad, long-term trends.

Statistics on Illegal Commerce

Statistics on employment and the gross national product are subject to another (little
noticed) problem, namely, that a good deal of employment and industry in the United

---

Dissecting the notion that continuous growth in the gross national product is
per se desirable, he emphasizes that the GNP is the sum of very different
quantities. Those quantities include costs associated with economic "throughput," such as mining of ores and the cleaning up of polluted rivers; additions to
capital stock, such as the production of automobiles; and services rendered by
the capital stock, such as auto rental fees. ("Throughput," a word difficult to
avoid in such discussions, refers to the flow of raw materials processed by the
economic system.) "It makes no sense," Daly writes, "to add together costs,
benefits, and changes in capital stock. It is as if a firm were to add up its
receipts, its expenditures, and its change in net worth. What sense could any
accountant make of such a sum?" And yet, in spite of numerous critiques of the
value of the GNP as a measure, both from economists and others, one continually hears economists talking solemnly about how important it is for the
GNP to grow. If its name were changed to the equally accurate gross national
cost . . . .

From a book review in *Human Nature* (August 1978) of Herman E. Daly's *Steady-State Economics*
(San Francisco: W. H. Freeman, 1978).

Within the next two years, Russian scientists will receive powerful radio signals from space—proof that an alien civilization is attempting to communicate with us.

We will accidentally discover the ruins of Atlantis deep in the sea between Cyprus and Turkey. Finely preserved tablets containing complicated symbols will reveal that the inhabitants of Atlantis were highly intelligent in mathematics and language. Several types of highly sophisticated construction tools will be found.

Prominent researchers and scientists will announce that they have proof that the Loch Ness Monster is a living creature. Photographs and recordings will be studied and they'll solve this ancient mystery.

UFOs will buzz Camp David while President Reagan is in weekend retreat there—forcing him to announce officially that they exist.

Jimmy Carter will announce he's running again for President.

A savage earthquake will hit San Francisco this summer, causing death and destruction.

Murdered Beatle John Lennon's son Julian will form a band called the New Beatles—featuring musicians who bear eerie resemblances to former Beatles Paul McCartney, George Harrison and Ringo Star.

The first female manager of a major-league baseball team will be named at the beginning of the 1983 season.

Two jumbo jetliners will collide at a major airport in West Germany, resulting in a huge loss of life.

The predictions on the left (above) were made by the famous metal-bending watch-starter Uri Geller ("FAMED PSYCHIC") in the National Enquirer *(November 9, 1976). Needless to say, none of them came true. The predictions on the right appeared in the* National Enquirer *on January 4, 1983 (for the year 1983). They were made by New York psychic Shawn Robbins, "who predicted with stunning accuracy one of history's worst airline disasters" (if you believe that, go back to square one), and were among 64 predictions by nine alleged psychics and astrologers in that issue. So far none of them have come true.*

The second edition of this text contained 13 predictions by perhaps the most famous of all seers, Jeane Dixon. None of them came true (although two were so general and ambiguous that some might claim they did). The third edition contained another Jeane Dixon prediction and seven by psychic Jack Gillen, alleged to have "correctly predicted the 1974 crash of the Turkish airliner near Paris." None of them came true.

You'd think that massive failure of this kind would tarnish the reputations of these "famous seers", but it doesn't. (Uri Geller has been exposed as an out-and-out fraud many times, yet he has millions of followers.) Those who want to believe, or need to believe, believe. Those who put their money on experience and use statistical induction to evaluate alleged psychics, don't believe. Since the National Enquirer *and similar publications are read by over 20 million people every week, it's clear that an awful lot of people choose to ignore the evidence and believe. Believe me. But if you want the opinion of this writer, "It don't even make good nonsense."*

States is illegal (racketeering, gambling, drugs, prostitution, migrant farm labor), so that figures on these activities must be either guesswork or based on tangential evidence (for instance, legal sales of gambling and marijuana equipment or records of convictions for prostitution). Further, the amount of otherwise legal commerce that is done "off the books," so that no taxes need be paid, has been increasing rapidly in recent years in the United States. (In some other countries this has been the custom for a long time.) No one can be sure of the true value of such transactions, in particular since money usually doesn't change hands (one sort of goods being bartered for another). And even rough estimates are bound to be mainly educated guesses (for instance, by insiders in the barter trade).

All of this does not mean that government statistics on commerce and the gross national product should be tossed in the wastebasket. But it does mean that precise official figures should be taken as merely rough approximations of true business activity, valuable primarily in showing long-term trends.

Polls

A well-conceived and well-executed poll is a useful way to find out all sorts of things, from the voter strength of a political candidate to Fido's tastes in canned dog food. Unfortunately, all polls are not created equal.

For one thing, many polls ask biased or loaded questions. That is, they ask their questions in such a way as to get more or less the answers they want to hear. Evangelist Billy James Hargis conducted a poll of 200,000 "subscribers to various publications . . . a sampling of 200,000 average Americans," and reported the results in a letter to the *Houston Post* (April 1979). Here are a few of the questions and the responses:

3. Are you in favor of the diplomatic death of Taiwan as the price of recognizing Red China? 111 said yes; 16,889 said no.

4. Do you favor retaining loud-mouthed, pro-terrorist, racial agitator Andrew Young as a U.S. ambassador to the United Nations? 564 said yes; 16,436 said no.

5. Are you willing to pull U.S. troops out of Korea and risk surrendering the country to the Communists after our boys bled and died on the Korean battlefield? 503 said yes; 16,497 said no.

9. Are you ready to surrender our way of life in order to "accommodate" left-wing forces here in America? 52 said yes; 16,780 said no.

While the extremely lopsided results are almost certainly due in part to an unrepresentative sample, in large part they result from the loaded nature of the questions. It takes some nerve to favor retaining a "loud-mouthed, pro-terrorist, racial agitator" or to be "ready to surrender our way of life in order to accommodate left-wing forces here in America."

While the Hargis poll contained grossly loaded questions, poll questions can be biased in more subtle, even unintentional ways. During the Watergate scandal, a Gallup poll question asked:

Do you think President Nixon should be impeached and compelled to leave the presidency, or not?

Thirty percent said yes. But a Pat Caddell private poll asked the question this way:

> Do you think the President should be tried, and removed from office if
> found guilty?

Fifty-seven percent answered yes to that one. How a question is worded is crucial to what sorts of answers will be obtained.

Another problem with polls is that respondents don't want to sound stupid (or prejudiced). A 1981 Cambridge Reports poll conducted for Union Carbide asked:

> Some experts say that there are 50,000 toxic and poisonous chemical waste
> sites around the country that pose serious health and safety threats to the pub-
> lic. Other experts say that . . . only a few of these sites pose a risk to the public.
> . . . In general, which view is closer to your own?

Doonesbury. Copyright, 1980, G. B. Trudeau.
Used by permission of Universal Press Syndicate. All rights reserved.

Common sense tells us that most Americans know next to nothing about the number of such sites, yet 52 percent answered that there were 50,000, 25 percent that there were hardly any, and only 23 percent admitted that they didn't know.[17]

An article in *Parade Magazine,* "Keeping Up with Youth" (March 11, 1979), contained the following gem:

> Census takers point out that the percentage of those [in census surveys] who say they voted is considerably higher than the official count.

People lie when they answer poll questions for all sorts of reasons—in addition to not wanting to look stupid—as this bit from *Scientific American* (August 1978) illustrates:

> The University of Arizona . . . project is an effort to get quantitatively reliable data on household food input and output. Some of the earlier results are striking. Poor people interviewed in Tucson say they never buy beer, but their garbage gives them away. The point is that beer cannot be lawfully acquired with food stamps.

Polls often are misleading because they tap an *unrepresentative* or *biased sample* of the population. Perhaps the most famous case of this is the 1936 *Literary Digest* poll, based on names lifted from telephone directories and auto registration lists. This poll predicted that Alf Landon would defeat Franklin Roosevelt, but the actual result, of course, was a tremendous landslide for Roosevelt. The magazine failed to realize that relatively few people with low or average incomes owned cars or had telephones in those depression days, so that their poll was far from representative of the voting population as a whole.

In a test of beer drinkers:

Drinking from a six-pack without labels, beer lovers decided the quality of the beer was not very good and showed no particular preference for one bottle over another—even though their favorite brand was included as one of the unlabeled bottles. Later, given the same six-packs, this time with the proper brand labels, the taste rating improved immeasurably and drinkers showed a definite preference for their own brand.

Jeffrey Schrank, Snap, Crackle, and Popular Taste (New York: Delacorte, 1977)

In assessing poll results, we have to bear in mind the various peculiarities of human nature which lead respondents to stray from the truth. Since most popular brands of beer of a given type (for example, regular, as compared to low-calorie) taste pretty much the same, factors such as snob appeal, pandered to by advertising ("Tonight, let it be Lowenbrau"—trading on the snob appeal of the name of a famous old, and excellent, German beer applied to an ordinary American beer), determine most beer preferences. But few beer drinkers are aware of being snobs—that's the sort of thing we tend to deceive ourselves about.

---

[17]For more on this, see "The Art of Polling," in *The New Republic* (June 20, 1981).

The Handbook of Political Fallacies, *by the English political philosopher and reformer Jeremy Bentham (1748–1832) is one of the classic works on political rhetoric and fallacies. Here are excerpts from his account of the first two of four "causes of the utterance of [political] fallacies" (taken from Chapters 2 and 3 of Part Five):*

First Cause . . . : Self-Conscious Sinister Interest

. . . [I]t is apparent that the mind of every public man is subject at all times to the operation of two distinct interests: a public and a private one. . . .

In the greater number of instances, these two interests . . . are not only distinct but opposite, and that to such a degree that if either is exclusively pursued, the other must be sacrificed to it. Take for example pecuniary interest: it is to the personal interest of every public man who has at his disposal public money extracted from the whole community by taxes, that as large a share as possible . . . should remain available for his own use. At the same time it is to the interest of the public . . . that as small a share as possible . . . should remain in his hands for his personal or any other private use. . . .

Hence it is that any class of men who have an interest in the rise or continuance of any system of abuse no matter how flagrant will, with few or no exceptions, support such a system of abuse with any means they deem necessary, even at the cost of probity and sincerity. . . .

But it is one of the characteristics of abuse, that it can only be defended by fallacy. It is, therefore, to the interest of all the confederates of abuse to give the most extensive currency to fallacies. . . . It is of the utmost importance to such persons to keep the human mind in such a state of imbecility that shall render it incapable of distinguishing truth from error. . . .

Second Cause: Interest-Begotten Prejudice

If every act of the will and hence of every act of the hand is produced by interest, that is by a motive of one sort or another, the same must be true, directly or indirectly, of every act of the intellectual faculty, although the influence of interest upon the latter is neither as direct or as perceptible as that upon the will.

But how, it may be asked, is it possible that the motive by which a man is actuated can be secret to himself? Nothing, actually, is easier; nothing is more frequent. Indeed the rare case is, not that of a man's not knowing, but that of his knowing it. . . .

When two persons have lived together in a state of intimacy, it happens not infrequently that either or each of them may possess a more correct and complete view of the motives by which the mind of the other is governed, than of those which control his own behavior. Many a woman has had in this way a more correct and complete acquaintance with the internal causes by which the conduct of her husband has been determined, than he has had himself. The reason for this is easily pointed out. By interest, a man is continually prompted to make himself as correctly and completely acquainted as possible with the springs of action which determine the conduct of those upon whom he is more or less dependent for the comfort of his life. But by interest he is at the same time diverted from any close examination into the springs by which his own conduct is determined. From such knowledge he would be more likely to find mortification than satisfaction.

When he looks at other men, he finds mentioned as a matter of praise the prevalence of . . . social motives. . . . It is by the supposed prevalence of these amiable motives that he finds reputation raised, and that respect and goodwill enhanced to which every man is obliged to look for so large a proportion of the comforts of his life. . . .

But the more closely he looks into the mechanism of his own mind, the less able he is to refer any of the mass of effects produced there to any of these amiable and delightful causes. He finds nothing, therefore, to attract him towards this self-study; he finds much to repel him from it. . . .

Perhaps he is a man in whom a large proportion of the self-regarding motives may be mixed with a slight tincture of the social motives operating upon the private scale. In that case, what will he do? In investigating the source of a given action, he will in the first instance set down the whole of it to the account of the amiable and conciliatory motives, in a word, the social ones. This, in any study of his own mental physiology, will always be his first step; and it will commonly be his last also. Why should he look any further? Why take in hand the painful probe? Why undeceive himself, and substitute the whole truth, which would mortify him, for a half-truth which flatters him?

Of course, the art of polling has come a long way since 1936, or even 1948, when polls predicted Thomas E. Dewey would easily defeat Harry Truman. (The *Chicago Tribune* was so sure Dewey would win that it misinterpreted early returns and printed one of the most famous headlines in newspaper history—"Dewey Defeats Truman"—which an exultant Truman held up to the crowd at his victory celebration.) Nevertheless, it still is difficult to get a representative sample of the U.S. voting population by polling only 1,500 or so people, which is the standard practice today. In theory, a very carefully selected sample of roughly this size should be almost as reliable as one of 15,000 people (polls this large would be much too expensive and are never conducted). But in practice, for all sorts of reasons, it doesn't always work that way. The result is that political polls occasionally are wrong by significant amounts.

In the 1980 presidential election, for instance, a *New York Times* and CBS News survey conducted between October 30 and November 1 showed Carter and Reagan only one percentage point apart. This was "too close to call," since the alleged margin of error of the poll was two percent. Yet on November 4, Reagan won in a landslide.[18]

---

[18]See the *Washington Star* or almost any major newspaper on November 1, 1980, for more on this.

11. False Charge of Fallacy

It's often easy, perhaps too easy, to charge others with fallacy. This is particularly true when they change their minds and embrace positions they previously denied. The temptation in these cases is to charge them with the fallacy of *inconsistency*.

But someone who makes a certain statement at one time and a contradictory statement later is not automatically guilty of the fallacy of *inconsistency*. That person may have rational grounds for a change of mind.

Take the person who argues, "I used to believe that women are not as creative as men, because most intellectually productive people have been men; but I've changed my mind, because I believe now (as I didn't then) that *environment* (culture, surroundings), and not native ability, has been responsible for the preponderance of intellectual men." Surely, that person cannot be accused of *inconsistency,* since he (or she!) has explained the change of mind, as say, Lyndon Johnson did not explain his switch on the question of civil rights.

Consider the charge that the philosopher Bertrand Russell was guilty of *inconsistency.* Soon after World War II, he advocated attacking the Soviet Union if the Russians failed to conform to certain standards, and yet in the 1950s he supported the "better Red than dead" position. Russell *would* have been guilty of *inconsistency* if he had not had, and stated, what he took to be good reasons for changing his mind about how to deal with the Russians. He felt, and stated, that Russian acquisition of the atomic bomb made all the difference in the world. Before they had the bomb, he believed it to be rational to deal with them in ways that became irrational after they had acquired such great power. Hence, Russell was not guilty of the fallacy of *inconsistency.*

Women in West Germany are limiting their families to an average of only 1.4 children. If that rate continues, the current population of West Germany will decline to about 49 million by the end of this century, and to 22 million 100 years from today. [The article implied that it will continue if West Germany doesn't do something about it.]

—Lloyd Shearer, in "Intelligence Report," *Parade Magazine* (March 1979)

A common trick of some "experts" is to make predictions simply by continuing current trends into the future. Population trends are a good example. But why assume they will continue? Who knows? We do know that some factors are very likely to change, the death rate being an important example. (If the death rate in West Germany continues to decline from now until the year 2000, and it's more likely that it will than that it won't, West Germany's population will have increased, assuming no nuclear war or other unknown factor arises.) Imagine trying to guess the population of the United States in 1980 simply on the basis of the 1880 birth and death rates. The result wouldn't be anywhere near the true figure. (This is one of those cases where background knowledge should lead us to suspect the results of low-level induction.)

Exercise item from the second edition of a textbook on logic and contemporary rhetoric:

Newspaper Story: Thor Heyerdahl has done it again, crossing the Atlantic in a papyrus raft designed according to ancient Egyptian tomb carvings. Landing in the Western Hemisphere on the island of Barbados, he was greeted by the Barbados prime minister, Errol Barrow, who declared, "This has established Barbados was the first landing place for man in the Western World."

The correct answer was supposed to be hasty conclusion, *but a student from Barbabos pointed out that the prime minister was known for his sense of humor. Another* false charge of fallacy.

On the contrary, it is his critics who are guilty of a fallacy, which we might as well call the **false charge of fallacy.** (Of course, falsely charging a person with *any* fallacy, not just *inconsistency,* makes one guilty of a *false charge of fallacy.*)

Quibbling

In deciding whether someone has committed a fallacy, we don't want to *quibble.* For instance, we don't want to take advantage of the fact that life is short and in everyday life we don't spell out every detail. Consider the AMA ad: "100,000 doctors have quit smoking. Maybe they know something you don't." Some students have said this ad is fallacious because it suppressed evidence as to what kind of doctors had quit ("Maybe it was horse doctors," "They don't say if they were doctors of medicine"). These students were quibbling, like the student who objected to Shakespeare's wonderful line, "He jests at scars that has never felt a wound" (*Romeo and Juliet*), on grounds that *he* had felt a wound (a mere scratch) and still jested at scars.

This concludes our account of fallacies. We've discussed only a few of the more common ones from among the hundreds mentioned in the literature (many others have never been catalogued). The point is to become sufficiently critical in your reading and reasoning so that you can spot fallacies more easily. But we'll soon see that spotting fallacies is only part of a larger enterprise, namely the analysis of more extended passages containing related arguments that are intended to form a coherent whole. *Extended arguments* of this kind are discussed in Chapter 6. But before getting to that material, we need to say a bit about language, since arguments after all are always couched in words. So on to the next chapter, on language, its uses and abuses.

Summary of Chapter Four

1. *Suppressed evidence:* The omission from an argument of known relevant evidence (or the failure to look for evidence likely to be available).
   Example: The failure of Shell Platformate commercials to indicate that most other standard brands of gasoline contain the ingredient Platformate.

2. *Slippery slope:* Failure to see that the first step in a possible series of steps does not inevitably lead to the rest.
   Example: Claims—unargued for—that Medicare would inevitably lead to complete socialism.
   a. *Domino theory:* The conclusion that if *A* falls, so will *B*, then *C*, and so on.
      Example: The belief that if South Vietnam went Communist, so would Laos, Cambodia, Thailand, the rest of the Far East, and so on.

3. *Hasty conclusion:* The use of relevant but insufficient evidence to reach a conclusion.
   Example: Concluding that today's students aren't as bright as in days of old on the evidence that SAT scores have declined.

4. *Small sample:* Drawing conclusions about a population on the basis of a sample that's too small to be a reliable measure of that population.
   Example: An Evans and Novak prediction based on a poll of 64 voters in one suburb.

5. *Unrepresentative sample:* Reasoning from a sample that isn't representative (typical) of the population from which it was drawn.
   Example: The article on primate mating habits based on a sample of three human couples, a pair of Gibbons, and a troop of baboons.

6. *Questionable classification:* Placing items in the same class although they aren't relevantly similar.
   Example: NOW's classification of divorcees in need of rehabilitation as divorced *women* instead of divorced *homemakers*.

7. *Questionable cause:* Labeling something as the cause of something else on the basis of insufficient evidence, or contrary to available evidence.
   Example: A magazine's suggestion that Vietnamese civilians were massacred by American soldiers because the soldiers were "trying too hard."

8. *Questionable analogy:* Use of analogy where the cases seem relevantly different.
   Example: DeCoster's analogy between customers washing their own hair at home before going to the beauty parlor and diners bringing their own salad to the restaurant to eat before ordering roast beef (questionable because it would be more like eating salad at home before coming to the restaurant just for the roast beef).
   a. *Faulty comparison:* A kind of questionable analogy.
      Example: Comparing crime statistics gathered in one way at one time and place with those gathered differently in another.

9. *Unknowable statistics:* Presenting unknowable statistics as though they are established facts.
   Example: Stating that in the past 5,000 years men have fought in 14,523 wars.

10. *Questionable statistics:* Using or accepting statistics that are questionable without further proof or support.
    Example: Statistics on illegal or off-the-book transactions.
    a. *Polls:* Statistics generated by polls should be questioned when their sample: (1) is too small, or (2) is unrepresentative, or (3) asks loaded questions, or (4) asks questions likely to embarrass respondents, or (5) asks questions respondents are not likely to know how to answer.
       Example: The Billy James Hargis poll that asked loaded questions about American attitudes.

11. *False charge of fallacy:* Fallaciously charging someone with a fallacy.
    Example: The charge that Bertrand Russell was *inconsistent* in advocating the use of force against the Russians at one time, while adopting a "better Red than dead" position at another; Russell explained this switch several times as being due to changing circumstances. (Quibbling often leads to commission of this fallacy.)

Exercise 4-1

Determine which fallacies (if any) are committed by the following, and carefully explain why you think so. (Some of these contain fallacies discussed in previous chapters.)

1. *Pentagon logic, from* The Progressive *magazine:* Defense Secretary Harold Brown, commenting on the failure of two submarine test firings of the Tomahawk cruise missile: "Failure in the past increases the probability of success in the future."

2. *John F. Keenan, New York Off-Track Betting Corporation chairman, responding to a question about whether licensed gambling casinos would cut into OTB revenue, in the* Washington Monthly *(August 1979):* Big business thrives on competition. When night baseball came, they didn't stop sex.

*3. Hartford Courant, *"Sunday Parade" (August 20, 1972):* [There was] a judge in Salisbury, Rhodesia, who had never driven a car. Someone in his court wanted to know how [he] could rule on motor accidents without first-hand knowledge of driving. "It's really no handicap," the magistrate explained. "I also try rape cases."

4. *Letter in the* Huntsville *(Texas)* Item *(September 27, 1974):* The Chamber [of Commerce] proposes taxing occupancy of the hotels to build occupancy [by advertising for tourists]. If the city adopts this policy, then it should tax bank deposits and use the proceeds to advertise for more bank depositors; it should tax professors' salaries and use the proceeds to try to attract more students; it should tax retail sales and use the proceeds to advertise for more shoppers.

5. *Howard:* You mean you take this Horoscope business seriously?
   Aunt: Yes, of course. Don't you see how today's horoscope fit you to a T?

Howard: Yes, but . . .
Aunt: No buts. There must be something to it.

6. In 1978, the National Highway Traffic Safety Administration placed a value on human life, for purposes of assessing the costs to society of an accidental death, of $287,175.

*7. Smoking marijuana definitely leads to heroin use. A report by the U.S. Commissioner of Narcotics on a study of 2,213 hardcore narcotic addicts in the Lexington, Kentucky, Federal Hospital shows that 70.4 percent smoked marijuana *before* taking heroin.

8. U.S. Customs officials justify their method of solving the heroin problem (catching drug smugglers) by citing the fact that heroin seizures are up sharply, from 210 pounds seized in 1969 to 346.8 pounds in 1970, to a staggering 1,308.85 pounds in 1971.

*9. *Column by James J. Kilpatrick (August 1970), in which he argued for more action on the drug problem:* J. Edgar Hoover released his 1969 Crime Report a week ago. Last year, for the first time, there were more arrests in the U.S. for violations of drug laws than for violations of liquor laws—223,000 drug offenses against 213,000 liquor offenses.

10. *Thomas O. Enders, Assistant Secretary of State for Inter-American Affairs under the Reagan administration (late 1981):* There is no question that the decisive battle for Central America is under way in El Salvador. . . . If after Nicaragua El Salvador is captured by a violent minority, who in Central America would not live in fear? How long would it be before major strategic United States interests—the Panama Canal, sea lanes, oil supplies— were at risk?

11. *Barstool economist:* Now is the time for some sure profit investing in stocks, because the stock market is at its lowest point in five years and so is bound to shoot up. (It then in fact did go up about 20 percent in less than a year.)

12. *Magazine article: Amen, Deacon.* It's time Christian people stand up for our rights. If we don't stand up for creation against evolution, we soon won't have any opportunity to worship. It'll be like Russia.

13. Texas Observer *(March 16, 1973), quoting State Senator Walter Mengden:* The base cause of inflation is an unbalanced federal budget. . . . "If the rate of inflation becomes too excessive, the result of this inflation is that the economy will stop . . . because the dollar will be losing value so fast people will stop exchanging goods of real value for dollars. . . . Now this isn't conjecture; this has happened before, many times. . . . If you don't control inflation, . . . you will destroy the economy, and in a few weeks there will be no food to buy, little water, no electricity and services, and there will be such panic and disaster that some hard-pants general is going to move in and say, 'I am now running the show,' and the Army or somebody like him will take over, and that's the end of the Constitutional Republic. And that's what's going to happen if we don't control inflation."

Raeside, Canada

14. What do you think of the analogy illustrated by this cartoon?

15. National Review *(June 11, 1982):* They were rudely rebuffed by the ruling feminist clique. The [Women's] Center's [of Princeton] director, Lila Karp, asked hostile questions about the supplicants' religion, and her cohorts screeched that for women to be against abortion was like Jews favoring Nazism. [The *National Review,* obviously, didn't agree with this sentiment.]

16. *From Dr. Joyce Brothers's column, in the* Houston Post *(October 3, 1976):* Question: You should be more fearful of rape at home because rapes occur more frequently in private homes than in back alleys.
Answer: TRUE. Studies indicate that more rapes are committed in the victim's home than in any other place. Almost half took place in either the victim's home or the assailant's; one fourth occurred in open spaces; one fifth in automobiles; one twelfth in other indoor locations.

17. *From article claiming to prove a causal link between junk food diets and antisocial behavior, in* Moneysworth *(November 1977):* If you project a curve showing the increase in behavioral disturbances and learning disabilities over the past 25 years, you will find that it parallels the increase in the dollar value of food additives over that time. . . .

18. *Item from* The Progressive *magazine:* New York State Senator James H. Donovan cited the Crucifixion as a rationale for capital punishment:

"Where would Christianity be," he asked, "if Jesus got eight to fifteen years, with time off for good behavior?"

19. *Allan Grant, president of the American Farm Bureau Federation, in the* Houston Post *(October 5, 1976), lamenting the forced resignation of Secretary of Agriculture Earl Butz for telling offensive ethnic jokes:* It's unfortunate and it shouldn't have been said, but most people are guilty of telling ethnic jokes at one time or another.

*20. *Start of letter from Anita Bryant Ministries arguing for harsh laws against homosexuals:* "When the homosexuals burn the Holy Bible in public . . . how can I stand by silently?" Dear Friend: I don't hate the homosexuals. But as a mother, I must protect my children from their evil influence. . . .

21. The universe, like a watch, must have a maker.

*22. *Nutrition expert Frederick Stare answering the charge that flaked dry cereals—Wheaties, Corn Flakes, and the like—are not sufficiently nutritious, in the* New York Daily News *(August 5, 1970):* Stare said cereals with milk "provide approximately the same amount of protein and calories as a bacon-and-eggs breakfast. And they also provide substantially more calcium, riboflavin, niacin, thiamin, and iron and substantially less saturated fat. . . . Popeye's spinach doesn't begin to compare with the over-all nutritional worth of breakfast cereal—any cereal. . . ."

23. *UPI story in the* Hartford Courant *(July 11, 1972):* A study completed by four University of Rhode Island researchers shows vitamin E may be a key to the secret of youth. . . . The research team said the vitamin . . . may be at work normally in humans to prevent aging. Working with a group of experimental rats, the scientists learned animals deprived of vitamin E seem to age faster and even become senile. Dr. Harbrans Lal of URI said that although the aging process is still a mysterious event, an "interesting relationship" had been found in the rats between the lack of vitamin E and old age.

24. *From the* American Sociological Review *(October 1950):* One of woman's most natural attributes is the care of children. Since the ill and infirm resemble children in being physically weak and helpless as well as psychologically dependent and narcissistically repressed, women are also especially qualified to care for the sick.

25. *From a* New Republic *(September 5, 1983) review of the James Michener book* Iberia: Michener leads off his chapter on bullfights with an argument between your quintessential American and Spaniard about brutal sports— which the Spaniard wins by pointing out that more young men get killed and maimed every year playing American football than in the bullring.

26. Parade Magazine *(September 25, 1983):* For a while, doctors argued over whether bypass surgery prolonged patients' lives. . . . Dr. [Michael] DeBakey recently completed a study of 3500 patients. "About 80 to 85 percent survived 10 years after their surgery," he told me, "and half of the

people under 65 years of age are working full time." [The implication is that bypass heart surgery does prolong life.]

27. *Richard Nixon, May 1974:* An historical assessment would be that [Watergate] was probably the broadest but the thinnest scandal in American history. . . . When they say this is like Teapot Dome, that is comparing apples with oranges. . . .

Exercise 4-2

*1. *W. Allen Wallis and Harry V. Roberts, in* Statistics: A New Approach: After the New Hampshire preferential primary in 1952, it was reported that Senator Taft, Ohio, had received a slightly higher percentage of the total vote in a group of 17 cities in which he had not campaigned personally than in a group of 15 cities in which he had. One newspaper jibed that "Senator Taft should have stayed at home."

2. *Ford campaign worker (fall 1976):* When you hear all those scare statistics about our economy and unemployment, just remember this: More Americans now have jobs than at any time in our history prior to Mr. Ford taking office.

*3. *From campaign literature of antiabortion candidate Ellen McCormack, in 1976 presidential race:* When pollster Louis Harris dismissed Mrs. McCormack's overall showing of better than 3 percent as insignificant, the candidate fired back: "The fact that 3 percent is insignificant will certainly be news to Ronald Reagan, who lost New Hampshire to Gerald Ford by less than 3 percent—or to George Wallace, who lost Florida to Jimmy Carter by that figure—or to Morris Udall, who lost Wisconsin by 1 percent—or to dozens of Congressional candidates in 1974 who lost by 3 percent or less. The presidential elections of 1960 and 1968 were also decided by less than 3 percent."

4. *Article in the* Boston Globe *(June 26, 1974), on youth, drugs, and alcohol:* "We're seeing a tremendous switch back to alcohol." Dr. Chafetz (of National Institute on Alcohol Abuse) cited a recent national survey of 15,000 boys and girls, aged 11 to 18, in which 92 percent reported alcohol use but only 38 percent said they smoked marijuana.

5. *Here is a student answer to the earlier question about 100,000 doctors having quit smoking:* "This ad is fallacious in its appeal to authority. The ad is made to make the reader think that the expert (the doctor) knows something the reader doesn't because he is a doctor. The problem with this is anyone can quit smoking if they have enough will power and really want to do it. The doctors don't know any more on the subject than the people."

6. *Ad for Honda motor cars:* Honda . . . has traditionally retained a high resale value. . . . Our first Accord model, the 1976 Accord Hatchback, has retained 107.8 percent of its original suggested retail price. And our first Accord 4-door sedan, introduced in 1979, has kept 89 percent of its original suggested retail price.

7. *W. Allen Wallis and Harry V. Roberts, in* Statistics: A New Approach: It is three times as dangerous to be a pedestrian while intoxicated as to be a driver. This is shown by the fact that last year 13,943 intoxicated pedestrians were injured and only 4,399 intoxicated drivers.

*8. Vancouver *(British Columbia)* Sun *(July 10, 1975):* Britain has a strong socialist tradition more preoccupied with the distribution than the production of wealth. But distributionist preoccupations are a luxury for rich nations, which Britain no longer is. Since 1945, while world living standards tripled and productivity increased more than it did in the preceding 10,000 years, Britain went from being the second richest nation in northwest Europe (behind Sweden) to being the second poorest (behind Ireland).

9. *From a National Rifle Association membership letter (objected to by the Reverend James Atwood in a letter to the* Washington Monthly, *June 1983):* We all know their Master Plan: First, outlaw all handguns. Then register all rifles and shotguns. . . . Make no mistake, these anti-gun and anti-hunting forces are working feverishly for the day when they can gather up your rifles, handguns, and shotguns and ship them off to gun melting furnaces.

   A letter in the same issue by Frank N. Egerton stated in part: Ten to 15 percent of the murders committed each year in the United States with guns are actually committed with shotguns and rifles. If we ever succeed in banning handguns in America, the number of crimes committed with shotguns and rifles is apt to increase. There might then be a new demand from liberals to ban all private ownership of guns.

10. *Robert Sherrill, in* Inquiry *(May 14, 1979):* The myth of Franklin D. Roosevelt as the savior of a depressed nation has been pretty thoroughly debunked. The welfare capitalism of his New Deal, his Keynesian orgy, has left us with a federal government dedicated to waste and corruption and corporate favoritism.

11. *Item in* Playboy *(February 1983), above a picture of Anita Bryant dancing with Russ McCraw: Shake it, Anita!* We all remember what Anita Bryant used to say about homosexuals, but here she is, discoing with gay evangelist Russ McCraw.

*12. *Michael H. Hart, in* The 100: A Ranking of the Most Influential Persons in History, *1980:* It's worth noting that over the past fifteen years—a period during which American women began using the pill regularly—life expectancy among American women has *increased* significantly. That fact alone should make it obvious that the pill is not a *major* health hazard.

*13. *Article in* Science 80 *(November/December 1979):* The chief trouble with the word "superstition" is that it always applies to the beliefs of someone else, not your own. The entire history of science shows that, in varying degrees, much that even the greatest dead scientists believed to be fact is today either false or else somewhat less than factual, perhaps even superstitious. It follows that what the best scientists today believe to be fact will suffer the same fate.

14. National Review *(April 2, 1982):* El Salvador is more decisively crucial than Vietnam ever was. If it is allowed to fall into Communist hands, the strategic balance in the Western Hemisphere will be dangerously, perhaps irretrievably, tilted against the United States. The credibility of American power would be gravely, perhaps fatally, affected. For if the U.S. were seen to be incapable of stopping a direct challenge in a minor country in its own backyard, what credence would be commanded by its will to act, say, in the European theatre?

15. *Article in the Marin County, California* Independent Journal *(February 4, 1983) on a proposed regulation of "prescription drugs or prescription devices" of a sexual nature:* We are stuck with trying to communicate two contradictory messages: Don't do it because it's premature, dangerous, stupid or immoral; but if you do, make certain that you use a contraceptive. It's like saying to your son: Don't shoplift; it's illegal, immoral and extremely dangerous. But if you do, here's how to avoid getting caught.

*16. *Article in* New York *magazine (September 12, 1972) on alcoholism:* A genetic biochemical deficiency could be the reason some persons become alcoholics while others don't. Dr. Stanley Gitlow, President of the American Medical Society on Alcoholism, [stated] that more than 80 percent of the alcoholics he has seen had a blood relative who also was an alcoholic.

17. *Richard C. Gerstenberg, General Motors Board Chairman, arguing against more stringent auto exhaust emission standards:* [The Clean Air Act would force auto makers to put out a car which] would emit fewer hydrocarbons per day than would evaporate from two ounces of enamel you might use to paint your shutters.

18. *Article in* Newsweek *(July 31, 1972) on a government program to give rent money directly to the poor to find their own housing:* Financially, the program is a definite success, because the cost to the government has averaged out at only $1,500 a year per family—a hugely favorable comparison with the $25,000 per unit cost of new low-income housing.

19. *Item from* Detroit Free Press, *by Ronald Kotulak, entitled "When Doctors Struck, Death Rate Fell":* If surgeons performed fewer operations more people would still be alive.

    This controversial conclusion, by a public health expert from the University of California at Los Angeles, is the latest and perhaps most serious attack on the surgical field. . . .

    The newest charge was made by Dr. Milton I. Roemer, professor of health-care administration at UCLA, after studying the effects of a five-week doctor strike in Los Angeles in 1976.

    Roemer and Dr. Jerome L. Schwartz from the California State Department of Health found that the death rate in Los Angeles County declined significantly during the strike.

    They said that fewer people had non-emergency surgery, so there was less risk of dying.

"These findings . . . lend support to the mounting evidence that people might benefit if less elective (non-emergency) surgery were performed in the United States," said Roemer. "It would appear, therefore, that greater restraint in the performance of elective surgical operations may well improve U.S. life expectancy."

*20. It's a well-known and much pondered-over fact that every United States president elected at 20-year intervals died in office, starting with William Henry Harrison, elected in 1840, and continuing with Lincoln in 1860, Garfield in 1880, McKinley in 1900, Harding in 1920, Franklin D. Roosevelt in 1940, and Kennedy in 1960. Only one other president, Zachary Taylor, has ever died in office. So the odds are pretty bad for Ronald Reagan.

21. *Jane B. Lancaster, in "Carrying and Sharing in Human Evolution," Human Nature (February 1978), in which she argued that some other primates are much more vicious than homo sapiens:* During the five years of observing the habits of a community of chimpanzees at the Gombe Stream Reserve in Tanzania, researchers witnessed eight attacks between the community and neighboring groups. These fights resulted in the deaths of at least two elderly males, an adult female, and four infants, the equivalent of an annual murder rate of 1,400 per 100,000 chimpanzees. The murder rate in the United States, 88 per 100,000 people in 1976, becomes insignificant in comparison.

22. *Article in* Baltimore *magazine (March 1979) on the social costs of drug use in the state of Maryland:* Start with the understanding that a so-called "dime" ($10) bag of heroin . . . today sells for $50. Some addicts need six bags per day to keep from going into physical withdrawal. Cost: $300 daily. At 365 days a year, this amounts to $109,500. . . .

How do you support a $110,000-a-year habit? One 28 year old . . . prostitute with three children . . . explains:

Normally, I'll turn anywhere from 6 to 12 tricks a day and shoplift at Hutzler's or any large department store. Other times we'll spend the day over in Rockville at White Flint Mall boosting [shoplifting] at Bloomingdales and Lord and Taylor's. Once a month we'll try and pull a con game . . . and at least once a week I'll pull a stick-up either around the Block or down off Park Avenue."

Suppose every addict supports his or her habit by stealing every day. Multiply, then, the $110,000 it costs the heroin addict to support his yearly habit by the 32,625 known narcotic addicts in the state and you get a figure of over $3.5 billion a year.

23. *Excerpted from a letter from Calhoun's Collectors Society, Inc.:* Back in April, 1971, I bought my first "collector's plate" for $25. . . . I made the mistake of mentioning to my husband that one day it might be worth a lot more than I paid for it. He laughed and suggested . . . he could recommend a good stock broker.

Well, getting to the "last laugh" department—that $25 plate now lists for $580. That's an increase of 2,300 percent in just six years. The Dow-

Jones in that same time has actually gone down from 950.82 as of April 28, 1971 to 769.92 on January 31, 1978. . . .

I'm now working for a company that's in the very thick of collectibles, and everyone here is excited about a new series of plates by the artist Yiannis Koutsis called "The Creation." This series is yours at a huge discount if you join Calhoun's Plate Collectors Club. The experts tell me this may be the most important plate series of the past ten years. But I don't want you to think I'm an expert. I'm still just a collector, but I've learned this lesson very well: Some plates, like some stocks, shoot up in value quickly. But even if they don't, collector's plates are works of art that you can enjoy as objects of beauty.

24. *Note from* High Times *magazine:* Even though they contain an illegal drug, *Psilocybe* mushrooms are legal in Great Britain, held the Reading Crown Court. . . . Judge Blomefield reasoned: "Psilocybin is a chemical; these mushrooms are mushrooms."

25. Public school textbooks inculcating the idea that the United States is a peace-loving nation point with pride to the fact that the border between the United States and "our friendly neighbor to the north," Canada, is the longest unprotected border in the world.

26. *Wayne W. Dyer, in* Your Erroneous Zones:[19] Here is a logical exercise that can forever put to rest the notion that you cannot take charge of your own emotional world.
    MAJOR PREMISE: I can control my thoughts.
    MINOR PREMISE: My feelings come from my thoughts.
    CONCLUSION: I can control my feelings.
    Your major premise is clear. You have the power to think whatever you choose to allow into your head. . . . You alone control what enters your head as a thought. If you don't believe this, just answer this question, "If you don't control your thoughts, who does?" Is it your spouse, or your boss, or your momma? . . .

27. *William Harsha, in the* Congressional Record: The city of Boston, the city of Philadelphia, the city of Chicago, the city of New York, all have rapid rail transit systems, and they have the highest congestion and traffic tie-ups in the country. Rail mass transit has not solved their problems. It is not the solution . . . to the problem.

28. A letter to the *San Francisco Examiner* from a physician argued that if juries award sums like $10.5 million to plaintiffs who have contracted toxic shock syndrome—even though that disease wasn't known to medical science when the damage took place—perhaps we can now expect lawsuits against pharmaceutical companies and physicians by the relatives of people who died of pneumonia before 1943, on the grounds that as yet undiscovered penicillin hadn't been prescribed.

---

[19]New York: Avon Books, 1977.

29. *Delta Rubber Company Chairman Richard Moe, quoted in* This World *(March 27, 1983), defending his ban on the parking of Japanese cars in the company parking lot:* As Communism has taken one country at a time, . . . so the Japanese are taking over one industry at a time: automobiles, motorcycles, television, electronics, clothes, lawn mowers, machine tools— you name it. They are making Scotch whisky now. It's the same way with the Communists. We just sit idly by and say: 'Oh, well, there goes Afghanistan.'

30. *William Shakespeare, in* As You Like It: Why, if thou never wast at court, thou never sawest good manners; if thou never sawest good manners, then thy manners must be wicked; and wickedness is sin, and sin is damnation. Thou art in a parlous state, shepherd.

Exercise 4-3

Find examples in the mass media of fallacies discussed in Chapter 4, and carefully explain why they are fallacious.

By permission of JULES FEIFFER. Copyright 1978. Distributed by Field Newspaper Syndicate.

It makes a great deal of difference what we call something. Political cartoonist Jules Feiffer suggests that military bureaucrats know this just as much as any other bureaucrats.

5

Language

1. Cognitive and Emotive Meaning

If the purpose of a sentence is to inform, or to state a fact, some of its words must refer to things, events, or properties. Some of its words thus must have what is commonly called **cognitive meaning**. The sentences made up of them also may be said to have cognitive meaning—provided, of course, that they conform to grammatical rules.

But words may also have **emotive meaning**—that is, they may have positive or negative overtones. The emotive charges of some words are obvious. Think of the terms *nigger, wop, kike,* and *fag,* or think of four-letter "sex" words, which even in this permissive age rarely appear in textbooks.

The emotively charged words just listed have negative emotive meanings. But lots of words have positive emotive overtones. Examples are *freedom, love, democracy, springtime,* and *peace.* On the other hand, many words have either neutral or mixed emotive meanings. *Pencil, run,* and *river* tend to be neutral words. *Socialism, politician,* and *whiskey* tend to have mixed emotive meanings.

In fact, almost any word that is emotively positive (or negative) for some may be just the opposite for others, perhaps because one person's meat is another's poison. *God,* for instance, has quite different emotive overtones for a sincere believer and for an atheist. Similarly, *dictatorship,* a negative word for most Americans, in some contexts has positive overtones in the Soviet Union.

Terms that on first glance appear neutral often turn out to be emotively charged, sometimes because the charge is fairly small. But even when the charge is quite large, we may fail to notice it. The terms *bureaucrat, government official,* and *public servant,* for instance, all refer to roughly the same group of people, and thus have roughly the same cognitive meaning. But their emotive meanings are quite different. Of the three, only *government official* is close to being neutral.

Emotive Meaning Is Not the Enemy

It is sometimes claimed that emotive meaning gets in the way of rational "objective" thought. According to this view, serious intellectual uses of language should be stripped of their emotive content so that we can deal rationally with their cognitive content. Thus, newspapers, textbook, political rhetoric, even advertisements, according to this view, should be written in emotively neutral language.[1]

But surely this view is not correct. Such large doses of emotively neutral language would bore most of us out of our shoes, and so fail to communicate effectively. And anyway, we want to know what the emotive responses of others are to claimed facts. So we don't want to discount the emotive side of language, but rather to become aware of how this otherwise useful feature of language can be used to con us into accepting unreasonable arguments. Emotive language, like cognitive language, is a tool. And like other tools, it can be used both for good and for evil purposes.

2. Emotive Meaning and Con Artistry

There are several ways in which the emotive side of language can be taken advantage of. One is to use emotively charged words to mask cognitive import. Another is to take an emotively favorable or "pro" word, like *democracy* or *republic,* and change its cognitive meaning while keeping its emotively "pro" overtones. Thus, the East German Communist dictatorship is called the *German Democratic Republic,* although it is neither democratic nor a republic (while the democratic republic in West Germany settled for the name *Federal Republic of Germany*); the Argentine military dictatorship is called the *Argentine Republic;* and the Communist dictatorship in China is officially known as the *People's Republic of China.* (All this makes the straightforward and accurate *State of Israel* and *Kingdom of Saudi Arabia* sound almost refreshing.)

Doublespeak, Jargon, Bureaucratese, . . .

And then there is the use of emotively dull or euphemistic language of the kind favored by government officials and professionals like doctors, lawyers, and academics. There are many names for this kind of language, each with slightly different cognitive and emotive meanings: *doublespeak, jargon, bureaucratese, newspeak, academese, professionalese, bafflegab, gobbledygook,* and so on.

Take the bureaucratic language of war—remembering that war, the real thing, is unvarnished hell. During the Vietnam War, we used particularly nasty weapons (for

---

[1]Proponents of this view often associate all evaluative language with emotive meaning, including that of ethics and aesthetics. This assumes that evaluative terms such as *right* and *good,* as used in sentences such as "Killing is sometimes morally *right*" and "That is a *good* painting," are basically emotive terms—a conclusion many would deny.

example, fragmentation bombs and napalm) in areas where they were certain to kill thousands of civilians. We dropped far more bombs on that small nation than on Germany and Japan combined in World War II. To make all this palatable, a double-speak language was developed. Here are a few examples (with translations):

Pacification center	Concentration camp
Incursion	Invasion (as in the "Cambodian incursion")
Protective reaction strike	Bombing
Surgical strike	Precision bombing
Incontinent ordinance	Off-target bombs (usually used when they kill civilians)
Friendly fire	Shelling friendly village or troops by mistake
Specified strike zone	Area where soldiers can fire at anything—replaced *free fire zone* when that became notorious
Interdiction	Bombing
Strategic withdrawal	Retreat (when our side does it)
Tactical redeployment	Retreat (when our side does it)
Advisor	Military officer (before we admitted "involvement" in Vietnam) or CIA agent
Termination	Killing
Infiltrators	Enemy troops moving into the battle area
Reinforcements	Friendly troops moving into the battle area
Selective ordinance	Napalm (also known as *selective explosives*)

George Orwell was probably right in arguing that the main point of bureaucratese is to numb the reader into submission by replacing succinct, pungent locutions with long-winded or dull ones. Typical examples seem to support his view: Bureaucrats speak of *undocumented workers,* not illegal aliens; of *termination with prejudice* rather than assassination (CIA lingo); of *end use allocation* instead of rationing; and of *diversion,* rather than theft (as in "200 pounds of highly enriched uranium *diverted* by Israel"). They speak of *plausible deniability* (as in "Once the White House tapes became known, Nixon lost his *plausible deniability* on the Watergate coverup"—the tapes were said to be a *smoking gun*). They write of being *selected out,* not fired (as in "Foreign Service Officer Smith was again passed over for pro-motion, and is therefore to be selected out"). And they use the phrase *program misuse and management inefficiency* in place of the old *fraud, abuse, and waste.* [2]

Here is George Orwell in his 1948 classic Politics and the English Language *explaining why politicians favor doublespeak:*

In our time, political speech and writing are largely the defence of the indefen-sible. . . . Thus political language has to consist largely of euphemism, ques-tion begging, and sheer cloudy vagueness. Defenceless villages are bom-barded from the air, the inhabitants driven out into the countryside, the cattle machine-gunned, the huts set on fire with incendiary bullets: This is called *pacification.* Millions of peasants are robbed of their farms and sent trudging along the roads with no more than they can carry: This is called *transfer of population* or *rectification of frontiers.* . . .

The inflated style is itself a kind of euphemism. A mass of Latin words falls upon the facts like soft snow, blurring the outlines and covering up all the details. The great enemy of clear language is insincerity. When there is a gap between one's real and one's declared aims, one turns as it were instinctively to long words and exhausted idioms, like a cuttlefish squirting out ink. . . .

And here is Albert Joseph in the Quarterly Review of Doublespeak *(July 1981) giving three reasons why so many people, politicians and the rest of us, use this obfuscatory language:*

People everywhere enjoy making their messages sound more complicated than necessary. In all professions, people enjoy using language to convey the feel-ing, "my field is so complex ordinary mortals could never understand it." Children establish superiority over peers with Pig Latin. Lawyers do it with gobbledygook, truck drivers with citizens-band jargon, and scientists (and educators) with the language of grantsmanship.

Now my main point is this. Misrepresentation is not the only reason so many people write in impossibly difficult language. In fact, years of study have convinced me it is not even the main reason. Many perfectly honorable people write in heavy language because it is an ego trip; they are writing to impress, not to express. They may not be writing doublespeak, in the sense that they are not deliberately concealing weak information, but the effect on language style is the same.

But the most common reason for heavy writing style is still more innocent: *most people honestly think they are supposed to write that way.* Who can blame them? They see it all around them—in government regulations, legal docu-ments, and in their professional books and journals. They see it, alas, even in the writings of their teachers of English, who set the model.

---

[2]See the *Washington Monthly* "Memo of the Month" (March 1981).

MEMO OF THE MONTH

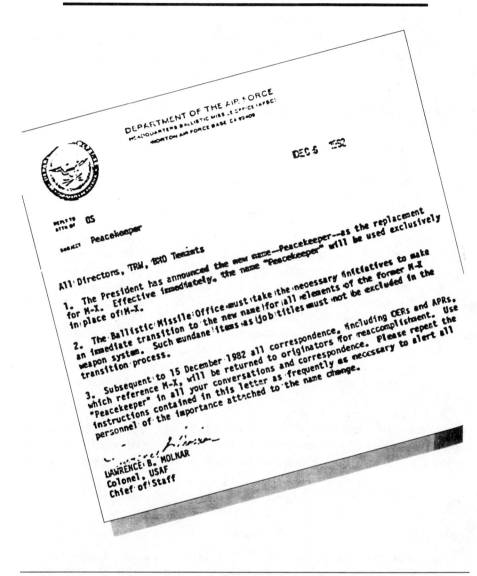

Replacing emotively charged names with emotively neutral ones is serious business in government, as this Washington Monthly *"Memo of the Month" (February, 1983) illustrates (the poor quality of the reproduction probably reflects a bit of bureaucratic leaking).*

But Albert Joseph is also right that people often think they're supposed to write that way.[3] How else explain this example from the Internal Revenue Code:

> The term "taxable distribution" means any distribution which is not out of the income of the trust, within the meaning of section 643(b), from a generation-skipping trust to any younger generation beneficiary who is assigned to a generation younger than the generation assignment of any other person who is a younger generation beneficiary.[4]

Apropos Al Smith's famous remark that law school is where you learn to call a bribe a fee, here is an item from *New Times* on illegal bribes by big business:

> Asked by a *New York Times* reporter about the recent bribery disclosures, a professor of management and business at the University of California replied, "At a high level of abstraction, it's clear that American companies should not engage in wholesale bribery abroad, but I can't pass judgment until I get down to the operating details and ask when a bribe is a tip or a commission."

Misleading language is apt to crop up almost anywhere. *The Congressional Record,* for example, isn't an accurate record of what goes on in Congress, or even of what is said on the floors of the House and Senate. Members of Congress have power, so they also have privileges—one being the privilege of changing what they actually say in Congress or adding to the "record" things they might have liked to say but didn't. (The folks back home will never know.)

The Group Health Association says that it believes "it is important for [ex-schizophrenic] patients to realize they are normal, average people who happen to have a medical illness called schizophrenia." That's like saying Siamese twins are "normal, average people" who just happen to be physically joined together at the hip so that they share the same circulatory system.

The nuclear age has generated a *nukespeak* to mask the risky nature of atomic energy plants and the horror of atomic war. In this lingo, *spent fuel* means radioactive waste, *thermal enrichment* means heat pollution, *breach of containment* means a leak of radioactive poisons, and *nuclear exchange* is used instead of atomic war.

Here is an example of critic doubletalk, a distinct dialect:

The Brahms sang with detachment as if the music were a coat-of-arms which he hung on the wall while he took the frame and exhibited it.

From a Harriet Johnson review in the New York Post

Possible translation: "The Brahms sang." (Metaphors do have content. We do know roughly what it means to say "The Brahms sang"; what all that business about a coat of arms hung on the wall means is anybody's guess.)

---

[3]For instance, see Gregory M. Jones's "Confessions of a Reg Writer," *Quarterly Review of Doublespeak* (July 1981).
[4]IRS Code, Chapter 13, Subchapter B, Section 2613.

D. C. REDEVELOPMENT LAND AGENCY

M E M O R A N D U M   May 4, 1972

TO : SEE ATTACHED DISTRIBUTION LIST

FROM: Harold D. Scott

SUBJ: Intra-Agency Communication

In order to avoid negative reflections as a result of dysfunctional internal communications, and in order to enhance the possibilities of coordinated balances I am strongly urging that any item having a direct or indirect affect on the NW#1 Project Area be made known to me before, rather than after it's occurence, when possible.

Your cooperation in achieving a better communication channel relative to NW#1 would be greatly appreciated.

Attachment

Washington Monthly "Memo of the Month." Reprinted by permission.

Government memos often use jargon to hide (relative) triviality—to make communications seem more important than they really are (and to protect the writer by getting a document "on the record"). The above memo, translated into plain English, seems to say simply this: "Please let me know when something is going to happen which concerns NW#1 Project Area *before* it happens rather than after, when it's too late." *But it all sounds so much more important and professional in doublespeak.*

Similarly, atomic weapon accidents are called *bent spears* or *broken arrows,* and the Three Mile Island near-disaster an *event, normal aberration* (literally contradictory, since by definition an aberration is abnormal), or *incident.* The Indians call their bomb a *peaceful nuclear device.* And in Washington, D.C., we encounter the phrase *fallout sojourn in the countryside* to describe people fleeing cities under atomic attack. (For more on this topic, see *Nukespeak: Nuclear Language, Visions and Mindset,* by Stephen Hilgartner, Richard Bell, and Rory O'Connor [San Francisco: Sierra Club Books, 1982].)

Now listen to Admiral Isaac C. Kidd, Chief of Navy Materiel, explaining a Navy memo urging contractors to spend another $400 million to keep Congress from cutting Navy appropriations:

> We have gone with teams of competent contract people from Washington to outlying field activities to look over their books with them . . . to see in what areas there is susceptibility to improved capability to commit funds.[5]

In other words, the Navy asked contractors to try to increase costs so the Navy could spend more money. Doublespeak masks the true import of language behind the dull mush of emotively neutral circumlocutions.

Here are a few more doublespeak examples:

Singularities	Miracles (used by "Creation scientists" —itself a euphemistic expression employed to appear scientific)
National species of special emphasis	Endangered species you can kill legally
Democratic Personnel Committee	Name of the U.S. House of Representatives Democratic party patronage committee (*patronage* has a foul odor)
Unacceptable borrowing	Plagiarism (used by the *New York Times* in investigating alleged plagiarism of some of its writers)

Sometimes people get the notion the purpose of EST is to make you better. It is not. I happen to think that you are perfect exactly the way you are. . . . The problem is that people get stuck acting the way they were instead of being the way they are.

—Werner Erhard, Erhard Seminars Training (EST), quoted in *Harper's* (October 1975)

Mumbo-jumbo con artistry used to get you to overlook the ambiguity in the phrase "the way you are." If you're "stuck acting the way you were," well, then, sorry, Charlie, but that's the way you are.

---

[5]*Washington Monthly* (May 1972).

Poorly buffered precipitation	Acid rain
Safety net programs	Veterans benefits, unemployment benefits, social security, and so forth—but not things like food stamps, Medicaid or school lunch programs (they're called *all other* in Reagan administration lingo, meaning they'll be cut if politically expedient)
Automotive internist	Auto mechanic
Scheduled person	Non-black (in South Africa)
Occasional irregularity	Constipation
Cult[6]	Group with a doctrine most "respectable" people reject (as in "the *cult* founded by James Jones," or "the Moonie *cult*")
Life insurance	Death insurance
Price enhancement	Inflation

Watergate-ese reached its peak with Richard Nixon's press secretary Ron Zeigler, who was responsible for the famous "All previous White House statements about the Watergate case are inoperative." Here is his reply when asked whether some Watergate tapes were still intact:

I would feel that most of the conversations that took place in those areas of the White House that did have the recording system would in almost their entirety be in existence but the special prosecutor, the court, and I think, the American people are sufficiently familiar with the recording system to know where the recording devices existed and to know the situation in terms of the recording process but I feel, although the process has not been undertaken yet in the preparation of the material to abide by the court decision, really, what the answer to the question is.

Zeigler's remark so impressed the Committee on Public Doublespeak of the National Council of Teachers of English that they gave him their first annual Gobbledygook Award for his effort. They also gave Colonel David Opfer, USAF press officer in Cambodia, an award for this gem:

You always write it's bombing, bombing, bombing. It's *not* bombing! It's air support.

---

[6]This isn't really doublespeak, but rather an ordinary term whose bias isn't generally recognized. The same is true of the example that follows.

Receipts strengthening or *revenue enhancement*	Tax increase
Internal Revenue Service	Tax collector
Totalitarian government	Dictatorship unfriendly to the U.S.
Authoritarian government	Dictatorship friendly to the U.S.
High mobility multipurpose wheeled vehicle	Jeep (Army lingo)
Deep chilled	Frozen, but not below 28°F (as in *"deep chilled* chicken")
Physically challenged	Handicapped (itself once a euphemistic term)
Negative economic growth	Recession
Department of Human Kinetics	Physical Education Department (at Rutgers University)
Member of a career offending cartel	Mobster (as in "Don Corleone was a member of a *career offending* cartel")
Incomplete success	Failure (used by Jimmy Carter to describe the failed Iran hostage rescue mission)
Combat emplacement evacuator	Shovel (Army nomenclature)
Speech Communication Association	Name of a language association
Vertical Transportation Corps	Insignia on uniforms of elevator operators at Hahnemann Hospital in Philadelphia
Ecology, Inc.	Name of the old *Nuclear Engineering Co.*, which runs waste disposal sites for chemical and atomic wastes

And then, in a class by itself, the crowning achievement of Nazi phraseology, purified of the stench and horror of extermination camps: *The Final Solution.*

Academese

Now for a bit of *academese,* which has a sleep-inducing quality all its own. First, a tiny snippet from Zellig Harris's well-known text *Structural Linguistics,* to give a feel for the genre:

> Another consideration is the availability of simultaneity, in addition to successivity as a relation among linguistic elements.

Which may or may not mean simply that we can simultaneously do things like wink an eye and talk and we can also say words one after another. You didn't know that, did you?

In his book *The Dragons of Eden,* Carl Sagan explains a bit of academese:

> With this evidence, paleontologists [titles in the professions rival those in gov-ernment] have deduced that "bipedalism preceded encephalization" by which they mean that our ancestors walked on two legs before they evolved big brains.

The *Washington Monthly* (February 1979) noted that writer Tom Wolfe referred to what he perceived as a very self-centered generation in America as the "me generation," but that when social scientists picked up the idea, they translated it as "the culture of narcissism."

Unfortunately, it may be that the best (that is, the worst) examples of academese come from the field of education itself, in particular education in coherent writing, perhaps explaining why so many people think doublespeak is the correct way to use language. A few examples are *evaluation tool* used to refer to a test, *needs assessment* to refer to a survey, and *transportation component* to indicte a bus.

The Associated Press reported that a school principal in Houston sent the following message home to parents:

> Our school's cross-graded, multi-ethnic, individualized learning program is designed to enhance the concept of an open-ended learning program with em-phasis on a continuum of multi-ethnic, academically enriched learning using the identified intellectually gifted child as the agent or director of his own learning.

One father responded as follows:

> I have a college degree, speak two foreign languages, and four Indian dialects, have been to a number of county fairs and three goat ropings, but I haven't the faintest idea what the hell you're talking about! Do you?

Inflation at the *Monthly*

As a long-time subscriber to your magazine, I'd like to ask if you don't feel just a wee bit hypocritical poking fun at bureaucrats with inflated titles (Administrative Assistant to the Deputy Assistant Administrator, etc.) when you have the same problem yourselves?

I recently noticed something interesting: you don't have any writers. You've got an "Editor in Chief." And you've got "Editors." You've got "Contributing Editors." You even have an "Editorial Advisory Board." You must have one hell of a lot of writers to need all that editing, but there are none listed on your masthead! So who *writes The Washington Monthly?*

—Doug Ellice

Letter to the editor of The Washington Monthly, *famous for its "Memos of the Month" and other battles against gobbledygook, inflated titles, and other linguistic monstrosities. (So who's perfect?) Reprinted by permission.*

And here's another example from the *Quarterly Review of Doublespeak* (July 1981):

> I cannot forget a recent statement by a Massachusetts educator on the teaching of writing:
>
>> The results (of declining writing skills) have catalyzed a societal dynamic which stimulated many school systems to adopt Back to Basics or Competency Based education schemes.
>
> One would have more confidence in that educator's ability to help others teach writing if the statement read:
>
>> Society has demanded that our schools go back to basics, and that they make sure students learn them.

It might be naïvely supposed that academics who write in academese would as a consequence not be read and thus have little influence in their fields. But that isn't the way it works. Here is a typical example of the writing of a very famous and extremely influential sociologist, Talcott Parsons:

> Skills constitute the manipulative techniques of human goal attainment and control in relation to the physical world, so far as artifacts for machines especially designed as tools do not yet supplement them. Truly human skills are guided by organized and codified *knowledge* of both the things to be manipulated and the human capacities that are used to manipulate them. Such knowledge is an aspect of cultural level symbolic processes, and . . . requires the capacities of the human central nervous system, particularly the brain. This organic system is clearly essential to all the symbolic processes. . . .

This passage was cited by Stanislav Andreski,[7] who translated it into: "A developed brain, acquired skills, and knowledge are needed for attaining human goals." Which sounds about right.

A common feature of academese, as of all jargon, is padding—adding significant-sounding sentences here and there which in fact say little or nothing. Here's one that occurs over and over, in this case in a *Human Nature* article (August 1978) on psychological causes of illness: "Although the effects of mental attitudes on

Reprinted by permission of Tribune Syndicate, Inc.

---

[7] In *Social Science as Sorcery* (London: Andre Deutsch, 1972).

> Some words are born pretentious (*ongoing ambience*). Some words achieve pretentiousness (*situation*). And some have pretentiousness thrust upon them (*charisma, parameter*).
>
> Philip Howard, in *Weasel Words*

bodily disease should not be exaggerated, neither should they be minimized." True. And here's one from *Psychology Today* (July 1979): "As soon as there are behaviors you can't generate then there are responses you can't elicit." Yes. And finally, in their article "Needs Assessment and Holistic Planning," in *Educational Leadership* (May 1981), Roger Kaufman and Robert Stakevas point out that "in order to achieve products, outputs, and outcomes through processes, inputs are required." Absolutely.

Legalese

Anyone who has spent much time perusing legal documents will agree that *legalese* is probably the deadliest variety of *professionalese*, itself a variety of *bureaucratese*. (This is nicely illustrated by the cartoon on page 148.)

But now, winds of change are beginning to blow in legal circles—gently, we don't want to get your hopes up too high—largely because of the demands of ordinary citizens and, in particular, the demands of insurance companies (responding to demands of their customers). A few legal contracts are now being written in something modestly resembling plain English. Here are two examples:[8]

Promissory Note

Old: "No extension of time for payment, or delay in enforcement thereof, nor any renewal of this note, with or without notice, shall operate as a waiver of any rights hereunder or release the obligation of any maker, guarantor, endorser or any other accommodation party."

New: "We can delay enforcing any of our rights without losing them."

Surrender of Lease

Old: Tenant "has not at any time heretofore made, done, committed, executed, permitted or suffered any act, deed, matter or thing whatsoever,

From *Non-Being and Something-Ness*, by Woody Allen. Drawn by Stuart Hample. © 1978 by I. W. A. Enterprises, Inc. and Hackenbush Productions, Inc. Reprinted by permission of Random House, Inc.

[8]Cited in *War on Gobbledegook, U.S. News & World Report*, November 7, 1977.

whereby or wherewith, or by reason or means whereof the said lands and premises hereby assigned or surrendered, or any part or parcel thereof are, or is, or may, can, or shall be in any wise impeached, charged, effected or incumbered."

New: "Tenant has done nothing which would give anyone a claim against the leased premises."

BEDTIME PRAYERS BEFORE MOMMY WENT TO LAW SCHOOL

AT THE PRESENT JUNCTURE, THIS DAY AND AGE, THIS HOUR, ON THIS, THE PRESENT OCCASION; I, MYSELF, THIS PARTICULAR INDIVIDUAL AND ENTITY, ALLEDGED TO BE MARY JOYCE HARCOURT AND SOMETIMES REFERRED TO AS "JOYCIE" OR "MOMMY" (MOTHER TO THE ALLEDGED LIBERTY REESE HARCOURT); REPOSIT, ASSIGN AND CONSIGN, FIX AND ESTABLISH THIS SAID PERSON, THE ABOVE AND AFORE-MENTIONED (SEE PARAGRAPH 1. LINE 3. WORDS 26, 27, 28) WHO SHALL BE REFERRED TO AS THE PARTY OF THE FIRST PART FROM THIS TIME FORWARD, IN A LOWERED (AS COMPARED TO UPRIGHT) RECLINED AND/OR PROSTRATED POSITION, LIKENED TO A TOP AND/OR LOG; PURPOSE OF SLUMBER, REPOSE REST IN THE ARMS OF MORPHEUS, SOUNDLY AND/OR HEAVILY, FOR THE SOLE NOT TO THE EXCLUSION OF DREAMING AND/OR SNORING WHICH SHALL REMAIN TO BE SEEN ON THE EVIDENCE OF THOSE WHO SHALL REMAIN ANONYMOUS AT THIS TIME; I, MYSELF, THIS PERSON, THIS PARTICULAR INDIVIDUAL AFOREMENTIONED AND NOW REFERRED TO AS THE PARTY OF THE FIRST PART, PROPOSE, REQUEST AND PETITION, MAKE BOLD TO ASK, PUT TO AND CALL UPON, COURT, SEEK TO ENTREAT, AND IMPLORE, BESIEGE, IMPORTUNE AND ADJURE, BEG AND BESEECH THE DIVINE DEITY, GODSHIP, GODHEAD, OMNIPOTENT AND OMNISCIENT SPIRIT i.e. SUPREME BEING, SOUL, HIGHER POWER, PROVIDENCE, KING OF KINGS, QUEEN OF QUEENS, LORD OF LORDS, ALMIGHTY ONE, ABSOLUTE BEING, INFINITE CAUSE, SOURCE, UNIVERSAL MIND, NATURE, ALL POWERFUL, ETERNAL BEING, ALL KNOWING, ALL WISE, ALL MERCIFUL, ALL HOLY, THE PRESERVER, MAKER, CREATOR, AUTHOR AND/OR CREATOR OF ALL THINGS, TRUTH AND LOVE; MY, THE AFOREMENTIONED PARTY OF THE FIRST PART, ESSENCE, FUNDAMENTAL TRUE BEING, INMOST NATURE, CORE, INNER AND ESOTERIC REALITY, VITAL CENTER, ESSENTIAL QUALITY AND SUCHNESS, QUIDDITY PITH, KERNEL, NUCLEUS, INMOST RECESSES OF THE HEART, SPIRIT, PRANA, LIFE FORCE; TO TAKE CUSTODY OF, GUARD, WATCH OVER, SUSTAIN AND PRESERVE FOR THE SAFEKEEPING OF, AUSPICIOUS AND SECURE AND CAUTIOUS SURVEILLANCE OF, TO PROTECT, HOLD AND KEEP. SHOULD CIRCUMSTANCES WARRANT THAT I, THE AFOREMENTIONED ONE, NOW KNOWN AS THE PARTY OF THE PART, SHOULD EXPIRE, END, CEASE TO LIVE, EXTINGUISH THE MORTAL LIGHT, LEAVE THIS PHYSICAL PLANE, EXPERIENCE MY DEMISE, DESIST, QUIT THIS WORLD, MAKE MY EXIT, PASS ON, PASS AWAY, MEET MY END, SHUFFLE OFF THIS MORTAL COIL, RELINQUISH OR SURRENDER MY LIFE, YIELD THE GHOST, GIVE UP MY BREATH, GO OUT LIKE THE SNUFF OF A CANDLE, BEFORE OR AT A TIME PRIOR TO THE TIME I REGAIN CONSCIOUSNESS, PASS FROM THE SLEEPING TO THE WAKING STATE, ROUSE MYSELF, WARM TO THE DAY, OPEN MY EYES, I, THE PARTY OF THE FIRST PART, IMPLORE, BEG, AND BESEECH, INVOKE AND ENTREAT, HUMBLY ASK THEE ALMIGHTY, EVER PRESENT UNIFYER OF ALL FAITH, HEALING SOURCE, ONE WHO GIVES ENDLESS BIRDS AND INSECTS, GIVER OF BOONS, INSTILLER OF FAITH, AS IN I, THE PARTY OF THE FIRST PART, OF LOVE UNCONDITIONALLY, MY, AS IN ME AND MINE, VITAL FORCE, INNER PRINCIPLE, HEART, MIND LOWER OR MORTAL NATURE, SPIRIT, ATMA, BUDDHI, VITAL FORCE, INNER PRINCIPLE, HEART, MIND AND EMBODIED BREATH, ANIMATING PRINCIPLE AND TRUE SELF, ESSENCE AND SUBSTANCE OF LIFE, THE DIVINITY THAT STIRS WITHIN, INNER FLAME AND SEAT OF CONSCIOUSNESS TO; (IF IT PLEASES THEE) APPROPRIATE, CAPTURE, SEIZE, ABDUCT AND TAKE RESPONSIBILITY FOR, AN INFINITE PERIOD OF TIME, ENTER INTO POSSESSION OF, AND CAPTURE AND SEIZE AND HOLD OBTAIN AND RESCUE, PICK UP, GLEAN, GATHER IN, CAPTURE AND SEIZE AND HOLD. AMEN. UNTIL SUCH TIME AS IT SHALL BE RELINQUISHED BY THE SAID HOLDER. AMEN.

BEDTIME PRAYERS AFTER MOMMY WENT TO LAW SCHOOL

Reprinted with permission from *29 Reasons Not to Go to Law School*, by Ralph Warner and Toni Ihara, illustrated by Mari Stein. © 1982 Nolo Press/Folk Law, Inc., 950 Parker Street, Berkeley, CA 94710.

Perhaps the deadliest variety of professionalese (a cousin of bureaucratese) is legalese (see, we can all play this game).

It would be a serious mistake (a kind of reverse provincialism) to think that the use of doublespeak is typically American or confined to the English language. Every human society engages in this sort of manipulation. During the reign of Idi Amin Dada in Uganda, the name of the government's dreaded murder squad translated into English as "Public Safety Unit." And the title of the first law in Japan regulating prostitution and establishing red light districts translated into "Regulation on Earning a Living by Renting Rooms."

In Communist-ruled Romania, food was in such short supply in the early 1980s that masses of people suffered from constant gnawing hunger. The government's response was a propaganda campaign for "scientific nutrition," which urged people to stay within minimum caloric requirements—in the interests of the "material and spiritual well-being of the workers"—so they could avoid illnesses brought on by overeating.

And here's an item from the CBS nightly news (December 20, 1981) which earned Poland a nomination for a doublespeak foreign award: "After the imposition of martial law in Poland, accompanied by the suppression of news media, the Polish government explained that the reduction of newspapers was justified because it created more paper for textbooks and literature."

Noun-Replacing Phrases

As times change, language changes also. Words and phrases come into existence to help us say what we want to say easily and succinctly. In particular, *nouns* are generated to name common things or classes. Thus we use the term *television set* or *TV*, not some longwinded expression that describes a television set, like "device to electronically reproduce ordered progressions of pictures."

One of doublespeak's interesting devices is the *noun-replacing phrase* (common name: *euphemism*), which describes (often with less precision) an item or class of items generally referred to by some perfectly ordinary noun. An example is the Army's *combat emplacement evacuator,* used to refer to a type of shovel. Another is the use of *medical care facility* for a hospital. Some of these noun-replacing phrases

---

In Chapter 3, we described inconsistency *as a serious fallacy to be avoided at all costs and* consistency *as a requirement of good reasoning. Yet others have railed against being consistent. Art critic Bernard Berenson, for instance, said that "Consistency requires you to be as ignorant today as you were a year ago." And according to Ralph Waldo Emerson's famous remark, "A foolish consistency is the hobgoblin of little minds, adored by little statesmen, philosophers and divines."*

But there need be no inconsistency in accepting both sides of this coin, provided we notice that consistency is an ambiguous concept. One sense requires us to be consistent with what we know at any given time. This is roughly the sense meant in Chapter 3. The other requires us to be consistent now and forever, to stick to our beliefs no matter what contrary evidence we encounter. This, presumably, is the sense intended by Emerson and Berenson. The moral is that we need to notice ambiguous uses of language so as not to be confused by them.

are used to avoid nasty or emotively charged terms (*passed gas, sanitation engineer*). But most are used either in ignorance, to impress, in an unnecessary attempt to gain precision,[9] or to obfuscate (look up that word in the nearest alphabetized basic linguistic component assemblage). Whatever the reason, they serve to make communication more difficult and to hide poor or trivial thinking.

Of course, there are lots of other obfuscatory devices similar to noun-replacing phrases. Here are a few items employed by Alexander Haig (try to figure out how they work and give them a noun-replacing phrase name of your own invention): "caveat my response" (Haig's most famous effort); "definitizing an answer"; and "epistemologicallywise." These brilliancies "won" Haig the 1981 Doublespeak award.

But Euphemisms Often Serve Good Purposes

Our desire to cleanse language of bad uses shouldn't blind us to the fact that euphemisms often serve good purposes. Those used to replace offensive four-letter words are an example. Why, after all, should we shock or offend others when we don't have to?

But there are surprisingly many other examples of good euphemistic language. For instance, the word *mature* often is used in the euphemistic phrase *mature adult movies* to mean a film with lots of explicit sex in it, and the phrase *for the mature figure* refers to attire for overweight people, usually women. Surely good usage should not require store owners to offend potential buyers of outsize clothes.

3. Those Who Control the Definitions, . . .

Calling something by just the right name, or legally shifting the meaning of a term in just the right way, is crucial when you want to bend the law to your own purposes. For instance, employers who want to pay employees less than the minimum wage laws require can call them "subcontractors" instead of "employees." *Employees* is a bad name, and *subcontractors* a good one, because the minimum wage laws apply to employees but not to subcontractors. Yes, the law in the United States does work that way.[10]

Of course, it operates pretty much the same way everywhere else. In Moslem Saudi Arabia, for example, the commandment not to make graven images is taken quite seriously; until recently photography was therefore forbidden. But aerial photography is such a boon to oil exploration that something had to be done. So:

---

[9]Every discipline needs some technical terms that are more precisely defined than their everyday counterparts. But noun-replacing phrases (to use a noun-replacing phrase) are another matter.
[10]However, on occasion scams of this kind are thwarted: As the fourth edition of this book was going to press, attempts in the Midwest to get around the minimum wage laws and avoid paying social security, unemployment, and workmen's compensation contributions by calling migrant workers "sharecroppers" were being challenged in the courts. And the courts recently thwarted attempts by Burger King to avoid minimum wage laws for overtime by calling low-level employees covered by the law *assistant managers*.

King Ibn Saud convened the Ulema [a group of Moslem theologians who have great power over public morals] and eventually prevailed over them with the argument that photography was actually good because it was not an image, but a combination of light and shadow that depicted Allah's creations without violating them.[11]

All sorts of organizations twist words for profit when they can get away with it. A certain large corporation defended the judgment of one of its employees whose mistake caused a great deal of trouble by arguing that the person was a "trained employee"—the implication being that a "trained employee" ought to know the right thing to do, so the company was not negligent. But as they were using the expression, *trained employee* meant just "employee put through a company training program." Whether the program was any good, or whether the employee actually learned what was being taught, is another matter. By the way, did you notice that among the tools used by the Reagan administration to fight unemployment was the redefinition of terms, so that 6.5 percent unemployment or less suddenly became known as *full employment*?

In 1979, striking public school teachers in Washington, D.C., defended their demands to remain just about the best treated and best paid grade school teachers in the country (in spite of the fact that D.C. public school students were near the bottom academically) by pointing out that all full-time D.C. teachers have teaching certificates qualifying them as trained grade school teachers. Again, what this really means is just that they all have completed a training program for grade school teachers—whether they're trained in the sense that they know how to teach small children is something else.

The Roman Catholic Vatican Council II declared that marriage is a permanent covenant of love resulting in an intimate union of persons and their actions, so that many Catholic priests and bishops have concluded that where love never existed, or has been extinguished, a marriage covenant never existed, or no longer exists.[12] So they remarry divorced people in some circumstances without in their own eyes violating the Catholic doctrine that marriage is forever and divorce impossible. They've reasoned that "till death do us part" refers to the death of love as well as physical death. And Church courts have sometimes declared that no marriage existed, even though the legally married couple had several children.

The United States Constitution grants Congress the sole right to declare war. But a president who wants to engage in a military venture without getting the consent of Congress need only *rename* his military escapade. Since our last war declared by Congress (World War II), United States military forces have been ordered to fight in several wars, the most prominent being the Korean and Vietnam "engagements." (The Supreme Court decided that the Vietnam war was legal even though no declaration of war had been made by Congress.)

For years, psychologist Thomas Szasz has been campaigning against the use of the expression "mental illness." Declaring John Hinkley "not guilty by way of

---

[11]Peter A. Iseman, "The Arabian Ethos." In *Harper's* (February 1978).
[12]See Francis X. Murphy, C.S.S.R. "Of Sex and the Catholic Church," in *The Atlantic* (February 1981).

> You can consistently win debates if you consistently use two words: "baby" and "kill."
>
> — Dr. J. C. Willke, Vice President, National Right to Life Committee,
>   at a pro-life (which means anti-abortion) convention, teaching others
>   to teach the pro-life position (St. Louis, 1978)
>
> ---
>
> *Choosing words and phrases with just the right emotive force is a vital part of the art of rhetoric.*

insanity" in his attempt to assassinate President Reagan is for Szasz just an extreme example of what happens when we take the analogy between physical illness and mental illness seriously. His view is that there is no such thing as mental *illness*.

Another consequence of this mislabeling, he claims, is that close relatives of the "mentally ill" (and others who don't want them around) often are able to have them "hospitalized for treatment" against their will. Forcing people into institutions in this way is a practice some see as not unlike the Russian habit of confining dissidents in "mental institutions." (Anyone who speaks out against the government in Russia today must be crazy.) In a similar vein, Szasz argues, "we call self-starvation either anorexia nervosa, a hunger strike, a suicide attempt, or some other name, depending on how *we* want to respond."

4. Common Rhetorical Devices

Mind-numbing language of the doublespeak variety is only one of many kinds of rhetorical devices used to obfuscate, deceive, or otherwise manipulate via language. Emotively loaded language is, obviously, another. Let's now consider a few more of these common rhetorical tricks.

Slanting

Slanting is a form of misrepresentation. In one version, a true statement is made in such a way as to imply or suggest something else (which usually is either false or not known to be true). For example, a defense lawyer may try to blunt damaging testimony by stating "All this proves is that . . ." or "Since we willingly admit that . . ." implying that the testimony was of little importance when in fact it was quite damaging. Or an advertisement may say, "Try our best quality knife, *only* $9.95," implying that the price is very low, whether it is or not. (Notice that this statement is

> Neurotic means he is not as sensible as I am, and psychotic means he's even worse than my brother-in-law.
>
> — Karl Menninger, of the famous
>   Menninger Clinic

literally true—the knife is being sold for only $9.95—but implies what is probably false—that the knife is usually sold for much more.)

Slanting also can be accomplished by a careful selection of facts. (So slanting often involves the fallacy of *suppressed evidence.*) School textbooks are almost always written so as to slant the history of a nation and its leaders. For example, history texts used in American public schools select facts so as to make the United States look as good as possible in the eyes of young readers. The point of public school history texts is, after all (note that slanting expression), to turn young people into good citizens by making them proud of their nation.

But slanting occurs just about everywhere. We all naturally try to arrange facts so as to support our own point of view and refute our opponent's. This is most obvious in advertisements (since they rarely tell what's wrong with a product), but political rhetoric also is a good case in point. And anyway (another slanting term), political rhetoric is largely just advertising for political candidates.

Obviously, writers and speakers aren't going to tell you how they've slanted what they say very often. Perhaps the best defense against slanting (as against the fallacy of *suppressed evidence*) is to ask yourself whether you've been given all available relevant information, or whether something important has been omitted. Are there some unmentioned things you would need to know before making an intelligent

---

Monroe C. Beardsley was one of the first to write a textbook dealing strictly with critical thinking (as opposed to formal logic). In this excerpt from Thinking Straight, *he explains an example of what he calls "suggestion" (a kind of slanting):*

On November 30, 1968, *The New York Times* reported on the construction site for a new jetport in the Everglades, 40 miles from Miami:

> Populated now by deer, alligators, wild turkeys, and a tribe of Indians who annually perform a rite known as the Green Corn Dance, the tract could some-day accommodate a super jetport twice the size of Kennedy International in New York and still have a one-mile buffer on every side to minimize intrusions in the lives of any eventual residents.

A more horrible example of suggestion could hardly be found. First, note that by putting the Indians in a list with deer, alligators, and wild turkeys, the writer suggests that they belong in the same category as these subhuman species. This impression is reinforced by the allusion to the "Green Corn Dance," which . . . (since it is irrelevant to the rest of the story) can only suggest that this kind of silly superstitious activity sums up their lives. And the impression is driven home sharply at the end when we get to the need to "minimize intrusions on the lives of any *eventual* residents"—the Indians, of course, can hardly be counted as real residents. . . .

Thinking Straight (Fourth edition). Englewood Cliffs, N.J.: Prentice Hall, 1975.

judgment? If so, would the author be likely to know them? (If he would, but didn't reveal them, that's good reason to think the information may be damaging to his claim.)

Another important question to ask is whether the slanted material would convince you if you wanted very much to believe it *false*. If the answer is "no," then perhaps there would be self-deception or wishful thinking involved in the acceptance of that material.

Weasel Words

Weasel words are words or phrases that appear to make little or no change in the content of a statement while in fact sucking out all or most of its content.[13] For example, an anthropology student, apparently unsure of her facts, wrote that "Economic success *may be* the explanation of male dominance over females" (italics added). Using the expression *may be* instead of the usual verb *is* protected the student from error by reducing the content of her statement to close to zero. After all, given what she said, the economic success of males may *not* be the explanation of male dominance. (Note the assumption that males *do* dominate females in the last analysis.)

Fine Print Qualifications

Another common device is to unobtrusively take back in the (usually) unread fine print what is claimed in the most easily read part of an argument or document. Schlock insurance policies are notorious for using this device. They tout wonderful coverage in large type while taking away most of it in the small-print explanatory qualifications. Advertisements regularly do this by using a small asterisk to direct you to the bottom of the ad—where you find, for instance, that you have to buy the

---

Here is an item that illustrates how the way things are counted can be used to mask unfavorable information:

. . . , the committee [on doublespeak] voted a third place award to the Nuclear Regulatory Agency for its method of counting accidents at nuclear power plants and reporting them to Congress. In one report the agency detailed 400 "events" at nuclear plants, naming two of them "abnormal occurrences." But one of those "abnormal occurrences" included accidents at 19 different reactors. The 19 plants had a common design problem and the agency counts "generic" problems such as design flaws built into many different reactors as one problem, not 19. Another "abnormal occurrence" occurred so frequently (in 12 different reactors) that it was called a "normally expected occurrence."

Quarterly Review of Doublespeak (January 1981)

---

[13]This expression, which originated with Theodore Roosevelt, suggests the practice weasels have of making a small hole in eggs and sucking out their contents, so that what appears to be a normal egg is in fact just an empty shell.

> *Language sometimes is so slippery that it confuses not just those who hear it but also the users themselves. For instance, pollsters employ the phrase* margin of error *in a way that is slightly different from its more common usage, apparently (?) without realizing how their usage is misleading. In its primary sense,* margin of error *refers to the limitations of a measuring or manufacturing device. To say that a ruler has a margin of error of ±.01 inch means that even when used properly, we can be sure of our measurement only to within a hundredth of an inch. Similarly, to say that a device for making machine screws has a margin of error of ±.0001 inch means that when working properly, the screws it turns out will be of the desired diameter give or take at most a ten-thousandth of an inch. (In other words, all the screws it turns out when working well will have diameters within two ten-thousandths of an inch of each other.)*
>
> *But the margin of error of a poll is different. A Gallup poll said to have a margin of error of, say, 4 percent may still be mistaken by more than that amount, even when the poll is conducted perfectly. (Of course, in real life, no polls are conducted "perfectly"—another reason they sometimes are off by more than their stated margins of error.) In fact, the principles used to calculate the margin of error of a poll also predict that errors greater than the margin of error* will *happen once in a while, even when the poll is conducted properly.*

ticket 45 days in advance and stay at least 10 but not more than 30 days to qualify for the low air fare shouted in the headline.

5. Sexism in Language

In the last ten to fifteen years, a minor language revolution has been taking place as a result of the demands of women's rights advocates and because of a quickly evolving consensus against sexist language. An early sign of this consensus was the publication of "Guidelines for Equal Treatment of the Sexes . . ." by the McGraw-Hill publishing company, guidelines that were quickly adopted by most publishers. Here are some dos and don'ts listed in various places in the guidelines which show how far this part of the language revolution has gone:[14]

NO	YES
mankind	humanity, human beings, human race, people
If a man drove 50 miles at 60 m.p.h.	If a person (or driver) drove 50 miles at 60 m.p.h.
manmade	artificial, synthetic, manufactured, constructed of human origin
manpower	human power, human energy, workers, workforce

[14]Reprinted by permission of the McGraw-Hill Book Co.

NO	YES
grow to manhood	grow to adulthood, grow to manhood *or* womanhood

(1) Reword to eliminate unnecessary gender pronouns.

NO	YES
The average American drinks his coffee black.	The average American drinks black coffee.
(2) Recast into the plural.	Most Americans drink their coffee black.

(3) Replace the masculine pronoun with *one, he or she, her or his,* as appropriate. (Use *he or she* and its variations sparingly to avoid clumsy prose.)

(4) Alternate male and female expressions and examples.

NO	YES
I've often heard supervisors say, "He's not the right man for the job," or "He lacks the qualifications for success."	I've often heard supervisors say, "She's not right for the job," or "He lacks the qualifications for success."
congressman	member of Congress, Representative (but Congress*man* Koch and Congress*woman* Holzman)
businessman	business executive, business manager
fireman	fire fighter
mailman	mail carrier; letter carrier
salesman	sales representative; salesperson; sales clerk
chairman	the person presiding at (or chairing) a meeting; the presiding officer; the chair; head, leader, coordinator, moderator

NO	YES
the men and the ladies	the men and the women; the ladies and the gentlemen; the girls and the boys
man and wife	husband and wife

NO	**YES**
Bobby Riggs and Billie Jean	Bobby Riggs and Billie Jean King
Billie Jean and Riggs	Billie Jean and Bobby
Mrs. Meir and Moshe Dayan	Golda Meir and Moshe Dayan or Mrs. Meir and Mr. Dayan

NO	**YES**
the fair sex; the weaker sex	women
the girls or the ladies (when adult females are meant)	the women
girl, as in: I'll have my *girl* check that.	I'll have my *secretary* (or my *assistant*) check that. (Or use the person's name.)

NO	**YES**
Pioneers moved West, taking their wives and children with them.	Pioneer families moved West. Or Pioneer men and women (or pioneer couples) moved West, taking their children with them.

On the other hand, things can be carried too far. It would be silly, for instance, for Germans to stop referring to their homeland as the "Fatherland," or Englishmen—that is, ah, citizens of England—to their "mother tongue." Nor does there seem to be anything wrong with the predominantly male members of a ship referring to their particular tug as *she*. There are also questions of aesthetic taste—of what sounds right, or wrong, rolling off the tongue. The expression *her or his,* for instance, rings false, perhaps because it calls attention to the avoidance of *his or her,* or *his* (used to mean his or her) and thus distracts from what's being said. Similarly for the terms "Congressperson" and "Chairperson."

A *Wilmington Comment* on Governor Tribbitt's appointment of Irene Shadoan of the Associated Press as his press secretary at $20,000 a year: "If he wants to pay $10,000 a mammary, that's his business."

—From *Delaware State News,* reprinted in *Ms.* magazine

Can you imagine a similar remark about paying a man $10,000 a testicle?

Summary of Chapter Five

1. Most words have emotive meanings (in addition to cognitive meanings). Words like *oppression, kike,* and *bitch* have more or less negative (con) emotive overtones: words like *spring, free,* and *satisfaction* have positive (pro) emotive overtones; and words like *socialism, marijuana,* and *God* have mixed emotive overtones.

   Words that have roughly the same cognitive meaning often have radically different emotive meanings; the words *bureaucrat, government official,* and *public servant* illustrate this.

   The point of becoming aware of the emotive side of language is not to learn to avoid such language—the emotive element gives language much of its charm, interest, and importance. Emotively neutral language is dull. The point is to learn to use the emotive side of language effectively and not to be taken in by its misuses.

2. Con artists use the emotive side of language: (1) to mask cognitive meaning by whipping up emotions so that reason is overlooked, and (2) to dull the force of language so as to make acceptable what otherwise might not be. The latter often is accomplished by means of euphemisms (less offensive expressions used in place of more offensive ones) or a kind of doublespeak that lulls the unwary into acceptance.

3. It should also be noted that the meanings of words and expressions sometimes are changed so as either to get around or to take advantage of laws, rules, or customs. (Example: calling an employee a *subcontractor* to avoid paying a minimum wage or social security.)

4. Common rhetorical devices are often used to obfuscate. Examples are slanting words and expressions ("All this proves is that . . ."), weasel words that suck the meaning out of a sentence ("Economic success *may be* . . ."), and fine print qualifications that take back part of what was originally claimed ("* . . . with ticket purchased before October 15 but not valid on flights starting Friday or Sunday").

5. The English language contains features that mirror sexist attitudes of our past. The McGraw-Hill guidelines have been adopted by most publishers to rid written English of these locutions. For example, they require us to replace the word *man* by *person* whenever gender is not an issue.

Exercise 5-1

1. Here is a *New York Daily News* editorial (April 5, 1972):

Any Old Jobs for Homos?

Herewith, a cheer for the U.S. Supreme Court's ruling Monday (with Justice W. O. Douglas dissenting—but you knew that) that states governments have a right to refuse employment to homosexuals.

   Fairies, nances, swishes, fags, lezzes—call 'em what you please—should of course be permitted to earn honest livings in nonsensitive jobs.

But government, from federal on down, should have full freedom to bar them from jobs in which their peculiarities would make them security or other risks. It is to be hoped that this Supreme Court decision will stand for the foreseeable future.

    a. List the heavily emotive words or expressions and other rhetorical devices you feel are used unfairly, explaining *why* in each case.

    b. Rewrite the editorial so that its cognitive import is the same, but the language used is as emotively neutral as possible. Compare your version with the original editorial for persuasive power.

2. Discuss what you think (and why, of course) of the following explanation (in Robert J. Ringer's *Looking Out for Number One*) of President Kennedy's famous statement, "And so, my fellow Americans, ask not what your country can do for you; ask what you can do for your country":

Ask what you can do for your *country?* Does this mean asking each of the more than 200 million individuals what you can do for him? No, individuals are not what Kennedy or any other politician has ever had in mind when using the word *country.* A country is an abstract entity, but in politicalese, it translates into "those in power." Restated in translated form, then, it becomes: Ask not what those in power can do for you; ask what you can do for those in power.

3. Try to find some examples of inappropriate names being applied to things so that the law, custom, or whatever will deal with these things differently, and explain the chicanery.

*4. Translate the following excerpt from *Usable Knowledge: Social Science and Social Problem Solving,* by Charles F. Lindblom and David K. Cohen (mentioned in a book review in the *Washington Monthly*):

By social problem solving, we mean processes that are to eventuate in outcomes that by some standard are an improvement on the previously existing situation, or are presumed to so eventuate, or are conceived of as offering some possibility to so eventuate.

5. Here is a passage from a United States history textbook, *America: Its People and Values,* by Leonard C. Wood, Ralph H. Gabriel, and Edward L. Biller:

A friendly Indian named Squanto helped the colonists. He showed them how to plant corn and how to live in the wilderness. A soldier, Captain Miles Standish, taught the Pilgrims how to defend themselves against unfriendly Indians.

    How is language used to slant this account? In what other ways is it slanted?

6. Translate the following quotation from Woodrow Wilson into the most succinct form you can, and compare both versions for persuasive power and understandability:

The men who act, stand nearer to the mass of man than the men who write; and it is in their hands that new thought gets its translation into the crude language of deeds.

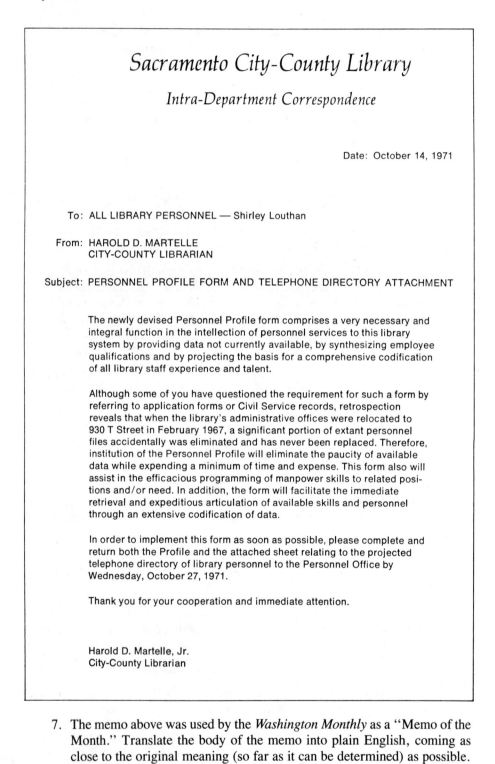

Sacramento City-County Library

Intra-Department Correspondence

Date: October 14, 1971

To: ALL LIBRARY PERSONNEL — Shirley Louthan

From: HAROLD D. MARTELLE
CITY-COUNTY LIBRARIAN

Subject: PERSONNEL PROFILE FORM AND TELEPHONE DIRECTORY ATTACHMENT

The newly devised Personnel Profile form comprises a very necessary and integral function in the intellection of personnel services to this library system by providing data not currently available, by synthesizing employee qualifications and by projecting the basis for a comprehensive codification of all library staff experience and talent.

Although some of you have questioned the requirement for such a form by referring to application forms or Civil Service records, retrospection reveals that when the library's administrative offices were relocated to 930 T Street in February 1967, a significant portion of extant personnel files accidentally was eliminated and has never been replaced. Therefore, institution of the Personnel Profile will eliminate the paucity of available data while expending a minimum of time and expense. This form also will assist in the efficacious programming of manpower skills to related positions and/or need. In addition, the form will facilitate the immediate retrieval and expeditious articulation of available skills and personnel through an extensive codification of data.

In order to implement this form as soon as possible, please complete and return both the Profile and the attached sheet relating to the projected telephone directory of library personnel to the Personnel Office by Wednesday, October 27, 1971.

Thank you for your cooperation and immediate attention.

Harold D. Martelle, Jr.
City-County Librarian

7. The memo above was used by the *Washington Monthly* as a "Memo of the Month." Translate the body of the memo into plain English, coming as close to the original meaning (so far as it can be determined) as possible.

8. Check the media (newspapers, magazines, television, radio, books) and find several examples of doublespeak or jargon, and translate them into plain English.

9. Check the media for sexist uses of language, and translate so as to remove the sexist connotations.

10. Find an article somewhere that's loaded with emotive or gimmicky language, and explain how this use of language would tend to be persuasive (or, perhaps, if overdone, backfire). Then rewrite the article in plain English and compare with the original.

11. Check your automobile insurance policy (or somebody's insurance policy). If it isn't written in the new clear style, rewrite the first 250 words or so to say the same thing in plain English. (Lots of luck.)

Good thinking requires being able to put two and two together to get four.

The prejudice against careful analytic procedure is part of the human impatience with technique which arises from the fact that men are interested in results and would like to attain them without the painful toil which is the essence of our moral finitude.
—Morris R. Cohen

There is no expedient to which a man will not resort to avoid the real labor of thinking.
—Sir Joshua Reynolds

6

Analyzing and Constructing Extended Arguments

So far we have considered relatively short arguments, and these mainly to illustrate fallacious reasoning. But in daily life we usually encounter longer passages, containing several connected arguments. It takes more than just the ability to spot fallacies to deal with such extended passages.

1. How to Analyze Extended Passages

There are almost as many ways to analyze extended arguments as there are analyzers. What works best for one person may not work well for someone else. And time and interest also play a role. Even so, there are guidelines that are useful for most people, in particular for those who initially have a bit of trouble handling lengthier arguments.

Find the Thesis and Keep It in Mind

The most important thing, obviously, is to find the author's main conclusion or **thesis.** (Occasionally there is more than one.) The thesis isn't always obvious, because the passage may be poorly written, or the author may build up to it and put it near the end. The thesis is the point of the passage, so you have to keep it in mind to determine whether the author provides sufficient *reasons* for accepting it. In sports, the trick is to keep your eye on the ball. In analyzing extended passages, it's to keep your mind's eye on the thesis.

Find the Reasons Supporting the Thesis

The next thing to do, obviously, is to find the *reasons,* or *premises,* supporting the author's thesis, or main conclusion. Again, this will be hard or easy depending on the author's style and competence. But it may also be hard because the reasons themselves are supported by reasons, and so on. A simple example is the newspaper columnist who argued that cigarettes should be made illegal because they kill so many people and anything so bad for us should be illegal. He then went on to argue for his claim that cigarette smoking is indeed deadly by providing overwhelming statistical evidence. So the logical structure of his extended argument was something like this:

> *Thesis:* Cigarettes could be made illegal.
> *Reasons:* (1) Cigarettes are deadly, and (2) anything so deadly should be illegal.
> *Reasons for (1):* Statistical proof linking smoking cigarettes with lung cancer, emphysema, and heart disease.

He took it for granted that anything so lethal should not be legal.

Skip Whatever Doesn't Support the Thesis

People write to persuade other people. So they include irrelevant material whenever they think that it will help convince others. This kind of "flavoring" material makes reading more fun, but you don't want to be influenced by it when analyzing a passage that you're serious about. Anecdotes and especially introductory flavorings are great but generally irrelevant to the job of proving the thesis.

Add Relevant Information

Everything needed to prove a thesis is never—that means *never*—included in any argument, no matter how long. To do that would require dragging in big chunks of a writer's world view, as well as proving things that are obvious or generally accepted. Good writers try to provide just the information their audience will need. Someone writing about education, say for an audience of teachers, generally wouldn't bother to prove that a great many public school students graduate from high school today without a solid background in reading, writing, and arithmetic. Proving this for that audience would amount to useless overkill.

In addition, being human, writers often neglect a point that they should have included or (worse) argue fallaciously when a cogent argument is available. So you should provide whatever reasons you know that support the thesis of the passage, as well as the things you know that contradict it. That is, you should analyze the best version of an argument you can think of, even if the writer's argument is less good.

Come to an Evaluation

While evaluation is logically the last thing we need to do in argument analysis, good argument analyzers tend to start evaluating as soon as they come across the thesis. They keep in mind questions like, Do I already accept this thesis? Does it fit well with what I already know? If not, what sort of evidence or reasons might change my mind? And they continue to evaluate as they go along, bearing in mind such questions as, Is this reason acceptable without further argument? Does that reason defend the thesis, or just a straw version of it? Do the facts referred to seem plausible, given my background beliefs? Is there some serious counter-argument the writer seems to be forgetting?

Of course, a completely confident judgment can't be reached until the whole extended argument has been gone through, and at least something of its structure has been figured out. When the entire structure of an extended argument has been figured out, all of its relevant passages will divide into those that are argued for within the argument as a whole and those that are not. The latter are the writer's basic "starting points"—assumed without being justified. When thoroughly evaluating an extended passage, you need to ask and answer three basic questions, corresponding to the three basic requirements of good reasoning (discussed in Chapter One): (1) Are the writer's starting points justified by what you already believe? (2) Do you know other relevant reasons or arguments? (If so, you should add them, of course.) And (3) Do the starting points (plus any relevant material you may have added) justify acceptance of the thesis? That is, is the reasoning valid?

If there is a starting point that isn't justified by your background beliefs, or if you know of relevant information that refutes or casts doubt on the thesis, or if the reasoning is not completely valid, then clearly you should not accept the thesis of the argument.

A note of caution: It's common for some of the subsidiary arguments in a lengthy passage to be cogent while others are fallacious. In these cases, the right thing to do is to accept only the untainted portions of the overall argument. You don't want to automatically toss out the whole extended passage, because in many cases other relevant information can be added from your store of background beliefs to make the main thesis of the whole passage acceptable.

It's also important to remember that the reasons given in an argument may, strictly speaking, not be premises of the kind given in formal logic texts. We're thinking here of *reasons* in the wide sense that makes any kind of support a reason. For instance, here is a passage in which the ancient Greek philosopher Plato used *examples* to support his conclusion:

> Take this matter of doing right. Can we say that it really consists in nothing more nor less than telling the truth and paying back anything we may have received? Are not these very actions sometimes right and sometimes wrong? Suppose, for example, a friend who has lent us a weapon were to go mad and then ask for it back. Surely anyone would say that we ought not to return it. It would not be right to do so; nor yet to tell the truth without reserve to a madman. Right conduct, then, cannot be defined as telling the truth and restoring anything we have been trusted with.

In this passage, Plato's reason for refusing to define right conduct in a certain way is that there are examples which don't fit that definition. Similarly, a writer may argue for a thesis by reminding the reader of something, by presenting a comparison or analogy, or by showing that an opposing view is incorrect. (Convincing people of something often requires forcing them to first give up wishful thinking, or at least to give up a contrary view.)

Exercise 6-1

For each of the following, find the thesis, find the reasons, explicit or implicit, supporting the thesis (and any reasons supporting the reasons), and isolate the extraneous material (whatever doesn't support the thesis or the reasons). Then rewrite the passage in your own words, as in the following example.

Example: Original Passage (from a speech by President Reagan):

As many of you know, our administration has . . . strongly backed an amendment that will permit school children to hold prayer in our schools. (Applause) We believe that school children deserve the same protection, the same constitutional consensus that permits prayer in the Houses of Congress, chaplains in our armed services, and the motto on our coinage that says, "In God We Trust." (Applause) I grant you, possibly, we can make a case that prayer is needed more in Congress than in our schools, but. . . . (Laughter, applause)

Rewritten passage:

Thesis: We should pass an amendment permitting prayers in public schools. *Reason:* School children deserve the same protection (he meant "*the same rights*") under the Constitution as it gives to Congress, the armed services, and coins. *Extraneous material:* We can probably make out a better case for the need for congressional prayers.

1. *Richard Nixon:* Some people, quite properly appalled at the abuses that occurred, will say that Watergate demonstrated the bankruptcy of the American political system. I believe precisely the opposite is true. Watergate represented a series of illegal acts and bad judgments by a number of individuals. It was the system that has brought the facts to light and that will bring those guilty to justice.[1]

2. *Baruch Brody* [on the abortion issue]: There is a continuity of development from the moment of conception on. There are constant changes in the foetal condition; the foetus is constantly acquiring new structures and characteristics, but there is no one state which is radically different from any other. Since this is so, there is no one stage in the process of foetal development after the moment of conception which could plausibly be picked out as the moment at which the foetus becomes a living human being. The moment of conception is, however, different in this respect. It marks the beginning of this continuous process of development and introduces something new which is radically discontinuous with what has come before it. Therefore, the moment of conception, and only it, is a plausible candidate for being that moment at which the foetus becomes a living human being.[2]

3. *Florida Democratic Senator Lawton Chiles:* Citizens have the right to know how their Government works; yet, lobbying is largely hidden from public view even though it has enormous impact on legislation. Of an estimated 15,000 lobbyists in Washington, only about 2,000 are registered and

---

[1]*The White House Transcripts* (New York: Bantam Books, 1974).
[2]*Abortion: Pro and Con,* ed. Robert Perkins (Cambridge: Schenkman Publishing, 1974).

little of an estimated $2 billion a year spent for lobbying is being reported. This is allowed by current law loopholes, loopholes that legislation I am sponsoring would plug. The public understandably is suspicious of that which is hidden from it, and this suspicion creates doubts about the integrity of both lobbyists and the legislative process. We must have greater lobbying disclosure.[3]

*4. *Thomas Paine, in his classic* The Age of Reason: Revelation is a communication of something which the person to whom that thing is revealed did not know before. For if I have done a thing, or seen it done, it needs no revelation to tell me I have done it or seen it, nor to enable me to tell it or to write it. Revelation, therefore, cannot be applied to anything done upon earth, of which man himself is the actor or the witness; and consequently, all the historical and anecdotal parts of the Bible, which is almost the whole of it, is not within the meaning and compass of the word 'revelation,' and therefore, is not the word of God.

5. *Astronomer Fred Hoyle:* Perhaps you may think that the whole question of the creation of the Universe could be avoided in some way. But this is not so. To avoid the issue of creation it would be necessary for all the material in the Universe to be infinitely old, and this it cannot be for a very practical reason. For if this were so, there could be no hydrogen left in the Universe. . . . Hydrogen is being steadily converted into helium throughout the Universe and this conversion is a one-way process—that is to say, hydrogen cannot be produced in any appreciable quantity through the breakdown of other elements. How comes it then that the Universe consists almost entirely of hydrogen? If matter were infinitely old this would be quite impossible. So we see that the Universe being what it is, the creation issue simply cannot be dodged.

6. *John Locke, in his classic* The Second Treatise on Government: Though the earth and all inferior creatures be common to all men, yet every man has a property in his own person; this nobody has any right to but himself. The labor of his body and the work of his hands, we may say, are properly his. Whatsoever then he removes out of the state that nature has provided and left it in, he has mixed his labor with, and joined to it something that is his own, and thereby makes it his property. It being by him removed from the common state nature has placed it in, it has by this labor something annexed to it that excluded the common right of other men. For this labor being the unquestionable property of the laborer, no man but he can have a right to what that is once joined to, at least where there is enough and as good left in common for others.

7. It also appears that suicide no longer repels us. The suicide rate is climbing, especially among blacks and young people. What's more, suicide has been appearing in an increasingly favorable light in the nation's press. When Paul Cameron surveyed all articles on suicide indexed over the past 50 years in the *Reader's Guide to Periodical Literature,* he found that volun-

tary death, once portrayed as a brutal waste, now generally appears in a neutral light. Some recent articles even present suicide as a good thing to do and are written in a manner that might encourage the reader to take his own life under certain circumstances. Last year, a majority of Americans under 30 told Gallup pollsters that incurable disease or continual pain confer on a person the moral right to end his life.[4]

8. *Ayn Rand:* By what conceivable standard can the policy of price-fixing be a crime when practiced by businessmen, but a public benefit when practiced by the government? There are many industries in peacetime—trucking, for instance—whose prices are fixed by the government. If price-fixing is harmful to competition, to industry, to production, to consumers, to the whole economy, and to the "public interest"—as the advocates of the anti-trust laws have claimed—then how can that same harmful policy become beneficial in the hands of the government? Since there is no rational answer to this question, I suggest that you question the economic knowledge, the purpose and the motives of the champions of antitrust.[5]

9. *From a speech by President Ronald Reagan:* I . . . strongly believe, as you have been told, that the protection of innocent life is, and has always been, a legitimate, indeed, the first duty of government. Believing that, I favor human life. (Applause) And I believe in the human life legislation. The senate now has three proposals on this matter from Senators Hatch, Helms, and Hatfield. The national tragedy of abortion on demand must end. (Applause) I am urging the Senate to give these proposals the speedy consideration they deserve. A Senate Committee hearing was held recently to determine, if we can, when life actually begins. And there was exhaustive testimony of experts presenting both views. And, finally, the result was declared inconclusive. They could not arrive at an answer. Well, in my view alone, they did arrive at an answer, an answer that justifies the proposed legislation. If it is true we do not know when the unborn becomes a human life, then we have to opt in favor that it is a human life until someone proves it isn't. (Applause)

10. Segregation of white and colored children in public schools has a detrimental effect upon the colored children. The impact is greater when it has the sanction of the law; for the policy of separating the races is usually interpreted as denoting the inferiority of the negro group. A sense of inferiority affects the motivation of a child to learn. Segregation with the sanction of law, therefore, has a tendency to [retard] the educational and mental development of negro children and to deprive them of some of the benefits they would receive in a racially integrated school system.[6]

11. *B. F. Skinner:* The concept of responsibility is particularly weak when behavior is traced to genetic determiners. We may admire beauty, grace,

---

[4]Elizabeth Hall and Paul Cameron, in *Psychology Today,* April 1976.

[5]*Capitalism: The Unknown Idea* (New York: New American Library, 1966).

[6]From the 1954 U.S. Supreme Court decision in *Brown* v. *Topeka Board of Education,* which declared segregated schools inherently unequal and thus unconstitutional.

and sensitivity, but we do not blame a person because he is ugly, spastic, or color blind. Less conspicuous forms of genetic endowment nevertheless cause trouble. Individuals presumably differ, as species differ, in the extent to which they respond aggressively or are reinforced when they engage in sexual behavior or are affected by sexual reinforcement. Are they, therefore, equally responsible for controlling their aggressive or sexual behavior, and is it fair to punish them to the same extent? If we do not punish a person for a club foot, should we punish him for being quick to anger or highly susceptible to sexual reinforcement? The issue has recently been raised by the possibility that many criminals show an anomaly in their chromosomes. The concept of responsibility offers little help. The issue is controllability. We cannot change genetic defects by punishment; we can work only through genetic measures which operate on a much longer time scale. What must be changed is not the responsibility of autonomous man but the conditions, environmental or genetic, of which a person's behavior is a function.[7]

12. *Howard K. Smith, in a commentary on* ABC Evening News: Our thinking about inflation is paralyzed by a cliché. It is, as repeated by Mr. Roy Ash today: "Inflation is too complex to understand, and there are no easy answers." I beg to argue that it is not that complex, and there are answers.

The trouble is too much money in the system chasing too few goods and services. So prices keep going up. There is too much money mainly because too many are getting more income than their production justifies. They get too much because they get from Congress subsidies, as in shipping and a hundred other industries, tax breaks as in oil and a thousand other industries, rulings by regulatory agencies allowing artificially high prices, as in trucking and other industries.

Probably most industries of any size are featherbedded by favors, allowed to be inefficient and to take more from the national pie than they contribute. A solution is a combing out of inefficient industries, stopping their breaks, subsidies, and fixed prices. Make them earn their way in free competition.

Of course, many of them would fail without artificial help. They won't let that happen while they have clout with Congress. The cause of inflation is not complexity. It is a want of political courage. It will remain as long as our politicians depend on special interests to get and hold office.[8]

13. *Thomas Szasz:* Psychiatry is conventionally defined as a medical specialty concerned with the diagnosis and treatment of mental diseases. I submit that this definition, which is widely accepted, places psychiatry in the company of alchemy and astrology and commits it to the category of pseudoscience. The reason for this is that there is no such thing as "mental illness." Psychiatrists must now choose between continuing to define their discipline in terms of nonexistent entities or substantives, or redefining it in terms of the actual interventions or processes in which they engage. . . .

---

[7]*Beyond Freedom and Dignity* (New York: Alfred A. Knopf, 1971).
[8]September 3, 1974.

Until the middle of the nineteenth century, and beyond, illness meant a bodily disorder whose typical manifestation was an alteration of a bodily structure: that is, a visible deformity, disease, or lesion, such as a misshapen extremity, ulcerated skin, or a fracture or wound. Since in this original meaning of it, illness was identified by altered bodily structure, physicians distinguished diseases from nondiseases according to whether or not they could detect an abnormal change in the structure of a person's body. This is why, after dissection of the body was permitted, anatomy became the basis of medical science: by this means physicians were able to identify numerous alterations in the structure of the body which were not otherwise apparent. As more specialized methods of examining bodily tissues and fluids developed, the pathologist's skills in detecting hitherto unknown bodily diseases grew explosively. . . .

It is important to understand clearly that modern psychiatry—and the identification of new psychiatric diseases—began not by identifying such diseases by means of the established methods of pathology, but by creating a new criterion of what constitutes disease: to the established criterion of detectable alteration of *bodily structure* was now added the fresh criterion of alteration of *bodily function;* and, as the former was detected by observing the patient's body, so the latter was detected by observing his behavior. This is how and why conversion hysteria became the prototype of this new class of diseases—appropriately named "mental" to distinguish them from those that are "organic," and appropriately called also "functional" in contrast to those that are "structural." Thus, whereas in modern medicine new diseases were *discovered,* in modern psychiatry they were *invented.* Paresis was *proved* to be a disease; hysteria was *declared* to be one.[9]

2. Quick Appraisals of Arguments

In real life, outside of the classroom, people seldom spend a lot of time on any particular extended argument. This is certainly true of the mass of readers. But even the most critical of us only occasionally go over a newspaper editorial, political column, or whatever with a fine-tooth comb. Exact analysis is regularly done only by lawyers and such types, or by someone commenting on or replying to someone else's arguments (as in a debate or school assignment).

This doesn't mean it isn't a good idea to develop the skill needed for close analysis. Aside from being useful in those few cases when close analysis is needed, practice at it will improve your general ability to more quickly assess extended passages.

The key to good, quick appraisals is the ability to do the basic processes of a more systematic appraisal informally and quickly.

First, you want to find the *thesis* (or theses), so that you can keep it (or them) in the back of your mind when reading the passage. Some people like to make a mark in the margin where the thesis occurs; others underline; still others just keep the thesis firmly in their mind.

When the thesis is stated right off, there's no problem in finding it. In other cases, you may have a pretty good idea what the thesis is anyway. For instance, if the first few sentences of an essay describe how human an aborted fetus looks, you can figure the thesis is going to be antiabortion. But if in doubt, skip around, especially to the last paragraph or two, to find the main point. That's one of the great advantages of written material over speeches, television, and radio, so take advantage of it. You don't have to read an essay in the order it was written.

Second, read the passage with an eye for the *reasons* given to support the thesis (and, when the reasons aren't acceptable to you straight off, for the reasons supporting the reasons). Again, some people like to mark the important reasons in the margin, others underline, and still others just firmly plant them in their mind. The point is to get an idea of the basic thrust of the extended argument without working out its complete structure and without putting anything down on paper.

And third, as you read, bring to bear your *background knowledge and beliefs,* making preliminary evaluations as you go along. Reasons pro or con may occur to you that the author of the argument has overlooked entirely. And bringing to bear what you already believe should guide your reading by helping you to know what you want to look out for.

Remember, in real life people read critical essays to find out things they didn't know before or to correct old ideas. Suppose, for instance, the thesis of an essay is that abortion should be made illegal because it's murder. You have probably already heard quite a few arguments pro and con and come to some conclusions on the issue. Perhaps you feel that abortion is all right—that arguments against it are wrong because they consider the fetus to be a human being (a baby), while you're inclined to think it isn't. If so, then for you the key question when reading an antiabortion tract is whether it gives any good reasons for thinking a fetus is indeed a human being. If it does, you may have to change your mind on the abortion issue (which means reading the article was very profitable, since the point of reading critical material is either to expand or to change your opinions). If it doesn't, you probably won't have to change your mind (which means reading the article wasn't very useful). Of course, there's always the possibility that the author will take a completely original tack, say by arguing that abortion is wrong even though a fetus isn't human. In that case, you want to bring your background beliefs to bear on the reasons presented for this unexpected way of looking at the issue.

So, quick appraisal boils down to swiftly doing the things that any good analysis must do: Keeping your eye on the thesis; looking for reasons to support it; and bringing your background beliefs to bear in evaluating or supplementing the reasons. This means not getting distracted or moved by flavoring material, fancy language, or irrelevant asides. Keep your mind's eye on the issue!

Oh, yes. One of the reasons for developing the knack of quick appraisal is to save time—to keep you from struggling through a whole extended essay only to find out that you've learned next to nothing. Quickly getting to the nub of an article often lets you know that the best thing to do is toss it aside and go on to something else. There are wonderful things out there to read on almost any topic, but there's much more chaff than wheat. Skipping the chaff is half the battle.

An Example of a Quick Appraisal

To illustrate how a passage can be analyzed rather quickly without formally laying out its entire structure, here is one person's quick look at a portion of a very famous political tract, Adolf Hitler's *Mein Kampf* (from the chapter called "Nation and Race").[10] The chapter starts out this way:

> There are some truths which are so obvious that for this very reason they are not seen or at least not recognized by ordinary people. They sometimes pass by such truisms as though blind and are most astonished when someone suddenly discovers what everyone really ought to know. Columbus's eggs lie around by the hundreds of thousands, but Columbuses are met with less frequently.

So far, all we have is flavoring material, but no substance. So we have nothing as yet to keep in mind.

> Thus men without exception wander about in the garden of Nature; they imagine that they know practically everything and yet with few exceptions pass blindly by one of the most patent principles of Nature's rule: the inner segregation of the species of all living beings on this earth.

Now, it's time to mark the page, or make a mental note. Is the thesis going to be the natural segregation of species? If not, is this going to be used later to support some other thesis? The title of the chapter, "Nation and Race," suggests the thesis may be that various human racial groups should not interbreed. (Those with background information about Hitler would be likely to reach the same tentative conclusion.) Let's see.

> Even the most superficial observation shows that Nature's restricted form of propagation and increase is an almost rigid basic law of all the innumerable forms of expression of her vital urge. Every animal mates only with a member of the same species. The titmouse seeks the titmouse, the finch the finch, the stork the stork, the field mouse the field mouse, the dormouse the dormouse, the wolf the she-wolf, etc. . . . .

Here we have evidence for the "thesis" (in quotes, because we can't yet be sure it *is* his thesis) that animals mate only with members of their own species. While not strictly true (lions and tigers have been mated in captivity), experience shows it is generally true.

> Any crossing of two beings not at exactly the same level produces a medium between the level of the two parents. This means: the offspring will probably stand higher than the racially lower parent, but not as high as the higher one. Consequently, it will later succumb in the struggle against the higher level.

Here is the first substantive statement that seems grossly wrong, in that it seems to contradict any reasonable interpretation of the theory of evolution. For instance, there is reason to say that mating a large dog and a small one will produce medium-

---

[10]From Ralph Manheim's translation (Boston: Houghton Mifflin, 1971), pp. 284–87. Reprinted by permission of Houghton Mifflin Co. and Hutchinson Publishing Group Ltd.

sized offspring on the average, but labeling one dog "higher" and the other "lower" seems to be an unwarranted value judgment. Is a Great Dane "higher" than a dachshund?

Notice also that at this point Hitler has to be talking about breeding *within* a species, because he's just argued that breeding doesn't occur between species. So he implies that some races or breeds within a species are "higher" than others. Will he provide evidence for this, showing, say, that German dachshunds are higher or lower than French poodles? Or that Aryans are higher than Latins, Slavs, or Jews? And will he use the idea of higher and lower races (within species) to support the thesis that human races shouldn't interbreed? If so, the acceptability of his reasons supporting his claim that some racial types are "higher" than others may be crucial.

> Such mating is contrary to the will of Nature for a higher breeding of all life. The precondition for this does not lie in associating superior and inferior, but in the total victory of the former. The stronger must dominate and not blend with the weaker, thus sacrificing his own greatness. Only the born weakling can view this as cruel, but he after all is only a weak and limited man; for if this law did not prevail, any conceivable higher development of organic living beings would be unthinkable.

Hitler saw animals evolving from a lower to a higher state, something most of us would deny, although we might agree that there is a tendency to evolve from the simpler to the more complex, as a fly is much more complex than an amoeba. But suppose we allow that more complicated animals are "higher" than less complicated ones. Then it will be true that higher animals don't breed with lower, since only animals of roughly the same complexity ever breed successfully (like a Great Dane with a dachshund or a lion with a tiger). In this sense, the "will of nature" is against the interbreeding of "higher" with "lower" animals.

> The consequence of this urge toward racial purity, universally valid in Nature, is not only the sharp outward delimitation of the various races, but their uniform character in themselves. The fox is always a fox, the goose a goose, the tiger a tiger, etc., and the difference can lie at most in the varying measure of force, strength, intelligence, dexterity, endurance, etc., of the individual specimens. But you will never find a fox who in his inner attitude might, for example, show humanitarian tendencies toward geese, as similarly there is no cat with a friendly inclination toward mice.
>
> Therefore, here, too, the struggle among themselves arises less from inner aversion than from hunger and love. In both cases, Nature looks on calmly, with satisfaction, in fact. In the struggle for daily bread all those who are weak and sickly or less determined succumb, while the struggle of the males for the female grants the right or opportunity to propagate only to the healthiest. And the struggle is always a means for improving a species' health and power of resistance and, therefore, a cause of its higher development. . . .

Putting aside Hitler's anthropomorphisms (he seems to think of "nature" as a living person), we can see what he's getting at. This is his way of saying that species evolve from lesser to greater complexity by competing for food and mates within a species, which certainly is in accord with the main thrust of the theory of evolution (there are exceptions, but they're not important here).

> No more than Nature desires the mating of weaker with stronger individuals, even less does she desire the blending of a higher with a lower race, since, if she did, her whole work of higher breeding, over perhaps hundreds of thousands of years, might be ruined with one blow.

Now he is talking about races, not species. So he seems to be saying that just as members of a higher species can't interbreed with those of a lower one, so members of a higher race shouldn't mate with those of a lower. Will he *argue* for this idea that one race is "higher" than another? (Remember, we were willing to allow that some species are higher than others only if he meant by this that they are more complex. But all human races are equally complicated.) And will he justify his move from what he claims *is* the case (that higher species don't interbreed with lower) to what he says *should* be the case (that higher races should not interbreed with lower)?

> Historical experience offers countless proofs of this. It shows with terrifying clarity that in every mingling of Aryan blood with that of lower peoples the result was the end of the cultured people. North America, whose population consists in by far the largest part of Germanic elements who mixed but little with the lower colored peoples, shows a different humanity and culture from Central and South America, where the predominantly Latin immigrants often mixed with the aborigines on a large scale. By this one example, we can clearly and distinctly recognize the effect of racial mixture. The Germanic inhabitant of the American continent, who has remained racially pure and umixed, rose to be master of the continent; he will remain the master as long as he does not fall a victim to defilement of the blood.

This is the second justification Hitler gives in this part of *Mein Kampf* for his ideas on racial superiority. (Elsewhere, he gives similar, equally bad, arguments to support this belief.) The trouble with this argument is that the North American "Aryans" (he thought of the English as Aryan cousins) have been happily interbreeding with Latin Italians, Slavic Russians, and all sorts of other non-Aryan groups, even occasionally including Jews, Orientals, and blacks, yet still are masters of North America. And worse still for Hitler's argument, those foolish Latinos who did interbreed with the natives became and still are the masters of Central and South America.

Anyway, immense amounts of history contradict Hitler's thesis about the superiority of the Aryans. To mention just one point, the most powerful civilizations up to about A.D. 1400 were Chinese, Indian, Egyptian, and so on, never German. So on Hitler's criteria these "races" were superior, or higher. Yet there is no significant genetic difference between, say, Chinese people in A.D. 1000 and today, or between Germans in A.D. 1000 and today. (Hitler also overlooked, assuming he knew, the fact that his beloved German "race" itself evolved from countless cases of interbreeding with surrounding groups, since all current human populations seem to have arisen in this way.) By bringing superior background beliefs to bear, we see that Hitler's main justification for his thesis is defective.

At this point, Hitler sums up his argument as follows:

> The result of all racial crossing is therefore in brief always the following:
> (a) Lowering of the level of the higher race;
> (b) Physical and intellectual regression and hence the beginning of a slowly but surely progressing sickness.
>
> To bring about such a development is, then, nothing else but to sin against the will of the eternal creator.
>
> And as a sin this act is rewarded.
>
> When man attempts to rebel against the iron logic of Nature, he comes into struggle with the principles to which he himself owes his existence as a man.
> And this attack must lead to his own doom.

We now can see that Hitler has given us essentially two arguments for his thesis. The first is that in nature higher races don't mix with lower, and so higher human races shouldn't mix with lower. This argument is doubly defective. For one thing, it constitutes a gigantic *equivocation* on the term *race,* which in one sense refers to a *species* (as when we say we all belong to the human *race*) and in another sense refers to groups within a species (as when we say that there are three or four basic human *races,* just as there are many breeds of dogs). He proves that species don't interbreed but not that races (in the latter sense) don't. And for another thing, his argument justifies the idea that races (meaning "species") *don't* interbreed, but it says nothing to prove that they (now meaning "races") *shouldn't* interbreed. He admits they *can* interbreed, because he wants to stop Germans from interbreeding with other races. (He thus commits the error philosophers describe as going from *is* to *ought* or *should* without explaining how the gap between the two is bridged.

Hitler's second argument is an appeal to what happened in the Americas, where Germans didn't but Latins did interbreed with the native populations. But as we just saw, this argument also is grossly defective.

Notice in parting that by trying to figure out where Hitler's argument was going to go as we were reading it, and by bringing our background knowledge and beliefs to bear, we were able to quickly dispose of his argument without using margin notes or a summary, and without analyzing every word and phrase. In real life, that's the knack needed to cope with the flood of "information" that washes past us every day.

3. The Margin Note-Summary Method

Although a quick analysis of reading material is satisfactory in most cases in every-day life, sometimes we need to use a better method. While there is no one method that is best for everyone, many people find that using margin notes, or combining margin notes with a summary, works well when a close analysis is required. (Even those who might naturally develop some other method will find that a margin note-summary method is very *effective*.)

The margin note-summary method is based on the idea that a summary is more easily digested than the original material and therefore more accurately evaluated.

(Of course, the summary must be accurate to begin with.) There are four basic steps in the margin note-summary method:

1. Read the material to be evaluated.

2. Read it through again, this time marking the important passages with an indication of content written in the margin, taking advantage of what was learned from the first reading. (Margin notes need not be full sentences, or grammatically correct, and may contain abbreviations or shorthand notations.)

3. Use the margin notes to construct a summary of the passage.

4. Evaluate the original material by evaluating the summary, checking the original to be sure there are no differences between the two which are relevant to the evaluation.

Two things need to be said about using the margin note-summary method. First, when we skip part of a passage, we make a value judgment that the skipped material is relatively unimportant. It takes practice and skill to know what to include and what to omit, and "experts" will differ on such matters. And, second, margin notes and summaries are shorthand devices and should thus be briefer than the passage analyzed. But any shortening runs the risk of falsification. When using margin notes or summaries to aid in reasoning, remember that we don't want to be guilty of the *straw man* fallacy by drawing conclusions from the shortened version that would not be valid for the original.

Let's use a newspaper editorial[11] to illustrate the margin note-summary method. The margin notes are already attached. (This editorial was written before the Hitler diaries were exposed as a fraud.)

Hitler Diaries Deduction

Rising controversy over authenticity of the newly surfaced diaries of Adolf Hitler was to be expected in view of the spectacular literary frauds of the recent past. And, if logic has any place in the arcane world of literary forgery, the certainty of this widespread doubt may be construed as an argument in favor of the diaries' legitimacy.

Certainty that doubts would be raised about Hitler's diaries favors authenticity.

Who, for example, would go to all the effort to fake the hundreds of pages of Hitler lore knowing that the world's foremost experts would be brought in to expose the hoax?

A forger would know that experts would expose a hoax.

In these days when wealthy publications are willing to pay ridiculous prices for just about anything that is journalistically titillating, there is extra inducement to attempt the big scam. But the danger of speedy exposure is equally high and the odds against success are overwhelming.

Possibility of large return is great, but the odds greatly favor exposure.

---

[11]In the *Salt Lake City Tribune* (April 27, 1983). Reprinted by permission.

In less intense times it was possible to phony up an old master or a million-year-old archaeological discovery or even an ambitious literary spoof with a good chance of getting away with it for years. But technological advances in communication and detection have changed all that. Instant publicity means quick and in-depth suspicion which fuels demand for proof of authenticity beyond any doubt.

You used to be able to get away with this kind of fraud, but now better communication means quick demands for proof.

In the case of the Hitler diaries there still are "missing links" in the story of how they were supposedly tracked down. And, as expected, the "experts" are divided pro and con on whether the material disclosed by the West German magazine Stern is the genuine article.

We still don't know how the diaries were tracked down. And the experts are divided on the parts they've seen.

We, of course, must attempt to reach a conclusion by pure deduction rather than examination of the physical evidence which is beyond our reach and ken. We conclude, therefore, that the diaries are either genuine or the clever output of a dedicated fool. Since they involve Adolf Hitler, they could be both.

Without seeing the documents, we conclude that they are either genuine or "the clever output of a dedicated fool," or both.

At this point, we can either use the material in the margin notes directly or rearrange it to form a summary that reflects the *logic* of the original argument. Let's do the latter.

First, we need to know the thesis or conclusion of the editorial. In this case, the thesis is obvious, since it's given in the last two sentences. Rephrased, it becomes:

> Therefore, either a dedicated fool forged them, or they're genuine.

Now we have to see how the reasons given support this thesis, and reconstruct the argument (tossing away anything not relevant to the thesis):

1. Doubts about the Hitler diaries' authenticity would be raised.

∴ 2. Experts would be called in.

∴ 3. The odds a forgery would be exposed are great.

∴ 4. Only a dedicated fool would have forged them.

5. But we still don't know how they were tracked down.

6. And the experts are divided on the part they've examined.

∴ 7. The diaries could be genuine (haven't been proved phony).

∴ 8. Either a dedicated fool forged them or they're genuine.

We've now figured out what the editorial says, putting it into our own words, and arranging the material in a logical order. The margin note summary made it quite easy to do this. Now we have to evaluate the argument, in order to decide if its conclusion should be accepted.

In the first place, we don't want to be worried about the fact that even in logical form the argument is invalid taken all by itself. If we can see a way to make the argument valid by adding things we believe to be true, we should do so by all means. It would amount to nit-picking to dismiss the argument just because everything is not nicely spelled out. Life is short, and everyday arguments rarely are that airtight.

Now take a look at the conclusion. Notice that its structure is what is called a *disjunction*. That is, it has the form: Either _____ or _ _ _ _ _. So to be acceptable, the editorial has to show that both of the disjuncts are possible and that nothing else is at all likely. Let's see if it succeeds.

1. The little said about past frauds, plus our general beliefs about how things work, should convince us that the first statement in our revised summary is acceptable. Doubts were sure to be raised about the document's authenticity.

2. And it's reasonable to conclude, therefore, that experts would eventually be asked to check the documents.

3. Further, the experts would almost certainly demonstrate that they are frauds, if they are (we know this because we know how much science can tell us about these matters nowadays).

4. But does this mean that *only* a fool would forge them? Doesn't our background knowledge (say of past forgeries, even recent ones), plus our knowledge of what motivates people and how they do all sorts of odd and amazing things, make it perfectly possible that an intelligent person or group of people might have forged a Hitler diary? They might, for instance, have planned to "take the money and run" before their handiwork was exposed. Or the forgers might be Nazis from the Hitler era who received help (and some genuine documents) from some of the top Nazis still at large in South America. Or they might be a neo-Nazi group that fabricated the documents for political reasons, say to make Hitler look better in the eyes of history. All of this creates suspicion concerning the conclusion of the editorial that only a dedicated *fool* would forge them. However, it must be admitted that the arguments given do lend some support to that idea, even if not enough.

5-6. Most people who kept abreast of this story were aware that *Stern,* the German magazine that bought the diaries, had refused up to the time of the editorial to tell how they were tracked down. They also knew that experts were divided on the basis of the few things they'd been shown. So Statements 5 and 6 are acceptable.

7. And these two statements do make it plausible to believe that the diaries might be genuine.

8. Finally, if Statements 4 and 7 are both acceptable, the conclusion that in all likelihood the documents either were forged by a fool or are genuine would be acceptable.

So, on the whole, the argument is pretty good, but it shouldn't quite convince us of its conclusion because it has one weak link (Statement 4). A clever group of people might well forge a Hitler diary, either in hopes of getting a quick fortune before the hoax is exposed or to make political hay. (As this text is being written, it still isn't clear who forged the diaries or why.)

Notice that to successfully evaluate the editorial, we needed to bring to bear all sorts of background knowledge and beliefs. This is almost always the case. A perfect reasoner who had no facts or theories to bring to bear and had to evaluate the argument as is could not do a good job on this editorial, or indeed on many arguments from daily life.

Analyzing Speeches and Debates

Political speeches and debates are generally listened to rather than read. This makes critical analysis much more difficult (because the arguments zing by too quickly for proper assessment), and margin notes become impossible (except on written versions).

One way to handle spoken rhetoric is to write down the point or points at issue and then write down the reasons given pro and con for each point as they are presented. The result will contain the essence of what has been said, which can then be analyzed when there is more time.

But another way to deal with spoken rhetoric is to get a written copy of the text. Written copies are usually quite easy to get by writing to the speaker (for instance, writing to the White House for a copy of a presidential speech) and often are printed in newspapers and magazines. Similarly, transcripts of television debates and issue programs (which are becoming more and more important) can be obtained by writing to the network or other originator of the material. When the issue is serious enough, it's worth the effort to obtain a written version of what was said.

Let's now look at some excerpts from the CBS *Sixty Minutes* program of November 5, 1978.[12] Only this time, let's use margin notes but not bother to put them together into a summary. The topic is the private enterprise, nonunion fire department of Scottsdale, Arizona. Here is the first excerpt, with margin notes attached:

Mike Wallace: In other cities Scottsdale's size, there are at least a hundred full-time fire fighters on the payroll. Scottsdale does it with forty-five career professionals, who work longer hours and make more than their counterparts in the area, and the twenty-six auxiliaries, who can earn an extra $200 a month above their regular city pay. The price tag for this manpower? It costs the taxpayers of Scottsdale a bargain $700,000 a year, compared to the national average of $2 million a year for cities Scottsdale's size.

> *(1)* Wallace: *Scottsdale's private nonunion fire department employs 45 full-time and 26 part-time fire fighters, far fewer and much less costly than the average for its size.*

William Howard McClennan: But Scottsdale is a glorified volunteer fire department.

> *(2)* McClennan: *But it's a glorified volunteer dept.*

---

[12]© CBS Inc. 1978. All rights reserved. Originally broadcast November 5, 1978 over the CBS Television Network as part of the *60 Minutes* program series. (*Sixty Minutes* has for some time been the most influential news program on television—there have been many weeks when it has won the highest Nielsen listener rating of any program.)

Wallace: William Howard McClennan, president of the strong and militant International Association of Fire Fighters —175,000 members. He despises Fire Chief Lou Witzeman's fire department. His union back in 1971 went out to Scottsdale, took a look, and then filed a report on Witzeman's nonunion outfit. It was not favorable.

(3) W.: Have they just been lucky not to have had a fire catastrophe?

He's been lucky you say. His fire defenses are all glitter and veneer, with no substance. The citizens are not properly protected. The stations are too far apart, the runs too long, the time factor too great, et cetera. . . . That was seven years ago. I would think that Scottsdale would be lying in ruins by now.

McClennan: Every one of those things you've just read off, Mike, the same is true. Hasn't changed any. He's been lucky. . . .

(4) McC.: They've just been lucky. Their luck will change some day, and they'll need a "real fire department."

Wallace: And you think that some day their luck is going to run out?

McClennan: That's right.

Wallace: And that's when they're going to need—

McClennan: A real fire department.

So far, the stage has just been set for the major exchanges. Wallace clearly is going to try to uphold the idea that the Scottsdale nongovernment, nonunion fire department does a good job at much less cost. McClennan is going to argue that their success so far has just been luck and that the department is not providing adequate fire protection, particularly because it is nonunion. But even at this point, McClennan has hit below the belt in calling Scottsdale's professional, paid fire department a "volunteer" fire department. It is nonunion, not volunteer; it has some part-time employees, not volunteer employees.

Now here is the next exchange:

Wallace: But other experts heartily disagree with McClennan. They found that Witzeman's Rural-Metro does provide effective fire protection, and economically. In fact, at a far lower cost than surrounding Arizona communities pay.

(5) W.: Other experts think Scottsdale's department provides effective protection at a lower cost than surrounding cities.

McClennan: You'd have to analyze that, and then take a city of the same size, with the same conditions, with a . . . paid fire department, and see what the difference is in . . . dollars and cents loss . . . by fire . . .

(6) McC.: You have to take a city with similar conditions and compare money losses from fires.

Wallace: The very thing that you've suggested, President McClennan, has been done by the Institute for Local Self-Government. It's been done by this outfit out in Berkeley, California. And I've got to tell you, Scottsdale comes up with very, very good marks on every point that you raise. . . .

(7) W.: That was done by the Institute for Local Self-Government in Berkeley, and Scottsdale does well.

McClennan: They couldn't put a match out, Mike, if there was a fire.

(8) McC.: The IFLSG couldn't put a match out in a fire.

Wallace: But putting a match out was not what the Institute had in mind. Their job was to rate the fire departments in Scottsdale and in three neighboring communities. And their professional survey concluded that Scottsdale's nonunion fire department performed just as efficiently and for far less taxpayer money than the other three union fire departments. That is what bothers President McClennan. For you see, McClennan's IAFF had tried but failed to unionize Scottsdale's Rural-Metro. And he has charged that because there is no union, Witzeman can cut his fire-fighting force to dangerous, unsafe levels.

(9) W.: That wasn't their job. They compared Scottsdale with three nearby communities and found the nonunion department just as effective at far less cost, apparently without being understaffed, as McClennan claimed they would be without a union.

McClennan: We feel, as members of a union, that our interests should be looking out for the guy that rides on the back step, and we should be fighting—they have the proper number of men there at all times. It takes X number of men to do this and to get that line of hose and to get that water operating on the fire.

(10) McC.: As union members, we should look out for the fire fighter's interests, and should want the proper number of fire fighters on trucks at all times.

In this exchange, McClennan is guilty of an interesting irrelevancy—that the IFLSG couldn't put a match out in a fire—since, as Wallace pointed out, their job was to evaluate fire departments, not put out fires. This irrelevant comment was intended as an attack on the credibility of an expert witness, the IFLSG, and thus indirectly (but no less falsely) charged Wallace with committing the fallacy of *appeal to authority.*

McClennan then attacked Wallace's claim that the Scottsdale department is doing a satisfactory job by arguing that they sometimes go to fires with fewer fire fighters than needed, that is, fewer than union rules require. And that certainly gets to the nub of one of the key issues in this as well as many other disputes concerning union and nonunion labor: whether union rules require *featherbedding* (that is, require more labor than is really needed, the classic example being the fireman required on diesel trains that have no fires to stoke).

So far, Wallace has argued that experience shows Scottsdale's department doesn't seem to need more men on fire trucks, indicating that union requirements do indeed constitute featherbedding. McClennan says they're just lucky. This means that the issue comes down to a question concerning statistics. Witzeman's private company has been fighting fires in Scottsdale for thirty years; is that enough time to get a representative sample of fire-fighting problems in the city of Scottsdale? Common sense says *yes.*

(In the next exchange, omitted here to shorten matters, Chief Witzeman also argued that union rules aim at having sufficient numbers of fire fighters at the biggest fires, while his rules require just the number needed for each fire. Witzeman also argued that rigid fire inspections and (as in the case of Scottsdale) a strict fire sprinkler code save a great deal on fire protection. This points the way to reducing fire damage without having a lot of fire fighters on each truck.)

Wallace: Are the taxpayers of Scottsdale really getting shortchanged . . . by having Witzeman's penny-pinching department protect them? One way to find out how good a fire department is is to check on that town's fire insurance rating. We did, with the Arizona Insurance Service Office. They told us that Scottsdale's insurance premiums for homeowners are no higher than those in surrounding towns. So a Scottsdale resident has got to say, . . . "Look, I'm getting good fire protection. My insurance premiums are the same. And I'm paying half the price they're paying next door. . . ."

(11) W.: Scottsdale's fire insurance premiums are no higher than for surrounding towns, evidence that insurance companies believe the risk is no higher.

McClennan: My answer is simple. If . . . it's all that you paint it to be, Mike, . . . how come there's only one in the whole United States?

(12) McC.: Then why is this the only one in the whole United States?

Wallace: You're a very powerful organization. . . . You support politicians. It's going to be very difficult for a . . . town to turn their back on the IAFF, and you know it.

(13) W.: It's hard politically to defeat an entrenched fire fighters' union.

McClellan: Public employees were always good at that, Mike. That's why they survived.

(14) McC.: Public employees survive because they have been good at that.

McClellan's first task was to counter Wallace's evidence concerning insurance premiums. He had to show that the insurance companies were wrong in this case. He tried to do this by appealing to the authority of a *common practice* —namely, the practice of having union fire departments. Wallace countered this by arguing in effect that insurance companies are better authorities than those who have unionized a fire department, pointing out that unionization often depends on political rather than just economic or safety factors. Is he right? For what it's worth, this writer's background information supports Mike Wallace; until quite recently, it would have been very hard for a city to oust a government employees union. So the expert opinion of insurance companies, who stand to lose a great deal of money if they're wrong, should weigh more heavily. Of course, cities that hire too many fire fighters also lose (waste) a great deal of money—but it's public money, nobody's in particular, which experience shows is another matter entirely.

Wallace: McClennan said his union would revisit Scottsdale to see what has happened there in the seven years since his union's last report.
McClennan: We're going to give it another look, no question about it. . . .
Wallace: Why?
McClennan: Because I want to see if some of these things that you've brought out here today are actually so.

(15) McC.: We're going to re-evaluate the Scottsdale fire department performance to see if anything you said about it is true.

Wallace: In other words, you're keeping an open mind?
McClennan: Yeah, sure, I'm keeping an open mind.
Wallace: You mean it's possible . . . that you're going to come down on the side of Scottsdale—
McClennan: No way! No way, Mike.

(16) W.: You're keeping an open mind?

(17) McC.: No way.

McClennan thus intended to keep an open mind while being sure all along that Scottsdale's department would receive low marks. Mike Wallace neatly trapped him into being *inconsistent* while admitting the truth that he didn't have an open mind on the merits of Scottsdale's privately owned, cheap (but effective) fire-fighting company.

So thanks to Mike Wallace, CBS, and *60 Minutes* for a pretty carefully researched and reasoned performance, quite unusual for the mass media.

Exercise 6-2

In Exercise 6-1, you were asked to rewrite several extended arguments in your own words. Now, using those summaries, critically evaluate each of these extended arguments, being careful to spell out your reasoning in a way that is likely, to convince others.

Exercise 6-3

Use margin notes (or whatever method works best for you) to construct a clear, accurate summary in your own words of each of the following extended passages. Then critically evaluate each summary, bringing to bear relevant portions of your background beliefs.

*1. Here is a Patrick J. Buchanan newspaper column:[13]

U.S. Blacks Would Fight in Africa

Washington. Of all the inane remarks our "point man" at the U.N. has made, none is more disturbing than the statement he made 10 days ago.

In the event of an East-West showdown in Africa, says Andy Young [at that time the U.S. ambassador to the U.N.]: "I see no situation in which we would have to come in on the side of the South Africans . . . You'd have civil war at home. Maybe I ought not to say that, but I really believe it. An armed force that is 30 percent black isn't going to fight on the side of the South Africans."

This is not some hotheaded young leader of SNCC [Student Nonviolent Coordinating Committee, a modestly radical civil rights group] talking. This is the United States ambassador to the U.N., who holds Cabinet rank. And he has warned publicly that if his president and Congress declare that America's vital interests require the use of military force guerrillas in southern Africa, black American soldiers will mutiny. And black American civilians will rise up in insurrection.

One wonders if Young—babbling away into every open microphone—is remotely aware of the slander he has leveled at the patriotism of black America.

---

[13]*New York Times* (March 26, 1977). Reprinted by permission of The Tribune Company Syndicate, Inc. (The last two paragraphs, which add nothing new, have been omitted.)

When the United States entered World War I, Irish-Americans died in the trenches alongside British soldiers whose fellow units were, even then, snuffing out the flames of Irish freedom. In that same war German-Americans fought and killed their own cousins fighting for imperial Germany and the Kaiser.

During World War II, German-Americans, Italian-Americans, Japanese-Americans fought loyally against Nazi Germany, Fascist Italy, Imperial Japan.

They all put loyalty to America above any residual loyalty to the homeland of their fathers and grandfathers. What Young is saying is that black Americans—who have been here centuries, not just decades—do not have that kind of loyalty to the United States. In a crunch, he is saying, black America will stand with their racial kinsmen in Marxist Angola and Mozambique—rather than with their white countrymen in the United States.

What makes Young's flippancy fairly chilling is that he has just confided to the editors of *Newsweek*, "I get the feeling that Jimmy Carter wants me to take charge of Africa. . . ."

Anti-white racism already seems to have become the determining factor in U.S. policy toward that continent.

Up at the U.N., Jimmy Carter, grinning away at the muted mouthpieces of some of the rankest, blood-stained ogres in history, announced that the United States had just rejoined the world conspiracy to strangle Rhodesia to death. Because Southern Rhodesia does not have "majority rule," we too will no longer buy Rhodesian exports. [This was before majority rule was won in Rhodesia.]

We will buy chrome instead from Soviet Russia, a hostile, totalitarian empire ruled by an elite party which claims the membership of less than 6 percent of the Soviet population.

How many countries in Africa, how many in the world, have majority rules with minority rights guaranteed?

Idi Amin comes from a small, dominantly Moslem tribe in Uganda which is mercilessly persecuting members of larger Christian tribes. Yet the United States, which now considers it illegal and immoral to buy Rhodesian chrome, is delighted to buy Idi Amin's coffee.

The most virulent strain of racism in the world today is not anti-black, anti-yellow, or anti-red; it is anti-white.

Reflect a moment: What makes the ruling tribes in Rhodesia and southern Africa so hated? Are they the most barbaric, repressive, dictatorial in Africa, and the world? Hardly! What makes them evil, unacceptable—what mandates their destruction—is that the skin of these particular ruling tribes is not black, but white. . . .

*2. This is a political column by Jeffrey St. John:[14]

Women's Lib Amendment Not Simple Legal Formula

"The legal position of women," observed the late Supreme Court Justice Felix Frankfurter, "cannot be stated in a simple formula, especially under a consti-

---

[14]*Columbus* (Ohio) *Dispatch* (May 9, 1972). © 1971 by Copley News Service. Reprinted by permission.

tutional system, because her life cannot be expressed in a single simple relation." A procession of contemporary legal scholars made much the same
argument prior to congressional passage of the Women's Equal Rights Amendment now before various state legislatures for ratification.

Political pressures in this presidential year have given a militant minority of
women powerful leverage for enactment. However, the respective state of the
Union may come to regret ratification, if the two-thirds majority approves.

North Carolina Democratic Senator Sam Ervin has argued, along with legal
scholars from the University of Chicago, Yale, and Harvard, that while the
amendment would have no effect upon discrimination, it would "nullify every
existing federal and state law making any distinction whatever between men
and women, no matter how reasonable the distinction may be, and rob Congress and the 50 states of the legislative power to enact any future laws making
any distinction between men and women, no matter how reasonable the distinction may be."

In the wake of any ratification, moreover, a legal avalanche would be
unleashed that is likely to overwhelm the already overcrowded courts of
the country.

In reality, the aim of a minority of militant women's liberationists is to bring
about just such a state of legal and social anarchy. Like the disciples of Lenin in
the early part of the century, Women's Lib seeks to use the law to destroy both
existing law and the social structure.

In abolishing a legal distinction between men and women, the way is paved
for sociological anarchy which militants can exploit for their own purposes of
achieving political power.

The profound effect the Equal Rights Amendment would have on marriage
contracts, the home and children is precisely what Women's Lib wants; to
sweep such established social units away as a prelude to pushing the country
headlong into a life-style not unlike that now practiced in hippie communes.

Philosophically, at the root of the women's liberation movement is an
attempt to destroy the family structure as a means of bringing down the whole
of society.

The form of "discrimination" upon which the Women's Lib movement
bases much of its false, misleading, and dangerous campaign is less in law than
in custom and social attitudes, especially in the fields of career and
employment.

Like the civil rights movement, Women's Lib is seeking, by using the power
of the state, to forbid individual discrimination as opposed to discrimination
legally enforced.

This crucial distinction has not been made by most in Congress who
approved the Equal Rights Amendment for Women. Nor has it been made by
the few state houses that have already ratified the amendment.

One can predict the same chaos will follow passage of this amendment as
that which followed the 1964 Civil Rights Act.

Legal scholars like the late dean of the Harvard Law School, Roscoe Pound,
have argued that the guarantee of "due process" in the Fifth Amendment and
"equal protection" clause in the Fourteenth Amendment provide the necessary
legal instruments for reform now demanded by women's liberationists.

But like some elements of the civil rights movement, militant feminists are not really interested in reform, but rather in revolution and destruction of the existing social fabric of the society.

3. Here are two letters to the editor on related topics (*New York Times,* December 12, 1982). In your evaluation of each one, be sure to take account of whatever is relevant in the other, and be sure to apply background information consistently.

To the Editor:

In "A Prescription for Heroin," his Nov. 19 Editorial Notebook article, Peter Passell writes about the benefits to be gained from a British-type model of supplying heroin legally to addicts. Fortunately for the British, they had our American-type model of heroin prohibition to study before they formulated their own policy.

In 1914, the United States Congress passed the Harrison Narcotic Act, which effectively stopped doctors from supplying heroin to patients. In 1922, the British sent Dr. Harry Campbell to the United States to observe what had been happening during the seven years of enforcement of the Harrison Act.

His report to the Rolleston Committee, a group of distinguished medical authorities set up by the British Government to study various policies, stated that ". . . not only has the Harrison law failed to diminish the number of drug takers—some contend, indeed, that it has increased their numbers—but, far from bettering the lot of the opiate addict, it has actually worsened it; for without curtailing the supply of the drug, it has sent the price up tenfold, and this has had the effect of impov-

erishing the poorer class of addicts and reducing them to a condition of such abject misery as to render them incapable of gaining an honest livelihood."

The Rolleston Committee wisely recommended that, since heroin addiction is an illness, physicians could legally treat it by supplying heroin to addicts. This medical model, that heroin is an illness, has been the over-arching philosophic approach to British policy.

Unfortunately for America, we will persist in using the criminal justice model—and thus turn the heroin problem into the heroin disaster. As Peter Passell points out, American society has asked a great deal of government control of heroin, and in the process gotten nothing at all.

The British saw the error of our ways and responded cleverly and humanely. Now, 60 years later and with no improvement in the "colonies," isn't it about time we look to heroin maintenance for addicts as a viable alternative to our present system?

MARTIN H. LEVINSON
Assistant Professor of Urban Health Management, St. John's University
Jamaica, NY, Nov. 22, 1982[15]

To the Editor:

Peter Passel argues in his Nov. 29 Editorial Notebook article for "regulation and taxation" of marijuana. Legalization would, he writes, produce tax revenues of up to $2 billion a year and provide uncontaminated and even "low tar" pot.

Many readers may have wondered, "Why not?" There are answers.

Before getting to them, however, several facts need to be understood. In the last decade, the catalogue of negative health effects of marijuana—once thought to be a "harmless giggle—has

---

[15]Reprinted by the permission of the author.

grown alarmingly, to include serious damage to the lungs, brain and reproductive organs as well as a wide range of behavioral toxicities whose ultimate effects range from decreased school and work performance to highway fatalities.

Along with the growing awareness of these serious health effects, marijuana use among the young, which had risen relentlessly for two decades, peaked in 1978 and now appears to be declining. Public support for legalization and even the less extreme "decriminalization" also peaked in 1978 and is now declining. No state has decriminalized marijuana possession since 1978.

Still, marijuana use remains unacceptably high. In 1979, 4 million of the nation's 12- to 17-year-olds smoked marijuana, while "only" 2.8 million smoked tobacco cigarettes. In 1981, 7 percent of American high school seniors smoked an average of 3½ marijuana cigarettes a day; "only" 6 percent of this group drank alcohol daily.

When considering legalization of marijuana, it is well to remember that the arguments favoring it apply to all other drugs, including cocaine, PCP and even heroin. If we are willing to legalize pot to provide possible tax revenues and to give the users a "pure" product, why not do the same for other drugs? It was once believed that marijuana was significantly less toxic than other illegal drugs. This comforting thought has been shown to be dangerously wrong.

What would the effect of legalization of marijuana be on the levels of use in our society?

For those who think legalization will not increase use, the American experience with repeal of Prohibition is instructive: Levels of alcohol use and the health problems associated with that use have risen steadily since 1933.

How many more children are we willing to lose to marijuana to get that hypothetical $2 billion tax windfall?

How many more families will we wreck? How much less productivity, how many more highway fatalities?

Any thought of legalizing marijuana leads to thoughts of our national experience with the two traditional legal drugs, alcohol and tobacco.

While these drugs are so common as to seem almost trivial, as a physician concerned with the public health I cannot dismiss the fact that fully 30 percent of all American deaths in 1982 will have been premature because of these two drugs. Is that a precedent we should follow with another drug, a drug that appears to be more toxic than either alcohol or tobacco?

But one answer to the question "Why not?" stands out beyond all others: Why give up the effort to turn around the epidemic of marijuana use in the U.S. just as it is, for the first time, declining?

I can think of only one reason: the marijuana lobbyists are desperate. The "reforms" of permissive marijuana laws touted in the 1970's are now politically dead, so all pretense of compromise is being dropped. With it goes the one best argument the pro-pot forces had, namely that legalization is inevitable.

Mr. Passell makes this argument clear when he concludes, ". . . marijuana is here to stay. Some day, some way, a prohibition so unenforceable and so widely flouted must give way to reality." Would he use the same argument in regard to highway speed limits, which are surely more "widely flouted"?

It is unlikely that marijuana will be eliminated from the American scene, but major reductions in its use, and in the problems caused by that use, are now being achieved. Why quit while we're winning?

ROBERT L. DuPONT, M.D.
President, American Council on
Marijuana and Other
Psychoactive Drugs
Washington, Dec. 3, 1982[16]

---

[16]*New York Times*, Dec. 12, 1982. Reprinted by permission of the author.

4. Here is a political column by Michael Novak.[17]

According to *Time* magazine, there are a reported 150,000 homosexuals in
Miami. Still, only 90,000 votes came out for the lavender against the orange in
Miami's thirty-day war. On June 7, Miamians voted down a "human rights
ordinance" for homosexuals by a 70–30 margin. The political question was
decisively resolved in Miami, but a philosophical question remains. In a
democracy, does anything go? Must citizens cease making moral discrimi-
nations? Does homosexuality make a moral claim on the Republic equal to that
of heterosexuality?

By all means, the state should not intrude on the private life of citizens. But
there is an entity more important than the state—call it the people, the culture,
the society. The state ought not to spy upon private sexual life. In the private
sphere, large tolerance ought to be promoted. But society—as distinct from the
state—has not only the right, but also the duty to make moral distinctions.

One great advantage to homosexuality is referred to constantly by homosexuals. Homosexual apologetics are full of "loving relationships,"
"warmth," "tenderness," and "loving touches." Married men and women
rarely speak that way.

Two basic deficiencies in the homosexual way of life lead many persons not
to wish it for themselves or their children, and to regard it as a flawed way of
life. The first is the narcissism of one's own sex. Heterosexuality is not just
"an alternative life-style." It is rooted in the cycle of the generations, that long
prosaic realism of familial responsibilities that is the inner rhythm of the
human race.

The second deficiency follows from the first. The relationship between two
males, or two females, may be loving, tender, and satisfying. It is quite
likely—far more so than among married men and women—to be transient.
There is a restlessness in homosexual life that is not accidental or fortuitous,
but structural.

The future of the human race does not depend on homosexuals as it does
upon the married union of men and women, with all the skills and necessities
acquired in such unions. Although the state need not interfere in homosexual
unions, it has a critical stake in heterosexual unions. These unions are difficult.
To help them to succeed is of indispensable priority.

At an early stage, all humans are polymorphous. Each of us could become
homosexual as well as heterosexual. In a world as sexually confused as ours, it
would be surprising if the number of homosexuals failed to grow. The young
today are in a more unsettled sexual state than in many other eras. The strong
patterns of socialization that lead to heterosexuality have been enormously
weakened.

A strange argument is advanced by homosexuals. We cannot, they say,
influence your children to follow our example. But this claim flies in the face of
social constraints in other moral matters. The individual homosexual may not

---

[17]*Chicago Daily News* (June 25, 1977). Copyright 1977, Universal Press Syndicate. All rights
reserved. Reprinted with permission.

influence a child, but public approval will. Does sex-role stereotyping make a difference? Does it make any difference which role models are set before the young? If not, then talk about women and blacks in textbooks, and violence in TV films, is beside the point.

The state should not legislate about private sexual life. But neither should it prevent society from withholding moral and public disapproval of what they regard as an undesirable form of living. Citizens should not be coerced into approving—in school courses upholding homosexuality, for example—what they do not approve.

Like war and the poor, homosexuals we shall always have with us. No matter what the socialization toward heterosexuality, on some it will fail to take. We cannot eliminate homosexuality. What we can do is to diminish the numbers it affects and the suffering it entails.

What society teaches about homosexuality makes a difference. To teach that it is a matter of preference is different from teaching that it is morally wrong. Homosexuals have a right to live what some people regard as a deficient life, if they so wish. A free society may permit decadence, on the grounds that efforts to eliminate it would cause more harm than good.

Only a repressive society would try to punish homosexuals. Only a decadent society would grant them status. A wise society would try to provide conditions under which the talents of individual homosexuals could flourish, without holding up their condition for equal emulation.

4. Constructing Good Arguments

Learning how to analyze extended arguments and learning how to construct them go hand in hand. Good writers lead their readers through their own reasoning processes.

Get Clear about Your Thesis

Whether analyzing someone else's work or doing our own, we need to get clear about the thesis of a passage. When reading what others have written, the question is what the author's thesis is. When writing our own arguments, we need to get clear as to what precisely we want to prove.

It's usually best to start right out with our thesis, perhaps in an interesting opening paragraph that introduces the topic. Here is an example:

> If there's one issue that divides Americans these days, it's the abortion issue. Arguments pro and con seem endless.

This tells the reader that the topic will be the abortion issue, and prepares the reader for our thesis:

> Yet there are two simple reasons why abortion should be made illegal.

Now, the reader knows what the thesis is and knows that there will be two basic reasons offered in its support.

Spell Out Your Reasons for the Thesis

Having informed the reader of the thesis, we need to give our reasons for accepting it. In our anti-abortion essay, we might continue:

> The first reason is that abortion takes the life of a human being. We sometimes hear that a fetus is not human, not a baby. Ridiculous. Look at a three-month-old fetus and you'll see what can't be mistaken for anything but a human baby. [And so on.]

How much detail we provide at this point depends on our intended audience, and how resistant they're likely to be at this point. We don't want to hit people over the head with what they already know or believe.

Now for our second reason, anticipating a possible objection:

> Of course, it isn't always murder when we kill a human being. Police officers kill in the line of duty. So do soldiers in wartime. But no one calls that murder. The same is true of those who kill in self-defense, or to defend innocent people.
>
> But if we look at these cases, we find that they involve killing an aggressor or someone who has done something seriously wrong. Killing in battle is not wrong, for instance, because the point is to defend the nation against attack. In the case of abortion, however, the fetus has harmed no one. The fetus is innocent. [And so on.]

Help the Reader to Understand

Merely giving reasons for a thesis generally isn't good enough to persuade the reader to your point of view. For one thing, your reasons themselves may need to be justified by additional reasons, for instance, by appeals to relevant facts or authorities. And for another, you may need to help the reader *understand* (or be moved by) your reasons. There are many ways to do this, for instance, by *comparing* and *constrasting* the case in point with similar ones. But perhaps the best way is by giving *examples*. For example, in our little essay on abortion, we explained what we meant in saying that killing isn't always wrong by giving the examples of killing in self defense, in battle, and by police in the line of duty. (This last sentence, in fact, is an example presented to help readers understand that they need to give examples to help readers understand.)[18]

Examples also are often useful in convincing readers to *accept* our claims, not just to understand them, In our abortion essay, for instance, we gave examples to convince readers that killing wrongdoers or aggressors isn't always wrong, preparing them for the contrasting case of abortion, where an *innocent* life is taken.

A Summary May be Helpful

Having presented our case, it's usually a good idea to remind readers of its main drift. For instance, in our abortion example, we might want to conclude this way:

---

[18]No doubt the most frequently used expressions in this book are *for example, thus,* and *for instance.*

So abortion should be illegal, because it amounts to the *unjustified* taking of a human life. After all, we're justified in killing human beings only when they're guilty of an extremely serious wrong, but a fetus is completely innocent.

Provide Transition Expressions

A good essay obviously has to have a logical structure. But it also has to make it easy for readers to follow that structure. So we need to use transition terms to tell readers what to expect. For instance, the sentence just before this one used the word *so* to indicate that that sentence would "follow" from the previous one. In general, we want to let readers know whether we're giving them reasons, or conclusions, by using expressions like *because, due to this, hence,* and so on.

But we also want to direct readers in other ways. In particular, we want to use words like *however, but,* and *and* when appropriate. In the abortion essay, we did this quite often, for instance, in the sentence "In the case of abortion, *however,* the fetus has harmed no one." (The word *however* here has the sense of "on the other hand.") Flavoring words of this kind help a passage to flow so that readers can follow it as the author intended.

Write for Your Audience

The point of a critical essay is to convince readers to accept some thesis or other. So we want to include only those things that readers will need in order to understand and agree with us. A common failing of college textbooks, for instance, is that they are written for the instructor or for experts in the field, rather than for the students who must learn from them. (Texts that presuppose knowledge most students don't possess are a case in point.)

While it's obvious that we should write for our audience, in practice it's sometimes hard to carry this out. The reason is that it's human nature to spend lots of time explaining and illustrating those things we ourselves understand best or are most sure of, while sliding quickly past the parts that we don't quite understand ourselves or are unsure of. What we should do, of course, is almost the exact opposite. Those things we think our readers will grasp clearly and easily need to be mentioned relatively briefly, with at most one example, while harder things should be gone into in more detail and illustrated by more (and more varied) examples. (How well *we* understand a point is generally a good rough measure of how well our readers will grasp it.)

Think Your Position Through Carefully

That's one reason why analyzing arguments and writing them go hand in hand. To write a good argumentative essay, we need to carefully analyze our own ideas and beliefs on the topic, to root out inconsistencies and dubious or fuzzy beliefs, and to arrange the various points into a coherent whole.

You'll Probably Need to Rewrite

And that's one reason why you'll no doubt need to write and rewrite several times. When writing a critical essay, most people find that their thoughts on the topic aren't as cogent or clear as they supposed. The writing process itself thus becomes part of the reasoning process.

That's why some writers deliberately construct the first draft of an essay as a learning or thinking device. They do the best job they can on the first draft and then critically analyze it as they would an opponent's essay. Their next draft then takes account of this critical evaluation, either by introducing new arguments that aren't open to these criticisms or by showing that the objections they've discovered can be overcome by further argument.

But one thing is clear. Only a few of the very best writers can construct a really good critical essay in one draft. (One writer who could do this was the philosopher Bertrand Russell.) The rest of us have to write at least two drafts, usually more, in order to get our thoughts into good order and to arrange our exposition so as to present these thoughts in a logical, understandable manner. And you won't be surprised to find out that this takes *practice, practice, practice.*

Exercise 6-4

So let's get some practice writing short critical essays. Here are several issues college students might be interested in. Select one and write a short essay (about 500–1,000 words), taking one side or another. Then write a critical analysis in reply to your own thesis (as though you were a fair opponent attacking your argument). And then, rewrite your original essay to take account of your own criticisms. (You may find that you've changed your mind and now want to defend a different thesis.) Think of your audience as your fellow students, *not* your instructor. When you've done that, then pick another topic (from the list that follows, or from your head) and do the same thing over again (hopefully finding that you can do the job easier and better the second time around).

1. Should all students be required to take at least basic introductory courses in math and science? In a foreign language?

2. Is the lecture method a good way to teach certain college courses?

3. Should we have a peacetime draft?

4. Should marijuana, cocaine, or other drugs be legal?

5. Should the United States supply military aid to anticommunist governments and/or rebels in Central America?

6. Should we have sex education courses in high school?

7. Does the United States government's announced policy of mutual assured destruction (MAD) make sense? (That is, does it make sense to have so many nuclear missiles that no nation would believe it could strike at us without receiving unacceptably horrible damage in retaliation?)

8. Should we raise (lower) the legal drinking age? Should convicted drunk drivers lose their licenses?

9. How can we improve the college curriculum?

10. Are there fair ways to make American industry more competitive with foreign industry?

11. Should we legalize prostitution?

Summary of Chapter Six

Chapter Six deals with the analysis and construction of extended arguments.

1. There are several guidelines to use in evaluating such passages:
   a. Find the thesis and keep it in mind as you read.
   b. Find the reasons supporting the thesis, and (sometimes) the reasons for the reasons, and so on.
   c. Skip whatever doesn't support the thesis.
   d. Add relevant information, pro or con.
   e. Come to an evaluation.

2. In everyday life, there usually isn't time to thoroughly analyze an extended passage. So it's useful to develop the knack of quick appraisal. The trick in quick appraisal is to learn how to informally and quickly do the basic things just mentioned *as you read the passage*. In particular, you have to learn how to bring relevant information to bear and to evaluate as you read.

3. When a more careful analysis is required, margin notes, with or without a summary constructed from them, are very useful. There are four basic steps in the margin note—summary method: read the material carefully; read it again and add margin notes at the relevant spots; construct a summary from the margin notes; and evaluate the summary.

4. Learning how to analyze extended arguments and learning how to write them go hand in hand. Some hints for writing good essays of this kind are:
   a. Get clear about your thesis.
   b. Spell out the reasons for your thesis.
   c. Help readers to understand your argument (and convince them of its cogency) by providing examples, facts, and so on.
   d. (Sometimes) summarize your argument at the end.
   e. Use transition expressions, such as *but, therefore,* and *for example,* so that your writing flows, and the reader can follow it more easily.
   f. Write with your audience in mind, in particular so that you tell them all and only those things they need to know.
   g. Think your position through carefully (you may find your ideas are changed by the writing process itself).
   h. Write and rewrite until your essay says just what you want it to say.

Exercise 6-5 (A Rather Difficult Exercise)

Here are two essays on related issues concerning national defense and atomic weapons. Critically evaluate each one, taking account of whatever is relevant in the other. (The second one in particular is going to make you do a bit of background digging.)

Secretary of Defense Weinberger's Letter of August 23[19]

I am increasingly concerned with news accounts that portray this Administration as planning to wage protracted nuclear war, or seeking to acquire a nuclear "war-fighting" capability. This is completely inaccurate, and these stories misrepresent the Administration's policies to the American public and to our allies and adversaries abroad.

It is the first and foremost goal of this Administration to take every step to ensure that nuclear weapons are never used again, for we do not believe there could be any "winners" in a nuclear war. Our entire strategy aims to deter war of all kinds, but most particularly to deter nuclear war. To accomplish this objective, our forces must be able to respond in a measured and prudent manner to the threat posed by the Soviet Union. That will require the improvements in our strategic forces that the President has proposed. But it does *not* mean that we endorse the concept of protracted nuclear war, or nuclear "war-fighting." It is the Soviet Union that appears to be building forces for a "protracted" conflict.

The policy of deterrence is difficult for some to grasp because it is based on a paradox. But this is quite simple: to make the cost of nuclear war much higher than any possible benefit. If the Soviets know in advance that a nuclear attack on the United States would bring swift nuclear retaliation, they would never attack in the first place. They would be "deterred" from ever beginning a nuclear war.

There is nothing new about our policy. Since the awful age of nuclear weapons began, the United States has sought to prevent nuclear war through a policy of deterrence. This policy has been approved, through the political processes of the democratic nations it protects, since at least 1950. More important, it works. It has worked in the face of major international tensions involving the great powers, and it has worked in the face of war itself.

But, for deterrence to continue to be successful in the future, we must take steps to offset the Soviet military buildup. If we do not modernize our arsenal now, as the Soviets have been doing for more than 20 years, we will, within a few years, no longer have the ability to retaliate. The Soviet Union would then be in a position to threaten or actually to attack us with the knowledge that we would be incapable of responding. We have seen in Poland, in Afghanistan, in Eastern Europe and elsewhere that the Soviet Union does not hesitate to take

---

[19]Letter from Secretary of Defense Caspar Weinberger, sent to 30 U.S. and 40 foreign publications (August 23, 1982).

advantage of a weaker adversary. We cannot allow the Soviet Union to think it could begin a nuclear war with us and win.

This is not just idle speculation. The Soviet Union has engaged in a frenzied military buildup, in spite of their economic difficulties. They have continued to build greater numbers of nuclear weapons far beyond those necessary for deterrence. They now have over 5,000 nuclear warheads on ICBMs, compared to about 2,000 only five years ago. They have modified the design of these weapons and their launchers so that many of their land-based missiles are now more accurate, more survivable and more powerful than our own. They have also developed a refiring capability that will allow them to reload their delivery systems several times. They have elaborate plans for civil defense and air defense against any retaliation we might attempt. And, finally, their writings and military doctrine emphasize a nuclear war-fighting scenario. Whatever they claim their intentions to be, the fact remains that they are designing their weapons in such a way and in sufficient numbers to indicate to us that they think they could begin, and win, a nuclear war.

In the face of all this, it is my responsibility and duty as secretary of defense to make every effort to modernize our nuclear forces in such a way that the United States retains the capability to deter the Soviet Union from ever beginning a nuclear war. We must take the steps necessary to match the Soviet Union's greatly improved nuclear capability.

That is exactly why we must have a *capability* for a survivable and enduring response—to demonstrate that our strategic forces *could* survive Soviet strikes over an extended period. Thus we believe we could deter any attack. Otherwise we would be tempting them to employ nuclear weapons or try to blackmail us. In short, we cannot afford to place ourselves in the position where the survivability of our deterrent would force the President to choose between using our strategic forces before they were destroyed or surrendering.

Those who object to a policy that would strengthen our deterrent, then, would force us into a more dangerous, hair-triggered posture. Forces that must be used in the very first instant of an enemy attack are not the tools of a prudent strategy. A posture that encourages Soviet nuclear adventurism is not the basis of an effective deterrent. Our entire strategic program, including the development of a response capability that has been so maligned in the press recently, has been developed with the express intention of assuring that nuclear war will never be fought.

I know that this doctrine of deterrence is a difficult paradox to understand. It is an uncomfortable way to keep the peace. We understand deterrence and accept the fact that we must do much more in order to continue to keep the peace. It is my fervent hope that all can understand and accept this so that we can avoid the sort of sensationalist treatment of every mention of the word "nuclear" that only serves to distort our policy and to frighten people all over the world. Our policy is peace, and we deeply believe that the best and surest road to peace is to secure and maintain an effective and credible deterrent.

The purpose of U.S. policy remains to prevent aggression through an effective policy of deterrence—the very goal which prompted the formation of the North Atlantic Alliance, an alliance which is as vital today as it was the day it was formed.

Now here is George F. Kennan on the related topic of nuclear missiles in Europe.

Zero Options[20]

Any consideration of the problem of the stationing of intermediate-range nuclear weapons in Europe must depart from the recognition that the nuclear weapon is, for war-fighting purposes, an unusable one. This is now so widely recognized in both East and West that the assertion needs little substantiation. This weapon is not a "defense" against itself. No one has ever found, nor will anyone ever find, a way to attain superiority in the development of it or a plausible defense against it. Attempts to use it as the basis of a national military-political strategy have invariably failed. There is no way of initiating its use in warfare among the major nuclear powers that would not invite upon the initiating party disasters of such enormity that they would make a mockery of all normal concepts of victory or defeat.

These considerations would alone strongly militate against the probability of any actual use by the Soviet Union of the intermediate-range missiles it now has, or might have in future, targeted on Western Europe. They might conceivably serve as instruments of political intimidation; but it takes two to make a successful act of intimidation, and the very improbability of the actual use of these weapons means that no one in Western Europe needs to be greatly intimidated by them unless he wishes to be. Smaller powers than Germany or France have stood up, manfully and successfully, to threats more real than this one.

This improbability of any use of these Soviet weapons is heightened, it might be well to remember, by the strong Soviet commitment against the first use of nuclear weapons generally. To the extent that this commitment has been noted at all in the West, the reaction has generally been one of cynical disbelief and derision. But one may question whether this sweeping dismissal is really justified. The unilateral renunciation of the "first use" by the Soviet government has been repeatedly and solemnly stated at the highest levels of governmental and Party authority, where it has been coupled with the most unambiguous recognition that no nuclear war could be anything but a disaster to all the warring parties. Beyond this, the Soviet Union in 1981 introduced in the Assembly of the United Nations, argued for, and voted for, a resolution declaring first use of nuclear weapons to be a crime against humanity. This resolution represented a Soviet commitment not just to us in the West but to the 17 million members of the Soviet Communist Party, to various satellite peoples, to Communist parties across the world, to the third world, and to the majority of the other members of the Assembly who voted in favor of it. The Soviet leaders, whatever else one may think of them, are serious people, not frivolous; and they do not undertake such public commitments lightly, or only for the sake of tricking us.

All this being the case, it may be asked: how much does it really matter whether Moscow has 300 ss-20 missiles trained on Western Europe, or only

---

150, or none at all? Western Europe was not immune from nuclear attack before the ss-20s were mounted. It would not be so immune even if they were all taken away. The fact is that there are today, in this threatened world of ours, no "windows" of vulnerability that could be opened or closed. We are vulnerable—totally vulnerable. There is no way that could be changed. It is today precisely to the *intentions* of the potential opponent, not to his *capabilities* (or to ours), that we must look for our salvation.

The greatest danger that faces any of us today is that an actual nuclear exchange might develop among the major nuclear powers when no one really wanted it. That sort of an exchange could be triggered just as easily by the firing of a single nuclear device as it could be by the firing of several hundred of them. From this perspective, one may well ask whether the short-range tactical or "battlefield" nuclear weapons now in American hands in Germany do not present a greater danger of unleashing a nuclear catastrophe than all the intermediate-range weapons that we or the Russians may finally choose to mount. Why? For the simple reason that they are more apt to be employed. The layman is of course not fully informed; but from all that one can learn, NATO plans envisage the introduction of the use of such weapons at a relatively early stage of hostilities in a conventional conflict, especially if that conflict should be seen as going against the Western forces. (To which consideration might be added the reflection that a large portion of these tactical nuclear weapons are reputed to be of such short range that they would not only be fired off from German territory but would land on it, with consequences incalculable for the safety and well-being of its inhabitants even in the absence of any hostile retaliation.)

In the face of these considerations the question may well be asked: if what one wishes to do is to promote the safety of Western Europe in the face of the nuclear danger, would it not make more sense to seek a real "zero option" for this region in place of the spurious one we are talking about today? This would presumably be one that would bar, for both the NATO and Warsaw Pact nations, not only most of the intermediate-range nuclear missiles now deployed in, or scheduled for deployment in, the Western European region, or trained on that region, but also all tactical weapons of this nature stationed within the area; in addition to which there would presumably have to be some sort of an agreement restricting the numbers and operations of the many floating missile platforms, Soviet and Western, from which intermediate- or short-range nuclear warheads could be fired at the area—in other words, a real nuclear-free Western European zone in place of the not-at-all nuclear-free one which Mr. Reagan's "zero option" envisages.

It would of course scarcely be possible to achieve any total removal of intermediate-range missiles from this region so long as the French and the British insist on retaining their own. The Russians have a point here which cannot be denied. Either those two powers are NATO allies or they are not. One cannot have it both ways. Particularly we in the United States, who insist on viewing every weapon of Soviet manufacture discovered in Nicaragua as being under direct Soviet control, no matter in whose hands it is encountered, are in a poor position to require of the Soviet Union that the weapons of *our* allies should not be counted in the balance at all.

Nor would it be possible to achieve any total removal of the various floating platforms. Too many of these latter are actually based in the area. The best one could hope to do would be to place restrictions on their numbers as well as on their freedom to maneuver within, or to pass in transit through certain maritime areas from which they could unduly threaten the region in question.

Even more important, however, than any of these measures, if one wishes to reduce the dangers confronting Western Europe, would be the determined and imaginative strengthening of NATO's conventional military potential. This is a much more promising course than a further attempt to rely on so-called nuclear deterrence, which is really not a deterrent at all, since almost everyone now understands that the actual use of nuclear weapons would not be a rational option for any party. The task of providing an adequate conventional deterrence is less formidable than is commonly assumed, because there has been much exaggeration of the Soviet superiority in this respect. That an imbalance exists, in certain forms of conventional weaponry and in other limited respects, no one would deny; but it would take less of an effort from the Western side, particularly financial effort, than is generally supposed to correct it.

Not only this, but if the NATO powers are seriously worried about the conventional balance, they could do more than they have done to date to explore the possibilities for agreement in the so-called MBFR (Mutual and Balanced Force Reductions) talks, in Vienna, on the reduction of the ground forces stationed in the Central European region. The disagreements on which these talks have so long been stymied are of very minor significance. The Russians have recently made interesting new proposals which, so far as the ordinary newspaper reader can ascertain, have not been explored in any serious way from the Western side.

What would seem to be needed, in short, is a little less preoccupation with the various imaginative nightmares of nuclear weaponry and a more serious application to the only real foundations of an adequate military balance, and hence of genuine deterrence, which lie in the conventional, and not the nuclear field.

A white-haired woman sits in an overstuffed chair and says, "All this talk of cutting Social Security is really making me nervous." She goes on to say that's why she's voting for Barney Frank. "How can I be sure Barney will do the right thing by us older people?" She smiles. "Because he's my son." It's irresistible.

This excerpt from a Harper's *magazine article on TV spot commercials* [1] *illustrates what has been happening to political campaigns in recent years. They are being won or lost primarily on television, and thirty- and sixty-second spots like the one above are perhaps the most important component of a TV campaign. Notice that the appeal is chiefly to emotions, not reason. And notice that it* is *irresistible. We're all suckers for Mom and apple pie. (Yes, Barney Frank won.)*

---

[1]Copyright © 1983 by *Harper's* magazine. All rights reserved. Reprinted from the April 1983 issue by special permission.

7

Advertising: Selling the Product

Advertising is so obviously useful that it's surprising it has such a bad name. Ads tell us what is new, what is available, where, when, and for how much. They tell us about a product's (alleged) quality and specifications, and sometimes they even show us the product itself (on television or in pictures). All for free, except for the effort of reading or paying attention.

Yet there are legitimate gripes about advertising. Ads often exaggerate or are otherwise misleading; some even lie. Surely that's not what we want. And since some products are advertised more heavily or more effectively than others, ads tend to skew our choices in an unreasonable way. And that too is undesirable.[2]

But let's move to the more pressing problem of how to best use advertising without getting used.

---

[2]A third common charge against advertising is that it increases sales costs and thus increases retail prices. But this charge is false. It's true that advertising costs a great deal of money, but not true that it raises prices. That would be true only if things could be sold more cheaply by some other selling method, and quite clearly there is no such other method. It's no accident that virtually all businesses advertise—they don't know a cheaper way to sell their products. Those who argue that advertising raises prices forget that if a company doesn't advertise it will have to increase other selling costs (for instance, sales commissions).

Here is ad executive Alec Benn explaining the difference between promise and identification advertising and why identification ads are so effective when done well.

How to Get People To Do What You Want with Words and Pictures

An animal learns in two ways. First, through identification: The cub sees what the mature animal does and does not do, and follows his example. He *identifies* with the other animal. Second, through promises: The trainer causes the animal to do what he wants by holding out the hope of food or [expectation of] punishment. No one has figured out any other way of influencing the behavior of an animal, even an animal as sophisticated as man.

It is easier to influence the behavior of men and women because of language. An animal must engage in random behavior in order to discover what he must do in order to gain the promised benefit. Men and women can appreciate what is required in seconds. An animal can only imitate what it sees and hears, while the wonders of language and the facility of the human mind make it possible for men and women to identify with an ideal and understand a promise.

Shakespeare, that master of audience communication, shows how to do it. Here's Henry Tudor, just before the key battle in *Richard III,* promising his troops just about all they could ever hope for:

If you do fight against your country's foes,
Your country's fat shall pay your pains the hire;
If you do fight in safeguard of your wives,
Your wives shall welcome home the conquerors;
If you do free your children from the sword,
Your children's children quit it in your age.

Look at the promises: money, love, a better life for their children! What life insurance copy Shakespeare could have written!

Advertising deals with more mundane matters, but the same emotion must be aroused: hope of a better life. The promise may be of something superior: "Get clothes whiter than white." Or something more: "Get four for the price of three." Or something cheaper: "Lowest fares to Europe."

The most successful promises aim directly at the audience's self-interest, the more physical the better: taste, comfort, easier life, health, security, the chance to save time, the chance to save or make money, pleasure, power, greater sexual attractiveness. And the promise is backed up by logic. The formula is: "To get what you want, do what I want." The technique is cerebral.

The identification technique is quite different. It need not be logical. It does not depend upon reason for success but upon instinct. It aims at the heart, not the brain.

Another example from Shakespeare may help make the technique clear. Here is Henry V to his men just before the battle of Agincourt. Note that Henry V even uses the word "imitate," and suggests identification with admirable animals and the audience's fathers and mothers. The emotional appeal is to pride—and there's hardly any logic to it at all.

> . . . But when the blast of war blows in our ears,
> Then imitate the action of the tiger;
> Stiffen the sinews, summon up the blood,
> Disguise fair nature with hard-favour'd rage;
> Then lend the eye a terrible aspect;
> Let it pry through the portage of the head
> Like the brass cannon. . . .
> On, on you noble English,
> Whose blood is fet from fathers of war-proof!—
> Fathers that, like so many Alexanders,
> Have in these parts from morn till even fought,
> And sheath'd their swords for lack of argument:—
> Dishonour not your mothers, now attest
> That those whom you call'd fathers did beget you!
> Be copy now to men of grosser blood,
> And teach them how to war!—And you, good yeomen,
> Whose limbs were made in England, show us here
> The mettle of your pasture; let us swear
> That you are worth your breeding: which I doubt not;
> For there is none of you so mean and base,
> That hath not noble lustre in your eyes.
> I see you stand like greyhounds in the slips,
> Straining upon the start. The game's afoot:
> Follow your spirit; and upon this charge
> Cry—God for Harry! England! and Saint George!

Ideals change, but the fundamental technique remains the same. Marlboro became the leading cigarette brand by causing smokers to identify with the masculine cowboy. Virginia Slims became a big seller by associating itself with the women's liberation movement—"You've come a long way, baby!" . . . The U.S. Marines modernized Henry V in billboards showing good-looking young Marines in their distinctive dress uniforms and the words: "We're looking for a few good men."

The 27 Most Common Mistakes in Advertising (New York: AMACOM, 1978). Copyright © Alec Benn. Used by permission.

One solution to that problem is to become familiar with the advertising devices and gimmicks used to con the unwary, or more politely, to appeal to our emotions, weaknesses, or prejudices. It should come as no surprise that these devices are pretty much the same as those used in most persuasive rhetoric (except that ad experts are the acknowledged masters).

1. Two Kinds of Advertisements: Promise and Identification

First of all, it's important to understand that virtually all ads are of basically two kinds (or combinations of the two). **Promise advertisements** promise to satisfy desires or allay fears. All you have to do is buy the product advertised (for instance, remove bad breath by using Listerine). Most promise ads, but not all, give "reasons why" the product will fulfill the promise or do it better than competitors (example: Kleenex tissues are softer).

Identification advertisements sell the product by getting their audience to identify with the product, to remember its name, and to think of it positively (for instance, "Come to Marlboro country"). (Some identification ads are designed to get you to identify with a particular company, not a special product.)

When we use ads to get information about a product, or when we're just looking at ads on TV, we should remember that ads manipulate us in these two ways.

People tend to identify with their own kind (or, in a slightly different way, with the rich and powerful), and identification ads frequently take advantage of this fact. Recall the Life cereal ads that featured an appealing little kid and the slogan: "Try the cereal Mikey likes."

Magazine ads, for example, are tailored to match their audience. The National Rifle Association's ads in *American Hunter* magazine showed a state trooper—very macho—over the line "I'm the NRA." But their ads in women's magazines featured a pediatrician and father under the same line, "I'm the NRA." Similarly, most Virginia Slims ads feature a dolled-up, foxy white lady and the slogan "You've come a long way, baby"; in magazines with primarily black readers, such as *Essence,* their ads feature a dolled-up, foxy *black* lady and the same slogan.

Reprinted with permission of J. Walter Thompson USA.

This is the successful Marine Corps identification *advertisement Alec Benn referred to in his remark on page 203 that "the U.S. Marines modernized Henry V in billboards . . ."*

2. Things to Watch Out for in Advertisements

The good feature of ads is obvious: As stated before, ads give us useful information about products and companies. It's the bad features we have to watch out for.

Ads Don't Say What's Wrong with the Product

No product is perfect. Hence the completely informative ad would mention at least some drawbacks of the product. But no one has yet seen an ad that deliberately said anything negative about a product.[3] This means that practically every ad invites the fallacy of *suppressed evidence* by concealing negative information about the product.

Movie and theater ads routinely quote the few nice words in a negative review while omitting all the critical ones. Here is a quote from an ad for a porno flick, *Sometime Sweet Susan,* which appeared in the *New York Post* (February 21, 1975):

> Shawn Harris is pretty . . . the lusty doings, of course, get the most screen time. —Judith Crist, *New York* magazine

And here's the entire Judith Crist review:

> *Sometime Sweet Susan's* press agent boasts that it is "the first hard-core film ever made with Screen Actors Guild approval." Lord knows there's little else to boast about in this dreary little film that tries to rise above its genre with superior performances, auspices, and production values. It succeeds only in being less ugly than some and as boring as most. Coproduced by Craig Baumgarten and Joel Scott, with a screenplay by Scott and Fred Donaldson, who directed and edited the film, it's a two-thirds rip-off of *The Three Faces of Eve,* with Susan a schizophrenic as a result of her inability to reconcile her lusty doings with her moral upbringing. It's *the lusty doings, of course,* that *get the most screen time,* with all the porn rituals (hetero- and homosexual wosomes, threesomes, and a dash of sadism) observed.
>
> Union membership does not guarantee quality of performance. As Susan, *Shawn Harris is pretty* and uninteresting, and Harry Reems, the biggie of *Deep Throat* and *The Devil in Miss Jones,* proves, as Susan's psychiatrist and sex-fantasy lover, that acting with clothes on is not his forte. Neil Flanagan, a professional nonporn actor, tries unsuccessfully to beat his low-comedy dialogue as the head of the mental hospital. And Baumgarten, an ex-Lindsay aide, shows small promise as an actor in his role as Susan's first lover, although a male critic thought he "makes a rather impressive debut as a hard-core performer." To each his impressions.[4] [Italics added.]

---

[3] Except when employing "reverse twist," that is, trying to make a virtue out of an apparent defect. The Avis Rent-A-Car campaign—"We try harder (because we're only number two)"—is an example.

[4] *New York* magazine (February 24, 1975), p. 66. Copyright Judith Crist. Reprinted by permission.

Ads Use Psychological Tricks
More than Direct Appeals to Reason

We said before that promise advertisements promise the product will satisfy some need or desire or alleviate some fear, and that they usually give reasons why the product can do this for us. (Listerine will cure our bad breath because it will kill millions of germs in our mouths.) Thus it would be reasonable to suppose that such ads appeal chiefly to the rational side of our nature, since that's what "reasons why" are all about. In fact, most ads are a blend of devices designed to appeal both to reason and, via nonrational psychological ploys, to emotions. And in most cases, the nonrational aspect predominates. This is even more true of identification than of promise ads.

Consider the very successful ad campaign for "Lite Beer" from Miller. The "reasons why" you should buy Lite Beer touted in that series of commercials were quite simple: Lite Beer is better tasting and has fewer calories than regular beers.[5] But the Miller commercials didn't just inform us of these two reasons for buying their product. Miller spent many millions to tell us this simple message in a way that's psychologically more likely to be accepted by us, as all good ads do. In the Lite Beer ads, the psychological devices are *identification* and *humor.* They feature famous athletes (identification) in endless variations on the theme of ridiculous (therefore funny) confrontations between one group of athletes who say they drink Lite Beer because it tastes better and another group who say they drink Lite Beer because it's "less filling" (has fewer calories). No halfway intelligent viewer actually believes battles of this kind ever do or could occur in real life. But that, obviously, isn't the point. The primary appeal here is to emotion, not reason.

That's also why the same ads are used over and over, and why the theme of the whole ad campaign is repeated endlessly. The average TV sports fan has heard this Miller pitch dozens, even hundreds, of times. Miller wanted beer drinkers to hear it so often because they know that human psychology (not human rationality) must be appealed to to make beer drinkers think of Miller Lite when they step up to the bar or go out to the supermarket.

I'm a salesman. Salesmen don't tell you things that will cause you not to buy a product. If you are buying a used car, the salesman won't tell you what is wrong with the car.

> —U.S. Army recruiter, Dallas Texas, answering charges that
> military recruiters mislead potential recruits,
> in *Moneysworth* (May 1979)

Anyone thinking of enlisting in the military should realize that military recruiters are sales representatives who get paid to sell their product and that they will not necessarily tell you the fine print that sometimes makes all the difference.

---

[5] Lite Beer does have fewer calories, but few beer aficionados would agree that it tastes as good as "regular" beer.

It's hard to be sure why this repetitive humorous identification really works, while telling us straight just once or twice doesn't (or doesn't as well). Scratch two psychologists and you'll get two different theories on the matter.[6]

However, one thing we can be pretty sure of is that merely knowing something generally isn't enough to make human beings *use* that information when it comes time to act in everyday life. There is a great gap between mere knowledge and *effective* knowledge. This is true in general, not just concerning advertising. (One reason public opinion in America turned against our participation in the war in Vietnam was that for the first time in our history the folks back home got to see just a little of the horror of war—brought into their living rooms in living color on television evening news. Seeing one soldier shot and killed on camera has more effect on most of us than merely being told about a hundred soldiers being killed in battle.)

So, if Miller just told us that Lite Beer tastes better and is less filling, without using humor, repetition, identification, or some other device, they wouldn't effectively bridge the gap between merely hearing or understanding the message and *acting* on that understanding. But this isn't a book on psychology (except perhaps indirectly). The point here is that to be effective, an ad has to take account of human psychology. Man is a rational animal, to some extent. But he is also an emotional cauldron.[7]

To (repetitively) illustrate the point about ads playing primarily to emotions, not reason, consider one of the classics of advertising history, built around a headline that for a time became part of the language:

> They laughed when I sat down at the piano—
> But when I started to play! . . .

The promise of this ad was that the product would satisfy the desire to shine at parties. In the fine print, having put prospective customers into the proper emotional frame, the ad promised to teach piano playing quickly and with "no laborious scales—no heartless exercises—no tiresome practicing." Reason would caution the reader. After all, how is it possible to learn to play the piano without lots of practicing? But no matter; emotions sufficiently aroused will override rationality—in a sufficient number of cases. This famous ad was a tremendous success.[8]

Here's an item that won one of Esquire*'s 1980 "Dubious Achievement Awards":*

When third grade students in a Connecticut grammar school were asked to spell the word *relief,* more than half of them answered R-O-L-A-I-D-S.

Esquire (January 1981).

---

[6]For the ad executives' view on this, see "Commercials. Can You Believe Them? . . . Why the Same Ones Again and Again?" in *TV Guide* (December 2, 1982).

[7]Note that in general this book doesn't just tell you something; it also illustrates it, sometimes repetitively. Miller similarly wants to "educate" you into preferring their beer.

[8]Frank Rowsome, Jr., used its opening phrase as the title of his delightful book on advertising, *They Laughed When I Sat Down* (New York: Bonanza Books, 1959). Some of the other examples used in this chapter also appear in Rowsome's book.

Ads Often Are Deceptive or Misleading

Among the three or four widely used deceptive or misleading devices, *false implication* —stating something that is (usually) true while implying something else that is false—is perhaps the most insidious.

London Fog commercials frequently are set in London, suggesting that London Fog raincoats and jackets are made in England. In fact, they're made in Baltimore, Maryland, U.S.A. The ads never say they're made in England, but some people are bound to think so, which is why the commercial makers went to the trouble of showing models standing in front of Big Ben.

Somewhere West of Laramie

SOMEWHERE west of Laramie there's a broncho-busting, steer-roping girl who knows what I'm talking about.

She can tell what a sassy pony, that's a cross between greased lightning and the place where it hits, can do with eleven hundred pounds of steel and action when he's going high, wide and handsome.

The truth is—the Playboy was built for her.

Built for the lass whose face is brown with the sun when the day is done of revel and romp and race.

She loves the cross of the wild and the tame.

There's a savor of links about that car—of laughter and lilt and light—a hint of old loves—and saddle and quirt. It's a brawny thing—yet a graceful thing for the sweep o' the Avenue.

Step into the Playboy when the hour grows dull with things gone dead and stale.

Then start for the land of real living with the spirit of the lass who rides, lean and rangy, into the red horizon of a Wyoming twilight.

JORDAN MOTOR CAR COMPANY, *Inc.*, *Cleveland*, *Ohio*

Appeals to emotion sell products. Reason gets left behind. See They Laughed When I Sat Down *for more on this extremely successful ad, one of the first auto ads of this kind.*

The Armour Star frank ads, which correctly stated that one pound of Armour franks and one pound of steak are equal in nourishment, implied that a hot dog meal is just as nourishing as a steak meal. But did you ever try eating ten Armour franks at one sitting?

Claude Hopkins (a great from advertising's past) was the first to understand and use a beautiful variation on the false implication gambit. Hopkins believed it was a waste of money to claim your product is the best, or pure, or anything so general. He tried to understand his product sufficiently to be able to provide more specific "reasons why" a person should buy that product. (This may sound as though his ads really did inform the public about the product, and Hopkins himself may have believed this. But it didn't work that way.)

One of Hopkins's early and famous ad campaigns illustrates this well. When he was put to work on Schlitz beer ads, he discovered that each Schlitz bottle was sterilized with live steam. So he built his campaign around headlines such as "Washed with Live Steam!", omitting the fact that all breweries used live steam. He knew that competitors could not then advertise that they too used live steam—that claim had been preempted for Schlitz. And he knew most readers would assume that *only* Schlitz washed their bottles with live steam. (Apparently, he was right; Schlitz's sales went from fifth to first in short order.)

Most ads claiming a certain quality for their product without explicitly asserting its uniqueness to that product are designed to make you *assume* that only their product has that quality. If you make that assumption, you reason fallaciously.

We Can't Tell a Lie about McDonald's Cherry Pie

When is a cherry pie not quite a cherry pie? Apparently, when it's a *McDonald's Cherry Pie*. Recently, a CU subscriber wrote us complaining that she'd bought a McDonald's pie that contained only 1½ cherries. She felt cheated.

So we investigated. We analyzed cherry pies from four McDonald's restaurants in the New York area. The pies contained an average of five cherries each—slim pickings when compared to the package photo, which shows more than 100 luscious-looking cherries.

McDonald's Cherry Pies appears to flout U.S. Food and Drug Administration regulations in two ways. First, they contain only about 20 percent cherries; by FDA regulations, a frozen cherry pie must contain at least 25 percent cherries by weight. Second, the photo on the package misrepresents what's inside. The package also appears to be in violation of the Fair Packaging and Labeling Act, since it contains no list of ingredients, no distributor's address, and no net-weight statement.

We wonder how many fast-food restaurants indulge in similar small deceptions. And at what point do many small deceptions add up to one big deception?

Another misleading or deceptive device frequently employed in ads is *ambiguity.* Fleishmann's margarine says on the package, "Fleishmann's—made from 100 percent corn oil." But on the side we read in the fine print that it's made from "Liquid Corn Oil, Partially Hydrogenated Corn Oil, Water, nonfat dry milk, vegetable mono and diglicerides and lecithin, artificially flavored and colored (carotene), Vitamins A & D added."

Well, did the statement mean that Fleishmann's is made from 100 percent corn oil and nothing else, or did it mean that the oil that is the main ingredient in margarine is 100 percent corn oil (instead of, say, partly soybean oil, as in many other brands)? If challenged, Fleishmann's can say they meant the latter while being confident that some consumers will take them to mean the former.

An interesting variation on the ambiguity theme is the *ambiguous comparison.* A Colgate fluoride toothpaste ad claimed that "Most Colgate kids got fewer cavities," but it failed to state fewer than who. Again, the hope was that readers would take the ad to claim that Colgate kids got fewer cavities than those using other fluoride toothpastes, such as Crest (by far the best seller at that time). But the *true* claim was that Colgate fluoride kids got fewer cavities on the average than they did before using Colgate, when, of course, some of them used a nonfluoride toothpaste, or perhaps didn't brush their teeth at all.

The use of *weasel words* is also common in advertisements. Words like *virtually, helps,* and *fights* almost always signal a claim that is smaller than it seems (as in "*helps* control dandruff with regular use").

Similarly, *evaluative terms,* like *good, better,* and *best,* are often used in sneaky ways. At the worst (itself a slightly sneaky expression), the word *best* translates into "tied for first with all the rest" or "tied for first with all major competitors." *Lowest* also is often misleading. The "*lowest* fare to Europe" may turn out to be the standard fare. And when they say, "No one sells _____ for less," the best inference is always that others sell for the same price.

Another deceptive device often used, especially in print ads, is the *fine print takeback.* Sometimes this device is used just for humor. An example is the TWA ad with a very large bold-face headline:

TWA announces the lowest price
to Europe in history
$0.

Below that is a large picture of part of a globe with a TWA plane superimposed, and below *that* we're told: "Only TWA offers two free tickets to Europe as a bonus for flying with us in the U.S.A." But it turns out still further down in the ad that to qualify

---

Schoolchildren might examine . . . the meaning of *free gifts* offered by savings banks in return for new deposits. Strictly speaking, if a gift is not free, it is not a gift. The bank's gifts, however, are not really free: If the deposit is withdrawn before a minimum period, the gift, or an equivalent amount of money, is taken back. The free gift turns out to be a conditional gift all along.

—Fred M. Heckinger, in *Saturday Review/World* (March 9, 1974)

you'd have to fly at least 60,000 miles on TWA in the U.S.A. (that's about twenty trips across the country).

More serious, because more genuinely misleading, are fine print takebacks like the one described in the April 1983 issue of *Harper's* magazine. A Schultz Cattle Company brochure (no, you'll never see their ads on TV or in the *Reader's Digest*) used a question-and-answer format to tout investments in their company as a tax shelter:[9]

> Q. I've heard a lot about abusive write-offs this year. Are you guys for real with this 8 to 1 write-off?
>
> A. The deductions you write off against your 1982 ordinary income are ordinary business expenses allowed by IRS tax code and court decisions affecting the cattle industry.
>
> Q. Why should I use this cattle feeding tax shelter?
>
> A. If you want a "zero" tax bill for 1982, cattle feeding can help you achieve it. . . .
>
> Q. The name of my game is cash flow! Can you help me?
>
> A. Yes! Your $7,000.00 cash minimum produces $56,000.00 of 1982 deductions that will save you $28,000.00 in taxes. Subtract the two and you have a $21,000.00 positive cash flow.

But in the complicated fine print of the legal opinion accompanying the brochure—which the Schultz people could be confident would be read less carefully, if at all—we find all sorts of hedging phrases that mask doubt as to the shelter's ultimate legality, like these:

> Nonetheless, there is a material risk. . . . While the matter is not free from doubt or controversy, we feel . . . depends on all the facts and circumstances . . . has been relied upon by various courts. . . . You have represented to us. . . . While the issue is not settled. . . . It is our understanding. . . . While no one factor is to be determinative. . . . However, while the issue is not free from doubt, it is our belief. . . . Any such changes may or may not be retroactive. . . . Moreover, it is not possible to comment on all of the federal income tax consequences of the cattle feeding business.

Puffery Is Legal

Most ads that are deceptive or misleading fall into the category of *puffery* or *puffing*, a category that has gained legal recognition. Ivan L. Preston[10] characterizes puffery this way:

> By legal definition, puffery is advertising or other sales representations which praise the item to be sold with subjective opinions, superlatives, or exaggera-

---

[9]In case you haven't heard about them yet, tax shelters are ways to use the tax laws legally (in ways supposedly not intended by Congress when it passed the relevant tax laws) so as to reduce the amount of your income tax. See the *Harper's* article for more on this tax dodge and why only the rich can take advantage of it.

[10]*The Great American Blowup* (Madison: The University of Wisconsin Press; © 1975 by the Regents of the University of Wisconsin).

tions, vaguely and generally, stating no specific facts. It appears in various verbal and pictorial forms, the best known being slogans which are used repeatedly, sometimes for years, on behalf of a throng of nationally advertised products and services. Perhaps the oldest of these still actively used is P. T. Barnum's "The Greatest Show on Earth." One might call it the king of them all, which would be puffing about puffing.

He then furnishes us with a lengthy list of one-line puffs, from which the following have been selected:

> "The World's Greatest Newspaper" (*Chicago Tribune*)
> "When you say Budweiser, you've said it all"
> "King of beers" (Budweiser)
> "You can be sure if it's Westinghouse"
> "State Farm is all you need to know about insurance"

Shoot-Out in Marlboro Country

A gathering storm darkens the desert sky. Heroic movie music. The TV screen shows the stark, barren mountains of northern New Mexico, and in their shadow, a lone cowboy slowly herding his cattle home. We first see him riding in the distance behind the ambling herd. Then closer; his head is bowed beneath a sweaty, broad-brimmed oversized hat. The scene could be straight out of one of the old Marlboro commercials . . . until the cowboy comes close enough for us to see the oxygen tank strapped to his saddle. Tubes from it run up his nostrils. "New Mexico rancher John Holmes has emphysema," the crisp British voice of the narrator informs us, "brought on by years of heavy smoking."

This scene is from a TV documentary called *Death in the West*. It is one of the most powerful anti-smoking films ever made. You will never see it. . . . [It was shown once in a few areas in 1983, and again seems to have disappeared back into the closet.]

Death in the West was filmed in 1976 by director Martin Smith, reporter Peter Taylor and a crew from *This Week,* a weekly show on Britain's independent Thames Television network. The show is roughly the British equivalent of *60 Minutes.* Taylor's searing half-hour film simply intercuts three kinds of footage. The first is old Marlboro commercials—cowboys lighting up around the chuck wagon, galloping across the plains at sunset, and so forth. The second is interviews with two Philip Morris executives who claim that nobody knows if cigarettes cause cancer. The third is interviews with six real cowboys in the American West who have lung cancer or, in one case, emphysema. And after each cowboy, the film shows the victim's doctor testifying that he believes his patient's condition was caused by heavy cigarette smoking.

After opening with a commercial showing Marlboro men around a campfire, the film cuts to another campfire, where narrator Taylor is interviewing cowboy Bob Julian. "For Bob," Taylor says, "the last roundup will soon be over."

"We try harder" (Avis)

"Toshiba—in touch with tomorrow"

"You can't get any closer" (Norelco)

"Allied Van Lines—We move families, not just furniture"

"With a name like Smucker's, it has to be good"

"Georgia, the unspoiled"

"Live better electrically" (Edison Electric Institute)

"Come to where the flavor is" (Marlboro)

"Breakfast of Champions" (Wheaties)

"Every kid in America loves Jello brand gelatin"

"Prudential has the strength of Gibraltar."

Preston then goes on to list several examples of puffery consisting entirely of names—"Wonder Bread" and "Super Shell" being two examples.

"I started smoking when I was a kid following these broncobusters," says Julian. "I thought that to be a man you had to have a cigarette in your mouth. It took me years to discover that all I got out of it was lung cancer. I'm going to die a young man." (He lived only a few months after the interview.)

Emphysema victim John Holmes, the man with the oxygen tank on his horse, tells what it's like to periodically gasp for breath. "It's hard to describe . . . it feels as if someone has their fingers down in my chest." Another man interviewed, Harold Lee, had only a few months to live, and you can see it in his stubbled, emaciated face.

Death in the West was shown only once, from London, to an audience of some 12 million TV viewers, in September 1976. It was high noon for Philip Morris, and the company walked in with guns blazing. Philip Morris promptly sued Thames Television and then got a court order preventing the film from being shown until its suit could be heard. . . .

Before the injunction, the American Cancer Society was eager to use the smoking program, and *60 Minutes* was negotiating to buy it from Thames TV. Officials at *60 Minutes* had seen a print of the film and were enthusiastic about using part of it on the air. "But then," explains the show's senior producer, Palmer Williams, "the people from Philip Morris—and I don't know how— heard we were interested. They came over here right away and wanted to know why. The very next day, out came this Queen's Bench Warrant or whatever the hell it was, barring Thames TV from selling the film anywhere in the world. So we couldn't get it."

Today, the film remains locked in a London vault, headed off at the pass.

Adam Hochschild, in *Mother Jones* (January 1979).
Reprinted by permission of *Mother Jones* magazine.

Compare this with the Marlboro ad on page 214.

Robert Glatzer called the Marlboro campaign the "campaign of the century."[11] *This is a typical ad from that campaign (generally credited with vaulting Marlboros from way back in the pack to the number one brand, in America and in the world. The Marlboro campaign is an excellent example of the power of* identification *advertising. (The warning note appearing in the lefthand corner is required by law and did not appear in earlier ads of the campaign.)*

---

[11]*The Great Ad Campaigns from Avis to Volkswagen* (New York: Citadel Press, 1970).

The law allows puffery because of an interesting line of reasoning, plus a good deal of fudging. It might be supposed that the law should prohibit most puffery in a general prohibition against false statements. But this would be a mistake. Truth or falsity is not the issue. *Deceptiveness* is. We don't want to forbid all false claims or even allow all true ones, for two reasons. First, a literally true claim may imply a false one. For example, a Bayer aspirin commercial pictured an announcer holding a bottle of Bayer aspirin while stating the truth that doctors recommend aspirin for pain relief, thus implying the falsehood that doctors recommend Bayer's aspirin. And, second, a literally false statement is not deceptive if hardly anyone takes it to be true. Here is Preston's example:

> The representation that you'll have a tiger in your tank when you use Esso (now Exxon) gasoline illustrates a kind of falsity which is not deceptive. There's no tiger, but regulators have never found anyone who expected a tiger. There was no disappointment and therefore no injurious deception, even though there was falsity.

So regulators are supposed to work on the theory that it is *deceptive* advertising that should be forbidden, not false advertising. So far, so good. Now comes the fudging. It has been decided in general, as a result of actual cases, that most puffery is not illegal because it is not *deceptive* (although there have been a few cases of successful prosecution for puffery, perhaps the best known being against Geritol). But, of course, most puffery *is* deceptive—that's the point of it. If it weren't, it wouldn't be effective in getting people to buy products; it wouldn't be one of the main ingredients in so many successful ads. For instance, the Esso ad just mentioned implied that their gas is peppier, or somehow better, than other brands, which is false and deceptive.

The moral is that we can't count on the government to protect us from deceptive advertising—so we have to learn to protect ourselves.

Ads Often Use Meaningless Jargon or Deceptive Humor

As language is used with less and less precision, it comes closer and closer to being meaningless noise or jargon (jargon fools us because it often sounds so sensible). Ads, of course, contain lots of examples, in some of which there is a kernel of sense to mask their general mindlessness. On the whole, jargon is used more in ads for products that either don't do the job well at all (cosmetics, hair restorers, weight reducers) or don't do it better than competing products (cigarettes, detergents, beer). But what does it *mean*, really, to say that a brand of detergent gets clothes "whiter than white," or "beyond white"? What does an ad ask you to do when it advises you to "recreate yourself"? These appeals use language more or less in a jargony, almost meaningless way, a way designed not to *inform* but to play on emotions.

In addition to jargon, ads often soften the pitch by using humor (especially plays on words—puns) to mask weak or ambiguous appeals. A full-page Eastern Airlines ad centered around the headline statement: "It is now within your means to live beyond your means. At least for a weekend." Stripped of ambiguity and humor, the ad's claim fizzles down to simply: "Fly now—pay later."[12]

---

[12]In other words, Eastern will extend you credit—if you're a reasonable risk, of course. If they thought it was really beyond your means, Eastern obviously wouldn't extend credit.

Ads Trade on Human Tendencies to Reason Fallaciously

In our discussion of advertising so far, only the major types of fallacious appeals have been mentioned (*false implication, ambiguity, suppressed evidence*). But others are used too. *Inconsistency* is an example. The following two blurbs for General Electric television sets (which both appeared in the same newspaper ad) illustrate this:

> The Black Matrix Advanced Spectra-Brite TV Picture Tube [jargon, jargon]—hundreds of thousands of time-colored dots are surrounded by a jet black background to give the crispest, brightest picture in GE history.

> Porta Color "In Line" Picture Tube System With Slotted Mask—Now. Rectangles instead of dots for the brightest sharpest color in GE history.

If having one brightest picture sells television sets, why not have two?

Now let's take a gander at this Baltimore radio commercial for the Maryland State Lottery:

Advertising is part of a modern package that is transforming human life, for good or evil. One of the evils is an increase in the number of essentially similar products available, taking away shelf space from genuinely different products, so that meaningful choice is reduced. Here are some excerpts from a well-researched, first-rate article on how beer and other products are advertised:

Market-Shelf Proliferation—Public Pays

Market segmentation, brand proliferation and advertising intensification—all part of the same marketing strategy aimed at increasing market share and profits—comprise the dominant form of competition in most consumer packaged goods categories. Price competition is passé. Manufacturers realize that if one producer cuts prices, competitors will be forced to follow, and this will hurt the profits of all without giving the initial price-cutter any lasting advantage. Producers seldom cut the price even of a failing brand, preferring to let it die and to replace it with a new full-priced brand. [This obviously is less true in hard times than in good, since price appeals are more effective in hard times.]

The FTC's seven-year-old antitrust suit against the largest cereal producers, Kellogg, General Mills, and General Foods, charges that they have used the proliferation and heavy promotion of . . . basically similar cereals to inflate prices and profits artificially. The cereal companies also are charged with discouraging new competition by making the pieces of the cereal market so small and costly to acquire that outsiders do not find entry attractive.

As some alarmed businessmen have pointed out, the FTC's test case against brand proliferation in breakfast cereals can be applied to nearly all consumer packaged goods, from cigarettes to chewing gum, from shampoo to soft drinks. In nearly every product category, the use of brand proliferation to maintain or increase market share has the effect, if not always the intent, of

Hi. Ol' Number Five here [Brooks Robinson, Baltimore Oriole baseball great] going to bat for the lottery. And speaking of five, I never hit five home runs in a row, but the lottery has scored with five straight championship years.

There's no definitive way to sort out a mess like this, but one way would be to say that it gently leads us into committing the fallacy of *irrelevant reason* (what's all that "five" magic?) and *appeal to authority* (what does Brooks Robinson know about lotteries that the rest of us don't?)

Ads Change Our Values

To judge by advertising, it would seem that keeping clothes spotlessly clean and linens absolutely white are among life's chief preoccupations, along with reducing cold symptoms and making absolutely sure to get the most potent pain reliever.

But ads for aspirin or detergent at least trade on genuine needs, even if played all out of proportion. Some ads generate "needs" that didn't even exist before, and

---

pushing up prices, increasing profits for those most adept at playing the game, discouraging competition, and in some cases even reducing meaningful product variety and innovation.

Although it has yet to run afoul of the FTC for proliferation, the generally acknowledged master at churning out essentially similar brands and using them to plug market holes and preempt shelf space is Procter & Gamble. Its multiple brand entries in dozens of food, toiletry and household products make it the market share leader or contender in just about every category it's in.

"Isn't free enterprise wonderful?" a Procter & Gamble public relations man says of the multiplicity. Yes, indeed. But while any enterprising individual is free to make soap—it can be done at home—trying to sell it nationally in competition with a marketing giant that spends half a billion dollars a year on U.S. advertising seems a freedom without meaning to all but a handful of similarly huge corporations.

Manufacturing efficiency, often reduced by the shorter production runs associated with multiple brands, is less important in giving Procter & Gamble and other large packaged goods manufacturers an edge over small competitors than economies of scale in marketing.

The main reason that consumer packaged goods industries are becoming more oligopolistic is that market fragmentation and the soaring costs of new product development and promotion are deterring new entrants. Most would-be entrants simply cannot afford the huge advertising outlays required to penetrate the existing noise level and break down loyalties to entrenched brands. Nor can they borrow the capital required, because lenders know they can't recover tangible assets from an unprofitable investment in advertising the way they can from an unprofitable investment in plant and machinery.

A. Kent MacDougall, in the *Los Angeles Times* (May 27, 1979).
Copyright 1979, Los Angeles Times. Reprinted by permission.

perhaps still don't (ads for vaginal deodorant sprays). And others tout products that satisfy us somehow but aren't really good for us (cigarette ads).

Still, most ads appeal to already existing genuine needs, desires, and fears. Ads that trade on our fear of offending are an example (mouthwashes, deodorants). The evil in this last (innocent-looking) type of advertising is mainly that it makes us spend more time, effort, and money on heavily advertised products that satisfy only marginal desires and fears, while spending less on things that might make our lives much more satisfying.

In other words, this kind of advertising—in fact, advertising as a whole—skews our values so that we tend to favor those needs that advertisers can make more money developing over our other, often more pressing ones. In fact, a serious charge against advertising is that it increases the already strong tendency of people in industrial countries to become preoccupied with the buying and consumption of goods. The point of advertising, after all, is to *sell products*.

3. Selling the Candidate: Political Rhetoric as PR

By now, just about everyone knows that political candidates are marketed pretty much like breakfast foods or laundry detergents.[13] And that might be all right if the appeals in breakfast food and detergent advertising were rational. But they aren't, a fact we have been taking pains to illustrate.

In recent years, radio and then television have transformed the political process. A candidate standing in front of a camera can influence more voters in one 30-second spot than candidates used to reach in a whole campaign. The result is a decline in the use of billboards, lawn signs, posters, newspaper ads, Fourth of July hoopla, and whistle-stop campaigns (but not in direct mail appeals). Television wins or loses most political campaigns. (But for some candidates, direct mail appeals raise most of the money. The trick in national campaigns in recent years has been for an "out" candidate to get a few "fat cats" to put up early "seed money" to finance direct mail appeals for the money needed to pay for the extremely expensive television exposure that determines who wins or loses.)

Advertising expenditures, for example, between 1970 and 1980 soared from $19.5 billion to $53.6 billion, totaling more than $362.5 billion for the decade. Over 42,000 *new* TV commercials are developed each year, adding to the hundreds of thousands already made. Some estimates claim the average American child sees 100,000 commercials before being old enough to go to school. In 1981, a Cap'n Crunch cereal contest, unnoticed by most adults, asked kids to respond by using an 800 phone number; in four months, the Captain and his crew were overwhelmed by 24 million phone calls. Such gee-whiz statistics can only suggest the scope of advertising's impact on our society.

—*Quarterly Review of Doublespeak*,
January 1983

---

[13]Except that laws regulating deceptive advertising don't apply to political rhetoric. The First Amendment to the Constitution prohibits restrictions on free speech.

All of us come from someplace else.

Just once, you should walk down the same street your great-grandfather walked.

Picture this if you will.

A man who's spent all his life in the United States gets on a plane, crosses a great ocean, lands.

He walks the same streets his family walked centuries ago.

He sees his name, which is rare in America, filling three pages in a phone book.

He speaks haltingly the language he wishes he had learned better as a child.

As America's airline to the world, Pan Am does a lot of things.

We help business travelers make meetings on the other side of the world. Our planes take goods to and from six continents. We take vacationers just about anywhere they want to go.

But nothing we do seems to have as much meaning as when we help somebody discover the second heritage that every American has.

America's airline to the world.

See your travel agent.

Compliments of Pan American World Airways, Inc.

Advertising tends to concentrate on marginal needs, desires, and fears at the expense of many more important ones. Occasionally, however, an ad comes along that reminds us of what (for most of us) are much more important values, even though we tend to forget them in the hustle and bustle of everyday life. This Pan Am ad is one of those rare ads that tend to push us in the right direction. Yes! If we can afford it (and more of us could if we spent less on lesser needs), just once, we should walk down the same street our great-grandfather walked.

The chief political ad device on television is the spot commercial, which generally runs from 30 to 60 seconds. It is almost impossible to say anything that is truly informative on any controversial topic in 60 seconds or less.

The first presidential campaign in which television ads played an important role was the 1952 Eisenhower–Stevenson campaign. In that campaign, General Eisenhower would read from letters received from "citizens" asking questions that Eisenhower then "answered." Here is an example:

> *Citizen:* Mr. Eisenhower, what about the high cost of living?
> *General Eisenhower:* My wife Mamie worries about the same thing. I tell her it's our job to change that on November 14th.[14]

The appeal here is to Eisenhower the father figure, who will set things right just as daddy used to. (Appeal to a father figure may well be the most effective version of *appeal to authority.*) You don't have to know *how* papa fixes things, and you didn't have to know how Eisenhower was going to reduce prices. (He didn't, of course, but that's hindsight.) All you had to know was that if you voted for him, he would be on the job after the election doing something about the high cost of living.

This Eisenhower example illustrates the fact that in presidential campaigns, at least, *identification* will win every time *if* you've got the sort of candidate people can identify with. Someone like John Kennedy, who had such tremendous charisma, illustrates this. But Eisenhower, the great father figure, would be hard for anyone to beat. (On TV, Walter Cronkite was impossible to beat for the same reason.)

Richard Nixon, on the other hand, always was handicapped by an image problem. ("Would you buy a used car from this man?") So he had to work much harder than

---

A Chinese View of Advertising

Hu Yun Huan, an English language specialist from China, spent the last year teaching in a private high school in Boston. When asked about American television, he commented:

> The advertisements are pretty fantastic. Sometimes, I admire these advertisement makers. How can they imagine to make propaganda this way?
>
> In China, the process of changing ideas reminds me very much of the television advertisements. The businessman doesn't force you to buy anything. But he gives you propaganda for his product. By and by, you believe you need this kind of thing.
>
> Now, people talk about mind control in China. Actually, you are being educated to make you believe what is good and what is evil. You are not controlled any more than the businessman controls the consumer.

> *New York Times* (September 6, 1981). Reprinted in the
> *Quarterly Review of Doublespeak* (November 1981).

---

[14]Quoted by David Ogilvy in *Confessions of an Advertising Man,* p. 159. Ogilvy quotes Eisenhower as moaning between television takes, "To think an old soldier should come to this." Notice again that the ploy used is to bring up a strong desire (for lower prices) and tie the product (candidate) to the satisfaction of that desire without giving a single "reason why" the product will satisfy it.

most on his image. (In a TV interview with Theodore White, he was quoted as saying "The main thing is to get a good picture, where you're not wiping your brow," which he then demonstrated by wiping his upper lip.)

One of Hubert Humphrey's commercials in the 1968 campaign played on the fact that Nixon had chosen as his running mate a man who was almost unknown outside of his home state of Maryland, a man who happened to have the unusual name "Agnew." Democrats at the time often bucked up their sagging spirits by asking each other, "Spiro who?" So Humphrey's television advertising geniuses concocted a television spot consisting of almost a minute of laughter, with a voice saying, "Agnew for Vice President?" and at the end of the video reading, "This would be funny if it weren't so serious. . . ." All of which amounted to nothing other than a vicious *ad hominem* argument against Spiro Agnew.

One of Lyndon Johnson's television spots in 1964 emphasized the claim that Johnson was a peace candidate, while the Republican candidate Barry Goldwater was a violent hawk. (Lyndon Johnson as peace candidate seems foolish now, but, again, that's hindsight.) The commercial shows a cute little girl plucking the petals from a flower one by one while on the sound track we hear, "Ten, nine, eight, seven, six, five, four, three, two, one," at which point an atomic fireball flashes on the screen. (This "informative" commercial was too much even for the American viewing public, and was withdrawn after one nationwide showing.)[15]

In 1972, Arch Moore ran for governor of West Virginia against Jay Rockefeller, obviously not a long-time resident of that state. Rockefeller desperately wanted to shake the image of an outsider, so that's exactly where media master Robert Goodman, in charge of Moore's campaign, attacked, in a famous commercial known as the "New York spot." Several New Yorkers were asked on camera: "Excuse me, what do you think of a West Virginian running for governor of New York?"; these questions were followed by close-ups of people laughing as they dismissed this idea. They were then asked, "What do you think of a New Yorker running for governor of West Virginia?"; this was followed by the New Yorker's reply, "Ridiculous."[16] Moore defeated "outsider" Jay Rockefeller (who later ran again and won).

By 1972, political spots on TV had reached maturity. The best spots by then were just about as good as the best ones today (however, average quality—read *persuasiveness*—has increased dramatically since then). On December 7, 1980, the

---

I'm not an old hand at politics. But I am now seasoned enough to have learned that the hardest thing about any political campaign is how to win without proving that you are unworthy of winning.

—Adlai Stevenson (1956)

What one (losing) candidate learned from two runs at the presidency.

---

[15]Goldwater's campaign slogan, "In your heart, you know he's right" was twisted by Lyndon Johnson supporters into "In your guts, you know he's nuts."

[16]From one of a series of articles on "media masters" in *The Washington Post Magazine* (March 11, 1979).

Washington Post gave its "Storck" award[17] for "Best Political Advertisement of 1980" to a Jay Rockefeller ad that was part of a series intended to turn Rockefeller's national ambitions from a liability to an asset (he'd already overcome his outsider image):

> The key to it is the idea that West Virginia is a state with a long-standing inferiority complex; Rockefeller, the ad implies, is turning West Virginia from a state of losers into a state of winners. . . . Our [winning ad] shows Arkansas's [Governor] Bill Clinton, who hits the point exactly: "My state is a lot like West Virginia, and I know how you feel when you think people around the country never know anything good about you, or perhaps don't know anything at all. But I can tell you that Governor Jay Rockefeller is a good spokesman for you. He's known and trusted and respected all over the country."

The *Post* also gave Ronald Reagan an award for the "Best Performance in a Leading Role in the 1980 Media Campaign." The ad in question was a five-minute biographical spot (unusually long) designed to show that Reagan was not (in the *Post*'s words) "a right-wing bomber-thrower," but rather "a super-competent professional administrator-cum-American hero":

> We begin with Reagan accepting the Republican nomination. Then back to his youth in, as the announcer puts it, "America's heartland, small-town Illinois." Then to Hollywood, where "he appealed to audiences because he was so clearly one of them." Then the obligatory military record. Then back to Hollywood as "a dedicated union man." Then taking over "a state in crisis" and getting things "back on track." Tax cuts. Praise from the AFL-CIO. Cut to 1980: Reagan asking us to look at Jimmy Carter's record. As the music swells, the announcer says, "Governor Reagan dealt with California's problems. He will do as much for the nation."

The *Post*'s assessment (which seems right to this viewer) was that the ad was successful because it moved so well, touched a lot of bases, and convinced viewers that "after five minutes you've come to know [Reagan] well and can trust him completely."

On the other hand, the *Post* awarded poor old Jimmy Carter the "League of Women Voters Award for Responsible but Dull Political Advertising." Of the winning (that is, losing) spot, the *Post* said (exactly on target in the opinion of this viewer):

> This one is a perfect example of the shortcomings of political advertising designed to appeal to the prejudices of good-government types who hate campaign razzle-dazzle. It shows Carter, in a red-white-and-blue tie, sitting in the Oval Office speaking with very little vocal inflection and looking straight at the camera. He's talking issues just like Adlai Stevenson did in the 1950s. That's what we all think candidates should do. It's deadly dull.

---

[17]The title harks back to the late Shelby Storck, whose legendary 1968 30-minute commercial "Man from Alaska" catapulted Mike Gravel from 30 points behind to 10 points ahead over one weekend in his campaign against Ernest Gruening, and convinced diehards that TV commercials were the key to political success in the electronic age.

After watching the expressionless Carter say, "On the economy, we've taken prudent steps to control both inflation and unemployment. . . . Present trends indicate that we've been on the right track," how much of the audience stayed riveted to its sets?

The *Harper's* magazine article[18] from which the following two spots are taken succinctly explained a serious consequence of the use of this TV device, namely

the way they encourage politicians to follow their constituencies rather than lead them. All political ads are based almost entirely on the results of polling, and they stress only those points that the pollsters tell the admen will evoke a response from the voters. So the ads tend to appeal to special-interest groups in the most chicken-hearted way.

Harper's is certainly right about the consequences of the use of TV spots. But is it chicken for politicians to want to *win*?)

Harper's gave its "Tylenol Triple Seal Award for the Best Repackaged Politician" to the makers of a spot for Tom Hayden of California:

Hayden's problem was his image as a leftover 1960's student radical who had made a propitious marriage [to Jane Fonda]. In the ad, Mrs. Hayden, a pert housewife [!], bids Tom and their son farewell. Tom and son drive off to school. Weirdos carrying picket signs confront them. They walk on. "I'm not the same angry young man I was in the 1960's," says Hayden in the voiceover. "I've changed. But I still care about people."

A typically informative commercial.

Harper's "Common Cause Medal of Honor for Most Substantive Advertisement" of 1982 went to the makers of a spot for Jerry Springer, of Ohio:

Here Springer faces the camera squarely and talks for thirty seconds about taxes, ending with the single most honest remark in any political ad [in 1982]: "But if there's still a deficit and you still want potholes filled and decent schools and more jobs, understand, you're talking state income tax. You can't have it both ways." Springer lost big.

Think about that ad the next time you criticize a successful politician for being gutless and telling the voters the lies they want to hear.

The one exception to the "tell them what they want to hear" rule of political rhetoric occurs when an elected official has to tell the people the truth "in the line of duty" (the extreme case being when the nation is threatened from without). In these cases, people want to close ranks against the common foe or to solve the common problem. The trouble is that politicians know it's relatively easy to get the electorate to *think* a crisis is at hand and to whip up public opinion; a classic case was Senator Joseph McCarthy in the early 1950s, and a more disputed one is the "missile gap"

---

[18]"Barney Frank's Mother—And 500 Postmen," by Nicholas Lehman. Copyright © 1983 by *Harper's* Magazine. All rights reserved. Reprinted from the April 1983 issue by special permission. Get this article from the library and read it for 15 or 20 minutes of entertainment that will tell you more about politics and political campaigns than all those civics books you were forced to wade through in junior high school. (You'll also find out about those 500 postmen.)

various politicians have been shouting about since the early 1960s. The incumbent gains even from minor or symbolic threats to public safety, as Ronald Reagan knew very well when he stepped in front of the cameras in 1983 and, wiping a smile from his face, announced in grave tones his feigned outrage at the bombing of the U.S. embassy in Beirut. (Do you think Reagan had PR in mind when he invaded Grenada?)

The only important campaign device other than television is use of the U.S. mails. Campaigning by mail begins the day after taking office for most elected officials and gives an incumbent a large head start over potential opponents (one reason why we're never likely to see Congress give up its franking privilege).

Of course, members of Congress aren't supposed to send out-and-out campaign literature free of charge, but they are allowed to frank letters containing question-naires and, in particular, answers to letters from constituents. A *Washington Monthly* article ("Mail Fraud on Capitol Hill," by Mark Feldstein, October 1979) argued quite plausibly that at least one United States senator, Milton R. Young of North Dakota, owed his repeated reelection to his considerable ability in talking out of both sides of his mouth when answering letters from constituents. (It can't be because of accomplishments or notoriety—Milton who?—yet he was reelected regularly, starting in 1945, until his retirement in 1980.)

The article described his (and some other senators') responses to twin letters, one favoring and one opposing abortion. (Of course, no senator could possibly compose an individual reply to each letter received; every senator thus uses standard replies,

---

I participated in preparations for nearly forty of John F. Kennedy's [extremely effective] news conferences and can recall only two questions that had not been anticipated and discussed; neither was very important.

—Robert Manning, editor of *The Atlantic* magazine, quoted in *The Atlantic* (February 1977)

Running for president is a long-term operation. If you're already president, the trick is to take advantage of the office in your campaign to win reelection. News conferences are scheduled primarily as an opportunity for the president to display presidential capabilities by being on top of whatever reporters are likely to ask—an easy task since what they ask is pretty much predictable, as Manning indicates. (Ronald Reagan is an exception, because of his tendency to disobey instructions and put his foot firmly in his mouth.) Imagery is so important in politics that a president is forced to integrate his plans for doing his job as president with his plans to get reelected. Jimmy Carter's handling of the Begin-Sadat Camp David agreement is a good example. The whole thing was planned so that the three leaders would sign on the dotted line and congratulate each other on national television programs which were watched by a very large international audience. Such exposure is free, of course, which is one reason it's so hard to beat an incumbent. (But media coverage of the Iranian hostage crisis, especially given the "incomplete success" of the rescue attempt, may have shot Carter down in 1980.)

classified by issue and by position taken on an issue.) Here is the main part of Young's standard reply to antiabortion letters:

> I thought you would be pleased to know that I have strongly supported the position you take. I have been a co-sponsor of a resolution in the Senate proposing a Human Life Amendment since the Supreme Court issued its decision liberalizing abortion almost six years ago.

But here's the sort of thing you got in reply to a pro-abortion letter:

> I appreciated hearing from you and receiving your views on this matter, . . . I agree with you that a woman should have a right to decide whether or not she wants an abortion.

All politicians have to do this sort of thing.

While TV is the principle ring in which political battles are fought these days, candidates still have to conduct grueling "grass roots" campaigns and thus be on almost continual public display for several months. (The main point of this, of course, is to get a minute or two on TV evening news programs.) This marathon campaigning doesn't leave much time for thinking about what to say. So a candidate is likely to have the same set items, which are juggled to fit each particular audience. Here, for example, is Jimmy Carter in his famous 1976 *Playboy* interview (in which he admitted he lusted in his heart after other women). The question was whether he didn't feel numb delivering the same speech over and over:

> Sometimes. But I generally have tried to change the order of the speech and emphasize different things. Sometimes I abbreviate and sometimes I elaborate. Of 20 different parts of a speech, I might take seven or eight and change them around. It depends on the audience—black people, Jewish people, chicanos— and that gives me the ability to make speeches that aren't boring to myself.

True. But it also gave him the chance to tell each group what it wanted to hear that other groups might not have wanted to hear.

About seven years ago Dialcom began working with Rep. David Emery (R-Maine), a former electronics engineer, to develop software that would allow a congressional staff to answer and file letters more quickly. Now, two-thirds of the House members pay Dialcom $1,000 a month for access to a system that allows staffers to compose letters by drawing from a bank of prewritten paragraphs relating to most political subjects in which their bosses have an interest.

The next step: computer terminals on every desk that would permit a staffer to type in a constituent's name and see a history of the constituent's correspondence. Which means a member of Congress about to talk with Joe Voter could instantly know Mr. Voter's pet peeves and prejudices.

—*Washington Post Magazine* (June 6, 1982)

Another Carter answer was revealing in what it said about reporters who cover presidential campaigns:

> The local media are interested, all right, but the national news media have absolutely no interest in issues *at all*. . . . The traveling press have a zero interest in any issue unless it's a matter of making a mistake. What they're looking for is a 47-second argument between me and another candidate or something like that. There's nobody in the back of this [campaign] plane who would ask an issue question unless he thought he could trick me into some crazy statement.

Reporters want confrontation and controversy, because that's what gets viewer or reader attention. Carter, naïve or idealistic as he was, wanted to talk about the issues, but was rarely able to.

Speaking of issues, they, too, can be advertised successfully by the standard Madison Avenue techniques. Here is Richard E. Smith, U.S. Corps of Engineers area engineer for the Tennessee-Tombigbee Waterway boondoggle, on the Corps's "public posture on costs": "I would recommend we hold the federal cost under $1 billion. Say $975,000,000. Considering the size of the estimate, $975 million is no less accurate than $1 billion and it has less emotional impact." Does this remind you of how businesses will price an item at $49.50 instead of $50 even? (At least businesses don't jack up the price as you're about to hand over the money. In the case of the Federal government, the price—called an "estimate"—is usually raised several times.)

Political image building is not restricted to candidates for office. J. Edgar Hoover, the first and for many years the only director of the FBI, was a master image builder, both for himself and for his baby, the FBI. The FBI's "Ten Most Wanted" list is one of the great image ploys of all time (no puffery here). In order to gain maximum publicity for the bureau, the list has had to mirror the interests of the times. Thus, in the 1950s, it ran to bank robbers and auto thieves, leaving organized mobsters and such types alone. As the sixties wore on, left-wing radicals like Angela Davis, Bernadine Dorn, and H. Rap Brown were featured. But today, that's passé. We now have accused sex killers like Ted Bundy and alleged porno kings like Michael G. Davis, along with an occasional big-time mobster. The Ten Most Wanted list is not an important part of the bureau's crime-fighting equipment, but it is great media hype.

Political rhetoric is not much different from other advertising when you get right down to it. The point is to manipulate the public to buy the product. For instance, vagueness and ambiguity are used, just as elsewhere—leading Jerry Brown to remark during his 1976 gubernatorial campaign, "In this business, a little vagueness goes a long way."

This is true in particular of the vague cliché—which is used even more frequently in political rhetoric than in soap commercials. Mike Royko (in his column of August 21, 1976) marveled at this string of clichés from just the first paragraph of a Repub-

---

The logic of campaign rhetoric is ruled by the psychologic of human nature.

—Harold Gordon

lican convention speech by vice presidential candidate Robert Dole: "Proud of the confidence. . . . Gratified by your trust. . . . Humbled by this new opportunity. . . . Determined to work with all my heart. . . ." Dole then topped himself with these dazzlers: "The eyes of the world are. . . . Weathered the storm of. . . . The future gleamed brightly for. . . . A long and noble chapter in. . . . Those principles upon which America was founded are. . . ."

Two college professors, John F. Cragan and Donald C. Schields, applied marketing research techniques to political issues and wrote a mock political speech conforming to what they had learned. The speech contains "no notion of a coherent policy. It is just telling people what they want to hear. The rhetoric does not flow from any thought-out foreign policy. These are just winning phrases." Typical are the following:

"America requires a President who is experienced in diplomacy and capable of managing world stability. The international scene demands a chief executive who carries out a coherent and consistent foreign policy that can be understood and respected by allies and adversaries alike."

"Today's international scene is one in which the major powers have reached military parity. What we must do is manage and stabilize our relationships with each other and maintain the balance of power. In a nuclear age we cannot escape the responsibility to build a safe future through wise diplomacy."

"The U.S. will continue to meet its responsibilities to its allies. However, to maintain world order, we will continue to seek and negotiate stable relationships with all nations."

"The U.S. is not a crippled giant. We are still a great economic and military power. In a showdown with communism, it will be American power that will determine the destiny of free men and women."

"The U.S. needs a President with a moral vision of promoting the welfare of mankind. America requires a leader who treats other nations with mutual respect; who promotes and encourages increased human rights and fundamental freedoms; who responds consistently in a calm, cool and reasoned manner."

"Detente means a state of affairs marked by the absence of significant tensions that could lead the U.S. to a nuclear confrontation. Detente does not mean that all differences will be resolved or that Russia no longer will attempt to expand her influence. It does mean that peaceful co-existence is the only rational alternative."

Bob Greene, *Chicago Tribune*, (October 23, 1980). Reprinted in the
Quarterly Review of Doublespeak (July 1981).

So they were shocked when several political candidates approached them to write speeches for them just like the mindless, computer-generated, market-tested speech they'd invented.

Why Pay Attention to Campaign Rhetoric?

If most campaign rhetoric is just PR, why pay attention to it? Good question. Perhaps the only reason for most people is to get a rough idea which groups and policies a candidate seems to be appealing to (and also to find out the mood of the nation—how they're responding to all that political rhetoric on TV).

For instance, in the 1980 election, it was useful to occasionally follow the presidential campaign to see which factions and ideas the "out" candidate Reagan favored (Carter had a track record as president, so his actions as president were much more important than his words). Similarly, it was useful to get an overview on local and state elections.

But finding out what candidates *say* they're going to do is useless by itself. The question is whether we can learn something from this about what they're actually going to do if elected. It's true, of course, that the better we are at reading between the lines, the more we can learn about what they're going to do from what they say they're going to do. But in nearly every case, we can learn more about what candidates are going to do from their track record (what they've actually done in the past) and from the discussions that go on in the more sophisticated non-mass media magazines. (Believing campaign rhetoric outright is just committing the fallacy of *appeal to authority.* For more on this topic, see the end of Chapter 8 on Managing the News.)

If the campaign rhetoric of TV spots is basically PR, there's little point in using high powered logic to analyze them. Of course, destroying campaign rhetoric can be great fun ("They laughed when I started to criticize, but when I tore Reagan's speech to bits, . . ."). But it amounts to overkill. We know ahead of time that most such rhetoric consists mostly of illogic designed to present the "right" image (so voters will identify with a candidate) or appeal to emotions in some other way. So we know it isn't likely to tell us right out what a candidate is going to *do* if elected, except in a very rough, general way. (On the other hand we can learn a bit from campaign rhetoric by reading between the lines.)

Summary of Chapter Seven

1. Advertising is useful because it tells us about products we may want to buy. There are two basic kinds of ads. *Promise* ads promise to satisfy desires or reduce fears and usually give us "reasons why" the product will do that. *Identification* ads sell the product by getting us to identify with it (or with a company). Of course, most ads contain a combination of both promise and identification devices.

2. But advertising has its drawbacks. We have to be a bit wary:
   a. *Ads don't tell us what's wrong with the product,* thus tempting us to commit the fallacy of *suppressed evidence.*
      Example: Ads for over-the-counter nonprescription drugs which rarely tell us about possible side effects.
   b. *Ads use psychological tricks more than direct appeals to reason.*
      Example: The Lite Beer TV commercials that use identification, humor, and repetition, while giving us the quickly stale "reasons why" over and over again.

c. *Ads are often deceptive or misleading,* in particular by making *false implications* while literally stating the truth.
   Example: The London Fog commercials that imply their raincoats are made in England.
      Note that all sorts of other devices, such as *weasel words* and *fine print takebacks* are also used.
d. *Ads commonly use puffery.* (Note that puffery is legal).
   Example: The *Chicago Tribune*'s motto: "World's greatest newspaper."
e. *Ads often use meaningless jargon or deceptive humor.*
   Example: Tide getting clothes "whiter than white."
f. *Ads tempt us to reason fallaciously.*
   Example: Testimonials inviting the fallacy of *appeal to authority.*
g. *Ads tend to twist our values* toward those values that an easily advertised product might satisfy.
   Example: Making us more concerned with buying just the right pain reliever or cold symptom suppressor than with the real necessities of life.

3. It's also important to realize that political candidates and policies are sold via advertising in much the same way as other "products." Identification, in fact image making in general, is the most frequently used device.
   Political campaigns nowadays are fought chiefly on television (although the mails are also important, especially to raise money). The quality of their TV spots, plus their ability to get coverage on TV news programs, wins or loses the race for most candidates.
   Example: The Barney Frank commercial featuring his mother.
   So it's a relative waste of time to spend great effort carefully analyzing political rhetoric meant primarily for the mass of voters, although paying rough attention is useful. (More important is to spend time and expend thought on serious political tracts and issues, of the kind more frequently encountered in the non-mass media.)

Exercise 7-1

Here are several ad snippets (usually including the main ad ploy). In each case, state: (1) whether the ad, if true, would provide a good reason for buying the product; (2) whether the ad contains questionable claims, and, if so, which claims are doubtful *and why;* (3) which, if any, of the devices employed were discussed in this (or some other) chapters (explain); and (4) which, if any, of the ads use emotive language unfairly (that is, so as to con).

1. Ad for Senator McGovern in 1972 presidential campaign: Nixon has a secret plan for ending the war. He is going to vote for McGovern.

2. *Rolaids television commercial, showing a Rolaids user rejecting another brand:* Rolaids active ingredient—medically recognized safe and effective.

3. CHEMICAL BANK has an answer to all your borrowing needs. The answer is "Yes." ("Yes" is a chemical reaction.)

*4. *Bloomingdale's Department Store ad, January 1975:* Our very finest sofas, now at our lowest prices in years.

5. *The Night Porter* —most controversial film of all time.

6. *Ad for James Buckley, conservative senatorial candidate from New York:* Isn't it time *we* had a senator?

7. Take my "Hundred Dollar Knife," yours for only $4.99.

8. The ingredient in Anacin *is* doctors' number one choice.

*9. Emeralds. $5 apiece. (This is not a misprint.)

10. There's only one King David, and there's only one King David Manor.

*11. Clorets has Actizol.

12. *Robert Morley, in a British Airways ad:* "If I didn't live in Britain, I'd take these tours myself."

13. *Ad for Toronto Dominion Bank:* We have a new way to lend you money.

14. *Sign on Highland Park, Illinois, retail establishment:* 100% Pre-Driven Cars.

15. I switched from sugar to Sweet 'n Low because I care.

16. *Sign on Royal Trust Bank in Vancouver, B.C.:* Trust Royal Trust.

17. *Ad for the new Olympic Towers Apartments:* A landmark ahead of its time.

18. *Fur sale ad:* Same styles sold by prestige furriers for $495 to $6,000!

19. *Soup Starter commercial:* It's so easy, I'll feel guilty. . . . But I'll get over it.

20. Just as you can depend on the sun to rise, you can count on Metropolitan [Life Insurance Co.].

21. *Ad for Calvert Gin:* Dry, Drier, Driest, Crisp.

22. *Greyhound Bus ad:* Say Hello to America. Say Hello to a Good Buy.

23. RCA—TV that "thinks in color."

24. *Mail ad:* Special collector's edition. Priceless recordings. $6.98 per album.

25. *Man speaking:* My boss was right [that I should use Sinutab]. That's why she's the boss [photo of smiling woman on screen].

26. Penthouse *ad:* Statistics show 100 percent of the readers of the biggest selling men's magazine on the newsstands [*Penthouse,* of course] . . . wear clothes.

27. Read *Time* —You'll understand.

28. When E. F. Hutton talks—people listen.

29. At Ford, Quality is job one.

30. Nothing beats a great pair of L'Eggs.

31. Help keep America beautiful. Wear Underalls.

*32. (*In this case, here's the whole ad.*)

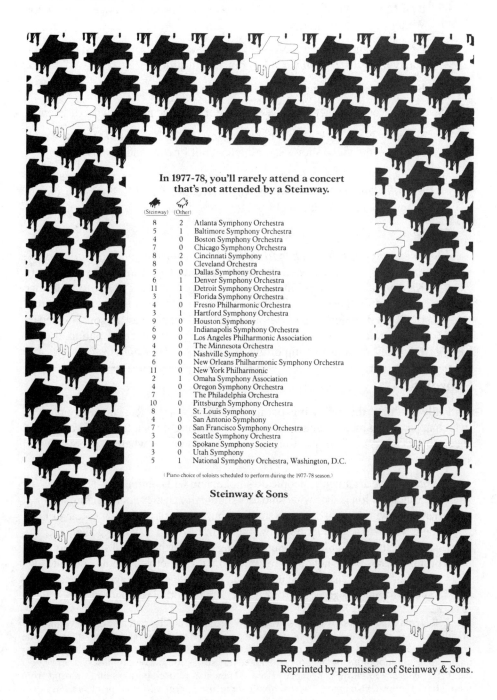

In 1977-78, you'll rarely attend a concert
that's not attended by a Steinway.

(Steinway) (Other)

8	2	Atlanta Symphony Orchestra
5	1	Baltimore Symphony Orchestra
4	0	Boston Symphony Orchestra
7	0	Chicago Symphony Orchestra
8	2	Cincinnati Symphony
8	0	Cleveland Orchestra
5	0	Dallas Symphony Orchestra
6	1	Denver Symphony Orchestra
11	1	Detroit Symphony Orchestra
3	1	Florida Symphony Orchestra
4	0	Fresno Philharmonic Orchestra
3	1	Hartford Symphony Orchestra
9	0	Houston Symphony
6	0	Indianapolis Symphony Orchestra
9	0	Los Angeles Philharmonic Association
4	0	The Minnesota Orchestra
2	0	Nashville Symphony
6	0	New Orleans Philharmonic Symphony Orchestra
11	0	New York Philharmonic
2	1	Omaha Symphony Association
4	0	Oregon Symphony Orchestra
7	1	The Philadelphia Orchestra
10	0	Pittsburgh Symphony Orchestra
8	1	St. Louis Symphony
4	0	San Antonio Symphony
7	0	San Francisco Symphony Orchestra
3	0	Seattle Symphony Orchestra
1	0	Spokane Symphony Society
3	0	Utah Symphony
5	1	National Symphony Orchestra, Washington, D.C.

(Piano choice of soloists scheduled to perform during the 1977-78 season.)

Steinway & Sons

Reprinted by permission of Steinway & Sons.

33. You're in the Pepsi generation.

34. There's a spirit in the air. The United States Air Force. Aim high—Air Force.

35. Paul Masson will sell no wine before its time [said dramatically by Orson Welles or John Gielgud].

36. *Le Sport* is more than a fragrance. It's a way of life. . . . Day and night, you play with style. *Le Sport.* Le fragrance with style.

37. Benson & Hedges Lights, B&H, I like your style.

*38. How'd you do it [get Kleenex even softer]? We've got it down to a science.

39. Some of New York's winningest players are playing at OTB [Off Track Betting—the video shows star athletes Walt Frazier and Sam Huff].

40. *Ad depicting a rich elderly gentleman talking to another one between their palatial homes:* "I was wondering if I could possibly borrow a cup of Johnny Walker Black Label."

41. Dodge trucks are ram tough.

42. *Beginning of a form letter from Teachers Insurance and Annuity Association of America (TIAA):* It simply wouldn't be true to say, "Howard Kahane [alias, Alfred Hitchcock] . . . If you own a TIAA life insurance policy you'll live longer." But it is a fact, nonetheless, that persons insured by TIAA do enjoy longer lifetimes, on the average, than persons insured by commercial insurance companies that serve the general public. Lower mortality rates are an important reason why TIAA policies cost less.

Exercise 7-2

Critically evaluate the following paraphrase of key arguments in a Vantage ad (which appeared in many magazines in 1979—you might want to track it down and check for accuracy).[19] The question addressed in the ad is whether people should smoke cigarettes:

> Whatever the arguments, people do smoke, and will continue to. The more relevant question is thus what smokers should do. Critics could recommend that those who want to continue smoking but are worried about nicotine or tar could switch to a low-nicotine, low-tar cigarette, such as Vantage. Vantage isn't lowest in tar or nicotine, but reducing them further would very likely compromise taste. We're not going to argue about whether you should continue smoking—the fact is that you do smoke. To reduce nicotine and tar, consider Vantage Menthol cigarettes (11 mg tar, 0.7 mg nicotine per cigarette).

[19] R. J. Reynolds Industries (which also makes Winstons, Camels, Salems, and several other brands) refused permission to reprint the Vantage ad verbatim, on the grounds that it is the policy of R. J. Reynolds not to do anything that might be construed as encouraging smoking among the young, pointing out that they do not advertise or promote on campuses, where *Logic and Contemporary Rhetoric* is primarily used. (They also refused permission to reprint from their letter of refusal.) No other advertiser has ever refused permission to reprint an ad in any of the four editions of this book, including Philip Morris (Marlboro's) and The Tobacco Institute. (You might want to critically evaluate Reynolds's reason for refusing to grant permission.)

Exercise 7-3

One-A-Day Plus Mineral tablets advertised that their product is more complete than several other major brands of vitamin tablets costing much more, and then went on to show that One-A-Day contains this mineral not in Brand *B,* that vitamin not in Brand *C*, and so on (thus providing evidence for the claim that their product is more complete). Would you trust this ad and switch to One-A-Day Plus Minerals, or would you figure there was probably a catch to it, and if so what catch?

Exercise 7-4

Here are two more advertisements. Check them for ad ploys and the like:

1. *From the side of a Cap'n Crunch cereal box:* THE SUGAR STORY. In considering presweetened cereals, there is no substitute for the facts: a serving of Cap'n Crunch contains 12 grams of sugar. That's about two rounded teaspoonsful, enough to make Cap'n Crunch's wholesome blend of corn and oats taste great and stay crunchy in milk. Yet a serving of Cap'n Crunch contains no more sugar than many other everyday foods. . . . [A comparison is made to one cup of canned spaghetti, half a peanut butter and jelly sandwich, one frosted "pop-up" fruit tart, and a half cup of flavored gelatin.] Served with ½ cup milk, one ounce of Cap'n Crunch provides 25% of the U.S. Recommended Daily Allowances of eight essential vitamins and minerals. . . .

2. *Headline on Monsanto chemical company ad:* Mother Nature is lucky her products don't need labels. [And then, below a picture of an orange with a long, fine print list of its ingredients:] All foods, even natural ones, are made up of chemicals. But natural foods don't have to list their ingredients. So it's often assumed they're chemical free. In fact, the ordinary orange is a miniature chemical factory. And the good old potato contains arsenic among its more than 150 ingredients. This doesn't mean natural foods are dangerous. If they were, they wouldn't be on the market. The same is true for man-made foods. All man-made foods are tested for safety. And they often provide more nutrition, at lower cost, than natural foods. They even use many of the same chemical ingredients. So you see, there really isn't much difference between foods made by Mother Nature and those made by man. What's artificial is the line drawn between them. Monsanto. Without chemicals, life itself would be impossible.

Exercise 7-5

Find two or more ads for the same product in different publications that are tailored to different audiences, and explain how it's done. (Example: the Virginia Slims ads containing a foxy white or black lady, depending on the expected audience.)

DOES THE GOVERNMENT SUPPORT THE TOBACCO FARMER?

NO, THE TOBACCO FARMER SUPPORTS THE GOVERNMENT.

Some people want to hear only one side of an argument.

That's not you, obviously—or you wouldn't be reading this.

You've heard the side of the anti-smokers—that the government is, in some way, "supporting" or "subsidizing" the tobacco farmer.

Here is the other side of that argument. And if you're not a tobacco farmer, you'll probably be surprised, maybe even pleased, to hear it.

Because the truth is the other way around: It's the tobacco farmer who's supporting the government.

There *is* a government program called the tobacco price support program. It began in 1933, and for the past 45 years it has been the single most successful farm program the government has ever had. It costs next to nothing, and it pays enormous dividends to all taxpayers.

The heart of it is a simple businesslike arrangement. The government offers the tobacco farmer what *he* needs: a guaranteed price for his crop. If commercial buyers do not meet this price, the farmer receives a government loan and surrenders his crop. And the government gets, in return, what the *government* needs: the farmer's agreement not to plant any more than the government tells him he can.

The government's interest, and the taxpayer's, is in preventing economic chaos. Without the weapon of the loan agreement, the government would be powerless to limit the production of tobacco. The results would be as predictable as any disaster can be: overplanting of the crop by big farmers with extra land and by

newcomers, a fall in the price of tobacco, a drop in the income of small farmers to the point where many would be squeezed off the land and onto welfare rolls, sharp decreases in tax collections in the 22 states that grow tobacco, widespread disruptions in the banking and commercial systems and, if you want to follow the scenario out to its grim conclusion, very likely a regional recession.

The value of the program to the government, and to the taxpayer, is thus very great. And the cost is unbelievably low. Over the entire 45 years of its operation, the total cost of the government guarantee has been less than $1¼ million a year, or roughly what the government spends otherwise every 79 seconds. This is because the government has been able to sell, at a profit, almost all the tobacco it has taken as loan collateral.

From the farmer's viewpoint, the tobacco support program might as easily, and more justly, be called a *government* support program, since it does more to support the government than it does to support him.

One fact above all others tells you the true story. For all his labors in planting, growing and harvesting his crop, the farmer receives $2.3 billion. And from the products of his labor, the government (federal, state and local) collects $6 billion in taxes.

It's enough to make even an anti-smoker, at least a fair-minded one, agree that, on balance, it's the tobacco farmer who's supporting the government. And doing it superbly.

THE TOBACCO INSTITUTE

1776 K St. N.W., Washington, D.C. 20006

Exercise 7-6

Evaluate the Tobacco Institute advertisement on the opposite page, following the instructions given for evaluating extended passages in Chapter 6. Also point out any ad ploys discussed in this chapter.

Exercise 7-7

Repeat the experiment described by Mark Feldstein in his *Washington Monthly* article (page 224), choosing a different topic than abortion. That is, write two letters to one of your senators or representatives in Washington, one letter taking a short, strong stand on some issue, the other letter taking an equally strong but different stand (opposite, if possible) on the same issue. Compare the two replies you get and draw conclusions. (Send each letter from a different address or at different times and use different names, because some members of Congress may be keeping track on computers.)

Exercise 7-8

1. Watch television for several hours, noting the main ploys of at least three or four commercials. Then analyze for fallacies, use of emotive language, and other advertising gimmicks discussed in this chapter.

2. Rewrite an advertisement containing highly charged emotive language ana fallacies (in other words, a particularly gimmicky ad). Once you have discovered its true informational content, compare your version with the original ad, and then critically evaluate the original ad.

Exercise 7-9

Do some research and find out what candidate Ronald Reagan promised the American public he'd do in the next four years if elected in 1980, and then compare that with what in your opinion President Reagan actually accomplished in those four years. (Support your research and opinions with evidence or reasons; don't pontificate or bullsling.)

Drawing by Richter: © 1975 The New Yorker Magazine, Inc.

"Attention out there! We now bring you an opposing viewpoint to a CBS editorial."

This cartoon effectively makes the point that the power of freedom of speech is relative. If you set policy for CBS news, your views will be widely heard and very influential, but if you're just one of the rest of us, you have no effective way to compete with the giants in the marketplace of ideas. You might just as well let off steam by shouting from the rooftops—or balconies.

8

Managing the News

Reasoning about political and social issues requires factual knowledge. That's why the success of a democratic form of government depends on a *well-informed* electorate. Unfortunately, the American mass news media (newspapers, television, mass magazines, and radio) do not adequately or accurately inform their readers or listeners. In particular, they fail to inform them of the great gulf between the way our society is supposed to work (the ideal—the "official story") and the way it actually works.

Yet we all have to rely on the mass media for news. Those who understand how and why things get reported as they do will be better able to evaluate that reporting, better able to read between the lines, separate wheat from chaff, and not be taken in by questionable reasoning or poor coverage. They'll also understand why the mass media have to be supplemented by selectively chosen non-mass media sources.

1. Television Channels, Radio Stations, Newspapers, and Magazines Are Businesses

The one overriding fact to bear in mind in trying to understand the mass media is that CBS, the *Los Angeles Times, Newsweek* magazine, and all the rest are *businesses,* intended to return a profit. They have two sets of "buyers"—their audiences (readers, viewers, listeners) and their advertisers. When they displease, annoy, or threaten either of these groups too seriously, they're likely to fail, or at least seriously reduce profits. *There is always more money in catering to both groups.*

We should expect, then, if our world view tells us businesses are run to maximize profits,[1] that media executives will shape the news so as to please their buyers. And this is just about what we find to be true.

News Selection Reflects the Interests, Opinions, and Prejudices of Its Audiences

Viewer and reader interests, opinions, and prejudices must be taken into account in reporting the news. Newspaper readers and television viewers are not captive audiences (as they were, say, in Nazi Germany and Fascist Italy, where outdoor loudspeakers blared the official line to the public). They can flick the switch or turn the page. The result is *provincialism* —news reporting that tends to reflect the interests and foibles of its audience, as world travelers often are amused (or dismayed) to discover. (That was the import of the Abbie Hoffman remark quoted at the beginning of the chapter.)[2]

The *New York Times* continues to adhere to high standards of dispassion. Take, for example, ABC's recent investigation of the secret maneuvers to obtain the release of the [Iranian] hostages. The *NYT*'s TV critic, John J. O'Connor, very reasonably felt that this was a major exposé which deserved notice and indeed praise.

A. M. Rosenthal, executive editor of the *NYT,* thought otherwise. Perhaps he felt that the *NYT*'s own efforts in this area would be diminished by such congratulation. At all events, the O'Connor review was killed.

—Alexander Cockburn, in *The Village Voice*
(February 11, 1981)

Why should the New York Times *praise a competitor's (in this case) superior product? (If you disagree with Cockburn's explanation, can you think of another plausible one?)*

---

[1]Fortunately, small-circulation political publications tend to be exceptions. While theoretically *in business,* they rarely make a profit or pay a dividend. People "invest" in such enterprises to champion a point of view or gain an outlet for their own opinions, not to make money.

[2]News reporting also reflects the prejudices and interests of media employees, top management, and owners. Run of the mill employees, including most reporters, tend to have the same biases as the rest of us. But owners and top brass generally see things from the point of view of the rich and powerful (with whom they associate).

The media cater to their audiences in all sorts of ways. For instance, they play up stories about alleged UFO citings (flying saucers and that sort of thing), often with an implication that there might actually be something to that nonsense. An example is the *U.S. News and World Report* article (February 20, 1978) titled "Is There Something to UFO's After All?" which gave the impression that reasonable people might differ on this topic. Here is a snippet giving the flavor of the whole (one-page) article:

> How many of these sightings are given much credence by UFO experts?
>
> Most can be explained. Among the objects that have been misidentified as UFO's are stars, planets, meteors, advertising planes, helicopters, balloons and even a street light.
>
> What about the others?
>
> Opinions differ sharply. Persons who advocate more research on UFO's contend that the unexplained sightings are an indication of life from other worlds visiting earth. Disbelievers argue that the phenomena either have logical explanations or are fabricated reports.

The reason for *U.S. News*'s "balanced" account of the UFO business is quite simple—large numbers of their readers would like to believe flying saucers really exist.

Similarly, the media tend to play into other audience prejudices. If a majority of Americans think marijuana and cocaine are much worse than alcohol and cigarettes, the media are bound to be swayed into portraying the drug scene in that way, even though all scientific evidence and several thousand years of experience indicate otherwise.

A large majority of the 1,500 or so daily newspapers left in the United States carry regular horoscope columns in which oracular advice (extremely general and likely

By permission of JULES FEIFFER. Copyright 1978. Distributed by Field Newspaper Syndicate.

Most of the U.S. media audience is white, in particular the portion with the most money to spend. The news in most papers thus gets slanted to their interests and prejudices.

to "fit" almost anyone and any situation) is dished out to the faithful. Yet astrology has no scientific validity whatever, and the basic objections to it were raised centuries ago,[3] a fact newspapers rarely tell their audiences. So long as astrology columns attract readers, newspapers will print them.

Similarly, so long as lots of readers are offended by words like *sh*t, f*ck,* and *f*rt*—to print them the way some publications do when it would be hard to avoid them altogether—the media will do their best to pretend these words don't exist. Which is fair enough, given that there isn't any reason to gratuitously offend audiences. But then you should realize that your favorite ball players, or politicians, probably didn't say "shucks," "darn," or "baloney."

The need for the media to cater to their audiences also is (partly) responsible for the general *lack of proportion* in media coverage. While it's true to some extent that an event becomes as important as the media decide to make it, it's even more true that they play stories up or down depending on audience interest. This is nicely illustrated by the way the media played up the 1982–83 Israeli "incursion" into Lebanon, while playing down the much larger and bloodier war between Iran and Iraq.[4] Or compare the vast coverage of the Iranian hostage "crisis" with either the war in Lebanon or the Iran-Iraq war.

The mass media also cater to their audience by means of *sensationalism,* in particular by picturing certain kinds of nasty extremes as common or even the rule. For example, *Time* magazine's cover story for April 11, 1983—"Fighting Cocaine's Grip—Millions of Users, Billions of Dollars"—started out with this extreme case, which actually fits only a handful of users:

Crashing on Cocaine

*Burnt-out cases proliferate, as drug-traffic cops
wage a no-win war*

Phil and Rita's life shimmered like an advertisement. Indeed, to an outsider it seemed less a life than a perfect life style: tree-lined California suburban street, tasteful $150,000 home (with piano), two sunny youngsters. Phil, 37, was a $30,000-a-year microchip sales engineer in Silicon Valley. Rita, 34, was a $20,000-a-year bookkeeper. Like their smart, attractive Northern California

---

In a media-dominated world, children who insist upon the actuality of the Bermuda Triangle, the reality of pyramid power, or the accuracy of astrological projections are quick to refer to having seen it on TV, having read it in a book, or having seen it in the newspaper. This presents a problem for skeptical adults. When the media uses such terms as "Bermuda Triangle" freely, they are, in effect, creating an air of legitimacy. Logically, children conclude that there must be some truth to the matter if they see it in their local paper.

Ray Hyman, in a book review in the *Skeptical Inquirer* (Winter 1980–81)

---

[3]Recall our discussion of astrology in Chapter 1, pages 31–32.

[4]Another reason for this great difference in coverage was the availability of motion pictures for TV news programs.

friends, Phil and Rita played tennis and ate interesting foods and knew about wine and, starting four years ago, sniffed coke.

And more coke. And then more. That is why several times last year Phil stood quivering and feverish in the living room, his loaded pistol pointed toward imaginary enemies he *knew* were lurking in the garage. Rita, emaciated like her husband, had her own bogeymen—strangers with X-ray vision outside the draped bedroom window—and she hid from them in the closet. The couple's paranoia was fleetingly sliced away, of course, as soon as they got high: they "free-based," breathing a distilled cocaine vapor, Phil alone all night with his glass water pipe and thimble of coke, Rita in another room with hers. In the mornings, Phil and Rita got back together, down on all fours, scratching and picking at the carpet for any stray grains of coke.

[Below was drawn an X ray of a man's head being blown apart (presumably by coke).]

News Is Simplified for the Mass Audience

Another of the standard ways in which the news is distorted is *simplification.* On the whole, media audiences are not sophisticated. They cannot, or at least will not, pay attention to complicated material (we saw the result of this in political spot commercials). The trouble is that almost all social and political issues are complicated, so that simplified accounts of events or issues must in general be distorted accounts.[5]

Take the ongoing question of an alleged "missile gap" between the United States and the Soviet Union. By some point in the 1950s, both nations had developed gigantic nuclear missiles capable of traveling thousands of miles to their targets. Within a very few years, all sorts of politicians found it expedient (particularly at election time) to shout from the housetops about how the Russians were getting ahead of us in "nuclear capability." John Kennedy was one of the first to use this ploy, and every president since then has played with this gambit at one time or another. The media have dutifully reported their allegations, but without a convenient exposition of the complex arguments on both sides of the issue that would enable the average person to come to a rational conclusion. There have been occasional exceptions, but they have had little effect on the mass of voters. (Note, however, that there are other forces tending to oversimplify reporting on this and other issues—some are discussed in the next few sections of this chapter.)

Organized Groups Apply Effective Pressure

The power of one person is small compared to that of an organized group. All but one advertiser withdrew its support from CBS's documentary *The Guns of August,* about World War I, after a letter-writing campaign organized by the National Rifle Association. Similarly, General Motors dropped out of the NBC mini-series *Jesus of*

---

[5]When considering this and other matters concerning the print media, it's important to remember that large numbers of Americans are functionally illiterate (estimates range to 40 percent), and many others are unable to read even modestly complicated sentences (like this one).

Nazareth in 1977 after criticism by Protestant church leaders. Even the PTA was powerful enough to pressure Sears, Roebuck into dropping sponsorship of *Charlie's Angels* (too much sex) and *Three's Company*. And no newspaper in Utah was foolish enough to run the 1979 Pulitzer Prize-winning exposé of Mormon Church power in that state.

In a reverse twist on the usual case where whites have their opinions pandered to at the expense of blacks, several black political groups were successful in suppressing a WNET (Channel 13, New York) Public Broadcasting System documentary, *Harlem, Voices, Faces.* PBS bowed to pressure generated by producer Tony Brown, who argued that ". . . the bigoted sector of white America will have its prejudices frozen in place and reinforced, and so many black people who need positive images so desperately to overcome the despair the film so ominously reveals will be even more psychologically destitute." No one claimed that the documentary was false or misleading. Harlem residents shown the film said that "that is how it is in Harlem these days."[6]

News Selection Reflects the Interests of Advertisers

The interests of advertisers are almost as important as viewer interests in distorting the news. It could hardly be otherwise given that most media revenue, and thus profit comes from advertisers. This is true even of newspapers, which charge for their product, (unlike television). In the late 1970s, the *Washington Post*, for instance,

---

Dart: to the Danbury, Connecticut, *News-Times.* The assistant copy-desk chief who ran this picture [of a disgruntled customer carrying a sign reading "Potential Customers *Beware* of Colonial Ford] in the February 18 Sunday edition was fired the next morning for "a gross lapse in judgment." The photo appeared at the end of a week in which the paper had been arranging for favorable coverage to soothe boycotting advertisers offended by its earlier used-car consumer guide. . . .

Dart: to *The Jersey Journal,* Hudson County, New Jersey, for fatuously recording in a six-column interview (with photo) on February 9 the observations of a local merchant following his return from a week's vacation in Egypt. Also carried in the same edition was a full-page ad for the man's furniture and appliance store.

Columbia Journalism Review (May/June 1979)

These "darts" were given by the Review *along with other darts and "laurels," including a laurel to the* Saginaw (Michigan) News *for a front-page exposé of racial prejudice in local housing. Those outside the news business may find it hard to appreciate the guts it takes for a local paper to buck the furniture, real estate, or auto interests that provide so much ad revenue.*

---

[6]*New York Times*, June 8, 1975.

Last year, 300,000 Americans were arrested for smoking an herb that Queen Victoria used regularly for menstrual cramps.

It's a fact.

The herb, of course, is *cannabis sativa.* Otherwise known as marijuana. pot. grass, hemp. boo. mary-jane. ganja—the nicknames are legion.

So are the people who smoke it.

By all reckoning, it's fast becoming the new national pastime. Twenty-six million smokers, by some accounts—lots more by others. Whatever the estimate, a staggeringly high percentage of the population become potential criminals simply by being in possession of it. And the numbers are increasing.

For years, we've been told that marijuana leads to madness, sex-crimes, hard-drug usage and even occasional warts.

Pure Victorian poppycock.

In 1894. The Indian Hemp Commission reported marijuana to be relatively harmless. A fact that has been substantiated time and again in study after study.

Including, most recently, by the President's own Commission. This report stands as an indictment of the pot laws themselves.

And that's why more and more legislators are turning on to the fact that the present marijuana laws are as archaic as dear old Victoria's code of morality. And that they must be changed. Recently, the state of Oregon did, in fact, de-criminalize marijuana. Successfully.

Other states are beginning to move in that direction. They must be encouraged.

NORML has been and is educating the legislators, working in the courts and with the lawmakers to change the laws. We're doing our best but still, we need help. Yours.

Used with permission of NORML.

Ad Censorship

NORML marijuana ad rejected by Time *and* Newsweek, *accepted by* Playboy. Time *and* Newsweek *readers tended to strongly oppose dope smoking.*

pulled only 15 percent of its revenue from sales to readers. Most of the rest came from advertising.

New York Times columnist Tom Wicker illustrated this in his book *On Press* by explaining how the power structure in Winston-Salem, North Carolina, influenced local news coverage. He concluded, (not surprisingly, in a town named "Winston-Salem") that "the cigarette-cancer connection got short shrift in [the *Winston-Salem Journal*] newsroom."[7]

On November 31, 1977, the Williamsburgh Savings Bank (of Brooklyn, New York) contracted to purchase ads in nine editions of a local paper, the *Phoenix*. This meant $2,000 in ad revenue. But on December 1, the *Phoenix* published a list of 166 directors of the 13 major savings institutions in Brooklyn accused of redlining (refusing to loan in certain areas, which generally results in deterioration of those areas—money deposited by people in redlined areas gets loaned out in other areas). On December 7, the Williamsburgh Bank canceled the last eight ads. (No, we don't commit the fallacy of *questionable cause* in concluding that this cancellation was almost certainly caused by the paper's publication of those 166 names.)

News Selection Reflects the Power of Government

Government has the right and often the power to regulate business activity. It can thus harass a news source that displeases it by being strict (as it usually isn't) about the rules it sets up and the licenses it requires.

Government officials also manipulate the news by playing favorites among reporters, leaking only to those sources who play ball in return. Since leaks are such a large source of media news, reporters have to think twice before crossing their government informants.

Henry Kissinger was famous for his use of selective leaks to keep the media in line. So was J. Edgar Hoover. Even Jack Anderson, who (along with his assistants) does as much real digging for news as anyone, is alleged at one time to have agreed to write only "nice things" about J. Edgar Hoover in exchange for access to FBI files.

But then the media often lack the information that might incline them to buck the official government story. The 1976 swine flu program is a good example. There was no swine flu epidemic and little reason to think there would be. But government experts did think there would be, or rather they were convinced it was prudent to think so just in case there was one (heads often roll when something like that is missed—from the bureaucratic point of view, it's better to err on the side of safety). So the media by and large played it that way—perhaps (let's be charitable) because they assumed without question that the government knew what it was talking about. It was primarily readers of non-mass circulation magazines and papers like the *Village Voice* (see, for instance, the December 6, 1976 issue) who were aware all along that the whole thing was a phony scare.

Governments also influence the media by selective exercise of their power to license. It surely was not lost on media moguls that the Pacifica Foundation, which runs left-wing, "unconventional" radio stations in Los Angeles, Berkeley, New York, and Houston, failed during the six years of the Nixon administration to obtain Federal Communication Commission approval for a station in Washington, D.C.

---

[7]*On Press* (New York: Viking Press, 1978).

Nor did they overlook the fact that during the same period, the pro-Nixon *New York Daily News* managed to hang on to its very valuable New York television channel in the face of extremely convincing evidence that it had failed to live up to the public service rules of the FCC.[8]

The United States Constitution guarantees freedom of the press as one of several freedoms needed to make representative government function. Nevertheless, governments do censor the media on occasion. Of course, the most common type of censorship is of alleged pornography (*Hustler* magazine's publisher, Larry Flint, got seven years for publishing material judged to be obscene). But on occasion they also censor political material (for instance, books critical of the CIA) and occasionally harass the media in other ways (for example, by forcing them to reveal the names of confidential sources). Recently, *Mother Jones* magazine charged, with some show of evidence, that the Internal Revenue Service tried to drive it out of business by rescinding its nonprofit tax exemption (an exemption most small circulation magazines enjoy). (See the January and April 1983 issues of *Mother Jones.*)

Inside Hollywood: Hollywood superstars are breathing easier now that congressional investigators have backed off a filmland drug probe. But there's more to the headline controversy: Narcotics experts confided that they had big names set to testify but that a lot of California biggies have backed off now that Ronald Reagan is in the White House. No one wants to be caught embarrassing the White House's tinseltown friends.

Item from The Investigator (September 1981)

Nothing a government does is as important as how it chooses to spend the taxpayers' money. Yet budgetary matters, particularly on the local level, are usually decided by bureaucrats and elected officials with little public involvement.

Not so in Clinton, Connecticut, thanks in part to the *Clinton Enquirer.* Each spring this small magazine prints its community's annual budget. The *Enquirer* doesn't stop with the largest figures: it prints everything from how much dog food the dogcatcher uses to the salaries individual teachers and policemen receive. By encouraging people to familiarize themselves with the details of how government operates in their own community, the *Enquirer* has set a highly useful example for other papers.

This daring practice won Jeanne and George Allardice the Washington Monthly*'s April 1982 Journalism Award.*

---

[8]The politically powerful have many ways to strike back at their opponents. The U.S. military establishment regularly makes its facilities available to movie makers who present the military in a favorable light, but denies them to those whose intent is critical. For instance, the producers of the movie *Limbo,* about the wives of men missing in action in Vietnam, were denied use of a U.S. Air Force base for background shooting.

Governments also put a chill on freedom of the press through court decisions in libel suits. *Fact* magazine went bankrupt when it lost a libel suit brought by Senator Barry Goldwater. And similar suits (such as those brought by actress Carol Burnett and writer Lillian Hellman) have made many newspapers leery of making unfavorable comments even about public figures.

Much Foreign Reporting Is Suspect

While it's true that government censorship happens on occasion in the United States, government officials here rarely threaten reporters with physical violence or death. Yet this happens quite often in some other countries, making the "news" from those countries extremely unreliable, even when it appears in the (usually) most reliable publications.

Here are excerpts from two *TV Guide* articles (October 23, 1982, and March 6, 1982) on foreign intimidation of American reporters and how it influences news coverage:[9]

> Four Dutch television journalists are killed and mutilated by government troops while on their way to a rendezvous with guerrilla forces in El Salvador. In the month before their deaths, 31 percent of the stories broadcast from El Salvador by the three American TV networks dealt with guerrilla activities. In the month after the killings, that percentage dropped to 3 percent. *Intimidation.*

> An American television correspondent is about to satellite a story from Libya. A man armed with a Kalashnikov automatic rifle says that if she does

By permission of JULES FEIFFER. Copyright 1978. Distributed by Field Newspaper Syndicate.

An attempt via humor to explain the insidiousness of government power over the press.

---

[9]See also Xan Smiley's "Misunderstanding Africa," in *The Atlantic* (September 1982), for an account of why lots of reporting from black Africa is mangled by government interference and intimidation. And for an account of the more subtle intimidation American reporters face at home, see *TV Guide* (October 30, 1982).

not alter her script, the story will not be transmitted. She changes the script. *Intimidation.*

Thirty-six hours after Metromedia reporter Christopher Jones was kidnaped in Argentina, three British correspondents also were seized, stripped naked and shoved out of a car in a Buenos Aires suburb. Before the two kidnaping incidents, says Jones, reporters would go out in search of stories by themselves. Afterward, "nobody traveled alone. And that had a tremendous effect. What can you learn, traveling six to a car? You can't talk to people. It becomes pack journalism." . . .

[During the 1982–83 Israeli invasion of Lebanon,] a number of broadcast correspondents left Beirut because they were threatened with death by Palestinian or Syrian groups. The BBC's Tim Llewellyn, for one, was evacuated because of threats against his life. It is rumored, but not confirmed, that ABC's Jerry King left Beirut for the same reason.

Of course, another country that makes it hard for reporters to get any information worthy of the name is the Soviet Union (and its satellites in Eastern Europe). But just about everybody realizes that in Russia "news" means propaganda. (The Russians even kill stories about commercial airline crashes.[10]) It's important to remember that lots of other countries (chiefly those with authoritarian regimes, like Argentina, or outright dictatorships, like Zaire) also consider news to be more or less a device to further the interests of government. The American tradition of freedom of the press is not universal; in fact, it's quite the exception.

Here is an excerpt from a Village Voice *interview with a reporter who had been to El Salvador and seen the news reporting from that war-torn land first hand:*

Alan Riding [of the *New York Times*] represented the only case in which a North American journalist did his work very competently. He used to visit places, travel places, and he had sources. But in the beginning of January 1980 the extreme right threatened his life. Since then he left El Salvador and he hasn't been back. So he reports from Mexico. . . .

Bernard Diederich of *Time* and the others. . . . They get to the airport, they go to the Camino Real hotel where all the newspaper people stay and they don't go out. Maybe they go to the Presidential House, to the headquarters of the armed forces or to the American embassy. We say they cover the war from the hotel. One cannot have an ample vision of what is going on in the country. Most American correspondents don't understand what is going on in El Salvador, that there is a class struggle. They see it as painted by the State Department, as a struggle of the superpowers.

The Village Voice (April 8, 1981)

---

[10]At first, they even killed the story on the Korean airlines commercial jet, flight 007, that they themselves shot down. Later they gave ridiculously false accounts of what happened.

News Selection Reflects the Power of Big Money

The economically powerful almost always receive better media treatment than ordinary folk. An example is David Rockefeller. He and his family control the Chase Manhattan bank, one of the largest banks in America, and David is the bank's chairman. Not surprisingly, the press treats the Chase and David Rockefeller with special deference.

In fact, all large banks get special treatment from the media. Stories with a negative image of banks are played down. For example, the *New York Times* ran only eight column inches on the U.S. Senate's 419-page report, "Disclosure of Corporate Ownership," containing a great deal of information on how huge institutions like Chase Manhattan and other super banks control most of the largest corporations in America. Stories favorable to banks or bankers are played up. For instance, the *New York Times* ran a 40-column-inch story plus pictures on page one of the Sunday Business Section (18 February 1973) on David Rockefeller's trip to Eastern Europe, entitled "An Eastern European Diary").

The powerful manipulate the media with the carrot as well as the stick. Media members at all levels become accustomed to their special little fringe benefits, and it *is* hard to write nasty things about someone who has just wined and dined you free of charge.

In 1972, Senator Fred Harris of Oklahoma campaigned briefly for the Democratic party's nomination for president. He gave up quickly, however, because he didn't have enough money for a media blitz and reporters just didn't pay much attention to him. (George McGovern, on the other hand, did get seed money that helped him raise lots more to finance his media blitz. He won the Democratic party nomination.)

Suppose Harris had been able to give a lavish party for Henry and Nancy Kissinger, celebrating their marriage. And suppose he had been able to invite all sorts of news people, like television personalities John Chancellor, Barbara Walters, and Howard K. Smith, editors Hedley Donovan (*Time*), Osborne Elliott (*Newsweek*), A. M. Rosenthal (*New York Times*), James Wechsler (*New York Post*), and Mike O'Neill (*New York Daily News*), columnists Marquis Childs, William F. Buckley Jr., Rowland Evans, and Joseph Kraft, and publishers Jack Howard (Scripps-Howard Publications), Thomas Vail (*Cleveland Plain Dealer*), Gardner Cowles (Cowles Communications), and Dorothy Schiff (*New York Post*)—to name just a few. It runs contrary to human nature to expect that coverage of his campaign would not have greatly improved. Yet this is exactly the party Nelson Rockefeller threw at his immense and lavish Pocantico Hills estate in June 1974, two months before President Ford chose Rockefeller to be his vice president.

News-Gathering Methods Are Designed to Save Money

If a newspaper or television station is a business, with a bottom line that determines eventual success or failure, it has to make sure that the bottom line is not written in red ink. Since it has to operate as economically as it can, just like other businesses, the news business cannot regularly spend more money on a story than is returned in reader or listener interest.

Regular News "Beats" Have Been Established

There are two principle ways in which the news is gathered, both designed to be efficient and to save money. One is through established news "beats." The two major wire services, the three big TV networks, and a few top newspapers routinely assign reporters to cover a few institutions that regularly generate news. For instance, they have reporters covering the United States Congress and Supreme Court (on days decisions are to be handed down.)

Most News Is Given to Reporters, Not Ferreted Out

The other important way the media gather the news is by having it given to them by government officials or by others who have power (or money—but money implies power). Since only those with power or money can call press conferences or issue press releases and attract attention from the mass media, the news is bound to reflect established powerful interests more than those of the rest of us.

Even a good deal of beat reporting results mainly in handouts. For instance, most of the news generated by reporters covering the coveted White House beat is given to them by White House officials. Similarly, most news from the local crime beats is told to reporters by district attorneys or local police officials.

The important thing to notice about all this is that *very few news stories result from true investigative reporting!*[11] (It's much easier and quicker to interview heads of government agencies than to find out for yourself what's going on in these agencies.)

It might be supposed that the media would routinely check up on stories given them by the high and mighty or by alleged experts. And they often do. Unfortunately, they often don't. This is illustrated nicely by the following snippet:

> In New York some years ago, special prosecutor Maurice Nadjari leaked to reporters of the more influential papers certain grand-jury proceedings. And they printed what they got. One unfortunate judge wound up on the front page of the *New York Times* as a suspect in a bribery case because of a Nadjari leak to reporters from a grand-jury session. A year later, when the judge was wholly exonerated, the *Times* gave him an inch of type deep inside the paper. . . .

The cover of the March 19 *U.S. News* asked, "Do Banks Make Too Much Money?" If the question persuaded you to look inside, you would have found an interview with the president of the American Bankers Association.

— *Washington Monthly* (May 1979)

The answer, incidentally, was that they don't. Surprise!

---

[11]Those that do tend to get buried back on page 49, and thus get read by fewer people. Recently, many newspapers that do little or no investigative or background reporting themselves have been reprinting more items from magazines and other newspapers (although so far they too tend to get buried in the back pages).

If the *Times* reporter who swallowed the Nadjari leak had bothered to do the most minimal checking, he would have found out that there was no way the hapless judge could have been involved in any bribery connected with the case at issue because he had never had the case before him. The special prosecutor had believed the court calendar, which did list this particular judge as hearing that case. But the assignment had been changed.[12]

While reporter bias is occasionally the reason for such inaccurate reporting (see below), the main reason is simply that it takes a great deal of time and money to verify information. (The only newspaper or magazine this writer knows about that tries to verify *all* alleged facts it prints is the *New Yorker* magazine. Not that this writer is in a position to cast stones at all the rest on that score.)

Those of you who have a special interest in journalism should give yourself a treat and verify something important about the newspaper business by going to the library and reading the September 28, 1981 *Wall Street Journal.* One of its front page articles describes how a journalism teacher, Joseph Skaggs, got United Press International (UPI), the *Chicago Tribune,* the *Dallas Times-Herald,* and lots of other newspapers (but not the *Wall Street Journal* !) to carry a phony story about ''Joseph Gregor'' and his organization ''Metamorphosis'' and how they were improving their health by chewing ''cockroach pills.'' Skagg's intent, of course, was to show how the media will fall for just about anything, and won't bother to verify a story, *if* you handle them

---

[12]Nat Hentoff, in *Inquiry* (January 11, 1982). He was responding to criticisms of the movie *Absence of Malice,* which itself was very critical of media coverage. (Could that be the reason the media attacked him?)

In the following interview excerpts, Congressman Les Aspin of Wisconsin explains his unusual success in getting the media attention necessary for reelection and for the political power needed to be effective in Washington:

A: If a congressman were to go out on the steps of the Capitol and set himself on fire, he'd probably get on the evening news, but otherwise it's really hard. If a congressman does something really bizarre—takes an absurd position or gets involved in Abscam—he'll get his name in the paper, but that doesn't help him. If a congressman is going to get on the wires, or in the *New York Times* or *Washington Post,* he's got to do something very different, put out something that wasn't there before—either more information, or a different point of view. So you have to anticipate a little bit. You can't take what's in the headlines today and do a report on that because by the time the reporting is finished, the story will have moved on. You've got to be able to anticipate where that story's going two weeks ahead. . . .

Q: Describe what you do with a press release.

A: You've got to release it on a slow news day—Monday. The press release has to go out Thursday by 2 o'clock, with a Monday a.m. embargo. I remembered sitting with Hubert Humphrey on the floor of the Congress before a State of the Union message, and he said, ''Say, I was just wondering how you

in the right way. (One bit from that story: UPI's managing editor saw no reason to correct the story when the hoax was revealed because, "The story was accurate at the time." Wonderful doubletalk. What he no doubt meant was that UPI reporters accurately relayed what the hoax perpetrators told them.)

2. The Media Operate According to Incorrect Theories and Practices

People don't often stand back and look at what they're doing from a wider context; they don't often theorize about their activities. Media workers on the whole theorize more than most workers. But when they do, their theories are frequently self-serving.

The Unusual Is News, the Everyday Is Not

Theory says that news is what's *new* — the unusual, not the commonplace. Yet what happens every day is generally more important than the unusual occurrence. Prison uprisings get big play, but the poor treatment prisoners receive every day, which leads to the uprisings, goes relatively unreported. Big court cases such as the Watergate trials receive much attention, but thousands of everyday cases in which justice is flouted tend to be ignored. (A whole disgraceful area of courtroom practice, plea bargaining, was pretty much ignored in the media until former vice president Spiro Agnew "copped a plea.")

---

get so much press. How do you get your staff to work on the weekends?" And I said, "What do you mean, work on the weekends?" "Well, you always get those stories to come out on Monday." I said, "No, no, no, you don't understand. The staff doesn't like to work on the weekends. Reporters sure don't like to work on the weekends. You've got to get the press release out on a Thursday afternoon, so the reporters get it Friday morning, and can write their Monday story and go away for the weekend. . . .

Q: Does anybody in the Pentagon do this kind of selective placing of stories, say on the MX? Is anybody over there doing the same thing?

A: Oh, yeah. They're planting stories. The whole operation there is a very different thing. They don't want their names on the stories. . . .

Q: What press release of yours got the most attention?

A: . . . The ones that got the most attention were the funny ones. The classic was the one we did that riled up all beagle owners. The Army was conducting poison gas tests on beagle puppies. We were mad at Eddie Hebert at the time, so we thought the way to really do him in was to send out a press release saying that Hebert [the chairman of the House Armed Services Committee] was the guy in Congress who could stop the gassing of beagle puppies. Gee, I went down there in Hebert's office and they were wig deep in bags of mail. . . .

Washington Journalism Review (June 1981). Reprinted with permission.

News Reporting Is Supposed To Be Objective, Not Subjective

Those who work on the news often say that facts are objective, conclusions or value judgments subjective, and that media workers are supposed to be objective. (Even J. Edgar Hoover subscribed to this view, although he didn't practice it. His motto was that the FBI does not draw conclusions, it only reports the facts.)

But this theory of objective reporting is mistaken. Reports of facts generally depend on someone's judgment that they are facts. A reporter must conclude that they are facts. Take the following excerpts from an Associated Press story carried in the *Lawrence* (Kansas) *Daily Journal World* (October 30, 1970) on an alleged riot in San Jose, California, before the November 1970 elections:

> President Nixon, the target of rocks, bricks, bottles, eggs, red flags, and other missiles hurled by antiwar demonstrators. . . .
>
> The San Jose violence was the most serious aimed at any president in this country since the assassination of President John Kennedy. . . .
>
> [Nixon's] limousine and other vehicles in the cavalcade were hit repeatedly by large rocks and other objects.

Clearly, the reporter did not actually *see* that the alleged attack on President Nixon was the worst attack on a president since the assassination of President Kennedy. He had to conclude this fact—if it is a fact—by using judgment as well as eyesight.

But we usually don't notice that judgment and conclusion drawing are required even in reporting immediate facts. Did the AP reporter—or any AP reporter— actually *see* rocks hit the president's limousine? If not, who did? Are those who think they did sure no visual distortion was at work? Did they hear a crunch as the rocks hit the car? These questions are not academic; it's well known that honest reports by onlookers frequently differ seriously as to what took place. In this case, many eyewitnesses, including television and newspaper reporters, said that nothing was thrown at the presidential limousine, although objects were thrown at the press corps bus.[13]

A great deal of reporting is of this kind. A reporter who is not an eyewitness must draw a conclusion about what happened from eyewitness accounts. Those who are not eyewitnesses need to compare different eyewitness accounts and draw conclusions as to what probably happened. For example, reporters who thought rocks were thrown at Nixon's car might have looked for rock fragments on the pavement at the correct location.[14] The idea that reporters must stick to facts and not draw conclusions is a myth. One must *reason to the facts* just as one reasons to anything else.

Similarly, the idea that newspapers should not make value judgments is incorrect. When we read of the death of a famous movie star on page one of our morning newspaper but read nothing of the death of an eminent philosopher, it becomes obvious that newspapers have to make value judgments to determine what is im-

---

[13]See, for instance, the *Village Voice* article by Tom Devries (November 5, 1970) in which Mike Mills, a television reporter, when asked why his films of the event show no flying objects, stated, "That is because nothing was thrown." The article quoted several other reporters who supported this statement. And the San Jose police chief confirmed reporters' claims.

[14]Mr. Devries, the *Village Voice* reporter, wrote that he later checked the area for loose rocks and broken glass and found none.

portant and what is not. The same is true when a hurricane on the Gulf Coast, which kills two dozen people, gets more space than reports of the My Lai massacre in Vietnam, or when the George Foreman–Muhammad Ali fight in Zaire gets more

---

The following review of Stephen Hess's book The Washington Reporters[15] *illustrates ways in which the normal workings of human nature influence news reporting (so long as it doesn't cost too much money):*

Washington reporters are like kids at a progressive school for the upper crust. They avoid the more difficult subjects. They groan at the very idea of doing research. They much prefer to cover political bull sessions. . . .

Drawing his evidence from what he sees as "an informal seniority system in the news business" that assigns younger reporters to the least desirable assignments, Hess concludes that the hierarchy of beats in Washington today runs like this:

High-prestige beats: diplomacy, Supreme Court, politics, White House.

Medium-prestige beats: Congress, science, energy.

Low-prestige beats: domestic agencies, regulatory agencies, economics, regional. . . .

Hess says "a beat is more desirable if *no documents research* [his emphasis] is required. Washington reporters use no documents in the preparation of nearly three-quarters of their stories. (Press releases are not counted as documents.)" Many reporters wish economics "would go away," says Hess, but since the subject can't be ignored it is palmed off on the youngest, most inexperienced reporters. . . .

Eighty-four percent of the reporters Hess talked with thought the regulatory agencies were not adequately covered and 51 percent thought this was a serious problem. But, because of those damned documents, few indicated any wish to take over the agency beat themselves. And, of course, it was commonplace for Hess to receive the same sort of appraisal and rejection of beats like Agriculture. Apparently, wheat subsidies aren't considered sexy. . . .

The best thing about this survey is that it occasionally captures so nicely the character of television. Hess points out that "in newspapers, senators receive only 5 percent more attention than House members; but on the television network evening news programs, 73 percent of the legislators mentioned are senators. Clearly, most House members lack the glitter that attracts a visual medium. Television, if it had been around in 1831, would have noticed Congressman John Quincy Adams, but only because he was an ex-president; in 1858, it would not have noticed Congressman Abraham Lincoln."

And especially this quote from a "veteran" television correspondent: "Reporters are in a tizzy when their faces are not on the tube at least once every few days. This is a reason why they do not want to do investigative pieces which may take months to develop. You can't blame them."

Robert Sherrill, in *Columbia Journalism Review* (May/June 1981). Reprinted with permission.

---

[15]The Brookings Institution, 1981. Hess was an aide to President Eisenhower and held other jobs where he observed the way the news is gathered.

space than mass starvation in Africa. In other words, *editing,* one of the chief tasks of any newspaper, requires value judgments about the relative importance of events.

So the media's theory about objective reporting is not correct. Of course, as we've already seen, real life practice differs significantly from this theory anyway.[16]

News Is Supposed To Be Separated from Analysis or In-Depth Reports

The theory of objectivity requires that facts be reported separately from conclusions or evaluations (which are thought of as "subjective"). But the separation of news from analysis further aggravates a defect already in evidence in most media reporting, namely their failure to tie what happens to some *explanation* of why it happened and why it's important. So those who stick to the mass media aren't likely to *understand* what happens or be able to *anticipate* the flow of events.

Most of the better "in-depth" or "analysis" reporting on television is done by the Public Broadcasting Service. But they too often fall into the same traps as do other media workers. A documentary widely shown on PBS in 1979 attempted to get behind the façade and show us how the U.S. House of Representatives really works (a marvelous idea). But it merely followed House Majority Leader "Tip" O'Neill around for a whole (supposedly) typical day of work. The impression given was that we were getting an inside glimpse of powerful people at work; we looked over their shoulders and heard what they told each other in the halls and behind closed doors.

To no avail. The members videotaped were aware of that fact and tailored their conversations accordingly. While it seemed that we were getting the real lowdown, we got instead lots of remarks like: "We've got to move that bill by the seventh," which revealed nothing about the true behind-the-scenes wheeling and dealing (still quaintly called "logrolling" in public school textbooks, where it's described with-

---

A Moment of Truth

It is obvious that we are lazy and superficial in much of our reporting. Often we do not even bother to challenge ourselves with the difficult question as to what really is going on. We rely, instead, on certain stereotypes as to what makes a news story. . . . Why is a speech, a press conference, a court decision, a Congressional hearing always news, while the real situations behind these surface things go unnoted? Why? Because it is easy that way, and because that is the way we have always done it. . . .

I think the worst of our lazy and superficial performance today is that we of the press are allowing ourselves to be manipulated by various interests. . . .

Newbold Noyes, president of the American Society of Newspaper Editors (April 14, 1971).
Reprinted in *The Washington Spectator and Between the Lines* (September 1, 1980).

---

[16]For what it's worth, this writer's opinion on the matter is that in everyday practice, the theory of objectivity requires only that reporters stay within the social consensus when they make judgments or draw conclusions. This means that the real point of the theory of objectivity is to discourage the reporting of radical, nonestablishment, or nonconsensual views—to placate the media audience and media advertisers.

out mention of mundane things like payoffs by lobbyists, campaign contributions, betrayals, or veiled threats).

Here are excerpts from ex- Washington Post *reporter Joseph Nocera's "Making It at* The Washington Post." *Nocera is describing one of the best newspapers in the United States, where "objective" reporting reigns:*

When [*Washington Post* reporter] Ron Kessler discovered three years ago that some of America's largest banks had been put on a secret list of problem banks by the Comptroller of the Currency, the *Post* had a field day running bank stories. There were a number of follow-ups by Kessler and a rising Metro reporter, Charles Babcock, who covered a series of congressional hearings on bank troubles. Then the scandal faded, as they eventually all do, and Kessler and Babcock went on to other things. The subject of banks dropped off the front page and back to the financial pages, where it was covered as it always had been—routinely. It wasn't that the subject of banks was any less news-worthy—certainly there were dozens of important stories the *Post* could have written about banks—it was just, well, the smell of scandal wasn't there any-more. Reporters lost their incentive to write about them; the subject didn't fit comfortably into the *Post*'s daily news coverage; it wasn't going to get on the front page; it wasn't going to help anyone's career. . . .

A few years ago, Barbara Sizemore was the Superintendent of Schools in Washington, and the Board of Education was trying to fire her. It was a story the *Post* was all over—a good political fight, with plenty of charges and coun-tercharges, hearings, and votes—and most of the coverage made the front page. But what was happening inside the schools? Why were Washington's teachers so uniformly mediocre? What was being taught? Why weren't kids learning? Seldom could these stories be found in the *Washington Post*. . . .

The concentration on beat reporting in the suburban counties means that *Post* reporters are missing a whole range of stories that could help explain how our government works. By using Arlington and Prince George's counties as barometers, reporters could discover whether a federal program was doing all the wonderful things some spokesman in Washington was attributing to it. They could tell us about welfare in ways much more meaningful than by cov-ering the latest from Capitol Hill and HEW. *Post* reporters could find out for themselves whether there was welfare fraud and how widespread it was, whether there were people unjustly denied benefits, whether welfare really did keep able-bodied people from working, and they could help us figure out how to make the welfare system work better. . . .

To get this kind of reporting, of course, a lot of what it takes to make it at the *Post* would have to change. . . . Above all, they would have to make judgments. Telling people what's wrong with [things] means coming to a conclusion.

Joseph Nocera, in the *Washington Monthly* (January 1979). Reprinted with permission from *The Washington Monthly.* Copyright 1979 by The Washington Monthly Co., 1611 Connecticut Ave., N.W., Washington, D.C. 20009.

The Opinion of Powerful Authorities Take Precedence

The reporters and editors who gather and assemble the news are not usually experts in the fields they cover. They couldn't be, given that they must deal with practically all the social and political questions of the day. It seems plausible, then, that they should seek out expert opinion on these matters. The trouble is that experts can be found on all sides of a really controversial issue. In everyday practice, *which* experts are consulted is determined by the other factors that influence the news.

In the first place, experts whose views are very unpopular with either the media's audience or their advertisers, or with media bigwigs themselves, will tend to be passed over or played down. Take the question of the safety of nuclear power. A great many top-notch physicists (and organizations, such as the Union of Concerned Scientists) have been shouting as loudly as they can for some time now that the current state of the art makes nuclear power plants inherently unsafe. But until the serious accident at Three Mile Island, Pennsylvania, in 1979, their voices were drowned out in the media, to the point where one supposed expert—Department of Energy boss James Schlesinger (what did he know about atomic physics or how nuclear plants produce power?)—received more coverage than all the protesting scientists combined. No, it was those scientists who stated that nuclear power was safe who were given the space—along with politicians like Schlesinger, of course. (When, if ever, did you first hear about the much more serious Russian nuclear disaster that occurred way back in 1957?)

Further, the fact that time is money means that the media will often as not take the first expert they can find—which most of the time means an expert in the employ of the rich or powerful, who are constantly being foisted on reporters via press conferences and other public relations operations.

Good Citizenship Requires Self-Censorship

Though unusual, self-censorship is not rare. Major newspapers and the TV networks tend to engage in self-censorship more often than other media sources, no doubt because they have access to more sensitive information. Perhaps the most famous example of this kind occurred during the Kennedy administration, when the *New York Times* decided not to print the Bay of Pigs story.[17]

In 1970, the *New York Times* killed a story by veteran reporter Tad Szulc which stated that the United States and South Vietnam were about to invade Cambodia.

The September 23, 1979 issue of the *Washington Post* magazine featured a cover story, *Hoover: Life with a Tyrant,* which disclosed lots of the nastiness, dirtiness, unfairness, and illegality of J. Edgar Hoover's long reign as FBI chief. But where was the *Post* (or any mass media outlet) when Hoover had power and was perpetrating all these crimes? (It wasn't until June 3, 1982, that ABC got around to telling its viewers about this.)

---

[17]President Kennedy is alleged later to have had the "chutzpah" to take the *Times* to task for this censorship on grounds that publication of the story by the *Times* might have resulted in calling off that ill-fated venture!

According to Roger Morris, Henry Kissinger asked that the story be killed for national security reasons (for we *were* about to invade Cambodia.)[18]

The problem of self-censorship is made particularly difficult by the counter tug of the right to privacy. A person in the public eye is still, after all, entitled to a private life. And yet it is difficult to know what bears on a person's public life (and thus can

---

The shock of Dec. 7 [1941] can be well imagined. When the last Japanese plane roared off, five American battleships had been sunk and three damaged, three cruisers and three destroyers badly hit, 200 planes destroyed, and 2344 men killed. For the loss of only 29 planes, Japan had virtually crippled the U.S. Pacific Fleet at a single blow.

The American service chiefs immediately decided that news of a disaster of such magnitude would prove unacceptable to the American people, and steps were taken to ensure that they did not learn about it. So effective were these measures that the truth about Pearl Harbor was still being concealed even after the war ended. The cover-up began with an "iron curtain" of censorship that cut off the United Press office in Honolulu from San Francisco in the middle of its first excited telephone report.

So drastic was the suppression of news that nothing further, except for official communiques, came out of Pearl Harbor for another four days. These claimed that only one "old" battleship and a destroyer had been sunk and other ships damaged, and that heavy casualties had been inflicted on the Japanese. It cannot be argued that these lies were necessary to conceal from the Japanese the extent of the disaster they had inflicted on the U.S. Pacific Fleet. The Japanese knew exactly how much damage they had done, and reports in Tokyo newspapers accurately stating the American losses meant that the Americans knew that the Japanese knew. The American censorship was to prevent the American public from learning the gravity of the blow.

After flying to Hawaii on a tour of inspection, the Secretary of the Navy, Colonel Frank Knox, held a press conference in New York at which, with President Roosevelt's approval, he gave the impression he was revealing the full extent of the American losses at Pearl Harbor. Colonel Knox told correspondents that one United States battleship, the Arizona, had been lost and the battleship Oklahoma had capsized but could be righted.

This must have made strange reading for anyone actually at Pearl Harbor, who had only to lift his eye from his newspaper to see five United States battleships—the Arizona, the Oklahoma, the California, the Nevada, and the West Virginia—resting on the bottom.

In wartime, truth is the first casualty, censorship the first expedient.

From *The First Casualty*, copyright © 1975 by Phillip Knightley. Reprinted by permission of Harcourt Brace Jovanovich, Inc.

---

[18]In the *Columbia Journalism Review* (May/June 1974). Also see John D. Marks, "The Story That Never Was," in *More* (June 1974), p. 20. (Incidentally, *New York Times* editor A. M. Rosenthal denies Szulc ever submitted the story to the *Times*.)

be exposed) and what does not (and thus ought to be censored). It was well known to newspeople, for instance, that as a Congressman and then as a Senator, John F. Kennedy was quite a lady's man (both before and after his marriage). The media, on the whole, chose not to report this feature of Kennedy's private life and were generally applauded for their restraint (after all, stories on Kennedy's sex life would have found an eager audience).

And yet, self-censorship of similar stories concerning Kennedy's brother, Edward M. (Ted) Kennedy, may well have been a mistake, given what happened at Chappaquiddick. Knowledge of a person's sex life *may*, after all, be relevant to character and thus to suitability for public office.

3. Devices Used to Slant the News

So far we have been considering *why* the media slant the news, and how that affects the selection of stories. Now let's look at a few of the devices used to slant stories (primarily in newspapers and magazines).

Stories Can Be Played Up or Down

If you like a story, you can play it up. If you don't, you can play it down. You bury it by putting it toward the end (relatively few readers get past the first few paragraphs) or by mentioning it in passing. You play it up by doing just the opposite. On TV, stories are buried by running them toward the end of the program when eyes have begun to glaze and by cutting them to run less than a minute.

The *Canton* (Ohio) *Repository* may have set some sort of record on this in its July 28, 1974 issue. Under the front page headline "Wowee. . . . What a Weekend," the *Repository* devoted most of the page to an account of the first National Football League exhibition game of the season, plus a description of ceremonies surrounding

---

Another night on the South Side [of Chicago] this guy went berserk and shot his wife and kids and himself—a quadruple murder and suicide. I was very excited. I went and reported the story, and there I was dictating it to a rewrite man [the common practice]. . . . All of a sudden the old editor at the news service . . . got on my wire and said to me, "My good, dear, energetic Mr. Hersh, do the poor, unfortunate, alas, victims of this crime happen to be of the American Negro persuasion?" I said they did. And he just said, "Well cheap it out," and hung up. Of course, to "cheap it out" meant that it would get only one paragraph for this whole murder and multiple suicide. Since then, I've had no illusions about the newspaper business. The experience gave me a cynical approach to what the news is, and what the news isn't.

—Seymour Hersh, at that time a *New York Times* reporter, whose earlier exposé
of the My Lai massacre and subsequent Pulitzer prize lifted him to fame,
quoted in *More* (September 1976)

the induction of four new members into Canton's Football Hall of Fame. Relegated to a bottom corner of page one was the decision of the House Judiciary Committee to recommend impeachment of President Nixon, a key event in one of the biggest ongoing news stories in American history.

Misleading or Sensational Headlines Can Be Used

Many more people read the headlines on a story than read the story itself. So even if a story is accurate, a misleading or sensational headline distorts the news for many readers. Here are a few examples:

New York Daily News:

Secret Bar Study Pounds Five Judges

New York Times (same general story):

Bar Report Clears 3 on State Bench
of Accusations Leveled in Mazagine

Chicago Sun Times (May 2, 1983):

Solidarity Backers Clash With Police

Chicago Tribune (same day):

Polish Throngs Routed

A later edition headlined a story on waste disposal, and directed the reader to page 6 for the story on Poland.

Sensational news reporting of the kind common in Britain and some other countries (for instance, African countries like Nigeria and Kenya) has never caught on in the United States. But there is one U.S. newspaper, the *New York Post,* [19] that specializes in sensational shlock. Here are some examples of *Post* front page headlines, all

---

Newspapers start when the owners are poor and take the side of the people, and so they build up a large circulation, and presently, as a result, advertising. That makes them rich, and they begin most naturally to associate with other rich men—they play golf with one and drink whiskey with another, and their son marries the daughter of a third. They forget about the people.

—Joseph Medill Patterson

The late newspaper mogul was in a position to know.

---

[19] Owned by Australian and British news magnate Rupert Murdoch.

from one week (collected by Rudy Maxa for his *Washington Post* column of November 29, 1981):

IRS Sex Ring Busted:
He spanked thousands of coeds, police say.

Death of a Hitman
Preppie Porn King Slain:
Smith College girl shot in head in Chelsea sex pad

Nun Rape Bombshell

Follow-up Stories Can Be Omitted

Follow-up stories rarely make headlines, primarily for two reasons. The first is that they are relatively difficult to obtain. It takes much less time and effort to report a prison uprising than to investigate day-to-day prison conditions. The second is that the public (and media) conception of "news" is what is *new,* and therefore different. Follow-up is reporting on "old news," which isn't really news. But isn't it news if, say, a president of the United States fails to keep his word, or a bill passed by Congress fails to get implemented?

The media covered Richard Nixon's political campaigns from 1946 through 1972. Stacked away in their files, their "morgues," were mountains of items on Nixon campaign rhetoric and performance, showing that Nixon's performance bore little relation to his campaign promises. Worse, it showed Nixon's attacks on his opponents *always* consisted primarily of *false dilemma, straw man,* and *ad hominem* arguments. Yet it was rare for a news outlet to follow through on the news and point out this great disparity between his words and subsequent actions, or between his portrayal of opponents' positions and their actual positions.

Emotive Language Can Be Used

Since we devoted a large part of Chapter 5 to the emotive side of language, let's give just two examples at this point from the media. First, the *Vancouver Sun* (July 15,

---

I think human beings are unpleasant and they should be shown as such. In my view we live in a banana-peel society, where people who are having a rotten, miserable life—as 99.9 percent of the world is—can only gain enjoyment by seeing the decline and fall of others. They only enjoy people's sordidness, their divorces, whether their wives have relieved them of $5 million, how their children turned around and beat the crap out of them. Then they suddenly realize that everything is well in the state of Denmark, that everyone else is leading a miserable, filthy life which—but for me and other journalists around—they would not know about. They see that those who obtain riches or fame or high position are no happier than they are. It helps them get along, and frankly that is what I give them.
                —British gossip columnist Nigel Dempster in *New York* magazine (May 3, 1976),
                                justifying having gossip columns in newspapers.

1975) headlined its story about American and Soviet spacemen: "Astronauts *Chase* Cosmonauts into Space" (italics added). This had a much better ring than the more accurate "American Astronauts *Follow* Soviet Cosmonauts into Space." Second, a *National Enquirer* article (September 7, 1982), headlined "A *Juicy* Way to *Waste* Your Tax Dollars," started out: "*Fruitcakes* at the National Science Foundation . . ." (italics added).

Ignorance Is Cloaked in an Aura of Authority

Television and newspaper reporters and editors are not generally experts on the topics they have to cover. How could they be when reporters may cover one thing one day and something much different the next, and can't spend much time on background digging (because it's too expensive). But it would be hard to guess at this ignorance when reading the polished stories the media turn out. On the contrary, reporters quote facts and figures (and the words of the high and mighty) in a way that makes them seem on top of their subjects.

However, closer investigation reveals cracks in the veneer of expertise. For instance, when Yuri Andropov became leader of the Soviet Union, the media ran a great many stories telling readers and viewers about this relatively unknown Russian figure, stories full of facts and figures. The trouble, unfortunately, was that the stories differed one from another and spouted off about all sorts of things that are probably not known in the West. The *Washington Post* said he was born in Karelia, near Finland; the *New York Times,* that he came from the Ukraine; and *Time* magazine, from the northern Caucasus.[20] The *New York Times* said he spoke fluent English, yet others had the former U.S. Ambassador to Moscow saying he never spoke to Andropov in English. Still other accounts had Andropov keeping a copy of Jacqueline Susann's book *Valley of the Dolls* in his library. The truth probably is that very little was known about Andropov when he took power. The press, of course, authoritatively pronounced on the subject anyway.

4. Television: Tail Wags Dog

Although still a relative baby, television, the newest of the mass media, is by far the most important. Television gives us the closest thing we have to a way of bringing a whole nation together. It's the town meeting, town crier, certifier, authenticator, grapevine of modern industrial life. That's why political campaigns are fought on it, the news is broadcast on it, and (more and more) a nation's mood and tone are set by it.

But before going into details about this new communications medium, perhaps we should stop for a moment and reflect on the wonder of it all. Television gives us the privilege of sitting in our living rooms and being magically transported down the Nile, through steaming African jungle, or parched Australian desert. It gives us the opportunity to see the famous figures of our time almost as though in the flesh, from the Pope to Jane Fonda, from Lech Walesa to Ronald Reagan. And so it gives us a much better chance to judge the character of our leaders than by just look-

---

[20]See Edward J. Epstein, "How a Short, Burly Thug Became a Tall, Dapper Chubby Checker Fan" (*The New Republic,* February 7, 1983), from which these examples are taken.

Political columnists who last long enough generally become "experts" just because they're well known. Here is Alexander Cockburn on these "experts" and their reporting of the 1980 political campaign:

"Bigfoot" was used to describe any senior officer of the press permitted by status and function to leaven fact with advertised opinion. . . . [T]he reaction provoked among the troops was analogous to that of a general visiting the trenches in the first world war. Among the smoke of press releases, . . . he would make a dignified tour of inspection, briefly confer with the candidate and senior officers on the spot, inscribe a few paragraphs of sagacious observation in his notebook, and return to the soft life in Washington.

When finally published, the Bigfoot's observations would be read by the troops left behind him with spite and derision. How could the Bigfoot know that the sentiments of the candidate he recorded in Pittsburgh as novel and refreshing insights had been daily staples of the stump for the previous six months . . . ?

Cockburn then went on to discuss one of the champion bigfoots, Walter Lippmann (often referred to in his day as the "dean of American journalists"), pointing out Lippmann's abysmal batting average. Here are a few examples:

"Democracy," [Lippmann] opined [in 1930], "cannot last long; it must, and inevitably will, give way to a more settled social order." . . .

In 1933, just after books were burned in the streets of Berlin, he solemnly wrote that repression of the Jews, "by satisfying the lust of the Nazis who feel they must conquer somebody and the cupidity of those Nazis who want jobs, is a kind of lightning rod which protects Europe." A week later he was praising Hitler for "a genuinely statesmanlike address" that expressed "the authentic voice of a genuinely civilized people." . . .

[In 1938], concerned with "distracted" Europe's overpopulation problem, he suggested that a million "surplus" Jews be sent to Africa. . . .

Knowledgeable of the corridors of power, he told Eric Sevareid and a CBS audience in [1965] that war hawks are "not found in the interior and at the top of the White House." In the same year, too, he endorsed the U.S.-backed coup in the Dominican Republic.

Then, somewhat late, he discovered that LBJ was a hawk, and that the war in Vietnam was a bad idea. Of the president he said sadly, in the distressed tones of a betrayed pundit, "He misled me." [But] disillusion did not lead to wisdom. In 1968 he reported that there was a "new Nixon, a maturer and mellower man."

ing at pictures or still photos. (That most viewers judge poorly reflects on them, not television.)

It's important also to see the political power this media "baby" possesses. All of the media have political power, because the power to expose the bad and publicize the good yields power automatically. But television's power to expose and publicize is vastly greater, more immediate, and more graphic than the other media, and so its political power is awesomely, indeed frighteningly greater. (The Polish government's control of television was one of its two main weapons in defeating Solidarity in 1981 and 1982.[21] The other, of course, was military power.)

So far, in the United States, this power has only been used sparingly, perhaps because of the opposing power of advertisers, the TV audience (that is, public opinion), and the power of government to regulate the media. TV has not as yet gone in for much serious investigative exposure of misuses of power in America. But the possibilities are occasionally illustrated on a small scale. An example is the TV exposure (in late July 1980) of the nastiness of police searches. TV *showed* a much larger audience than ever was told by newspapers or magazines how disruptive and unfair such searches can be—how difficult, if not impossible, they make it to continue normal routines of life. (This "legal" search was of station KBCI-TV in Boise, Idaho, to find film taken of a prison riot. See the *Washington Post* editorial of July 30, 1980, if you missed the TV coverage.)

The point here is that the power of TV, especially national TV, to expose chicanery is bound to have an effect on the behavior of government officials (as it did during the Vietnam war, when TV brought the war into everyone's living room).

To illustrate this TV power further, consider what Americans know about Nazi Germany's extermination camps, compared to what they know about Soviet slave labor camps. Russia, of course, is pictured on TV as a very nasty dictatorship, which it is, but very few of us know that many more people have died in Soviet labor camps than were murdered by the Nazis in their World War II extermination camps. In the early 1980's, millions of Americans learned about or were reminded of the "Holocaust"—the killing of almost 6 million Jews by the Nazis—when the plight of European Jews in World War II was portrayed graphically on TV. Few of us know of the Russian camps. But just one TV epic similar to *The Holocaust* could make the barbaric Russian camps and the millions worked to death in them common knowl-

---

The medium of television has so taken over the country that it has become our *only* mass medium. The number of people who read a best-selling book, the subscribers to the most successful magazines, the listeners to even the most powerful radio stations, and the readers of the most popular newspapers, the pre-TV film crowds, are all statistical gnats when compared to the viewers of a network series canceled for lack of an audience.

Jeffrey Schrank, *Snap, Crackle, and Popular Taste* (New York: Delacorte Press, 1977)

---

[21]See, for instance, "Polish Government vs. the Workers: Why TV Is the Prized Weapon." In *TV Guide* (November 7, 1981).

edge in America (as it is in Russia—via the grapevine, *not* Russian TV!), so that the name *Kolyma* would be as familiar to us as is *Auschwitz* or *Treblinka.*

TV Entertainment Gives a Juvenile Impression of Life

Going from horror to the ridiculous, . . . most television entertainment programs give us a hopelessly juvenile impression of human nature and human society. Hollywood endings are almost the universal rule—the good guys win in the end, or the foolish misunderstandings that sustained half an hour of comedy are cleared up, and everyone is happy (except for a few villains).

Even *All in the Family,* praised widely for its exposure of bigotry (in particular racial bigotry), bore little resemblance to the genuine article. It's hard to imagine Archie Bunker killing anyone, even indirectly. He *talked* against blacks but never *ever* raised his fist against them, or anyone else. He was a friendly bumbler. Real-life bigots are another matter. They frequently do things that *kill* as did U.S. State Department bigots during the Nazi period who refused entry into the United States to thousands of Jews trying to escape from Hitler's horror.[22]

In his book *The View from Sunset Boulevard,* Benjamin Stein discusses the "cleaned-up" world of television entertainment programs:

> Today's television is purer, in terms of backdrop and story endings, than the lines of a Mercedes convertible. Every day's shows bring fresh examples. A while ago, I saw an episode of "Charlie's Angels" about massage parlors that were really houses of prostitution. The three beautiful "angels" of the show were compelled to pretend they worked at massage parlors in seamy areas. Anyone who has ever passed by a massage parlor knows that they are invariably dirty, shabby places, with pitiful and degraded denizens. On "Charlie's Angels," the Paradise Massage Parlor compared favorably in terms of cleanliness with the surgical theater at Massachusetts General Hospital. The girls were immaculate and well-groomed, soft of speech and clear of eye and skin.

But Television Tends to Break Down Ethnic Prejudices

Still, the television picture isn't all dark. In helping to shape our world views, television has done much to reduce prejudice against blacks, women, and other groups, one of the great improvements in life that has taken place in post–World War II America.

Television is chewing gum for the eyes.

—Frank Lloyd Wright

But then, how many viewers ever heard of Frank Lloyd Wright?

---

[22]Arthur D. Morse's *While Six Million Died* (New York: Random House, 1969) has the grisly details.

The record-breaking docudrama *Roots* let Americans know how hard and unfair everyday life has been for blacks through most of our history by showing relatively simple things, like the difficulties Alex Haley and his family had in finding a motel room, and also more serious things, like the humiliating treatment blacks received in the segregated (until after World War II) United States Army. Many white Americans learned about the extent of these lapses from the American ideal of equality and freedom for the first time—they didn't read about them in their school textbooks.[23]

We don't want to go overboard about the power of television to shape American beliefs and practices. For instance, since World War I, and especially since World War II, a sexual revolution has taken place in the United States. But TV's role in that revolution has been spotty, to say the least. The reason is primarily the desire not to offend its audience, as these two snippets illustrate:

In the early 1960s, Grant Tinker, . . . a programming vice president at NBC, . . . became concerned with the plague of venereal disease among American teen-agers. He saw an opportunity for the network to do a bit of public service through its series *Mr. Novak,* in which James Franciscus played a high-minded high school teacher. . . . Tinker proposed the creation of a two-part episode dealing with VD, and was immediately and adamantly shot down by the higher-ups. They would agree to a VD documentary in a 10-to-11-P.M. time slot, but definitely not in a family-oriented series, and not at 7:30 while children were at the set.

Incensed, Tinker boarded a plane to New York and confronted a major NBC executive. This was vitally important, he coaxed, it was good television, and he *wanted* kids to be watching it at 7:30—that was, in fact, the whole point. The major NBC executive responded with one of the classic lines of contemporary broadcasting. "Grant, please," he said. "Forget it. They're eating in Chicago." . . .

Tom Kersey is . . . Vice President [of] Broadcast Standards and Practices, West Coast, for ABC. . . . He says: "We will not purposely go out and offend a significant segment of our viewership. TV goes into your home like an invited guest, into the privacy of the family unit. You wouldn't want a guest in your home who said and did vulgar things."

In his view the two most sensitive subjects right now are incest and masturbation, and he would not permit them on his network. "Maybe someday we can do them, at some time in the schedule, but not now."

Panorama (November 1980). Reprinted by permission of
Triangle Communications, Inc. and the author, Marcia Seligson.

---

[23]Not that television docudramas are all that accurate. Historians railed against the inaccuracies and distortions of *Roots*—forgetting how accurate it was compared to what most people are generally exposed to. For more on the negative side of the docudrama drama, see "Docudramas Unmasked," *TV Guide,* March 4, 1979. (The TV sitcom *Condo* is a more recent example of a TV program designed to break down ethnic prejudices and help unify this ethnically diverse nation.)

Television news reporting also helped to break down prejudices. It was an important event when the first woman, Barbara Walters, and the first black person, Max Robinson, read the evening news to us on national TV.

But TV shapes our ideas in more subtle ways also. Take the way several scenes were handled in a *Colombo* TV movie. Trying to solve a murder case, Colombo had to wait in a long line at a government office to find out the answer to a question that took just a minute or two. Then he was instructed to go down the hall to wait in another line. Then he went back to the first office with the document in hand, but the clerk was now out to lunch and Colombo had to wait. The point was obvious, and made much better than by just saying it: bureaucracies are a pain in the neck and aren't run for *our* convenience. Very true, and very important.

TV Presents the News More Effectively for a Mass Audience

When we think of the mass media, it's important to remember that about two out of five American adults are functionally illiterate. For them, and lots of others, a picture really is worth a thousand words, and a sound motion picture is worth more than any number of printed words. So for the mass of people, television is the best news source of all the media.

Capturing and informing a mass audience requires extremely tight editing (matched in print only by advertisements). The average attention span is short and comprehension limited. TV does a better job than the other media in editing the news so that it can be understood by most Americans.[24]

TV Documentaries Are a Mixed Bag

A careful television viewer can get a remarkable amount of accurate background from TV documentaries, as well as from programs like CBS's sometimes excellent

[24]For a maverick view on this topic, see James David Barber's "Not the *New York Times:* What Network News Should Be." In the *Washington Monthly* (September 1979), Barber argues that the "trouble with television news is that it is . . . too intellectual, too balanced. It passes right over the heads of the great 'lower' half of the American electorate who need it most. If [it] stopped thinking in terms of . . . the *Encyclopaedia Britannica* or the *New York Times,* it could realize its enormous, unexploited potential for reaching and enlightening voters who now do not know what it is talking about."

60 Minutes (the only news or information program that has ever topped the Nielsen ratings) and ABC's *Nightline*.

On the other hand, some of the documentaries on network television are absolutely awful, pandering to the worst irrationalities of their audience. Some examples are the ones on the Bermuda Triangle (trying to make a case for the silly idea that something funny is going on down there in the Atlantic Ocean) and on Eric von Daniken's even sillier ideas about astronauts having visited the Earth in ancient times, being responsible for humans having had the knowledge to build the Maya pyramids and move the Easter Island stone figures. (In fairness, the networks also have run occasional rebuttals, shredding this nonsense with scientific evidence and accurate facts—after protests from the scientific community.)

Even when they try to present a true picture, they sometimes fail. (The job *isn't* easy.) An ABC *Close-Up,* "State of Washington vs. Jack Jones," presented an actual court case videotaped while in progress; viewers even got to listen in on ordinarily confidential conversations between Jones and his lawyers. The trouble was that the case, supposedly typical, wasn't. Because they knew they would be on TV, all those involved were scrupulously fair, and acted in accord with standard theory of good courtroom procedure. Even the Seattle cops behaved themselves. Since that isn't at all what happens 99 percent of the time, this "totally accurate" portrayal of a court case was extremely misleading.[25] (Recall the discussion in the advertising chapter about the requirement that ads not be *deceptive.*)

The brightest spot on television is PBS, the Public Broadcasting Service. In a typical week, PBS carries about (depending on who's counting) ten informative and interesting evening documentaries.

One of their best series is *Nova.* Most *Nova* programs are well organized and easy to watch; they're also pretty accurate, according to the best expert opinion available. (They do run an occasional klinker, however.) An example is the *Nova* cosmology documentary, which explained the big bang theory of the universe and the discovery of low-frequency background radiation that confirmed it. Another superb *Nova*

Looking backward, it is easy to see now that while "CBS News" excelled at big set-piece journalism of the 60s and 70s—space, the political conventions, the Kennedy assassinations, the civil rights march on Washington—the news organization floundered when it came to enterprise or investigative reporting. The Pentagon papers, My Lai, the Tonkin Gulf fakery, Michigan State University's CIA connection, auto safety, the perils of DDT, and Watergate itself were all stories that we who worked at CBS in those years were frustrated to find had shown up first in such magazines and newspapers as *The Nation, Ramparts, The New Yorker, I. F. Stone's Weekly, The New York Times* or *The Washington Post.*

—Desmond Smith, veteran ABC and CBS news reporter, quoted in *The Nation* (September 16, 1978)

---

[25]This suggests a small point to add to world views. When people (in particular, elected officials) expect the world to notice what they're doing, they behave much more honorably and conscientiously than when their actions will be hidden.

feature, "The Miracle of Life," featured stunning motion pictures of living cells in action, from fertilization of the egg to the development of a human being. Some other fine PBS series that ran in 1983 were the *Wild World of Animals,* a National Geographic series, and Masterpiece Theatre.

From *Penthouse.* Reprinted by permission of Edward Sorel.

Truth at the Movies. *Motion pictures have an important influence on cultural standards and world views (although not as important as before television.) This Sorel cartoon makes the point that their portrayal of the FBI hasn't been exactly accurate (nor has TV's—think of the series* The FBI), *and suggests that fat-cat movie moguls know there's more money in going along with public opinion and power than in bucking it.*

In contrast, NBC's documentary "Reading, Writing, and Reefer," on marijuana, was so bad, so prejudiced, so false, that Henry Lewis's characterization of it (in the *Libertarian Review,* February 1979) as "ignorance, innuendo, and intolerance" erred only in being too mild. (Stoned potheads found NBC's effort hilarious.)

5. The Non-Mass Media to the Rescue

We've just gone on at great length about the limitations of the mass media. But two basic reasons stand out. The first is that the media select the news to appeal to a mass audience and the interests of that audience run to spectacle, to individual events, and to short term, on-going crises (like the Iranian hostage crisis—Americans spent an incredible amount of time listening to the details on that one). The media thus aren't correctly selective in what they report, since unreported, underlying trends and events are usually more important.

The second reason is that the mass media tend to give us secondhand opinions gleaned from the powerful and the rich, not those of more serious thinkers. Politicians are in the business of getting elected and running a government, not theorizing about what's going on. And to be crude, but accurate, Walter Cronkite, Dan Rather, and company (there are a few exceptions) are in the business of news entertainment. They aren't great theorizers and rarely penetrate behind the day-to-day individual events to give us a focused big picture.

When young people come to realize the limitations of the mass media, they often become disillusioned or cynical. If you can't trust good old CBS, *Time* magazine, or the *Lawrence Daily Journal World* who can you trust?

Fortunately, this cynicism is hasty (and often a reaction to an overly rosy world view that needs amending, anyway). In fact, more solid information and sensible opinion is available in the United States today than anywhere else in the history of the world. Books of all kinds are full of it (no pun intended). Of course, the "it" varies from book to book—you have to pick and choose. And the rest of the non-mass media, in particular magazines, provide a rich and (for many) more succinct and convenient mother lode. Trading in ABC, *U.S. News and World Report, The New Britain Herald,* or the *Chicago Tribune* for *Harper's, PBS,* the *Washington Monthly,* or the *Wall Street Journal* is bound to give you a better picture of what's going on. (Or if you're industrious and willing to dig on page 49, try the *New York Times, Los Angeles Times,* or *Washington Post.* And remember that the difference between these compendious newspapers and your local paper may not be all that great. Your local rag *may* have lots of goodies in it—stashed away towards the back—but then again it may not.)

Selectivity Is the Key

The point is that it isn't exactly a matter of mass versus non-mass media. It's a matter of learning how to be *selective*—learning to separate pearls from schlock. The non-mass media contain lots more pearls per square inch and are, on the whole, much more sophisticated.

Take books. On the whole, popular books on social-political matters of interest can be expected to be rather shallow—long on "human interest" but not very penetrating. Even the excellent and very important popular book *The Final Days,* by *Washington Post* reporters Bob Woodward and Carl Bernstein (Avon paperback, 1977) isn't all that authoritative. While it can be trusted concerning the basic facts of Nixon's final days in office, its portrayal of most of the characters in the drama is close to being naïve. In particular, Woodward and Bernstein write as though the public stances of these sophisticated politicians were their true responses to the Watergate revelations. When Senator Hugh Scott expressed public dismay, or Senator Barry Goldwater mouthed platitudes, the authors take them at their word. Here are a few examples to illustrate:

> Few of the President's men were as shocked by the transcripts as the senior academic-intellectual members of the Nixon administration: Arthur F. Burns, the Chairman of the Federal Reserve Board; Daniel Patrick Moynihan, ambassador to India and formerly advisor on domestic policy; George P. Schultz, formerly the President's economic counselor. They read the [Watergate] transcripts in different parts of the world. They heard a Richard Nixon they had never been exposed to before. [page 175]
>
> [Gerald Ford's] belief in Nixon's innocence remained steadfast: Watergate was a political vendetta conducted by Nixon's old enemies in the press and the liberal wing of the Democratic Party. The impeachment drive was not motivated by considerations of law or justice or principle. . . . The Vice President was showing signs of uneasiness. He hadn't planned to become President, and he wouldn't plan for it now. He had wanted to be nothing more than Speaker of the House, and he had accepted the Vice-Presidential nomination largely because it seemed a fitting way to end his political career. Now events were spinning out of control. Though the reality of the situation pressed itself on his logical mind, emotionally he succeeded in pushing it away. [Page 184]

That makes President Ford different from just about any other American you'll ever encounter. Which of us didn't dream as a kid of becoming PRESIDENT OF THE UNITED STATES? Of course, the Vice President couldn't lick his chops in public, but isn't it likely he did in private? Anyway, how did Woodward and Bernstein find out that "emotionally he succeeded in pushing [thoughts of the reality of the situation] away"? Even a mildly sophisticated world view concerning human nature contradicts the portrayal of these battle hardened politicians as kindergarten characters the way Woodward and Bernstein sometimes pictured them.

Of course, books that aren't likely to have a mass audience aren't likely to be widely advertised. A good way to find out about smaller circulation books with more serious and sophisticated content is to read the book reviews (or book excerpts) in non-mass media magazines (such as *The Atlantic,* the *New York Review of Books,* the *Washington Monthly,* the *Skeptical Inquirer,* and so on).

For example, if you're interested in the U.S.–U.S.S.R. arms race (and if you're not, you should be), you might have read the review of two books—*The Soviet Estimate: U.S. Intelligence Analysis and Russian Military Strength* and *Russian Roulette: The Superpower Game* —in the October 1982 issue of *Inquiry* magazine (and, if they sounded interesting, you might have gone out and bought them). Or you might have read the *Harper's* (March 1983) excerpt from *The Threat: Inside the Soviet Military Machine.* Or lots of others.

Of course, for those who don't have the time or inclination to read *whole books* (for gosh sakes!), and also for those who do, the non-mass magazines are the thing to read if you really want to find out what's going on in the world and improve your world view and background knowledge. That means weaning yourself from news on the tube, or better, cutting down on *The Love Boat, Dallas,* and fluff of that kind. Do it.

Summary of Chapter Eight

1. The news media are businesses. So they have to satisfy advertisers, their audience, and the government.

   They cater to their audience in two ways that affect the news: they simplify the news to make it more easily understood, and they slant coverage to reflect audience prejudices and interests (in particular, those of organized pressure groups).

   They cater to advertisers primarily by suppressing news that reflects badly on advertisers and their products (for instance, suppressing news of the cigarette–cancer connection in Winston-Salem). And to a lesser extent they cater to government power so as to avoid harassment (for example, over licenses) and in return for favors (for instance, to obtain leaks and other handouts).

   Being businesses, media news gathering methods are designed to save money. (They usually want to get the truth, but not at any cost.) So most news is gathered from regular news beats or from handouts (or both—much news beat news consists of handouts). It thus reflects the opinions and interests of the rich and powerful who can gear up to give them handouts much more than those of the rest of us. (In addition, it should be noted that much foreign news is suspect because of the ways that foreign governments intimidate reporters—including threatening their lives. The American principle of a free press is the exception in the world.)

2. Media theorizers tend to draw the wrong conclusions about what makes for good journalism. The usual (usually) is not considered news, because it isn't *new,* however important it may (cumulatively) be. Reporters are supposed to be objective, not subjective, and to separate analysis or in-depth reports from objective straight news stories. The opinions of recognized authorities are supposed to take precedence (in practice, this tends to mean authorities who agree with powerful political factions). In addition, theory requires the media to be good citizens and to censor news that might be bad for society.

3. The media use several standard devices that slant the news (inadvertently or otherwise). They play up stories they like and play down those they don't. They use misleading, sensational, or slanted headlines, omit follow up stories (even corrections), and use emotive language to con. (It should be noted that they tend to cloak their ignorance of the subjects on which they report in an aura of authority.)

4. Television is the newest and by far the most important of the mass media. It's the chief way in which the whole nation comes together. Its power to expose,

or inflate, is so great that important political events are arranged so as to have the greatest possible impact on tube watchers.

But television has its drawbacks as a source of information. TV entertainment programs give a juvenile impression of life and how people really act. And news programs on the tube suffer from all the defects of the other mass media (simplifying the news for an unsophisticated audience, using handouts to save money, bowing to government power, not following up on stories, and so on).

However, television also has been a strong force breaking down ethnic prejudice, and it does present the news in a way that is more easily understood by the masses. In addition, TV gives us the privilege of occasionally seeing stunning documentaries (for instance, *Nova*'s "The Miracle of Life").

5. On the whole, the non-mass media are better, more sophisticated sources of information, not so much for finding out which particular events occur on a given day, but rather for learning about the underlying forces that shape these individual events, so that we can come to understand what is happening during our lifetimes. (Several of the mass media newspapers also contain a good deal of solid information, although it tends to get buried amidst the usual news stories. Perhaps the best of these are the *Los Angeles Times*, the *Washington Post*, the *New York Times*, and the *Wall Street Journal*.)

The point is that we have to be *selective* in what we read and listen to. And we might even consider reading whole books once in a while. (!!?!)

Exercise 8-1

1. Evaluate the coverage of a particular event or issue of national importance covered in your local newspaper with respect to: (a) objectivity; (b) original vs. second-hand reporting of the news; (c) use of headlines; (d) "establishment" viewpoint; and (e) other matters discussed in this chapter.

2. Do the same for a recent issue of *Time* or *Newsweek*.

3. Do the same for an ABC, NBC, or CBS evening news program.

4. Listen to several episodes of some television series and determine what world view is illustrated (for example, "Marcus Welby, M.D." presented a world in which doctors are conscientious, professional, and successful in treating patients, a world in which all who need medical attention get it).

5. Check the front page of a single issue of your local newspaper and determine as best you can the sources of their stories. (In the case of things like wire stories, try to determine their sources.) How many of these stories are based on a single handout or speech, how many are compiled from several such sources, and how many resulted from reporters finding out for themselves what's going on?

6. How do you think the news would be different if the federal government controlled and managed it the way, say, it's done in the Soviet Union? Try to be specific, and back up your answer with reasons.

7. Compare the way in which the three major news magazines (*Time, Newsweek,* and *U.S. News and World Report*) report an important news event (such as American involvement in some foreign country, unemployment, government attempts to enforce drug laws, and so on).

8. Compare articles on the same topic in three magazines, one liberal (for instance, *The New Republic, Washington Monthly,* or *Harper's*), one conservative (say the *National Review, Wall Street Journal,* or *Conservative Digest*), and one libertarian (for example, *Inquiry,* the *Libertarian Review,* or *Policy Report*). Is their bias evident? What about quality?

9. How are the elderly and teenagers portrayed on television, both in news stories and especially in popular entertainment programs? Back up your conclusions with details.

10. Go to the library and get a copy of the James David Barber *Washington Monthly* article in the September 1979 issue mentioned in the footnote on page 266 (or if your library has no copy, write to the *Washington Monthly,* 2712 Ontario Road, N.W., Washington, D.C., and ask for a copy, explaining your classroom purpose). Then explain in more detail what Barber's view is on how television news could be radically improved, and give your opinion of his view (backed up by your reasons).

11. For the energetic: Dig through back issues of some mass media publication (guided perhaps by the *Reader's Guide to Periodical Literature*) and evaluate their coverage of some important, long-term national issue (such as nuclear disarmament, unemployment, America's reduced industrial strength, and so on).

12. Also for the energetic: Write your own news story about a personal event that in truth makes you look bad. Write it as though it would appear in your local paper, including headlines and everything else. Now rewrite the story so as to make your part appear in the best light possible without actually lying. Compare the two.

Community Up In Arms Over School Textbooks

BY MANNIX PORTERFIELD

CHARLESTON, W. Va. (UPI) — "Edith is the 'saved' broad who can't marry out of her religion . . . or do anything else out of her religion for that matter, especially what I wanted her to do.

"A bogus religion, man!

"So dig, for the last couple weeks, I been quoting the Good Book and all that stuff to her, telling her I am now saved myself, you dig."

When Charleston school bells rang this month, such passages from a new series of textbooks set off a controversy that spread from this capital city to the nearby coal camps and farmlands of Appalachia.

The furor generated closed schools and mines and inspired shootings, beatings and other violence.

Hundreds of outraged parents poured into the streets, chanting "burn the books." Book advocates within the education system saw shades of fascism, not unlike the fever that swept through Nazi Germany.

The school superintendent moved his family into hiding, fearful of the anonymous death threats he received. Police forces were strained beyond their capacity, dashing from one hot spot to another to quell disturbances.

"It's mob rule," one official said at the height of the protest.

Kanawha County School Board member Alice Moore, a minister's wife, was the first to say the books, for all grades from kindergarten through senior high school in Language Arts classes, were unfit for classrooms. They quickly became the reading material most in demand. Many parents became incensed by what they found.

A poem in one text reads:
"Probably you were a bastard
"Dreaming of running men down in a Cadillac,
"And tearing blouses off women . . ."

One book compares Daniel and the lion's den from the Bible with a fable. Another likens the Genesis account of creation to a myth. Another tale is concerned with a young boy's thoughts on suicide.

Parents feel other passages instill contempt for American leaders and encourage the use of marijuana.

Parental unrest, however, runs deeper than the pages of the texts.

Beneath the protest beats another and louder drum — one that fundamentalist Christians have been sounding in the hills and hollows since their ancestors arrived on the Atlantic Coast to escape religious persecution.

Fearing a new surge of religious intolerance, the fundmentalists thus have engaged in another confrontation — another clash between Christians who believe the Bible in its entirety as the literal truth of God, and those inclined to a liberal interpretation of the scriptures.

Such forces have collided before in West Virginia. They fought in the 1950s when fundamentalist preachers successfully waged war on liquor-by-the-drink and again during the next decade over Sunday closing laws.

The textbook row began weeks before schools opened Sept. 3.

Parents organized a boycott against a store where one of the school board members who supported the texts had connections. When that failed to bring a reversal of the board's 3-2 decision to adopt the books, parents elected to keep their children home,

fearing they would be exposed to antibiblical and un-American teachings.

Fundamentalist preachers led the protest. On the first day of school, nearly one-fourth of the students stayed home.

Armed with picket signs, parents roamed the county in search of support. They found it at coal mines and some industrial plants. Public buses became targets of pickets and 11,000 daily commuters were deprived of transportation.

Thousands of miners, traditionally reluctant to step across picket lines, refused to work. When the protest crusade showed signs of sagging, the miners shored it up.

In the center of the turmoil was Indiana-born Kenneth Underwood, the county schools superintendent.

"It's like a nightmare," he told UPI. "I wonder, when people tell me to burn books, whether we live in Nazi Germany. But I have faith in the democratic process. It will work out."

But at one point, fearing a new outbreak of violence, Underwood closed all county schools for two days. He reopened them after Gov. Arch Moore agreed to use 200 state troopers in roving patrols to guard bus garages and school property.

Supporters of the books view them as harmless, they defend the off-color language and passages from revolutionaries as chronicles of contemporary America.

Disgruntled parents view things differently.

"Anti-Christian, un-American, filthy and rotten," declared protest leaders, such as Rev. Marvin Horan.

By the end of the first week of the boycott, the protest had escalated from minor pranks to shootings incidents and beatings. Philip Cochran, 30, a United Parcel Service truck driver who was not involved in the protest, was wounded seriously at Rand, near Charleston, by a protester shooting at random. A picket received superficial wounds when shot by a janitor whose path to work was blocked by demonstrators.

Underwood and Horan then announced that they had reached a compromise in which the board agreed to a 30-day moratorium on the books.

Horan's followers, however, refused to bend, and the minister backed out of the agreement. He said the board would not put its promise in writing.

Two days later, the board consented to a signed offer, and Horan relented.

Not all clergymen and not all parents sided with dissidents.

Rev. James Lewis, one of 10 Episcopal clergymen who publicly deplored the violence, chided Gov. Moore for his initial reluctance to beef up sheriff patrols with state troopers.

Lewis said he read some of the books and saw nothing objectionable, but rather found the material "conducive to the kind of freedom our country was based on."

"The material opens up all kinds of human concern and godly concern," he said. "There is a lot of potential in it."

During the third week of the controversy, nearly 1,000 parents, waving American flags, demonstrated on the Capitol lawn and shouted down the 30-day moratorium. They demanded books be stricken on a permanent basis, without benefit of a review.

Two parents decided to set wheels in motion for a legal settlement and filed suit in U. S. District Court.

The easiest way to change history is to become a historian.

—Anonymous

Probably all education is but two things: first, parrying of the ignorant child's impetuous assault on the truth; and second, gentle, imperceptible initiation of the humiliated children into the lie.

—Franz Kafka

The less people know about how sausages and laws are made, the better they'll sleep at night.

—Bismarck

And the crowd was stilled. One elderly man, wondering at the silence, turned to the child and asked him to repeat what he had just said. Wide eyed, the child raised his voice and said once again, "Why, the Emperor has no clothes. He is naked."

—The Emperor's New Clothes

To limit the press is to insult a nation; to prohibit reading of certain books is to declare the inhabitants to be either fools or slaves.

—Claud Arrien Helvetius

9

Textbooks: Managing World Views

First, the bad news. The textbooks on United States history, civics, and world history that you read back in public school weren't just dull, dull, dull. They also suppressed evidence, pulled their punches, lacked a sense of proportion, and in general gave you a distorted view of history, your country, and the world.

Now for the good news. While public school textbooks still tend to be dull, otherwise they've been getting better and better. In particular, the minor revolution started in about 1960 (because of changing American attitudes toward blacks and other minority groups) has reached maturity, producing texts that slant history and how our system works much less than they used to. It would not be a case of puffery to say that some of the recent public school history and civics texts are the best of their kind in history, anywhere.

1. Textbooks Are Intended to Indoctrinate (Educate)

The first thing we have to remember is that the ultimate purpose of public schools is to educate the young to fit into adult society. That means, first, giving them the knowledge they'll need to be productive citizens, and second, inculcating in them the values, attitudes, and practices that will make them good citizens. Education thus inevitably involves a certain amount of indoctrination.

Applying these thoughts to public school textbooks yields some tentative conclusions as to their likely content. The first is that noncontroversial topics, like mathematics, will be presented in a more or less straightforward way, with indoctrination at a minimum.[1] Society wants just about everybody to be able to read and to do arithmetic.

The second tentative conclusion is that history and civics texts are bound to distort their material. The history of any nation has its dark spots as well as bright, and no system works the way it's supposed to. These social studies texts thus deal with extremely sensitive political and social issues. (Also, even the best scholars disagree on these topics, so it's hard to present a true account of them.) Public school history and civics texts therefore inevitably have to distort their subject matters so as to make "Our Great Nation" appear better than it really is. (No society wants to raise disaffected citizens.) Controversial and embarrassing points have to be papered over somehow or other. Exactly how and to what extent this is done depends on social and political factors that change from time to time. Today, these factors are more favorable for providing students with greater accuracy and less indoctrination than ever before in our history.

2. Textbooks Are a Commodity

We also have to remember that textbooks are a commodity very much like newspapers and magazines. So we should expect that the various parties involved in their production, sale, and use will have power over their content. It turns out, however,

---

The first requirement of any society is that its adult membership should realize and represent the fact that it is they who constitute its life and being. And the first function of the rites of puberty, accordingly, must be to establish in the individual a system of sentiments that will be appropriate to the society in which he is to live and on which that society itself must depend for its existence.

—Joseph Campbell, in *Myths Men Live By*

Throughout history, . . . people have had to be taught to be stupid. For to permit the mind to expand to its outermost capabilities results in a challenge to traditional ways. . . . A certain amount of intellectual sabotage must be introduced into all educational systems. Hence all educational systems must train people to be unintelligent within the limits of the culture's ability to survive.

—Jules Henry, in *On Sham, Vulnerability, and other Forms of Self-Destruction*

---

[1]Texts used in private denominational schools (in particular Catholic schools) are exceptions. Some of their texts intrude religious indoctrination into almost every subject.

that the relative power of each faction is a bit different than in the case of the mass media.

There are six groups who have an interest in textbooks: authors, publishers, state regulators, local buyers, teachers (and principals), and students. All exercise power in some way or other. But those who actually buy a product in a relatively open market have the largest share of say as to what the product will be like.

In the United States, local school boards are the ones who ultimately spend the cash that feeds the textbook industry. So in a sense local boards have the most power in determining textbook content. But they're constrained in their choices. First, state regulating agencies limit the books local boards can select from. Second, local boards almost inevitably delegate authority for textbook selection to local teachers (and principals), retaining only indirect control. And third, personal scruples and professional standards keep textbook authors from straying too far from the straight and narrow. (Remember too that local boards are elected by local citizens whose taxes buy public school textbooks. For what happens when local public opinion is thwarted, see the UPI article that introduces this chapter.)

Oh, yes, students also have an indirect say in textbook style and (to a lesser extent) content. Unliked books tend to be less effective, and that's bound to influence selection somewhat. But student power is smaller than that of any of the concerned groups. That's why the term *indoctrination* isn't far off the mark. In the case of the mass media, the ultimate user of the commodity wields the greatest power, as should be evident from the discussion in the last chapter. In the case of public school

---

The House of Representatives of the State of Texas, in a 1961 Resolution, desires ". . . that the American history courses in the public schools emphasize in the textbooks our glowing and throbbing history of hearts and souls inspired by wonderful American principles and traditions."

—Jack Nelson and Gene Roberts, Jr., in *The Censors and the Schools*

Philosophy of History–Social Science Education in California

The central purpose of history–social science education is to prepare students to be humane, rational, understanding, and participating citizens in a diverse society and in an increasingly interdependent world—students who will preserve and continue to advance progress toward a just society. (From the 1981 History Social Science Framework for California Public Schools Kindergarten Through Grade Twelve, the basic document governing California schools.)

Notice that the purpose of history and civics texts is not to tell you the history of the nation or how things really work, except incidentally as these serve other purposes. (Texas and California statewide selecting agencies have more influence on public school textbooks than all the other state agencies combined.)

textbooks, the ultimate user has the least say. (But then, most mass media audiences consist of "responsible" adults, while public school textbook audiences consist of "children.")[2]

3. Textbooks Are Censored

It's very difficult to distinguish censorship from the ordinary pressures on textbook content. But however it's defined, we have to realize that government agencies do in fact force changes in the content of public school textbooks (and also of nonprint material). This is particularly true of the state agencies in Texas and California, since no publisher wants to be shut out of the two most lucrative markets.

Prior to 1960, minority groups, in particular blacks, tended to be invisible in public school textbooks, as they were also in the mass media. But now, no major publisher will publish a United States history or civics textbook that does not give lots of space to minorities. They won't, for one reason, because such a book wouldn't satisfy the California state board's criteria and so would be a victim of California censorship.

Even biology texts are sometimes censored. In earlier editions of this text, we showed how Houghton Mifflin was forced to revise one of its biology texts[3] so as to satisfy the Texas State Textbook Committee. Powerful groups in Texas, who objected to its straightforward account of the scientific theory of evolution, forced changes in the text to make it appear that evolution is just a theory, an assumption that we might reasonably doubt, rather than what it is—an established, well-confirmed set of scientific principles. The point was to protect students from a scientific challenge to their religious beliefs about the creation.

Non-textbooks Are Also Censored

But by the early 1980s, fundamentalist attacks on evolution had become relatively unsuccessful. Recently published biology texts do usually make reference to "Creation Science," the fundamentalist theory of the origin of the universe (the account given in *Genesis*). However, they do so only to show that creation science is *not* a science and in fact runs counter to well-confirmed scientific discoveries. (It's hard to say why fundamentalists have been losing. But in this writer's opinion a strong force has been exerted by an awakened scientific community, effective at all levels—from author to teacher. For instance, when a flock of eminent scientists testified very effectively in a case in which the court struck down an Arkansas statute requiring

---

[2]In recent years, power has been shifting away from local school boards to state agencies that set uniform state requirements for textbooks. This trend has been influenced, surprisingly, by federal government actions, such as the 1967 ruling that all schools meet statewide requirements to get federal aid. See, for instance, the June 1982 *Policy Report* article, "Bureaucrats and Education," by Eugenia Froedge Toma.

[3]*Biological Science: Molecules to Man*. For details on this and many other cases of textbook censorship, see Hillel Black's *The American Schoolbook* (New York: William Morrow, 1967), Jack Nelson's and Gene Roberts, Jr.'s *The Censors and the Schools* (Boston: Little, Brown, 1963), and Edward B. Jenkinson's *Censors in the Classroom* (Carbondale, Ill.: Southern Illinois University Press, 1979).

Creation Science to be taught in science classes alongside the theory of evolution, the court held that Creation Science was not science but a religious doctrine.)

Some books still fudge slightly. But basically, they hold the line against religious challenges to accurate portrayal and assessment of evolutionary theory. Here, for instance, is how a 1980 biology text[4] dealt with the issue:

Theories of Life's Origin on Earth

There have been many suggestions as to how living organisms first appeared on Earth.

One of these says that life or living things were specially created. In the Christian tradition the special creator is God. In other traditions the creator has other names. The ideas of special creation, regardless of the tradition from which they come, are not scientific ideas. If special creation were a scientific hypothesis, it would have to be testable. Explanations are tested by making predictions from them and then seeing if the predictions are true or false.

So far, no one has been able to find a testable prediction that comes from special creation. Thus, special creation appears to be an untestable explanation or hypothesis. The subject matter of this book is limited to what can be known using the method of learning called scientific inquiry. From that point of view, special creation is an explanation that is neither right nor wrong. It is scientifically untestable as far as we now know. . . .

There is a hypothesis about the origin of life that can be tested. It states that life arose naturally from conditions on the earth. This . . . hypothesis is the subject of the next section. [The following sections deal with the history and details of the theory of evolution.]

Censorship occurs more overtly in the case of nontexts used in classrooms or shelved in school libraries. The censor in most of these cases is the local school board.

Almost any book may be censored. The principle reasons for censoring a book are obscenity, favorable portrayal of an immoral lifestyle, and racial or ethnic bias. A Tennessee county school board removed the old standby *Drums along the Mohawk* from the assigned list of books in local schools because it contained words they judged to be obscene like *hell* and *damn*. Shakespeare's *The Merchant of Venice* is censored occasionally because Jewish groups object to its portrayal of Shylock.

But perhaps silliest of all, one of the most frequently censored books is *The Adventures of Huckleberry Finn*. It has two groups on its back: blacks offended by its portrayal of blacks, and others offended by Huck's throwing off of conventional morality, glorifying "immoral conduct." (Irony of ironies, one of the schools censoring *Huck Finn* at one time or another turns out to be Mark Twain Intermediate School in Fairfax County, Virginia.)

It would be provincial to conclude that book censorship in public schools is an American phenomenon. On the contrary, school censorship in the United States is less frequent and much less severe than in most, perhaps all, other countries.

---

[4]*Biology: The Science of Life* (Houghton Mifflin, 1980), by Earl D. Hanson, J. David Lockard, and Peter J. French.

Recently, for instance, Japanese textbook censorship raised quite a storm, even involving Japanese Prime Minister Zenko Suzuki. Until a few years ago, Japanese texts portrayed Japan's aggression before and during World War II in a modestly accurate way (no doubt under the prodding of Allied occupation officers after the War). But then changes in textbook content, allegedly engineered by Japanese hawks, produced new history texts in which, for instance, Japan's invasion of China was called an "advance" and the 1919 rebellion in Korea against Japanese rulers was referred to as a "riot."[5] The hawks had one textbook changed because it stated that there have been significant changes in the way Article Nine of the Japanese constitution is being interpreted. The textbook's statement was a rather gentle way of pointing out the truth that this important article in their constitution has been violated in recent years. (Article Nine requires that military forces "never be maintained" by Japan. In one recent year, Japan spent $11.5 billion on its "peacekeeping" force—which sounds like pretty good evidence that Article Nine *is* being grossly violated.)

Even paintings of the catastrophes following our dropping of atomic bombs on Hiroshima and Nagasaki were censored by the Japanese Ministry of Education.

The number of books and magazines censored out of public school classrooms and libraries runs into the thousands every year. Here are a few examples:[6]

The Sun Also Rises (Ernest Hemingway)
The Catcher in the Rye (J. D. Salinger)
The Grapes of Wrath (John Steinbeck)
Andersonville (McKinley Kantor)
Look Homeward Angel (Thomas Wolfe)
1984 (George Orwell)
Brave New World (Aldous Huxley)
The Invisible Man (Ralph Ellison)
Native Son (Richard Wright)
Slaughterhouse Five (Kurt Vonnegut, Jr.)
Marjorie Morningstar (Herman Wouk)
Ms. magazine
The Naked Ape (Desmond Morris)
The American Heritage Dictionary (banned because it included "gutter words" like *ball, nut,* and *tail*)

If you were wondering why you read books like say, Sir Walter Scott's Ivanhoe *in high school, or Charles and Mary Lamb's cleansed versions of Shakespeare, maybe the answer is that they were the only ones left.*

---

[5]Public outcry in Far Eastern countries overrun by Japan during its "expansionist" period forced the Japanese government to promise reinstatement of the censored material. For more on this, see *The Nation* (December 19, 1981).

[6]The American Library Association's *Newsletter on Intellectual Freedom* contains a list in each issue of "Titles Now Troublesome," which means books somebody or other is censoring.

They forced elimination of pictures of crowds of people being burned alive, screaming, collapsing, and dying, saying that "Extremely tragic subjects will be removed from textbooks."

Nothing even remotely like that sort of national government interference in textbook content ever occurs in the United States. However, every U.S. public school textbook this writer has ever seen fudges the analogous issue of the allegedly illegal war we fought in Vietnam (illegal, it is claimed, because our Constitution gives Congress the sole power to declare war, and Congress hasn't done so since World War II).

Drawing by David Levine. Copyright © 1969 NYREV, Inc.
Reprinted by permission from *The New York Review of Books*.

Hamburger Hill

David Levine's drawing of Hamburger Hill (a hill in Vietnam on which many soldiers lost their lives) pictures two American presidents as jolly mass murderers. Would the Texas State Textbook Committee give its approval to a book containing this caricature?

In the United States today, banning books outside of public schools is much less common than censorship within educational walls. But it does occur, and obviously limits what students as well as adults can read. Favorite targets are books with sexual content and those affecting national security. (For more on the history of book censorship, see *Banned Books,* by Anne Lyon Haight, revised by Chandler B. Grannis.) However, in the history of censorship, all sorts of things have been banned or censored. For instance, in 1933 the U.S. customs office confiscated copies of "obscene photo books" it described as "Ceiling Sistene Chapel Filles Michael Angelo." In 1961, Canadian customs officials confiscated as obscene the official report of the trial in England in which D. H. Lawrence's *Lady Chatterley's Lover* was held to be *not* obscene. Not long after that, Ralph Ginsberg went to jail in the U.S. because the *advertising* for his magazine *Eros* was judged to be obscene. Way back in 1526, the first English translation of the *New Testament* was banned and copies burned; in Spain, a similar fate awaited the first translation into Spanish. In more recent times, several states have banned *Fanny Hill* as obscene; material dealing with our defeat at Pearl Harbor was censored during World War II; and just in the past few years, the U.S. federal government has forced censorship of several books dealing with the CIA and its clandestine operations.

4. Textbooks Distort History

Public school history texts are more accurate today than they've ever been before. But they still distort history, in particular the history of the United States.

United States History Is Sanitized

History texts "clean up" our past in order not to reduce student pride in America. Our leaders are pictured as better than human, all dressed up and minus their warts.[7] Take the way in which President Theodore Roosevelt, affectionately called *Teddy* in many texts (the teddy bear was named after him), is spruced up for textbook readers. In textbooks, Roosevelt is pictured as energetic, hard driving, exuberant, brave, a trustbuster, conservationist, big-game hunter, reformer, and progressive who was against big business and for the workers, although (in some recent texts) a bit of an imperialist who made the Panama Canal possible as an American enterprise—a great man well deserving of his place on Mt. Rushmore.

And perhaps he was. But no textbooks say much about another side of good old Teddy. They don't describe him as a bloodthirsty bigot who, though unusually brave, reveled in the slaughter he personally dealt out and witnessed during the Spanish-American War; a man who expressed pleasure that thirty men had been shot to death in the Civil War draft riots—"an admiral object lesson to the remainder"; a person who justified slaughtering Indians, on the grounds that their lives were only "a few degrees less meaningful, squalid, and ferocious than that of the wild beasts," and said that "no triumph of peace is quite so great as the supreme triumph of war." Not exactly a teddy bear, this Teddy Roosevelt.

---

[7]There are a very few obvious exceptions—villains who can't be dolled up to look virginal. Richard Nixon is the best example. But then, how do you picture the only president driven from office as a saint?

America's Role in History Is Distorted

Public school textbooks can't use puffery the way ads do. But they use other devices to accomplish a similar end—in particular, the simple *omission* of historical events and the distortion of those that are covered by careful control of *emphasis*. Both of these are very hard for uninformed or unsophisticated readers to detect.

Take the way that America's role in World War II is exaggerated, omitting all but a few of the details of the Russian role and playing down those that are mentioned. Although reliable statistics on World War II are sometimes difficult to find, common estimates place the total killed in that war at between 40 and 50 million, and the Soviet Union's dead at 15 to 20 million, almost half of the total. The United States lost 322,000 soldiers (almost no civilians), about 88 percent of them in the European theater of war. The Germans were defeated by a combination of British, American, and Soviet military action, but the Russian effort was incomparably greater than that of Britain and America combined. From June 1941, when Germany invaded Russia, to the end of the war in Europe, the largest and most powerful element of the German Army fought on the Russian front against the Soviet Army. The overwhelming majority of German military losses, in equipment and men, were inflicted on them by Russian forces on the Eastern front, not by British and American forces in Africa or Western Europe. There were several times more Russian *civilian* deaths than all the American deaths in all the wars in our history.

But public school textbooks don't play it that way. They emphasize our role in Europe in World War II and play down the Soviet role. One reason for this is to make our own country look better than other countries. Another is to prejudice readers against Communism, Communist governments and countries, and in particular the Soviet Union. (The Cold War had to be fought in textbooks as well as elsewhere, and it was. It still is.)

Here is how a reasonably typical junior high school text, *America's Heritage,*[8] portrays the Russian effort against Germany. The text allots about 16 pages (487–503) to World War II, including photos and maps. The first reference to Russia fighting in World War II is on page 493:

> By June 1941 the Germans had taken control of nearly all Europe except the Soviet Union and Britain. Then Hitler broke his agreement with Stalin and launched a surprise attack on Russia. The Nazi war machine needed Russian oil and wheat. Also the defeat of the Soviet Union was part of Hitler's long-range plan to become master of Europe. Churchill welcomed the Russians as an ally even though he distrusted the Communists. . . . By the time the U.S. entered the war, the Nazis were deep into Russia. . . .

We then are treated to a section entitled "How Germany Was Defeated," which starts out:

> The long bloody struggle to regain Europe began first in North Africa. There British troops were able to stop the German drive for the Suez Canal. Allied forces drove the Axis forces out of North Africa. Then they began the bitter task of driving the Axis soldiers out of Italy. (See map, p. 494.) At the same

---

[8]By Margaret Stimmann Branson (Boston: Ginn & Co., 1982).

time that land battles raged all over Europe and North Africa, a desperate struggle went on at sea. German submarines roamed the North Atlantic Ocean and even went into the Gulf of Mexico and the Caribbean Sea. Gradually, and at great cost, the Allies turned the tide of battle against these deadly underwater sharks.

The Russians don't enter the picture until over a page later:

Everywhere, the Germans met defeat. The Nazis tried one last desperate attempt to save themselves in a counterattack. They drove a fifty mile . . . bulge into the Allied lines. This "Battle of the Bulge" caused some of the fiercest fighting of the war, but it was no use. The Nazi forces were cut to ribbons. . . . General Eisenhower's troops reached the Elbe River in April 1945. There, they met the Soviets, who had come from the East. The Russians were first to enter Berlin, however.[9] Hitler . . . committed suicide in his underground shelter in Berlin before the Soviets could capture him.

One of the great improvements in public school texts since about 1960 has been the treatment of minority groups, in particular blacks and women. This improvement mirrors the change in attitudes that has been taking place in America since World War II. In previous editions of this text, we showed how American history was doctored so as to mask the essential fact that white Europeans who had no claim to even a foot of the North American continent defeated its legitimate owners (the Native American "Indians") and stole the whole continent from them. To mask this fact, or at least to blunt it, textbooks had to make Indians as invisible as possible, except for the "good" Indians (Pocahontas, the Thanksgiving Indians, Indian guides) and for the few cases where land may actually have been bought instead of just taken by force (Manhattan Island). Today's textbooks don't exactly shout grand theft on every page, but they do give some specifics concerning the suffering of the Indians (the "Trail of Tears") and a pretty good idea that the Indians didn't willingly give up their land to the Europeans.

In previous editions, we also showed how history and civics texts in the 1960s had to change their treatment of blacks so as to keep up with public opinion and the increased power of blacks. For instance, we showed cases where the only significant differences between old and new editions were in photos—replacing pictures of whites with those of blacks—and in mentioning more blacks— Frederick Douglass, Harriet Tubman, W.E.B. DuBois—than just the standard or token blacks, the Uncle Toms like Booker T. Washington who had always been mentioned.

Let's look at one particularly obvious (some would say hilarious) example of this from earlier editions, to illustrate the cleansing process established texts

---

[9]Even this bit, favorable to Russia, is misleading. American forces could have taken Berlin first, since the disintegrating German army still had its largest force facing the Russians. We didn't take Berlin because of a political decision by the American government, not because of military factors.

(After this, we get three pages on G.I. Joe, the home front, and Rosie the riveter.)

In addition, a map of Europe shows the general paths taken by Allied armies, including Russian armies (with an inset showing details of the American and British advances through France into Germany). And that's it for Russia's monumental sacrifices and their defeat of the bulk of the German army in World War II.

The point of all this detail is to show how omission and emphasis can add up to a monstrous lack of proportion that completely distorts history and puffs up the United States at the expense of other countries. Even the brightest students, reading between, over, and around the lines of the text just discussed, could not get a reasonable picture of what happened in those fateful times. They would have to conclude that the Americans and British did most of the fighting and winning against the German army, with Russian participation a vague blur on the periphery. How then can we expect today's students to understand the postwar period and the cold war that has been going on since then between the U.S. and the U.S.S.R.

It should be noted that the history text just discussed is a junior high school text.

---

underwent during that period (and thus to illustrate indirectly the way in which local political power translates into changes in textbooks). The text Building Citizenship[10] *had the following snippet on President Theodore Roosevelt in its 1961 edition:*

> Some people found fault with Theodore Roosevelt because they said he acted as if he had discovered the Ten Commandments. Quite likely, however, many more people became interested in applying the Ten Commandments to present-day life because they admired something in "T.R."

This is changed in the 1966 edition (same page, same exact spot on the page) to read:

> Some people find fault with [brace yourself] Martin Luther King because he acts as if he had discovered the Ten Commandments. Quite likely, however, many more people have become interested in applying the Ten Commandments to present day life because they admire Dr. King's fight against racial discrimination.

This was one of very few changes introduced in the 1966 edition. Most of the others were changes in photos to include blacks who had been invisible, or in tiny paragraphs like the one in question. In this context, the purpose of the switch from "T.R." to "M.L.K." becomes obvious—say something about a black leader that will fit a particular spot so the new edition can be published as quickly and cheaply as possible and the book can catch up to public opinion. (None of this had to do with anything so crass as making textbooks come closer to the truth.)

---

[10]This text was in use for a long time. The original author was Ray Osgood Hughes (Boston: Allyn & Bacon, 1921); it has been revised by C.H.W. Pullen and by James H. McCrocklin, the latter being responsible for both of the versions considered here.

Senior high school books have much more space to spend on World War II, as on everything else, and do generally give a few details of the fighting on the Russian front. The German defeat at Stalingrad is usually mentioned. And statistics on losses suffered by the various participants also are sometimes included. So a smart student might be able to read between the lines and see that the Russians at least did most of the suffering and may even have done lots of the fighting that eventually defeated the German armies. But it would have to be a pretty bright student. The general impression given by almost every high school history text is that the United States and Britain were primarily responsible for defeating Germany in World War II.

It also should be noted that grade school history texts distort the history of World War II (and everything else) even more. Students thus are exposed to the worst account of history when just starting out.

5. Textbooks Minimize the Gulf between Theory and Practice

In the constant struggle for power and wealth that goes on in America, as just about everywhere else, national ideals and standards get violated. Thus a great gulf is going to exist between the theory as to how our system is supposed to work and the actual everyday practice. It is terribly important that we know about this gulf, so that we can get a better idea as to what is in store for us under various possible circumstances. For instance, it's important for us to know our chances of getting justice when arrested, or when going to court, and of knowing the chances that our elected representatives will represent *us* as well as they do large election campaign contributors.

But civics texts have to skip most of these questions, and when they touch on them, they have to pull their punches. So they play up the wonders of our official story—the ideal way our system is supposed to work—while sweeping most of the battle dust under the rug.

For instance, one of our official myths[11] is that no one is above the law—that a Rockefeller can't break into someone else's property with impunity any more than you can. Civics texts have to stress the positive and play down the negative, so they don't tell students that this particular official myth really *is* a myth—that the rich sometimes are above the law in ways we common folk never are, and that a Rockefeller can (because one actually did) at least sometimes break into someone else's property and get away with it. Here, for instance, is a *Washington Post*[12] tidbit you're not likely to run across in any civics texts, although it reveals a great deal about privilege differences between rich and poor:

Rules Are Made to be Broken, for Some People

> Late one night in Kansas City, [Nelson] Rockefeller couldn't find his Water Pik. "He had dental work that debris would catch in sometimes," recalls Hugh Morrow, the former Rockefeller spokesman. "So with the aid of the local police, [aide] Joe [Canzeri] broke into a drugstore, got the Water Pik and left the money on the counter—including the local sales tax. . . ."

---

[11]Recall Mark Twain's colossal lies of silent assertion mentioned in Chapter 1.
[12]December 1, 1981. Reprinted in *Policy Report,* January 1982.

During the 1968 New York City garbage strike, Rockefeller was once in all-night negotiations with the union. By 5 a.m. the group was tired and hungry. Canzeri broke a kitchen lock at the nearby Gotham Hotel, then made bacon, scrambled eggs, coffee and toast for the group of 30.

Speaking of great wealth, here is how one secondary school text, *The Young American Citizen* (New York: Saddlier-Oxford, 1978), mentioned the problem of big money buying the votes of elected officials (most texts just slide past this question altogether):

> Organizations, groups, or corporations that take a great interest in a bill can spend large sums of money trying to persuade Senators and Representatives to vote for or against it. This is called *lobbying*. While citizens have the right to lobby Congress, few individuals can afford the great amount of money that some *pressure groups* can. Because members of Congress do not have time to get the opinion of everyone on a particular bill, they often rely heavily on the arguments of lobbyists. This is helpful when the pressure group represents a large number of citizens. Sometimes, however, lobbyists representing only a small number of powerful people can have laws shaped to further their interests.

This makes it sound as though the problem results from the pressure of time, and that lobbyists influence legislation chiefly by providing timely information, not by taking advantage of the human tendency to line one's own pockets at the expense of the general public. (The word *bribe* is not mentioned in this context in any text this writer has seen.)

Another secondary school text, *Free Enterprise in America* (New York: Harcourt Brace Jovanovich, 1977), describes supply and demand in terms that would have delighted Adam Smith (and set someone like John Kenneth Galbraith to howling), explaining how a small onion crop resulted in higher prices while a high tomato yield resulted in lower prices for tomatoes—supply and demand in the classic sense. The implication was that this is the way all markets operate—supply and demand. No mention here about international conglomerates or OPEC creating artificially controlled prices for major items like oil and gas; nothing here about collusion to fix prices (*à la* the 1960s electrical conspiracy) or how price competition is a negligible factor in marketing retail items like cigarettes, cosmetics, and beer, whose supply is generally greater than demand (for instance, they fail to point out the common interests of, say, beer manufacturers in keeping retail beer prices high).

Even the best texts fall down in reporting on actual practice. For instance, lots of civics and economics texts tell students about income taxes, and all civics texts explain the mechanics of how tax laws are passed by Congress. But none of them provide students with the crucial fact that a large majority of Americans cheat on their income tax (so that if you don't, you get ripped off by those who do), and only a very few hint at the fact that tax bills are tailored so that lots of rich people pay a smaller percentage of their income in taxes than the average taxpayer, some paying no income tax at all (so that, again, the average taxpayer, having fewer loopholes, gets ripped off).

The relatively excellent secondary school text *Foundations of Our Government* (New York: Scholastic Book Service, 1977), which does mention some of the evils and problems of our court system, our system of justice, does so while at the same time stressing the good in everyday practice. It lets readers know about the problems poor people have in getting decent legal help by way of introduction to the Supreme Court *Gideon* decision, which states that an accused person has a right to a lawyer, court-appointed if necessary, in order to assure equal protection of the law. Similarly, it lets its reader know about police tactics designed to worm or force "confessions" out of innocent suspects while introducing students to the Supreme Court *Escobedo* decision, which declared such confessions illegal. (No, they didn't tell students how often both of these Supreme Court decisions are flouted, especially when a defendant is poor or powerless, and they didn't say anything about the quality of court-appointed lawyers as compared to, say, the lawyers a member of Congress hires when charged with a crime.) The practice of telling about nastiness at the point something is being done about it is one of the standard ways used in textbooks to soften the blow for students.

When J. Edgar Hoover was alive and the head of the FBI, no textbook could say anything seriously nasty about him or his organization. Hoover was too popular with right-wing Americans and had the goods on too many public officials, as well as more ordinary folk. Now that Hoover has departed the scene, the mass media feel easier about taking pot shots at him, and occasionally at the FBI (recall the *Washington Post* item on tyrant Hoover reprinted in the last chapter). But so far public school texts still treat the FBI with kid gloves. None of them mention FBI illegal wire taps, burglaries, or the harassment of civil rights leaders (like Martin Luther King and Medgar Evers) in the 1960s and 1970s. No text explains how the FBI and many local police forces did their best to thwart the civil rights movement. Similarly, no public school textbooks mention CIA clandestine operations in Latin America, or how the CIA had a large part in overthrowing the legally elected government of Chile and in the murder of its legally elected president. (It doesn't make for pride in one's country to hear about such things.)

By concentrating on how things are supposed to work, while slighting how they actually work, textbooks color their accounts of nearly everything. Take labor unions. No longer relatively invisible in textbooks as they used to be, they now are treated in an idealized way that would delight someone like Jimmy Hoffa, were he around today. For instance, the text *Free Enterprise: The American Economic System* [13] spent a good deal of space on labor unions, mentioning their history from the late 1700s, how they've grown, how minorities and women "in recent years have come to play a more important part," and how the AFL and CIO finally joined forces. But the only criticism of labor unions is given in a discussion of the Taft-Hartley Act of 1947:

> Many Americans began to feel that the unions had become too powerful. [No explanation of why or how.] These people blamed some post war problems, such as rising prices, on the unions. In response to this feeling, Congress passed the . . . Taft-Hartley Act. . . . Most labor leaders were opposed to the Taft-Hartley Act. They called it a "slave labor law." However, other Americans saw the act as setting a balance of the power between labor and manage-

---

[13] By Robert F. Smith, Michael W. Watts, and Vivian D. Hogan [River Forest, Ill.: Laidlow Brothers (Doubleday), 1981.]

ment. . . . As opposition to organized labor grew, the AFL and the CIO began to think of joining together. . . .

Nothing is said of the racial discrimination that kept blacks and other nonwhites out of construction unions (and thus out of most construction jobs). There is not a word about crooked union leaders colluding with management against their own members, or those who siphoned off union funds for personal purposes, or mine workers with black lung who were cheated by their own union. Nothing is said of organized crime infiltration or control of some unions. "Good guys" George Meany, John L. Lewis, and Walter Reuther are mentioned, but not corrupt leaders like Dave Beck or Jimmy Hoffa. (Notice also that this text definitely did not take sides on the issue of the *merit* of the Taft-Hartley Act. Public school texts rarely risk taking sides on controversial issues—that is, on most issues—since that would only lose sales to the offended parties.)

6. Textbook Style Is Deadly

Textbooks also fail to truly educate young people because of their (lack of) literary style. Since they're supposed to be objective, emotively neutral locutions are the rule, especially where anything controversial is mentioned. Facts and details roll on, one after the other, with all of the life squeezed out of them. Atrocities are mentioned the way one might discuss the weather or a math problem. The idea is not to get students upset or disaffected, say by letting them find out the true horror of "Indian removal" as carried out by the white man. Injustices that are mentioned are discussed so as to be minimized, or when pointing out how they are being corrected (recall the snippet on the *Gideon* and *Escobedo* decisions in the last section).

After a few pages of such writing, eyes begin to glaze over and true understanding goes out the window. At best, most students will start reading for "facts" they may

---

At this point, some readers may be wondering whether all that much progress has occurred in recent years. So here's a little excerpt from a really bad textbook that was in circulation until a few years ago, to give you an idea of how much things have improved:

As you ride up beside the Negroes in the field they stop working long enough to look up, tip their hats and say, "Good morning, Master John." You like the friendly way they speak and smile; they show bright rows of white teeth. "How's it coming, Sam?" your father asks one of the old Negroes. "Fine, Marse Tom, jes fine. We got more cotton than we can pick." Then Sam chuckles to himself and goes back to picking as fast as he can.

Mentioned in the TRB column of the *New Republic* (July 25, 1970) and best left anonymous here.

If that sort of writing doesn't make every current civics text look good, nothing will.

need to regurgitate on exams. So they may hardly notice when something they really need to know about is discussed. Reading between the lines is discouraged by boredom and is made harder by the upbeat or even-handed style in which controversial topics are discussed.

Here, for instance, is how one civics text, *Civics For Americans*,[14] talks about courtroom justice:

Equal Justice for All

Our legal system is based on an important ideal—**equal justice** for all under the law. The goal of the legal system is to treat every person the same. Under the Constitution, every person accused of breaking the law has the right to a public trial. Every accused person has the right to a lawyer. If an accused person cannot afford a lawyer, the courts will appoint one and will pay the lawyer's fee. Every person is considered innocent until proven guilty. And a person has the right to ask for a review of his or her case if, in that person's view, the courts have made a mistake.

The ideal of equal justice is a difficult goal to reach. Judges and juries are not free from the prejudices of their communities. Poor people do not have the money to spend on legal help that wealthy citizens or large companies do. Nonetheless, Americans believe in the ideal. There are some countries in the world where prejudice is legal and where there are different laws for different groups of people. In the United States, all people are equal before the law. If injustice occurs, citizens have the right to speak out and correct it.

Even those students who are paying attention are unlikely to get much of an idea from this about the gulf between the theory of equal justice and the reality of everyday practice. So they're not going to learn about their chances of being treated fairly if they sue or are brought into court when they become adults. But if we don't tell students that, what good are all the details about the theory of jury selection or which courts handle what? (The text follows this snippet with almost two pages of forgettable details, including, for instance, a paragraph called "Disputes between States or People from Different States," which tells us things even most lawyers don't remember, such as "Such suits must involve a sum of at least $10,000 to be handled in Federal Court.")

7. Textbooks Fail to Give Students Genuine Understanding

From what has been said so far, it should be clear that textbooks fail to give students true understanding of the history and function of their society. They fail, to put it in a nutshell, because the various relevant pressures force them to be "goody-goody." Since our society is far from perfect and our history somewhat tarnished, textbooks have to pull their punches, reveal injustice primarily as it is being corrected, and in general puff up our society as much as they can in order to mold young people into loyal citizens.

---

[14]By John J. Patrick and Richard C. Remy (Chicago: Scott, Foresman, 1980).

Revised Texts

School History Books, Striving to Please All, Are Criticized as Bland

"America! America!" isn't a traditional history book. In its pages are black cowboys, woman pirates, Haight-Ashbury hippies, an Indian boy, a Chicano grandmother and a middle-aged Oriental.

There's something for everybody in this two-year-old American history textbook for eighth-graders, and that's by design.

"We don't want to get complaints from anybody," says Landon Risteen, editorial vice president at Scott, Foresman & Co., the book's publisher. "No matter where you come from, you're going to find yourself in this book."

His concern is understandable. Scott, Foresman shelled out $500,000 and four years of effort to put out "America! America!" With 20 other eighth-grade history texts battling for shares of the $7 million-a-year business, the competition is fierce. Morever, the competition is fierce throughout the $700 million elementary and high-school textbook market. . . .

Publishers feel they are being forced to please the parents, religious groups, political organizations, and state and local authorities that are wielding increasing influence over textbook selections. If a book should offend any group—veterans or war protesters, smokers or non-smokers—its chances of being a big winner are narrowed. So publishers carefully consider their presentation of minorities, treatment of Vietnam and pictures of tobacco fields, aiming to mollify as many of these groups as possible.

"There are all those people out there who will go through our books, so we have to judge what the market will accept," says Ralph Sterling, director of marketing at Houghton Mifflin Co. in Boston. "We can't afford to have a book sit on the shelf." . . .

[But many critics claim that the result is an] uninspiring blandness of American history textbooks. The problem, they say, is that by trying to please everyone, publishers take the edge off history, eliminating the exciting stuff that the past is made of.

"Textbooks minimize the real conflicts in history, like pretending the Civil War solved the problem of race relations in this country," says Douglas Price, a former high-school history teacher and current manager of Jocundry's bookstore in East Lansing, Mich. "If the real regional and racial tensions were written about," he adds, "the textbooks wouldn't sell to all the markets."

Justin Kestenbaum, a professor of history at Michigan State University, agrees. He says, for instance, that while textbooks describe the reform movement of the 19th Century, they ignore "its ugly overtones, like the anti-Catholicism. They don't want anybody to appear in an unfavorable light."

Balking at Blandness

In Stanford, Calif., historian Thomas Bailey refuses to write for the high-school and junior-high markets because of publishers' attitudes. "If you want to sell a maximum number of books, you have to make them so bland that you don't get into the tougher issues," he says. "But you also don't tell the truth."

Mr. Bailey grouses that efforts to include women and minorities make the books more ideological than intellectual. He admits that he grudgingly included 1972 presidential candidate Shirley Chisholm in one of his college books, even though "she was so unimportant that I wouldn't have normally put her in. When you write history, you should write about the main actors in the show."

Publishers argue that it isn't their place to take stands on controversial issues. Besides, they say, just presenting ideas is, for some readers, tantamount to condoning them. "Authors may want to tell it like it is, but with the constraints on us, we really can't do it that way," says Dorothy Collins, an executive editor at Allyn & Bacon Inc. in Boston. . . .

The emphasis on [minority] groups is also said to have dispelled many of the stereotypes that filled history books just a few years ago. Dorothy Davidson, an associate commissioner for general education in the Texas Education Agency, recalls a book that quoted a letter written by Abigail Adams to her husband, President John Adams. "Abigail says things like, 'I hope to get the drapes up,' " Miss Davidson says. "You know she must have had some thoughts on the administration, but the publisher instead chose to show her as a housewife at the White House, waiting for the furniture to move in."

"America! America!" with its black cowboys and female pirates, reflects concerns that were uppermost in Mr. Risteen's mind when work on the project began in the early 1970s. Scott, Foresman's market research had shown that the public was looking for a book with "more variety exemplifying the pluralism of America," Mr. Risteen says, and "we were determined to have that in there."

A Group Project

The idea was to come up with three or four historians and school administrators who could work with the editors on the book. "The day of the single author is past" in history textbooks, says Gordon Hjalmarson, president of Scott, Foresman. "We feel a group authorship brings various strengths."

These strengths include more than the author's field of interest or his or her familiarity with American history programs. Authors are also considered for their regional popularity. A professor from Texas, for instance, may help sell the book in that big market, and a Hispanic teacher could make a book more marketable in New York City.

In the case of "America! America!" four authors were finally selected: two male university history professors, a male school administrator and a woman who had worked as a consultant to schools in curriculum development. A professor from Texas who was originally part of the group dropped out, Mr. Risteen says, because he wasn't "willing to let us run the show."

Influence of States

The influence of the large states goes beyond the selection of authors; they also have a major effect on a book's content. "We are very sensitive to the big markets, particularly Texas and California," Mr. Risteen says. "It wouldn't make sense to publish a book and leave out the history related to those states." He says, for instance, "We made sure we didn't underplay the Texas independence."

The power of these two states is magnified by the fact that they are two of about twenty-six states that have state-wide "adoption committees." These committees select a certain number of books from which local school boards can choose and still receive state funds. While "adoption" doesn't guarantee that the book will sell in the state, exclusion of the book guarantees that it won't. . . .

Publishers admit to spending a lot of time gearing their books to meet the guidelines of states. The Texas rules call for textbooks to "promote citizenship and understanding of the free-enterprise system." One editor says of these rules, "They hang over our heads all the time. We try to give the books as nationalistic a feel as possible."

In California, "a book is almost automatically thrown out if it doesn't have ethnic balance," says James Eckman, a high-school teacher who was on the textbook committee that evaluated "America! America!" two years ago. Not surprisingly, "America! America!" is the biggest seller for eighth-graders in the state today.

A book is also dumped in any state if its reading level is too high. Authors typically have trouble "writing down" to a young audience, and editors must often rework manuscripts.

Scott, Foresman tests its books by counting the number of words in a sample section that aren't on a list of "appropriate" words and by counting the number of words in sentences. The editors then can come up with a number indicating the book's reading level. Mr. Risteen's staff took 70 samples of 100 words each to ensure that "America! America!" would be acceptable among eighth-grade teachers.

That approach, which is taken by practically all publishers, is assailed by many critics. "The publishers write to such a formula that they lose sight of conveying facts in an interesting manner," says Barry Fetterolf, an editor at Random House Inc., which publishes primarily college books. "If a kid who reads on a ninth-grade level finds his parents' sex book which is on a fifteenth-grade level, he will read it and understand it," Mr. Fetterolf says. "But they can't read a history text on a seventh-grade level because it's so boring." Still, he concedes, "you have to look at it, since that's what the market asks for."

Big Seller

Indeed Scott, Foresman has been giving the market what it wants. "America! America!" is one of the biggest sellers on the eighth-grade market today. The book, selling at about $10 each, came out in September 1977 and sold 67,000 copies that year, Scott, Foresman says. The company estimates that it sold 160,000 copies last year. Competitors say the 1978 figure seems a bit high, but they agree that "America! America!" is doing well. . . .

The book, meantime, has received its share of complaints. The first edition of "America! America!" had a special section on countercultures, but it was criticized for "glorifying hippies," Mr. Risteen says. So in a new edition, out this year, that section was changed to one on people discovering their roots.

Primarily, though, users say the book's faults are much the same as those of all textbooks. "While it isn't as much of an absolute history of the perfecting of America as are some books," it still suffers from some of that, says Henry Hicks, a director of social studies for the Needham, Mass., public schools. . . .

Significantly, one of Mr. Hicks's reasons for liking the book—its limited listing of facts—may work against it over the next few years. The "fads in American history textbooks change quickly, and publishers currently are seeing a swing back toward the more traditional approaches that dominated until the late 1960s.

Mr. Risteen expects to undertake a major revision of "America! America!" in about two years, and the inclusion of more hard facts may be part of that revision. "I hope we don't get to the point where we think to be good a book has to be big and grim," says Mr. Risteen. "But I see some signs that we might be."

Of course, it could hardly be otherwise, and in fact it's the same or worse in every other country. (Read a Soviet text on the 1956 Hungarian uprising—which they call "the events of 1956"—and you'll gain new respect for the American educational system.) The point is not to knock the United States, but rather that a society's textbooks are going to be slanted in favor of that society. All have the same goal: to make their youth into good citizens. That may or may not be best for a nation as a whole, but it does make it hard on those students who would like to know the true history of their countries or the way their system actually works. Public school textbooks are not going to tell them right out. But perceptive, selective readers can learn a great deal from slanted texts—in particular naked facts, like dates—so that all is not lost by any means. A careful reader can get a good deal of information even

---

Public school textbooks don't have to be as dull and uninformative as they are. The proof is that a very few texts are not. To illustrate, here is a page from an exceptionally good high school text, Understanding Mass Media.[15]

Economic Control

Magazines, newspapers, television, and radio stations, book publishers—all, with a few rare exceptions—share one common goal; to make money. This fact controls to some extent the content of what these media produce.

With the exception of book publishing, all these media receive most of their income from advertising. The question thus arises: Does advertising in any way influence the content of mass media?

One illustration of economic influence is the true case of the Car-Puter Company's attempt to buy ads in major newspapers and magazines. Car-Puter is a company that supplies customers with a computer read-out of dealer costs on any new car they may want to buy, including options. The company also supplies the name of a local automobile dealer who, through a special arrangement, will sell the customer the car for about $150 over dealer cost. The company charges the consumer $5 for this service, which is legitimate and helpful to consumers. However, when Car-Puter attempted to run a small ad, they were refused by most newspapers as well as by some magazines.

The ads were refused without a detailed explanation. The newspapers claimed they had a right to turn down any advertising—and they do. But the reason for the refusal most certainly is related to the fact that automotive ads are an important source of income for newspapers and magazines. Car-Puter Company would not be approved of by other auto advertisers.

As another example, sponsors of television programs are not likely to buy time for programs that attack business. Sponsors carefully monitor network TV shows. A group called "Stop Immorality on Television" asked major TV sponsors about their "moral stance" on the programs they sponsored. Gillette replied that "we try to see that our advertising runs in programs which are suitable for general family viewing.

---

[15]By Jeffrey Schrank (Lincolnwood, Ill.: National Textbook Company, 1975). Schrank did have to pull punches a bit (compare his style in the adult book *Snap, Crackle, and Popular Taste,* (as quoted in Chapter 8), but he still manages to tell students lots of things they need to know.

from Russian textbooks, compared to which ours are treasure troves of information. (Of course, anyone who wants a sophisticated knowledge of these matters has to go to the other sources.)

If the test of true education is understanding, and not mere digestion of facts, the best test of understanding is the ability to foresee events, or at least not be unduly surprised at their occurrence. If American public school textbooks had helped students to achieve a true understanding of their own system and how it really works, would the Watergate scandal have been such a shock to them? Would they have accepted our government's denial that we had interfered in the internal affairs of Chile (and then later accepted the clearly untrue explanation of *why* we had in fact interfered)? Would they have been so surprised by the overthrow of the Shah of Iran

---

Under this policy we have declined to participate as sponsors in programs such as *The Smothers Brothers* and *Laugh-In.* " Eastman Kodak commented that they preview all scripts before the airing of a program: "If we find a script is offensive, we will withdraw our commercials from the program."

Although advertisers have no formal censorship power, they can exert great influence on the kinds of programs that networks will offer the viewers. A TV network would think twice before showing a documentary exposing the faults of the over-the-counter drug industry, because so much of its advertising revenue comes from pain-killers and headache remedies.

A question often asked at networks is "Will the show gain sponsors?" The importance of this question can easily limit consideration of another question: "What is in the best interests of the public?"

Newspapers and magazines vary widely in the amount of control they allow advertisers to exert. Some keep "news" and ads completely separate and will report the problems and failings of local food chains or auto dealers even though these provide the paper with thousands of dollars yearly in advertising revenue. Some newspapers, however, still have a policy of not "biting the hand that feeds them." If the health department closes or issues a warning to a local food store or restaurant, such papers will ignore the story for fear of "hurting" the advertiser's reputation. A story about a shady car dealer or home builder might go unreported if that company is a large advertiser in the newspaper.

Such control is less frequent now than it used to be, but it still exists, especially among smaller newspapers struggling to stay in business.

Record companies put pressure on radio stations to play their records. Every time a radio station plays a record, the "exposure" is as good as or better than an ad for the record. The more radio stations play any given song or record, the more it sells. Record companies can give away free records but are not supposed to give money to stations as an inducement to play the records. There have been many instances, though, of record companies slipping a little extra money ("payola") to disk jockeys to gain air time for a song. As with newspapers, this practice is less common among the largest stations and offers a greater temptation to small stations.

and the odiousness of this regime of one of our "allies"? (Of course, textbook indoctrination is only one reason so many Americans were taken in by their leaders on these issues.)

It should be clear now that the author of this college text doesn't like the idea that public school textbooks and education use large doses of indoctrination in lieu of useful truth. He realizes, of course, that indoctrination can't be entirely eliminated, but he believes that it can be reduced to some extent and that students can be taught to guard against it.

This text was written in a completely different spirit from that of indoctrination. A student who accepts its contents uncritically has missed its main point, which is that in controversial social and political matters free men and women must be their own experts, or at least must be able to judge for themselves the opinions of those who call themselves experts. A free society does, after all, depend on a correctly informed and thinking electorate, not an indoctrinated one.

8. Postscript on College Texts

The question naturally arises about college textbooks. Do they distort American history and practice, as do public school texts? If the forces at work are the same in both cases, we should expect the results will be roughly the same (taking into account the greater maturity of college students). If they aren't, we should expect the finished products to be different. What do our world views tell us about this question?

The first thing to notice is that the sellers of college texts have exactly the same motives as those who sell public school texts. In fact, many publishers in one field also publish in the other. The second key point is that most college texts are adopted by the teachers who will use them in their own classes (or, in the case of large classes with several sections, by group faculty decisions), not by school boards or state agencies. (Students then buy them but can't choose which one to buy.)

The reason for this important difference is the history (and current funding) of higher education in America, as compared to primary and secondary education. Primary and secondary school traditions are largely "homegrown" and intended for a mass audience. Public school teachers have always had their rights to academic freedom infringed by local school boards, or, more accurately, never had such rights. But American colleges and universities evolved on the model of their European counterparts (chiefly in Germany and Britain), which were intended for an elite clientele. Professors, at least, were granted a great deal of academic freedom. The result of transplanting this tradition into the United States, the freest Western society, has been academic freedom for almost all college faculty members; thus college teachers themselves select the texts they and their students will use. It follows, then, as night follows day, that college textbook publishers will try to produce books that please college faculty members, their potential buyers.

And that's the main reason why college texts, wherever they may rest on an absolute scale, are unlike their public school counterparts. College teachers want widely differing things from their textbooks, creating a split market in which all sorts of views (and to a lesser extent qualities) find a constituency. College texts even tend to be less dull than lower level counterparts, a happy note on which to end this particular college textbook.

Summary of Chapter Nine

1. Every society needs to indoctrinate its young. Public school textbooks are just one device used in this educational process.

2. But textbooks are a commodity. So in the United States they are tailored by publishers to reflect buyer preferences, which means the preferences of local school boards and state agencies responding to local citizens (in particular, organized citizens). We should expect, then, that texts will reflect the views of local citizens. And they do.

3. What public school students read is censored in two ways. First, the truth is bent or omitted to conform to local or state pressures. Those texts that fail to conform are not permitted to be used. (*Example:* No text that slights minority groups is likely to be used in California schools.) And second, certain nontext books are not permitted space on library shelves or allowed to be used in classrooms. (*Example:* The removal of *Drums along the Mohawk* from reading lists because it contains words like *hell* and *damn.*)

4. Public school texts distort the history of our country by omitting as much as possible that is bad in it and playing down the rest, and by generally puffing up our role in history. (*Examples:* Portraying just the good side of Teddy Roosevelt; puffing up our role in World War II at the expense of the Russians.)

5. Civics texts tend to cover up the gulf between theory—the way our system is supposed to work—and practice—the way things really work—as a way of papering over injustice and evil in our society. (*Example:* Telling students lots of good things about labor unions but few of the bad things, so that they don't learn about corrupt labor leaders, collusion with management, and so on.)

6. Textbook style is necessarily bland or dull. Emotive language is kept to a minimum and is rarely used to get students excited about injustice or other ills in our system. Evils tend to get slipped in only as they are being corrected or so as to have minimal effect. (*Example:* Snowing students with lots of dull and soon-forgotten facts while pussyfooting around the basic issue of how much justice there is in our court system.)

7. The upshot of all this is that students are given lots of dull facts but little understanding, either of their country's history or of how their political-social system works. Everything comes out goody-goody. Which means that education in public schools tends to contain a large dose of indoctrination.

8. But college texts are different. (*Vive la différence.*)

Exercise 9-1

In college, the subject matter dealt with in high school civics classes becomes the province of political science, history, and (to some extent) other social science courses. Along with this change in title, there is a broadening of subject matter and a change in motive (indoctrination with the "American way" surely is not attempted in the typical college-level social science course or text). But some college texts still display a few of the defects we have been discussing, including an "objectivism" that hides a controversial point of view, a distortion of the difference between theory and practice (often by ignoring practice that doesn't conform to theory), and an unconscious bias against certain groups (for example, women). College history texts also often display these defects.

Examine one of your history, political science, or other relevant social science texts (or get one from the library) for evidence of bias, distortion, suppressed evidence, or "textbook objectivity," and write a page or two on your findings. Be sure to *argue* (present evidence) for your conclusions, trying, of course, to avoid fallacious argument.

---

*Exercise for the Entire Text

This text, as all others, is based on certain presuppositions (only some of them made explicit) and no doubt contains fallacious reasoning, in spite of the author's best efforts to reason cogently. So, as the final exercise, write a brief critique of this textbook with respect to: (1) its major presuppositions (that is, the world view of the author as exhibited in the text), (2) possible fallacious arguments, (3) biased selection of material, and (4) rhetorical devices used to convince the reader to accept the author's opinion on this or that. (Be sure to *argue* for your findings.)

Answers to
Starred Exercise Items

These answers certainly are not presented as revealed truth. They represent one person's thoughts on the matter, which it is hoped will prove useful to the reader.

Chapter One, Exercise 1-1

1. *Premise:* At the present rate of consumption, the oil will be used up in 20–25 years.
   Premise: We're sure not going to reduce consumption in the near future.
   Conclusion: We'd better start developing solar power, windmills, and other "alternative energy sources" pretty soon.
3. No argument. Just a list of things the student doesn't like.

Chapter Two, Exercise 2-1

1. *Popularity.* On this planet, all sorts of things, some quite monstrous, have become popular. *Example:* Daughter to mother (Berlin, Germany, 1932): "Nazism is the coming thing."

7. *Traditional Wisdom.* But for some, given their world views, it isn't fallacious. Suppose Smith believes that God transmits his wishes by means of long-term traditions. Then, the fact that long Catholic tradition excludes women from certain roles would be a good reason for continuing to do so, since the tradition would be a sign of God's will. The point is that for most of us, including most Catholics, accepting this argument is fallacious.

15. *Equivocation.* Roche meant political repression—for instance, of limiting freedom of speech or movement. Freud was talking about psychological repression—for instance, of the desire to sleep with one's mother.

22. Reverse *Appeal to Authority.* If even the *Devil* believes there's a God, well, by God, there must be a God!

26. *Equivocation.* To imagine our own death is to visualize what it would be like to experience it. In this sense we can and do imagine our own death. Freud changes the meaning of the word *imagine* so that to imagine it we would have to *not* visualize it, which of course is impossible.

28. *Irrelevant Reason.* Suppose the police mistakenly charge you with murder. In defending yourself, you don't have to prove that someone else, Smith, did it; you just have to prove *you* didn't do it—say, by providing an air-tight alibi. Why, then, should Warren Commission critics have to prove who did murder John Kennedy, if they can show Lee Harvey Oswald couldn't have done it alone?

Chapter Three, Exercise 3-1

2. *Begged Question.* She wanted to know why the mechanism that produces saliva wasn't working and was told that it wasn't working.

6. No fallacy; certainly not *inconsistency.* Aristotle intended to point out to his friends that in this harsh world, friendship, alas, has its limits—that even good friends can be counted on only so far. This sour view has its exceptions, but on the whole is true.

11. *Inconsistency.* If not enough studies have been done, how can there be no question about marijuana relieving eye pressure? If there is no question that it does relieve eye pressure, then enough studies have been done.

15. *Inconsistency* (between words and actions). While allowing a 15-minute tape to be shown wasn't *exactly* crossing a picket line, it's in the same spirit. The point of Hope's not crossing a picket line was to show solidarity with ordinary laborers—in this case, by depriving those inside of the benefit of Hope's entertainment. (People who sneak out of obligations this way are derisively called "legalists.")

16. *Begged Question.* The question was whether reporters should be an exception to the rule. To point out that it would be an exception thus begs the question.

28. *False Dilemma.* The Creator might have intended sexual intercourse to have both of these consequences, reproduction and pleasure, or perhaps some other function.

Chapter Four, Exercise 4-1

3. *Questionable Analogy.* Depending on the kind of accident, knowing how to drive *is* a help, as every driver knows, even though not absolutely essential (say, in judging a case of alleged negligent driving). The line also suppresses a bit of evidence—namely, that judges who drive are easily obtained to try auto accident cases, but judges who have been raped (or mugged, or murdered) are in very short supply.

7. *Questionable Cause.* An even greater percentage of heroin addicts first drank milk, coffee, tea, and booze, and smoked cigarettes. (And, as the greeting card noted, they all are habitual breathers). To support a causal connection, we need evidence showing that all or most pot smokers go on to heroin, but in fact we have all sorts of statistics proving that the vast majority who smoke dope never even try, much less get hooked on, heroin.

9. *Suppressed Evidence* and *Faulty Comparison.* As Hoover and Kilpatrick knew very well, practically all uses of certain drugs (marijuana, LSD, heroin, cocaine) are illegal in the United States today, while almost all alcohol consumption is perfectly legal. (What if Hoover had compared 1920s drug and alcohol arrests, when alcohol was illegal while pot was legal?)

20. *Questionable Classification.* Homosexuals burned the books. But so did males, human beings, people between the ages of 16 and 60, and so on. The *relevant* classification of those against whom Ms. Bryant has brought evidence is *Bible burners*, since most homosexuals would no more burn Bibles than anyone else.

22. *Suppressed Evidence.* Stare knew, as did others who were informed, that (1) it's mainly the milk, not the cereal, that makes, say, a Wheaties and milk breakfast in the same league with bacon and eggs as a source of protein and (to a lesser extent) of minerals and vitamins; (2) while some vitamins and minerals are now commonly added to such cereals, even more nutrients (for example, most of the protein) are usually taken out in processing the grain; (3) most of these cereals contain gobs of unhealthy refined sugar; and (4) no expert would think of spinach (much overrated as a food anyway) as a complete breakfast—spinach is recommended for roughage and some vitamins and minerals (it has next to no protein), so that Stare's comparison of cold cereal and milk with spinach was faulty.

Exercise 4-2

1. *Questionable Cause.* It's plausible for a candidate to campaign harder where support is weak rather than where it is strong. The relevant figures to prove he should have stayed at home would have to show, say, that his popularity dropped in a given area after Taft campaigned there—figures not provided, one suspects, because they don't exist.

3. *Faulty Comparison.* Three percent is insignificant as the total support a candidate receives, but quite significant as the difference between one candidate and another in an election, since even a one-vote margin wins an election, while a 3 percent total vote wins only a booby prize.

8. *Faulty Comparison.* Britain is wealthier than it ever was. It is, however, poorer relative to other northern European countries. (Their economies have been growing much faster.) The comparison relevant to whether Britain can still afford to be preoccupied with distribution is between the wealth she had then (when she could afford that preoccupation) and now, not between what she has now and what other nations have, since the latter is irrelevant to the consumption of goods in Britain.

12. *Suppressed Evidence* and *Hasty Conclusion.* (1) Many other factors are believed to have been at work reducing mortality, for instance, improved diet and more exercise. (2) There are known side effects of the pill. (This indicates that the pill was a health hazard, but *we'd* be guilty of *hasty conclusion* if we concluded from this that the pill was a *major* health hazard.) (3) There were other health hazards at the time. If increased female longevity proved the pill was not a major health hazard, it would equally prove no other health hazard was major. But there seem to have been several other major health hazards, for instance, cigarette smoking. (4) By the same reasoning, we could conclude that cigarettes were not a major health hazard even for males, since male longevity also increased. Since cigarettes certainly were a major health hazard for males, the original reasoning must be fallacious.

13. *Suppressed Evidence.* (1) Superstition is more accurately defined as belief without good evidence, or in the face of contrary evidence. (So the article changed the meaning of the term *superstition.*) (2) Some of the greatest scientists may have been superstitious—Newton being an example (the line between superstition and mysticism is not sharp). But the part of their beliefs that became part of science was not superstitious—Newton again being a good example. (3) In addition, a great deal of what scientists once accepted, *on good evidence,* they now reject, or have modified or sharpened, because of better evidence (for instance, the rejected aether theory and the modified Newtonian theory of the 19th Century). But rejecting or modifying a well supported theory because of better evidence for a more accurate theory is the heart of science, and is definitely not superstition.

16. *Hasty Conclusion.* The statistic quoted certainly is evidence for the conclusion. But it isn't sufficient. It still could be that similar family environment is the principal reason why alcoholism tends to run in families (example: the higher incidence of alcoholism among present-generation Jews in America as compared with the incidence among their genetically similar grandparents).

20. *Questionable Cause* and *Suppressed Evidence.* This is one of those cases where background information and world views are crucial. Each of these presidents died under different circumstances—Kennedy was shot, Roosevelt had a stroke after twelve health-destroying years in office. Further, we have vast amounts of higher-level evidence and theories to the effect that mere passage of time cannot cause anything so complicated as the death of an incumbent president.

Chapter Five, Exercise 5-1

4. (Simplifying translation): We shall use the expression "social problem solving" to refer to cases where an actual or expected result will (possibly) solve a problem. (Put that way, it doesn't sound like much.)

Chapter Six, Exercise 6-1

4. *Thesis:* None of the historical or anecdotal parts of the Bible are the word of God.

Reason: What I've seen (or know?) needs no revelation.
Conclusion: Revelation is that which reveals what we didn't know (haven't seen) before.

Reason: Revelation is that which reveals what we didn't know (haven't seen?) before.
Conclusion: Revelation can't tell us about earthly things men could witness.

Reason: Revelation can't tell us about earthly things men could witness.
Conclusion: None of the historical or anecdotal parts of the Bible count as revelation.
(Paine assumed an equation between revelation and the word of God.)

Exercise 6-3

1. Here is the Patrick J. Buchanan article with margin notes attached.[1]

Of all the inane remarks our "point man" at the U.N. has made, none is more disturbing than the statement 10 days ago.

(1) Our U.S. Ambassador, Andrew Young, makes inane and very disturbing (false?) statements.

In the event of an East-West showdown in Africa, says Andy Young: "I see no situation in which we would have to come in on the side of the South Africans. . . . You'd have civil war at home. Maybe I ought not to say that, but I really believe it. An armed force that is 30 percent black isn't going to fight on the side of the South Africans."

(2) In particular, he said: (a) no situation will arise forcing U.S. troops to fight against blacks in southern Africa; (b) civil war would result here; and (c) a 30 percent black army won't fight against blacks on the side of the South Africans.

This is not some hotheaded young leader of SNCC talking. This is the United States ambassador to the U.N., who holds Cabinet rank. And he has warned publicly that if his president and Congress declare that America's vital interests require the use of military force against guerrillas in southern Africa, black American soldiers will mutiny. And black American civilians will rise up in insurrection.

One wonders if Young—babbling away into every open microphone—is remotely aware of the slander he has leveled at the patriotism of black America.

(3) Young has slandered the patriotism of black Americans.

---

[1]Patrick J. Buchanan, *New York Times,* March 26, 1977. Reprinted by permission of The Tribune Company Syndicate, Inc.

When the United States entered World War I, Irish-Americans died in the trenches alongside British soldiers whose fellow units were, even then, snuffing out the flames of Irish freedom. In that same war German-Americans fought and killed their own cousins fighting for imperial Germany and the Kaiser.

During World War II, German-Americans, Italian-Americans, Japanese-Americans fought loyally against Nazi Germany, Fascist Italy, Imperial Japan.

(4) In the past, ethnics fought loyally, even when fighting against soldiers from the ethnic groups of their origin: for example, Irish and Germans in WWI and Germans, Italians, and Japanese in WWII.

They all put loyalty to America above any residual loyalty to the homeland of their fathers and grandfathers. What Young is saying is that black Americans—who have been here centuries, not just decades—do not have that kind of loyalty to the United States. In a crunch, he is saying, black America will stand with their racial kinsmen in Marxist Angola and Mozambique—rather than with their white countrymen in the United States.

What makes Young's flippancy fairly chilling is that he has just confided to the editors of *Newsweek,* "I get the feeling that Jimmy Carter wants me to take charge of Africa. . . ."

(5)(a) Those groups put American loyalty above all else; (b) Young says black Americans instead will stand with racial kin in southern Africa.

Anti-white racism already seems to have become the determining factor in U.S. policy toward that continent.

(6) Anti-white racism has become the determining U.S. African policy.

Up at the U.N., Jimmy Carter, grinning away at the muted mouthpieces of some of the rankest, blood-stained ogres in history, announced that the United States had just rejoined the world conspiracy to strangle Rhodesia to death. Because Southern Rhodesia does not have "majority rule," we too will no longer buy Rhodesian exports. [This was before majority rule was won in Rhodesia.]

We will buy chrome instead from Soviet Russia, a hostile, totalitarian empire ruled by an elite party which claims the membership of less than 6 percent of the Soviet population.

How many countries in Africa, how many in the world, have majority rules with minority rights guaranteed?

(7) Pres. Carter told the U.N. we won't buy (chrome) from Rhodesia because they don't have majority rule. Yet we'll buy from totalitarian Russia, controlled by Communist party of less than 6 percent of population.

Idi Amin comes from a small, dominantly Moslem tribe in Uganda which is mercilessly persecuting members of larger Christian tribes. Yet the United States, which now considers it illegal and immoral to buy Rhodesian chrome, is delighted to buy Idi Amin's coffee.

(8) Idi Amin's Uganda is ruled by small Moslem tribe persecuting larger tribes, yet we buy their coffee.

The most virulent strain of racism in the world today is not anti-black, anti-yellow, or anti-red; it is anti-white.

(9) Worst form of racism in world now is anti-white.

Reflect a moment: What makes the ruling tribes in Rhodesia and southern Africa so hated? Are they the most barbaric, repressive, dictatorial in Africa, and the world? Hardly! What makes them evil, unacceptable—what mandates their destruction—is that the skin of these particular ruling tribes is not black, but white. . . .

(10) Southern Africa is hated so much because whites rule there, not blacks.

First, note how much less convincing the summary is stripped of emotively charged words and expressions like "flippancy," "chilling," "babbling," "grinning away," and "blood-stained ogres."

It should be clear that Buchanan has several fish to fry in this column. He wants to argue, first, against Andrew Young as U.N. Ambassador, on grounds of his having a big, inaccurate, intemperate mouth—point (1) in the summary; second, against U.S. policy toward southern Africa, which in effect means toward Rhodesia and the Union of South Africa, on grounds that it is inconsistent with the rest of what we do—points (7) and (8) in the summary; third, that U.S. policy is anti-white—points (6) and (9) in the summary, as well as, indirectly, (7) and (8); and, finally, that Young was wrong to doubt black patriotism—point (3) in the summary. Bearing this in mind, let's look at each of the eleven points in the margin note-summary:

(1): The first point just sets the tone for the article, charging that Young is an irresponsible blabbermouth. He did do a lot of talking; the question is whether it was the wrong kind. Anyone who doesn't already believe it was wrong should be looking for Buchanan's reasons for making that judgment.

(2): The second point gives part of the relevant quote from a Young speech. It certainly supports the view that he uttered rather contentious remarks for an ambassador. The question is whether his remarks, in particular the one Buchanan quoted from, were "inane," "disburbing," or some such.

(3): The third point in the summary is that Young's remarks slandered the patriotism of black Americans, who would and ought to fight where told to. If true, it lends support to the charge made in (1) that Young said things he shouldn't have.

(4) and (5): Buchanan then argues for point (3) by analogy: white ethnic Americans fought against their ethnic kin in past wars, so black Americans ought to be prepared to fight against their racial kin in southern Africa, and will in fact fight against black southern Africans if required to do so (which is why Young's remark was a bad one—it was just plain false).

But Buchanan's analogy is not a good one, because the cases compared are not relevantly similar. His analogy is thus *questionable*. Take the German-Americans who fought in World War II against their ethnic kin in Nazi Germany. This was a case where the security and even survival of the United States was believed to be at stake—a Nazi victory could have meant the end of the United States as we know it. That is definitely not the case with southern Africa.

Further, although the Nazis persecuted over a million Germans (including 600,000 German Jews), on the whole it was non-Germans (Poles, Russians, and others) who were their targets. But when Young made his comment, southern Africa was ruled by white minorities who enslaved black majorities. Having black American soldiers fight in support of such white minorities thus would be more like having had Christian Americans (white or black) fight in Uganda on the side of Idi Amin's government against persecuted Christian religious kin (black or white). Suppose in that circumstance a Christian ambassador in the U.N. said: "I see no situation in which we would have to come in on the side of Amin [meaning, as Young meant in the case of Rhodesia and South Africa, on the side of the enslaving ruling minority]. You'd have civil war at home. An armed force that is 80 percent Christian isn't going to fight on the side of a Ugandan minority persecuting our fellow Christians who are its majority." (Buchanan passed over the fact that Young was talking about siding with an enslaving small minority against an enslaved large majority struggling for freedom.) Would Buchanan have argued that such a comment slandered the patriotism of Christian Americans? Or that it was "inane" and "disturbing"?

This last brings us to another problem with his column. There are at least two complaints Buchanan can be making: first, that Young is too outspoken to make a good ambassador; and second, that what he says is far from the truth. The first is a claim for which he provides evidence; let's grant it, although there are arguments on the other side (for instance, that Young's outbursts were good for relations with black-ruled African countries). The second (that Young strayed far from the truth) Buchanan backs up by his analogy with other ethnic Americans, an analogy we argued above was not cogent. This means he has not successfully defended his claim that Young's remarks were false, or "inane," or whatever.

(6) and (9): The second half of Buchanan's column argues for the conclusion that American policy in southern Africa is anti-white (the implication being that that's why we had talkative Young as U.N. Ambassador). Point (6) merely states this conclusion; point (9) restates it.

(7) and (8): This is Buchanan's defense of point (6), that our policy is anti-white. He argues that support of majority rule cannot be the real reason for our not buying chrome from Rhodesia, contrary to President Carter's claim, because we buy chrome from Russia and coffee from Uganda where no majority rule exists. So it must be that we're anti-white in our policies.

But this argument is poor. In effect its form is this: either it is our African policy to support majority rule or else our policy is anti-white. It can't be that our policy is to support majority rule, because we don't do so in general (think of Uganda and Russia). Therefore, our policy must be anti-white.

The argument has the form *disjunctive syllogism,* introduced in Chapter 1, and is deductively valid. But its premises are not warranted. Its first premise is questionable because there are many other policies we might have toward southern Africa (for instance, to support anti-communist governments, or to support stable or reliable governments), and so sets us up for a *false dilemma.* And its second premise also is questionable. Buchanan does show that our policy cannot be *merely* to support majority rule, since we support minority governments elsewhere. But he doesn't show that our policy is not, say, to support majority rule when we can afford to. It could have been, and in fact seemed to have been the case, at least with respect to Rhodesia and the chrome-buying problem, that support of majority rule fitted nicely with other policy objectives, while in the case certainly of the Soviet Union— and plausibly of Uganda—supporting majority rule would have meant sacrificing all sorts of other objectives.

General conclusion: Buchanan manages to provide good evidence (but perhaps not conclusive) for at best only one of his conclusions—that Young was too talkative and contentious to be a good ambassador. He didn't prove that Young's remarks were inane or that they should be disturbing (he didn't even prove they were false or give reason to doubt them). He didn't show that Young had slandered black Americans, since he never showed that what Young said was false. (*Slander:* a false report maliciously uttered, tending to injure reputation.) And finally, he didn't show that American policy toward Africa (or anywhere) is anti-white. (Without mountains of evidence to support such a charge, the ironic idea that U.S. policy is or ever has been anti-white is ridiculous.) A typical political column?

2. Here is a summary of the arguments given by Jeffrey St. John in his column (margin notes have been omitted) in support of his conclusion that the Equal Rights Amendment (ERA) to the Constitution should not be passed:

   a. Legal scholars believe that the legal position of women cannot be stated in a simple formula. The reason Justice Frankfurter gives—that a woman's life cannot be expressed in a simple relation—comes close to just saying the same thing (*appeal to authority* —because their reasons are not provided, and other experts disagree).

   b. Senator Sam Ervin and legal scholars argue that the amendment will have no effect on discrimination (*appeal to authority*).

    c. And would nullify all existing (possible or future) laws that made distinctions between men and women (*appeal to authority*).

    d. Passage of the ERA would create a great court backlog of cases leading to legal and social anarchy (*questionable premise*).

    e. Which is the aim of a minority of women's liberationists, who intend to exploit this result to achieve political power (very *questionable premise*. Also a bit of *straw, uh . . . person,* because not true of the great majority of those favoring ERA.

    f. The effect of ERA, desired by Women's Liberationists, would be to do away with marriage contracts, the home, and children, and push us into a lifestyle like that in hippie communes (extremely *questionable premise*. St. John apparently believes marriage contracts would be illegal because entered into between *men* and *women*!)[2]

    g. Women's liberationists desire this in order to bring down the whole of society (another extremely *questionable premise*).

    h. The women's liberationist campaign is false, misleading, and dangerous (*questionable evaluation*).

    i. The discrimination it is against is based not in law but in custom and in social attitudes, especially concerning careers and employment. [see below]

    j. Women's lib wants to use the power of the state to forbid individual discrimination (as opposed to discrimination forced by law). [see below]

    k. A distinction not made by those who favor ERA (*questionable premise* —in fact just plain false).

    l. The same chaos will follow passage of the ERA that followed the 1964 Civil Rights Act. (*Begged question:* Did chaos result from the 1964 Civil Rights Act? *Questionable analogy:* Even if it did, why compare that to the ERA?)

    m. Legal scholars argue that the "due process" and "equal protection of the law" clauses of the Fifth and Fourteenth amendments are sufficient for the reforms demanded by Women's Libbers (i.e. ERA is not necessary). *(Appeal to authority* —other experts have challenged this—and *irrelevant reason* —if true it shows ERA to be superfluous, not wrong.)

    (Most of the persuasive emotively charged words—"*militant* minority of women"; "*legal avalanche* would be *unleashed*"—have been omitted from this summary along with the low blow analogy comparing political feminists with Lenin.)

    Item (c) is the crux of St. John's argument against ERA. Is it true that passage of ERA would make laws that distinguish between men and women illegal? Since many believe it would, we should not say dogmatically that it would not. Yet, there are simple arguments (none mentioned by St. John— *suppressed evidence?*) indicating it would not, which must be refuted or at least examined, before (c) can be accepted. For ERA only provides women what one would have supposed they, as do men, already have, namely equal protection, or equal rights, before the law.

    Rational discrimination always has been thought to be legal. Lenders and borrowers, for instance, have equal rights under the law, as do adults and children. This means that they cannot be discriminated against (or for!) *without a relevant reason.* A child cannot be treated differently from others except for good reason; for instance, lack of experience or developed intelligence may lead to laws instructing courts to provide legal guardians to protect the eco-

---

[2]However, it is *possible* that courts would hold marriages between homosexuals legal. Why he thinks this would be a threat to heterosexual unions only St. John can say.

nomic or legal rights of children (exactly as it does for senile adults). But no one would suppose this automatically violates a child's or adult's right to equal protection of the law. Similarly, it would seem plausible to suppose that laws distinguishing between the child-raising duties of a husband and wife based on the wife's special ability to provide mother's milk, or laws providing separate rest rooms for men and women on grounds of social custom, or laws forbidding women the right to engage in professional boxing on grounds of anatomical differences, would *not* violate women's rights to equality before the law. In short, it seems plausible to hold that equality before the law does not rule out *relevant* or *reasonable* discrimination, whether towards women, children, bankers, or thieves, but only irrelevant or irrational discrimination, again whether directed against women, children, bankers, or thieves.

The interesting aspect of (i) and (j) is that they muddle the issue, (i) because most but not all of the relevant discrimination is individual as opposed to forced by law, and (j) because women's liberationists want ERA to help fight against both kinds of discrimination. Moreover, it is curious to be against rectifying individual discrimination by law since that is the way most harms done by individuals are rectified. Rape, for instance, is not a harm required by law—it is an unfair harm done by one individual against another, which is the main reason why there are laws against it. Of course, it does not follow that we should try to rectify all unfair harms by law. For one thing, a danger of greater harms may result; for another, it depends on one's overall political and moral theories. But surely the reverse does not hold either, and that is what Jeffrey St. John has to claim.

Chapter Seven, Exercise 7-1

1. *Deceptive Humor.*

4. *Questionable Statement.* With prices going up and up, their very finest almost certainly costs more, not less.

9. *Misleading Statement.* When you think of emeralds, you think of gemstones. But these emeralds are not of gem quality. (The point is that you should realize *no one* would sell gem quality emeralds for $5. If you saw an ad for a 1983 Cadillac for, say, $500, wouldn't you assume it had been wrecked, or some such?)

11. *Meaningless Jargon.* "Actizol" is just one of those phony names, like "Plat-formate," for a widely used ordinary ingredient.

32. Definitely not a fallacious appeal to authority. Concert pianists tend to be extremely fussy about pianos, and while the sheer availability of Steinways tends to increase their use, there can be no doubt that concert pianists prefer Steinway over-whelmingly *and* are more likely to know piano quality than thee and me.

38. *Begged Question.*

Exercise for the Entire Text

I'll never tell. (*Hint:* Look at the first full paragraph on page 98 and notice uses of the words *blackmail* and *extortion* in connection with OPEC. Since these terms are emotionally very negative, the reader can conclude—by reading between the lines—that the author must feel a certain way about OPEC and have certain opinions about the causes of oil shortages, and so on.)

Bibliography

Good Reasoning (Chapter One)

Baker, Samm Sinclair. *Your Key to Creative Thinking.* New York: Harper & Row, 1962.
*Blair, J. Anthony, and Johnson, Ralph H. *Informal Logic: The First International Symposium.* Inverness, Calif.: Edgepress, 1980.
Carroll, Lewis. *Symbolic Logic and the Game of Logic.* New York: Dover, 1958.
Damer, T. Edward. *Attacking Faulty Reasoning.* Belmont, Calif.: Wadsworth, 1980.
Gardner, Martin. *Science: Good, Bad, and Bogus.* Buffalo, N.Y.: Prometheus, 1981.
———. *Fads and Fallacies in the Name of Science.* New York: Dover, 1957. (The classic debunking of pseudoscience.)
*Henry, Jules. *On Sham, Vulnerability and Other Forms of Self-Destruction.* New York: Vintage Books, 1973.
*Kahane, Howard. *Logic and Philosophy.* 4th ed. Belmont, Calif.: Wadsworth, 1982. (A mostly formal logic text.)
Lemmon, E.J. *Beginning Logic* (revised by G.N.D. Barry). Indianapolis, Ind.: Hackett, 1978. (A strictly formal logic text.)
Marks, David and Kammann, Richard. *The Psychology of the Psychic.* Buffalo, N.Y.: Prometheus, 1980.
Nickell, Joe. *Inquest on the Shroud of Turin.* Buffalo, N.Y.: Prometheus, 1982. (An example of sanity on a foolishness-provoking topic.)
*Peirce, Charles Sanders. "The Fixation of Belief," *Popular Science Monthly,* 1877.
Radner, Daisie, and Radner, Michael. *Science & Unreason.* Belmont, Calif.: Wadsworth, 1982. (Explains lots of pseudoscience.)
Randi, James (The Amazing). *Flim Flam! Psychics, ESP, Unicorns and Other Delusions.* Buffalo, N.Y.: Prometheus, 1982.
*Rice, Berkeley. "O Tempora, O Cult." *Psychology Today,* March 1979.
*Twain, Mark. *Mark Twain on the Damned Human Race.* Edited by Janet Smith. New York: Hill & Wang, 1962.

Fallacies (Chapters Two–Four)

*Bentham, Jeremy. *The Handbook of Political Fallacies.* New York: Harper Torchbooks, 1962.
Chase, Stuart. *Guides to Straight Thinking.* New York: Harper & Row, 1962.
Hamblin, C.L. *Fallacies.* London: Methuen & Co., 1970. (A wonderful history of fallacy theory.)
Horwitz, Lucy, and Ferleger, Lou. *Statistics for Social Change.* Boston: South End Press, 1980.
Huff, Darrell. *How to Lie with Statistics.* New York: W.W. Norton, 1954.
*Kahane, Howard. "The Nature and Classification of Fallacies." In *Informal Logic: The First International Symposium,* edited by J. Anthony Blair and Ralph H. Johnson. Inverness, Calif.: Edgepress, 1980.
Kinsley, Michael. "The Art of Polling." *The New Republic,* June 20, 1981.
*LaBrecque, Mort. "On Making Sounder Judgments." *Psychology Today,* June 1980.
Morgan, Chris, and Langford, David. *Facts and Fallacies: A Book of Definitive Mistakes and Misguided Predictions.*
*Morgenstern, Oscar. "Qui Numerare Incipit Errare Incipit." *Fortune,* Oct. 1963.

---

*Asterisks indicate items mentioned in the text.

Smith, H.B. *How the Mind Falls into Error.* Darby Books (1980 reprint of 1923 edition).
Thouless, Robert H. *Straight and Crooked Thinking.* New York: Simon & Schuster, 1932.
Wheeler, Michael. *Lies, Damn Lies, and Statistics: The Manipulation of Public Opinion in America.* New York: Dell Laurel Edition, 1977.

Language (Chapter Five)

*Bolinger, Dwight. *Language, the Loaded Weapon.* New York: Longman, 1980.
Burns, Roger, and Vogt, George. *Your Government Inaction: or In God We'd Better Trust . . .* New York: St. Martin's Press, 1981. (A collection of examples of bureaucratese "from desks and cabinets throughout government.")
Carroll, Lewis. *Alice's Adventures in Wonderland.* New York: New American Library, 1960. Reprint. (Figure out why Alice and the residents of Wonderland often fail to communicate.)
*"Guidelines for Equal Treatment of the Sexes in McGraw-Hill Book Company Publications." (Eleven-page in-house statement of policy that has been generally adopted throughout the publishing business.)
Hall, Edward T. *The Silent Language.* New York: Doubleday, 1973.
Jones, Gregory M. "Confessions of a Reg Writer." *Quarterly Review of Doublespeak,* July 1981.
Mitchell, Richard. *Less than Words Can Say.* Boston: Little, Brown, 1979.
Orwell, George. *Nineteen Eighty-Four.* New York: New American Library, 1949. (Shows how control of languge helps control thoughts, and thus behavior.)
*——. "Politics and the English Language." Reprinted in *A Collection of Works by George Orwell.* New York: Harcourt Brace Jovanovich, 1946.

Analyzing Extended Arguments (Chapter Six)

Cavender, Nancy, and Weiss, Len. *Thinking in Sentences: A Guide to Clear Writing.* New York: Houghton Mifflin, 1982. (Basic composition book linking thinking and critical writing.)
——. *Thinking/Writing* (tentative title). New York: Houghton Mifflin (to appear approximately December 1984).
Flew, Antony. *Thinking Straight.* Buffalo, N.Y.: Prometheus, 1977.
Lanham, Richard. *Revising Prose.* New York: Charles Scribner's Sons, 1979. (A good guide to clear writing.)
Scriven, Michael. *Reasoning.* New York: McGraw-Hill, 1976.

Advertising (Chapter Seven)

Albion, Mark S., and Farris, Paul. *Advertising Controversy: Evidence on the Economic Effects of Advertising.* Boston: Auburn House, 1981.
Baker, Samm Sinclair. *The Permissible Lie.* Cleveland: World Publishing, 1968.
*Benn, Alec. *The 27 Most Common Mistakes in Advertising.* New York: AMACOM, 1978.
*Feldstein, Mark. "Mail Fraud on Capitol Hill." *Washington Monthly,* Oct. 1979.
*Glatzer, Robert. *The New Advertising: The Great Campaigns from Avis to Volkswagen.* New York: Citadel Press, 1970.
Gunther, Max. "Commercials. Can You Believe Them?" *TV Guide,* Dec. 2, 1982.
*Hopkins, Claude. *Scientific Advertising.* New York: Crown Publishing, 1966.
*Lemann, Nicholas. "The Storcks." *Washington Post Magazine,* December 7, 1980.

*———. "Barney Frank's Mother and 500 Postmen." *Harper's,* April 1983.

McGinniss, Joe. *The Selling of the President 1968.* New York: Trident Press, 1969.

Napolitan, Joseph. *The Election Game and How to Win It.* Garden City, N.Y.: Doubleday, 1972.

Newsom, Doug, and Scott, Alan. *This Is PR: The Realities of Public Relations.* Belmont, Calif.: Wadsworth, 1981.

*Ogilvie, David. *Confessions of an Advertising Man.* New York: Atheneum, 1963.

*Preston, Ivan. *The Great American Blowup: Puffery in Advertising and Selling.* Madison: University of Wisconsin Press, 1975.

Price, Jonathan. *Commercials: The Best Thing on TV.* New York: Viking, 1978.

*Rowsome, Frank, Jr. *They Laughed When I Sat Down.* New York: Bonanza Books, 1959.

Schrank, Jeffrey. *Deception Detection: An Educator's Guide to the Art of Insight.* Boston: Beacon Press, 1975.

*———. *Snap, Crackle, and Popular Taste.* New York: Delacorte Press, 1978.

*———. *Understanding Mass Media.* Lincolnwood, Ill.: National Textbook Co., 1975.

Watkins, Julian L. *The 100 Greatest Advertisements, Who Wrote Them and What They Did.* 2nd ed. New York: Dover, 1959.

Managing the News (Chapter Eight)

Asimov, Isaac, ed. *TV: Two Thousand.* New York: Fawcett, 1982.

*Barber, James David. "Not the *New York Times:* What Network News Should Be." *Washington Monthly,* September 1979.

Barnow, Erik. *The Sponsor: Notes on a Modern Potentate.* New York: Oxford, 1979.

Bates, Stephen, and Diamond, Edwin. "How Accurate is the Network News?" *TV Guide,* Feburary 27, 1982.

Breslin, Jimmy. "Guilty Makes Larger Headlines than Innocent." Syndicated column, June 19, 1980.

Clark, Roy P., ed. *Best Newspaper Writing 1982.* Modern Media Institute, 1982.

*Cockburn, Alexander. "The Pundit's Art." *Harper's,* December 1980. (Review of Ronald Steel's *Walter Lippmann and the American Century.*)

English, Deirdre. "Brokaw: Seen But Not Heard?" *Mother Jones,* July 1983. (What happens to reporters who speak out.)

Euchner, Charles. "Questions the Press Didn't Ask About the Atlanta Murders." *Washington Monthly,* October 1981.

Fallows, James. "The President and the Press." *Washington Monthly,* Oct. 1979.

"Grief and Exploitation." *New Republic,* March 28, 1981. (How the media distorted and exploited the Atlanta murders mystery.)

Hentoff, Nat. "Fair Play on the Printed Page." [*MORE*], January 1972.

*Hersh, Seymour M. *My Lai 4: A Report on the Massacre and Its Aftermath.* New York: Random House, 1970.

*Hess, Stephen. *The Washington Reporters.* Washington: The Brookings Institution, 1981. (Reviewed by Robert Sherrill, *Columbia Journalism Review,* May/June 1981).

Hickey, Neil. "Henry Kissinger and TV: 'Did I Sometimes Use the Press? Yes.'" *TV Guide,* April 2, 1983.

*Knightly, Phillip. *The First Casualty.* New York: Harcourt Brace Jovanovich, 1975.

Lapham, Lewis H. "Gilding the News." *Harper's,* July 1981.

Levine, Richard M. "Polish Government Versus The Workers: Why TV is the Prized Weapon." *TV Guide,* November 7, 1981.

McIntyre, Mark. "Muting Megaphone Mark." [*MORE*], July 1974.

Merrill, John C., and Fisher, Hal. *The World's Greatest Dailies: Profiles of Fifty Newspapers.* New York: Hastings House, 1980.

Michaels, Marguerite. "Walter [Cronkite] Wants the News to Say a Lot More." *Parade,* March 23, 1980.

Newfield, Jack. "Bill Moyers Dazzles Gradually." *Village Voice,* February 20–26, 1982. (Story by a good reporter about a good TV reporter.)

*Nocera, Joseph. "Making It at the Washington Post." *Washington Monthly,* January 1979.

Panem, Sandra, and Vilcek, Jan. "Interferon and the Cure of Cancer," *Atlantic Monthly,* December 1982. (Documents poor media coverage of a science story.)

The Periodical Report (of the United Nations Staff Union). May/June 1981. (Exposé of how the *New York Times* distorted a news story.)

Powell, Ron. *The Newsmakers.* New York: St. Martin's Press, 1977. (Good analysis of how TV news programs function.)

Rhoades, Lynn, and Rhoades, George. *Teaching With Newspapers: The Living Curriculum.* Phi Delta Kappa, 1980.

———. *Discovering the News: A Social History of American Newspapers.* Basic Books. New York.

*———. "Sundays at Seven." *The Nation,* September 5, 1981. (Exposé review of *60 Minutes Verbatim.*)

*Seligson, Marcia. "The Sexual Revolution: Is TV Keeping Pace with Our Society?" *Panorama,* 1980.

60 Minutes Verbatim. New York: Arno Press, 1981.

Stein, Benjamin. *The View from Sunset Boulevard.* New York: Basic Books, 1979.

Toffler, Alvin. *The Third Wave.* New York: William Morrow, 1980. (Interesting ideas on the import of the media.)

Turovsky, Ronald. "Did He Really Say That?" *Columbia Journalism Review,* July/August, 1980. (How the media doctor and invent quotes.)

Weisman, John. "Stories You Won't See on the Nightly News." *TV Guide,* March 1, 1980.

*———. "Intimidation." *TV Guide,* October 23–30, 1982. (How brutal treatment of foreign correspondents intimidates the media and forces them to slant or not report the news.)

Westin, Av. "Inside the Evening News: How TV Really Works." *New York,* October 18, 1982.

Textbooks: Managing World Views (Chapter Nine)

*American Indian Historical Society. *Textbooks and the American Indian.* San Francisco: Indian Historical Press, 1970.

Barzun, Jacques. "The Wasteland of American Education." *New York Review of Books,* November 5, 1981.

*Black, Hillel. *The American Schoolbook.* New York: William Morrow, 1967.

"Creationism, Censorship, and Academic Freedom." *Science, Technology and Human Values,* Summer 1982.

*Elson, Ruth M. *Guardians of Tradition: American Schoolbooks of the 19th Century.* Lincoln: University of Nebraska Press, 1964.

Epstein, Noel. "Stop Giving a Bad Name to Schoolbook 'Censorship.'" *Washington Post,* March 14, 1982.

FitzGerald, Frances. *America Revised.* New York: Random House, 1980.

Guidelines for Selecting Bias Free Textbooks and Storybooks. Council on Interracial Books for Children. CIBA, 1980.

*"Governments Flunk History . . . Rewriting the Textbooks." *Inquiry,* October 1982.

*Haight, Anne Lyon. *Banned Books.* New York: R. R. Bowker, 1978. (The fourth revision is by Chandler B. Grannis.)

Harrison, Barbara G. *Unlearning the Lie: Sexism in School.* New York: William Morrow, 1974.

Harty, Sheila. *Hucksters in the Classroom: A Review of Industrial Propaganda in Schools.* Center for Study of Responsive Law.

Hentoff, Nat. "The Right to Read." *Inquiry,* December 11, 1978.

*"History/Social Science Framework for California Public Schools, Kindergarten through Grade Twelve." (The basic document governing California schools.)

*Kirk, Donald. "Japan Rearms Its School Books." *Nation,* December 19, 1981.

"Mind Control Through Textbooks." *Phi Delta Kappa,* October 1982.

*Nelson, Jack, and Roberts, Gene. *The Censors and the Schools.* Boston: Little, Brown, 1963.

Popovitch, Luke. "Realerpolitic: The Texts Are Getting Better." *Washington Monthly,* March 1973.

*Rout, Lawrence. "School History Books, Striving to Please All, Are Criticized as Bland." *Wall Street Journal,* September 5, 1979.

*Schrank, Jeffrey. *Understanding Mass Media.* Skokie, Ill.: National Book Co., 1975. (Example of an excellent public school textbook.)

"Vietnam Revised: Are Our Textbooks Changing?" *Social Education,* May 1982.

Non-Mass Media Periodicals

One of the themes of this book is that good reasoning requires good information sources. Here is a selected list of (primarily) non-mass media periodicals (mostly on social political issues, or science) with one person's brief comments on them:

Armed Forces Journal International.   Prints details on military issues most others just skim.

Atlantic Monthly.   Good; middle to left wing; long-established.

Columbia Journalism Review.   Now that [*MORE*] is no more, the best journalism rag.

Commentary.   Neoconservative, formerly left wing; overrated; too establishment-oriented for some tastes.

Conservative Digest.   One of the few reasonably interesting conservative magazines.

Consumer Reports.   Publication of Consumers Union, an unbiased, nonprofit organization.

Discover.   Popular science magazine.

Foreign Affairs.   Establishment quarterly; very influential in government. Tends to be right wing or establishment-oriented.

Harper's.   Center to left of center; very good lately. Has been published for over a hundred years.

Harvard Medical School Health Letter.   Reasonably reliable medical news.

Inquiry.   Libertarian; occasionally excellent.

Libertarian Review. Libertarian; will appear conservative to some, because of free enterprise, anti-big government view.

Matchbox.   Amnesty International publication. Gives the gory details about atrocities by governments around the world.

Mother Jones.   Successor to *Ramparts;* radical left publication.

Ms.   Magazine of the women's movement; sometimes good, sometimes too doctrinaire.

The Nation.   One of the oldest political journals, and very good.

National Geographic.   The most successful special-topic magazine.

National Review.   Bill Buckley's conservative magazine; occasionally interesting.

The New Republic.   Very good, long-established liberal magazine.

Newsletter on Intellectual Freedom.   American Library Association newsletter; contains list of censored books.

New Yorker.   The main long article in each issue sometimes stunningly good, although usually written in dull *New Yorker* low-keyed style.

New York Review of Books.   Left-wing; very good. (Good reviews of non-mass-media books.)

Policy Report.   Libertarian publication of the Cato Institute.

The Progressive.   Interesting left-wing publication.

Psychology Today.   With the demise of *Human Nature,* the best popular psychology magazine; getting better.

Science Digest.   Fair to middling science magazine.

Science 84.   Popular science magazine. Date in title changes yearly.

Science News.   Weekly on what's new in science; useful.

The Sciences.   New York Academy of Science publication.

Scientific American.   The best science journal; the trick for a lay reader is to learn how to glean knowledge from articles over one's head.

Skeptical Inquirer.   Excellent debunking of pseudo-science.

Soviet Life.   Interesting to read this slick, picture-filled propaganda product to see how schlock (the current Soviet system) can be made to appear wonderful.

Technology Review.   Massachusetts Institute of Technology publication.

TV Guide   Perhaps the only valuable, informative mass publication; ironically, the largest-selling magazine in the United States.

Video Review.   Keeps up with the home video revolution.

The Village Voice.   Left wing; more on New York than national scene, but filled with exposés by such as Jack Newfield and Nat Hentoff, plus Feiffer cartoons.

Wall Street Journal.   The best of the business publications; chock full of interesting facts, figures, and ideas.

The Washington Monthly.   This writer's favorite political magazine about how our system works.

Washington Spectator and Between the Lines.   Attempt to continue tradition started by *I. F. Stone's Weekly.* Four-page, basically one-person operation.

World Press Review.   News and views from the foreign press.

Indexes

Index of Topics

Index of Magazines and Newspapers

Index of Names